Out of Stock

Out of Stock

The Warehouse in the History of Capitalism

DARA ORENSTEIN

The University of Chicago Press
Chicago and London

The University of Chicago Press, Chicago 60637
The University of Chicago Press, Ltd., London

Published 2019
Printed in the United States of America

28 27 26 25 24 23 22 21 20 19   1 2 3 4 5

ISBN-13: 978-0-226-66287-9 (cloth)
ISBN-13: 978-0-226-66290-9 (paper)
ISBN-13: 978-0-226-66306-7 (e-book)
DOI: https://doi.org/10.7208/chicago/9780226663067.001.0001

Library of Congress Cataloging-in-Publication Data

Names: Orenstein, Dara, author.
Title: Out of stock : the warehouse in the history of capitalism / Dara Orenstein.
Description: Chicago : The University of Chicago Press, 2019. | Includes bibliographical references and index.
Identifiers: LCCN 2019018458 | ISBN 9780226662879 (cloth : alk. paper) | ISBN 9780226662909 (pbk. : alk. paper) | ISBN 9780226663067 (e-book)
Subjects: LCSH: Warehouses—United States—History. | Free ports and zones—United States. | Manufacturing industries—United States. | Trade regulation—United States.
Classification: LCC TS189.6 .O74 2019 | DDC 388/.0440973—dc23
LC record available at https://lccn.loc.gov/2019018458

♾ This paper meets the requirements of ANSI/NISO Z39.48-1992 (Permanence of Paper).

For Ron and Bruno

CONTENTS

INTRODUCTION

"My Brain Hurt Like a Warehouse"

It is hoped that the illustrations will help the reader understand what is new and strange to him, better than mere description could.

—Edwin J. Clapp, *The Port of Hamburg* (1911)

The 20 acres with the big warehouse on them looked just like any other part of New Orleans' busy river front.

—"Port of Dreams," *Time* (1947)

Nowadays, if you stop by a dealership in the United States to shop for a new car, and you kick the tires and peek in the windows of a model that you fancy, you might notice a sticker that tells you where the car was made. Listing percentages, it identifies where the majority of the parts originated and where the car was assembled. Maybe you decipher this sticker as a response to worries about the decline of the American auto industry; maybe you even know that Congress initiated it, in 1992, to force automakers to account for their increasingly extensive supply chains.[1] As you read it, probably you picture a map of Asia and the Pacific Ocean. If you learn that the car was assembled in, say, Tennessee, and that 45% of the parts were sourced from other countries, then probably you assume that those parts traveled from foreign territory to domestic territory before they were incorporated into the car. That's what the sticker says, right?

Not so simple. While the car was assembled at a plant in Tennessee, the sticker neglects to inform you whether or not that plant was in a foreign-trade zone, as it undoubtedly was. Nearly every car that is "assembled in the United States" is assembled in a foreign-trade zone—which, from the perspective of US Customs and Border Protection, is not "in" the United

States. When parts from Japan or South Korea arrive in a zone, they enter, essentially, "Shangri-la."[2] They remain foreign. Jurisdictionally speaking, they are "landed" on US soil only once they exit the zone as parts of a car. This legal fiction incentivizes the automaker not to uproot its assembly plant to foreign soil by allowing it to pay the relatively low tariff that applies to the car as a whole in lieu of all of the tariffs that apply to each of the parts. Business consultants recommend the foreign-trade zone as an "offshore-onshore" device: it brings "the benefits of offshore, onshore."[3]

"Offshore" conjures the specter of livelihoods washed away, of "manufacturing jobs" shipped off to China and later spirited back in boxes of T-shirts and yellow rubber duckies.[4] "Offshore" is the horizon of the global assembly line. Yet what of the manufacturing jobs that stay "onshore"? And what is meant by "manufacturing"? This term is perhaps the most fluid of all. As sentimental as it is empirical, *manufacturing* is more a floating signifier than a reference to a specific type of labor or a specific type of relationship between labor and capital. Its malleability is ideal for political theater. Shouted through a loudspeaker, "manufacturing" is the white man's birthright, weaponized against "illegal aliens" to make America great again.[5] Whether trumpeted in 2016 or in 1980, the surreal mantra of "manufacturing jobs" has attended the dislocatedness of production in the age of global capitalism. Think back to 2011, for instance, and the Chrysler commercial "Imported from Detroit." In that zeitgeistian classic, a white rapper gives props to the resilience of a black city from behind the wheel of a transnational sedan. While the Chrysler 200 he drives is not "imported from Detroit," it is imported from a US foreign-trade zone in Detroit, Subzone 70H.

We should not be surprised to hear "manufacturing" as a dog whistle for nationalism. Nostalgia for it acknowledges, unwittingly, that the geographies of production and circulation each have their onshore and offshore dimensions. Production is not confined to the homeland. And circulation is as provincial as it is cosmopolitan. Examining how an entity like the foreign-trade zone reconfigures these geographies helps us to appreciate how the nation-state has managed the accumulation of capital to constitute a national economy. Shady as it might sound, a foreign-trade zone is nothing more than an idea expressed in brick and mortar, a spatial form, and as such it is an attempt to resolve a social contradiction: it mediates between the nation-state's—or empire-state's—need to impose borders and capital's need to surpass them.[6]

This tension between the sovereign and the capitalist logics of territory has shaped the United States since the very first session of Congress. In

1789, in the third section of the second law ever enacted, the basis for the foreign-trade zone was established in the policy of the "drawback," which to this day refunds tariffs on imports if those imports are used in "manufactured" exports.[7] Manufacturers of sugar were early converts to the drawback policy; they imported molasses from Havana, refined it in Brooklyn, and then exported it as white sugar, afterward filing with the Treasury Department for "drawback" on the duties on the molasses. What the United States lost in duties, the rationale went, it gained in jobs and property taxes and other agglomeration effects—better that the sugar refinery be located in Brooklyn than in Havana. Insofar as it concerns the nation-state, then, *Out of Stock* begins in 1789. The zone concept is an extension of the drawback principle, as the US Tariff Commission noted in 1966, in that it facilitates "temporary entry" of the foreign into the domestic, a transitory blurring of offshore and onshore that nonetheless shores up the authority of the United States and of the US Custom House.[8]

Out of Stock concludes in 1989, an epic year for geopolitics that also capped off a contentious and pivotal decade for the foreign-trade zone. Two separate committees in the House of Representatives held hearings on the zone concept, responding to years of complaints about the perversity of a national policy that pitted city against city, sector against sector. These hearings were noteworthy for two main reasons. First, they were rare. Congress had debated the merits of the foreign-trade zone in just four other sessions: 1919, 1934—when it passed the Foreign-Trade Zones Act—1948, and 1968. (No other hearings have happened since 1989, as the zone system has grown routine.) And, second, they were supremely anticlimactic. The year 1989, like 1789, rang out with revolution. Everywhere, people were smashing things—walls in Berlin, guitars in Seattle, pizza parlors in Spike Lee's Brooklyn—but in Congress no one was toppling the zone system.[9] The hearings resulted in no additional legislation, and the zone system continued to mushroom. In 1989, there were 164 general-purpose zones and 181 subzones on the books, up from 8 general-purpose zones and 3 subzones in 1965 (fig. i.1). By 2019, these numbers had spiked to 296 zones and 772 subzones. Each state counted one or more general-purpose zone, with thirty-two in Texas alone.[10]

Americans have tended to apprehend foreign-trade zones as somehow foreign or un-American. "The residents of Boise, Idaho," one nativist website warned in 2011, "are about to have a 50-square mile self-contained communist Chinese city plopped right into their backyard" (fig. i.2).[11] That assumption is no less true for being so paranoid. The foreign-trade zone is, to be clear, the American version of a global disposition. Duty-free zones of

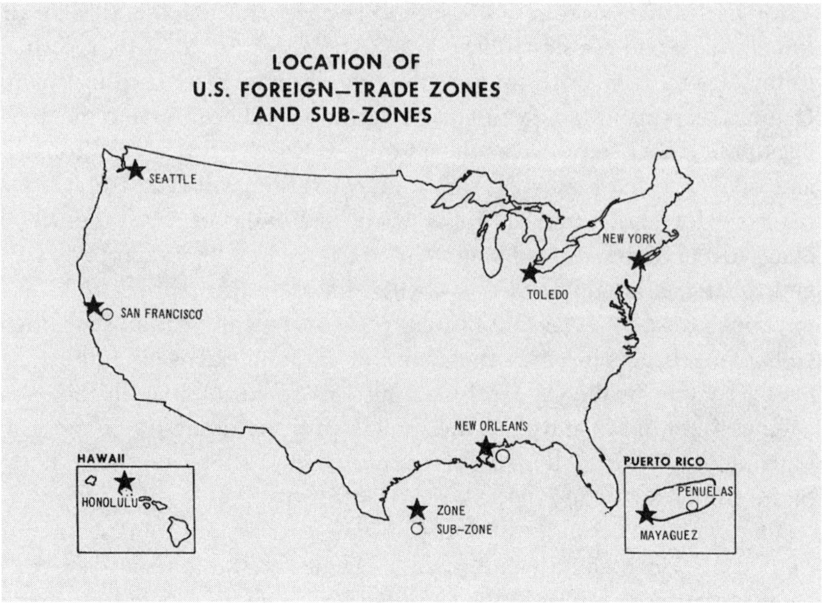

Figure i.1. In 1965, the FTZ system spanned eight general-purpose zones and three subzones. A version of this map appeared in every annual report from 1958 to 1972. No other map has been issued by the FTZ Board in the decades since. *Annual Report of the Foreign-Trade Zones Board* (Washington, DC: Government Printing Office, 1966).

varying sizes and configurations dot every continent save Antarctica. Currently, there are at least 3,000 zones in 135 countries, employing more than 43 million workers.[12] They range from swaths of cities in China ("special economic zones" as in Shenzhen) to gated compounds in the Caribbean and Central America ("export-processing zones" as in Kingston, Jamaica, or "*zonas francas*" as in Managua, Nicaragua). You may recognize these terms in the wake of investigations by antisweatshop activists in the early 1990s. The targets were the "labor warehouses" patronized by apparel lines like Kathie Lee Gifford's and Walt Disney's.[13] Or you may know of them simply because zones have proved to be a constitutive feature of global capitalism. They have borne out the prediction of a "U.S. businessman," who vowed in 1979 that they would "revolutionize international industry like Hilton hotels did for international tourism—free trade zones are also identical, self-enclosed, where the outside world doesn't touch you."[14]

Catalogers at the Library of Congress first started tracking the phrase *free ports and zones* in the mid-1940s.[15] As a spatial form the zone is most associated with the post–World War II era and decolonization.[16] But promoters

Just ask the residents of Boise, Idaho - they are about to have a 50 square mile self-contained communist Chinese city plopped right into their backyard.

NOW FOR A MAP OF THE FREE TRADE ZONES... YEP FOLKS IT ISN'T JUST IDAHO

Foreign Trade Zones

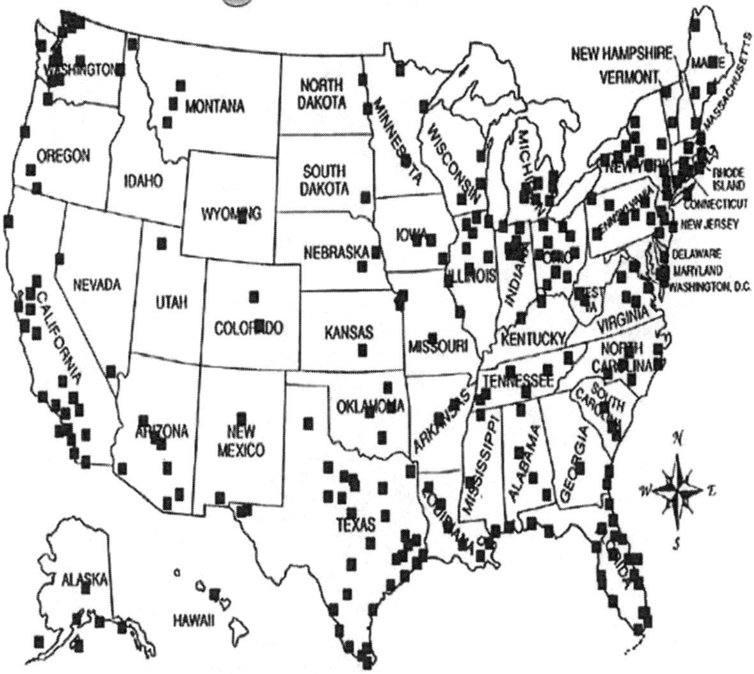

Source FTZ List: http://ia.ita.doc.gov/ftzpage/letters/ftzlist-map.html

The map is not to scale. The purpose is to show the approximate location and number of Foreign Trade Zones in each state. Foreign Trade Zones are considered foreign soil. As such, they do not contribute to the local economy in terms of property taxes – and it's not known how income earned in an FTZ is treated for tax purposes.

NOTE FOREIGN TRADE ZONES ARE CONSIDERED FOREIGN SOIL !

IF YOU DON'T CHANGE THIS NOW YOUR CHILDREN AND GRANDCHILDREN WILL BE LIVING IN A 3RD WORLD COUNTRY, FILTHY, POOR, HUNGRY AND DOMINATED BY THE ELITE, GROVELING JUST TO SURVIVE without even a weapon to defend themselves with.

Figure i.2. This map—unofficial (indeed, hostile) and an imperfect substitute for an official map in that it shows general-purpose zones but not subzones—is one of only a few in existence at present. Conspiracy theorists singled out the FTZ system in 2011, to incite protest about reports of a joint venture between Idaho and a Chinese state-owned corporation. End of the American Dream, "China Wants to Construct a 50 Square Mile Self-Sustaining City South of Boise, Idaho," June 8, 2011, http://endoftheamericandream.com/archives/china-wants-to-construct-a-50-square-mile-self-sustaining-city-south-of-boise-idaho.

Figure i.3. Four clocks from four corners decorate a wall in the headquarters of the Ras Al Khaimah Free Trade Zone, which I visited during an annual meeting of the World Free Zone Convention. Based in London, the WFZC is a for-profit consultancy that hosts trainings. I wired my payment for the conference fee to Barclays Bank in the Channel Islands. Photograph by author, November 2, 2010.

of the zone prefer to retail a premodern lineage. *It harkens all the way back to the Phoenicians!* they say. *To the dawn of capitalism!* Which is a way of mythologizing it—that is, naturalizing it by transposing it from genealogy to ontology. The zone, they would have you believe, is in the DNA of *Homo economicus*. That was the message at the 2010 summit of the World Free Zone Convention, which I attended at a golf resort in Ras Al Khaimah, an hour north of Dubai (fig. i.3). The CEO of Ras Al Khaimah's zone spoke to the audience's cosmology when, praising zones as "islands of efficiency and freedom," he rejoiced in that day's milestone, "the 1,012th birthday of the Gdansk Free Zone."

In this light, it is impressive that the United States boasts the largest and longest-running zone system in the world. None rival it in breadth or depth. And yet its history has gone untold.[17] President Franklin D. Roosevelt signed the Foreign-Trade Zones Act six days after the Reciprocal Trade Agreements Act (RTAA). But scholarship on the RTAA never mentions it. Neither do any of the studies of the New Deal's impact on cities, save one.[18] It earns no more than two sentences in *The Encyclopedia of New York City*, even though "the United States' first foreign-trade zone" debuted on Staten Island in 1937 with ample publicity (fig. i.4).[19] Likewise, it is overlooked in analyses of capital flight, despite the velocity with which it took off during the 1980s (fig. i.5). A more curious slight is its standing in the memoir of the "Father of the FTZ Act," the man who hustled to enact it and then to defend it over the next four decades, Congressman Emanuel "Manny" Celler (1888–1981). He utters not a word about it.[20] Semantically, I bury it as well, by omitting it from the title of this book.

Among the most durable traits of the foreign-trade zone has been its illegibility, even to its promoters, who have lamented straining to communicate what it is and what it offers. "There is a woeful lack of knowledge, Gentlemen," Manny Celler swore to federal officials in 1935, "and I want to say this with all the emphasis within me—a woeful lack of knowledge on the part of the public as to what a foreign-trade zone really is." People who should have heard of it "know nothing," Celler said. "There is a lack of knowledge even among experts."[21] Forty-one years later, Celler was still harping on this disconnect, imploring zone operators to innovate in their publicity efforts. "The press is silent. Television? Nothing," he scolded them, pleading for fresh solutions: "I can see in my mind a documentary, exciting and nourishing, telling the story to the public."[22] This litany hit the usual notes: the zone is off the radar not because it is dull but because it is tough to fathom. As a director of the zone system was wont to say, "No federal statute was ever enacted which has been so misunderstood as the Foreign-Trade Zones Act."[23]

For the record, this lack of understanding was not due to a lack of reporting. No media blackout has plagued the foreign-trade zone, as Celler well knew from his collection of thousands of newspaper and magazine articles. What's more, the coverage has been markedly consistent in play-

Figure i.4. The author has said that he chose this poster as his marquee because he found it attractive and resonant, not because of the FTZ, of which he knew little. Christopher DeNoon, *Posters of the WPA* (Seattle: University of Washington Press, 1987).

ing up the zone's oddity. Many a profile leads with a bait and switch: what sounds like an ordinary warehouse in an ordinary port is, in reality, a no-man's-land! A prototypical piece from 1942 hooked the reader with a nine-paragraph tour of a tungsten refinery with a metallurgist named "Dr. Li," who details the jobs of the refinery's technicians, "his Chinese countrymen." That ninth paragraph ends, "As in China, nothing is wasted." The next paragraph starts—*gotcha!*—"I say 'as in China' because this unique plant is at the New York Foreign-Trade Zone and not in China."[24] Abruptly the author steps from China to Staten Island.

If such exoticized reportage has been so pervasive, then why has the zone been so elusive in public culture? It's the exoticizing, stupid. Accentuating and thereby exaggerating the zone as unreal encourages readers not to grapple with how it functions, not to reckon with its real impact on real people. Real money is absconded with behind the smokescreen of "China." Still, while the zone's fictiveness is more superficial than substantive, it's important to register this fixation on the trope of "as in," for it's a sign of a deeper misrecognition. The history of knowledge about the zone reminds us that, in the culture of capitalism, even when something becomes visible, it is no less prone to mystification.

The "as in" had me fooled at first too. When I embarked on this research, I expected to unearth a hard-wired link between the precarity of

Figure i.5. Shown here are remnants from Zone 76. Dubbed the "Foreign-Trade Zone Industrial Park," this site had repurposed a shuttered Remington Arms ammunition plant in Bridgeport, Connecticut. I first learned of the FTZ system when I stumbled upon this site in 2003, while researching the deindustrialization of Bridgeport. Photograph by author, October 15, 2012.

labor and the foreign-trade zone. I *wanted* to discover it, that whopper of a punch line, the master code of late capitalism. Instead, I came to realize that zones require more nuance. Despite their flagrant liminality, zones are not lawless or "denationalized."[25] Quite the opposite—they are domains of the nation-state, in the United States overseen by the Foreign-Trade Zones Board, an agency in the Department of Commerce. They conform to strict parameters, and they entail no small amount of hassle to set up. They are staid, not free-wheeling. "If Bay City seems like an unusual place for a foreign-trade zone, don't err by imagining white slave traffic, multilingual spies, and hot cargo," as the *Detroit Free Press* put it in 1965, rejecting the "as in" cliché. "A foreign-trade zone is not like Singapore on the late-late show. It is somber, like nothing more than a fenced-off factory district."[26] And when it comes to violations of labor laws and mistreatment of workers, zones—defined as spaces in which customs duties are deferred or dodged—are not determinative. Certainly, surveillance of workers is heightened in zones, since surveillance of goods is intensified (to prevent smuggling). But surveillance and other abuses are endemic to capitalist workplaces, whether in zones or not.

If lawlessness is one aspect of the exoticism, then impartiality is the other: the foreign-trade zone is declared to be tantamount either to Singapore or to Switzerland. As prevalent as the yarn that it's a free-for-all is the vow that it's an apolitical machine.[27] This notion contributes to the zone's obscurity, and it is perplexing, because the zone is the epitome of politics—a political compromise: we cannot eliminate the rule (tariffs), but we can grant an exception to it (zones). The zone system owes its existence to the tariff system. A tipoff here is how regularly and assuredly people have professed that zones have not a whit to do with tariffs. Whether Democrat or Republican, "a rampant free trader or a rabid protectionist," insisted a port official from New York City in 1919, all parties could endorse the zone system. "It is a clean-cut business proposition," echoed a senator from Louisiana in 1922. "It is not a political one in any sense of the word." Congressman Celler never deviated from this script. "No question of the tariff is involved," he lectured his colleagues in 1948. "Whether a man is a high protectionist or a low-tariff man, there is no conflict between the principle of the foreign-trade zone and our tariff laws."[28] It is in this vein that we can reconcile inconsistencies such as when, in 1992, the billionaire presidential candidate Ross Perot applied for zone status for his industrial park in Fort Worth, Texas, even as he vilified the North American Free Trade Agreement.[29]

"A clean-cut business proposition," "not a political one." Zone promoters have threaded this needle by separating ends from means, legislation from

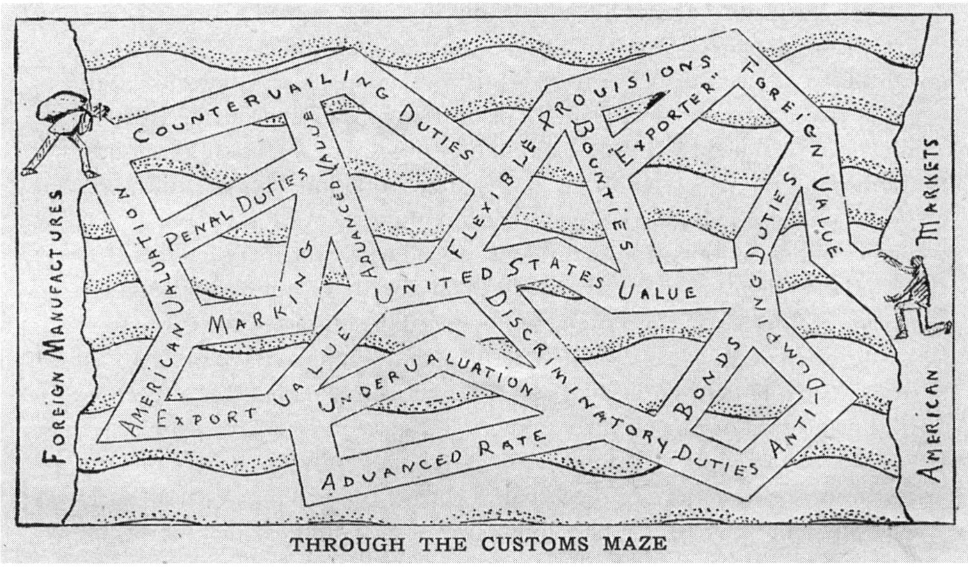

Figure i.6. Benjamin A. Levett, *Through the Customs Maze* (New York: Customs Maze, 1923).

administration. Whether to impose tariffs was a question for politicians; how to implement them, and whether to carve out exemptions, was a question for bureaucrats. In 1934, when Congress signed on, this split was feasible because of the design of the foreign-trade zone and the urgency of the moment. The foreign-trade zone was said to jibe with the tariff in that it would aid the transshipment business, with no impact whatsoever on domestic industry—oriented offshore, it would enable the specialized activity of importing for exporting, outside of the tariff system. With the Great Depression at full tilt, advocates were contending that the labyrinthine "customs maze"—the manifestation of the "elephantiasis" of the regulations of the Smoot-Hawley Tariff Act of 1930—was hindering traffic (fig. i.6). The foreign-trade zone would streamline the administration of the tariff. In short, it was smart government, prefiguring post–New Deal denunciations of "fat, sloppy, and smug bureaucracy," and the cherry on top was that it was said to cut out Washington, DC.[30] As a port manager in Chicago exulted in 1981, "It was the only New Deal program not funded by the federal government."[31]

There is an adjective that zone promoters have long favored to distinguish this "Shangri-la" of pure, politics-free transactionality: frictionless. "Frictionless" is a buzzword of our Digital Age. Computers are advancing civilization by eliminating intermediaries, from customs clerks to travel agents, according to Microsoft founder Bill Gates, who, in 1995, opined about "friction-free capitalism." But it is equally an artifact of a century earlier. Like "overhead" and even "work," "friction" was a factor in the physics of the assembly line. It was a gauge of movement, or of resistance to movement, as in the friction generated by unlubricated ball bearings. For the urban economist Robert Murray Haig, writing in 1926, "transportation," semantically, covered "all means of overcoming the friction of space." A river was not a body of water but "an opportunity to choose a road where the friction is less."[32]

The foreign-trade zone supposedly, and cleverly, minimized this friction of space through a fiction of space. It reduced the obstacles that the nation-state, often despite itself, planted in the path of capital—the tariff wall, red tape. The internet went further and seemingly deleted obstacles altogether. With the ease of one-click shopping, cyberspace, a cousin of zone space, elides the materiality of immateriality.[33] It partakes in the charade of automation. It tempts you to forget that as your Roomba Robot Vacuum sucks up dust bunnies and dog hair and you kick back on the couch for a game of Words with Friends, technicians repair cables damaged by hurricanes, and server farms drain electrical grids.[34]

The household is apropos because its marginality parallels that of the foreign-trade zone. Both have been positioned on the edges of capitalism, included as excluded.[35] And both have resisted scrutiny by political economists because both have featured a type of labor not embraced by the standard measures of productive economic activity—in the case of the zone, the labor of distribution. Like the household, the zone has been a workplace, yet not readily recognized as such by those not toiling in it. Except by zone promoters. Here lies the answer to the riddle of the zone's vaunted neutrality. When zone promoters maintain that the zone is immune to the politics of the tariff, they mean that it is apolitical precisely because it is a workplace, anterior to the nation-state. In their minds, its allure has hinged less on how it has offered a haven from tariff conflicts between national or regional economies and more on how it has offered an escape from labor. Zone promoters have spoken of not strictly "frictionlessness" but "frictionless handling," which is a fable about easing rules on handling as a prelude to clearing away handlers. The goal has been to bring offshore onshore and to liquefy the port into a steady stream of capital flows.

The bedrock of the foreign-trade zone's unintelligibility, then, has been a veneer of extraordinariness, of extraterritoriality and hyperefficiency, which has distracted observers from what transpires inside. To gauge the zone's worth, we need to assess it as a workplace, not as a den of thieves. The scholars of post-1945 political economy who gesture to US foreign-trade zones tend to treat them as tax havens.[36] Initially, I planned to investigate them through that lens, with "offshore" as a euphemism for fugitive dollars. What I found was far more mundane: catalogs of forklifts and hand trucks, engineering blueprints for sprinklers and refrigeration—files one would encounter in the archives of warehouses (if such archives existed). No traces of backroom rackets. No suspicious bookkeeping. No Panamanian stock certificates. As hinted by the epigraph above that describes the zone as resembling "any other part of New Orleans' busy river front," the zone looks "just like" the rest of the port because, for all intents and purposes, it is "just like" the rest of the port. The zone is, basically, a warehouse with a funky address, and therefore off the grid.[37]

Warehouses have tended to lurk in the shadows of the folklore of workplaces, overrun with objects, not with workers. As David Bowie belts out in "Five Years" (1972), "My brain hurt like a warehouse / It had no room to spare / I had to cram so many things to store / Everything in there." Inasmuch as any drama has surrounded these vaults, it has stemmed from the ominousness of places without people. Maybe the building was a warehouse owned by the government, and, as in the final shot of *Raiders of the Lost Ark* (1981), a precious object has vanished within its warren of crates, where the ark is wheeled into oblivion. This slow pan was filmed with a matte painting: so axiomatic was it that warehouses were inhumanly static that the filmmakers saw fit to simulate one with oil paint on glass rather than to construct a set (fig. i.7).

If people lurk in warehouses, the stereotype goes, they tend to be thugs. Warehouses have been the consummate settings for gun battles and scuffles, from *Angels with Dirty Faces* (1938) to *The Amazing Spider-man* (1980) (figs. i.8 and i.9). Such portrayals have been pervasive enough that life has imitated art, as in 1975, when police in Washington, DC, masqueraded as mafia "dons" and staged a stolen-goods venture in a warehouse in order to entrap petty thieves.[38] On the whole, the warehouse has epitomized the antithesis of the social. Putatively inert and all but empty of workers, it has furnished a narrative container for murder and mayhem, to a degree that has haunted warehousemen themselves.[39] "The trouble with 'warehouse,'" grumbled a Toledo-based warehouseman in 1966, "is that it makes you think of a spooky ruin you would be scared to walk past at night."[40]

The eeriness has had to do with the common perception of warehouse work, synonymous with insensate tedium. In American letters, the deathly aura has been as palpable when workers have punched in as during

Figure i.7. The original virtual warehouse: For the closing scene of *Raiders of the Lost Ark* (1982), Mike Panagrazio painted the interior of the government warehouse on glass, leaving the aisle unpainted as a kind of aperture, through which the cinematographer filmed an actor pushing the crated ark.

Figure i.8. In *Angels with Dirty Faces* (1938), James Cagney's character dodges the police by seeking shelter in a building captioned "Warehouse" and "Storage."

Figure i.9. A panel from *The Amazing Spider-Man* 1, no. 200 (1980). Spider-Man, a.k.a. Peter Parker, hunts down the Burglar at the Acme Warehouse.

off-hours. Arthur Miller's description of the set for his play *A Memory of Two Mondays* (1955), which takes place in an auto-parts warehouse, is a testament to this reputation for devitalization: a "box," "where these people are caught, caught by necessity and by their lives" (fig. i.10).[41] Or consider Tom, a character in Tennessee Williams's *The Glass Menagerie* (1944). "Most young men find adventure in their careers," Amanda says. "Then most young men are not employed in a warehouse," Tom replies. Dreary warehouses have bred dreary men, like the peeping Tom in the B-movie horror classic *Carnival of Souls* (1962). And this gloominess has become emblematic of a past we do not cherish.[42] Decrepit, dirty, these architectural relics have stood for history in the metropolitan consciousness, help-

Figure i.10. Boris Aronson's set design for a warehouse in Arthur Miller's *Memory of Two Mondays* drew grid-like lines in the guise of shelves, windows, and ceiling rafters so as to circumscribe the lives of the characters (1955). Harry Ransom Center, University of Texas at Austin.

ing to bring the present into focus (fig. i.11).[43] Some of us squint at them from the sidewalk and entertain the digger's dream—a trove of decades-old model trains or vinyl albums. Warehouses have loomed as time capsules, harboring childhood treasures, as in the final scene of *Citizen Kane* (1941). The world is in flux (or chaos) around them, and within them the air is still. When we picture people working in them, we picture those people all but mummified too.

But this perception of warehouses is receding. Lately, warehouses have shifted from backstage to frontstage—or, more accurately, backstage has morphed into frontstage, amid mounting interest in the infrastructure of the market, and in how T-shirts and yellow rubber duckies wind up in dollar stores. Mutations in the parameters of seaports are partly responsible for this new visibility. Seaports—the picturesque sort with sand and seagulls—have long offered optics on the world of goods. Articulating the local and the global, they have enchanted us as hubs: "Across the mind's eye sweep images of rare, precious goods," effused a writer from New Orleans in 1947. "Whether the cargo is coffee or ivory, a dismantled factory or a herd of cattle, it cannot help but excite the imagination because it is on the move."[44] Now, though, seaports themselves are on the move, multiplying and spreading thanks to containerization and to their nineteenth-century legal framework. A city as emblematic of amber waves of grain as Peoria, Illinois, is a seaport (and a foreign-trade zone—Zone 114, established in 1984). Correspondingly, the trappings of seaports have gone viral, well beyond the kitsch of Long John Silver's and Red Lobster. We dine on tacos in repurposed shipping containers. All the world's a seaport, and warehouses, as anchors of seaports, have risen to prominence. Now their impenetrability intrigues us. Amazon, for example, offers tours of its "fulfillment centers" four times per month (no photographs allowed). When I went to reserve a spot, in the fall of 2015, the first available date was seven months out. Demand for this opportunity to "see the magic that happens

Figure i.11. *Brooklyn Bridge, Water and New Dock Streets*, May 22, 1936.
Berenice Abbott (1898–1991) for Federal Art Project /
Museum of the City of New York, 43.131.3.87.

after you click buy" falls shy of the Model T mania that prompted Henry Ford to employ twenty-five full-time tour guides at River Rouge by 1916. But it is not trivial, either.[45]

A wait list for a warehouse tour? That is as good an indicator as a Federal Reserve balance sheet that capitalism is reconfiguring. Warehouses are beckoning us because warehouses are invading our daily lives. A longtime ambition of warehousing companies has been realized at last: the warehouse is understood as a space of flows—and frequently goods are not only flowing through it but also metamorphosizing in the process. To grasp this point, it helps to ponder the mechanics of warehousing and to sweep away Hollywood's cobwebbed caricature of "pure storage," which no entrepreneurial warehouse company has ever endorsed (as we'll see, there's no windfall in dust). Warehousing is a facet of the circulation of capital.[46] As such, it is distinct from the production of capital, or so we are accustomed to believe. It is a space of transmission, we presume, not of transformation—objects exit the warehouse in the same state they enter it. A warehouse is not a factory. Yet transformation *is* occurring during transmission. While the divide between circulation and production has never been absolute, in the age of just-in-time production it is shakier than ever, and the imperatives of circulation are dictating those of production. Efforts to shrink inventories and to compress the space-time between production and consumption are resulting less in a global factory than in a global warehouse. And this subordinating of production to circulation is why activists are increasingly targeting warehouses and ports—chokepoints—more than factories. Occupy a factory, and production is reallocated to another factory, like a game of whack-a-mole. Blockade a warehouse or a port, and circulation is stalled.

The foreign-trade zone has intersected with this advance in warehousing both because the zone is, effectively, a warehouse, and because the zone has been a pioneer in the privileging of flow. It has been a site of experimentation, where the line between circulation and production has been drawn and redrawn—consciously and literally. It's not as if there's a perimeter spray-painted on the asphalt around a warehouse or a factory, indicating that here you are engaging in circulation and here in production. This caveat is so obvious as to be strange to bother to clarify, except that when the zone was authorized in the United States, such a line *was* drawn. Congress delineated it so as not to undermine "American labor," agreeing for the zone to be a space of commerce, not industry—transmission, not transformation. Congress explicitly outlawed "manufacturing" in a zone.

This delinking of commerce from industry in the zone paralleled the segregating of the zone from US customs territory: commerce was offshore, and industry was onshore.

Then the line was redrawn because zone operators balked at it. For all their talk of "frictionless handling," they knew that the money was in the friction of handling, and so they pushed back on what was permitted in a zone, battling over the language of customs law and the meaning of keywords like "manufacturing."[47] They so groused that Congress relented and lifted the ban on manufacturing in 1950. Yet, make no mistake, this capitulation was not a way of converting the zone-warehouse into a zone-factory; it was a way of enfolding production into circulation. Subzone 70B, the Chrysler assembly plant in Detroit that President Barack Obama visited in 2010 to celebrate "manufacturing," is a space of transmission.[48] Obama was at a kind of warehouse. As a zone operator from Pennsylvania divulged to me at the World Free Zone Convention in Ras Al Khaimah, "I can't remember the last time I used the word *factory*."

The payoff from this book is not in the numbers. *Out of Stock* describes a global phenomenon, but not in the manner of a book that recounts the quantifiable, immediate effects of Walmart, or guns, butter, and steel. While there are thousands of zones in hundreds of countries (and colonies), with the biggest zone system in the United States, zones are small, autonomous parcels of land. In the United States, they are not lucrative for zone operators. Their benefits are claimed to ripple into the communities that host them, although no one can say definitively whether they "create" employment. Whatever impact can be attributed to them is indirect. Their significance, instead, lies in their very premise and in how it illuminates the lineaments of the US economy writ large. Taking stock of the zone helps us to divine how economic processes are territorialized. The characteristic that lends the zone such an eye-catching weirdness—the artifice of an enclave, set off by a barbed-wire fence—alerts us to the pervasive role of bordering in capitalism.[49] The border between foreign and domestic is most glaring, but others have given shape to economic processes in the United States: the borders between commerce and industry, public and private, city and country, white and nonwhite, male and female, human and nonhuman.[50] The zone demonstrates that these domains are social constructs—legal fictions—as well as physical environments (whether banks, bathrooms, or zoos). Perceiving them as both ideal and material heightens our awareness of the contingencies in how the circulation of capital and labor is compartmentalized and controlled. The zone, as a state-backed warehouse, offers a rare peek at the trial and error entailed in the governance of capitalism.

In that last sentence I decenter the people who govern capitalism. In the same sense that this book is not about the numbers, it is not about the number crunchers. At its core, *Out of Stock* is about a spatial form. It is about a "humble thing," in the mold of Siegfried Giedion's "anonymous history."[51] It is about a space of capital that is hidden in plain sight, present but absent—out of stock. In this respect, it departs from what has been called "the new history of capitalism," which has refocused attention on the agency of capitalists in a neoempiricist bid to slay the "abstraction of capital-C Capital."[52] Not only do I embrace abstraction—I fail to see how we can probe a set of operative and lived abstractions without deploying abstractions of our own—but also I minimize agency.[53] I do not regard capitalists as claiming a greater purchase on intentionality and "choices" than do their hirelings. I regard them as "conscious bearers of unconscious processes."[54] Hence the people who populate this book are not fully fleshed-out characters. They are "the warehouseman" and "the zone operator," not individuals, with the capitalists as inscrutable as the laborers whose names scarcely surface in the archive of the zone. I consider them all to be ciphers, as mysterious as a person walking into Zone 1 with no mark of identification (fig. i.12). *Out of Stock* is a history of the labor of distribution in which

Figure i.12. A quiet day at Zone 1 in 1960. Collection of Historic Richmond Town.

laborers and their bosses command few pages (and unions even fewer). It concerns the way that labor is abstracted—exchanged as a commodity, and (in an earlier sense of the word) stolen—in the spatial form of the warehouse.

Photographs are fundamental to my method. They are artifacts, not illustrations.[55] They help make the abstract concrete.[56] It is not that they are more "real" than other types of evidence, or any less abstract, for that matter. It is that they have tutored me in a language that textual evidence on its own can obscure. In the ephemera stuffed into the files of zone operators—the photographs, maps, blueprints, and diagrams, as well as the curated collections thereof, the catalogs, brochures, pamphlets, and scrapbooks—I have come to recognize symbols, codes: a semiotics of the supply chain. In the archive of the zone, these records are abundant. Visual thinking has dominated the fabrication of the foreign-trade zone because zone operators have strained to stake out the zone concept with words alone, much less to sell it to clients or funders. Both the irregularity of its location and the murkiness of its rules have left them casting about for ways to make the zone look like what they believed it to look like. Their strategies for configuring the field of vision give insight into what mythologies of capitalism told them they were gazing at. Specific tableaux have been favored, possibly for how they have accommodated the zone's ambiguity. One such hieroglyph is a photograph from Zone 1, "originally" from 1945, an aerial shot of women packing boxes, arrayed like an assembly line ("borderline manufacturing"), with men behind them sorting boxes and men in customs uniforms standing watch. I say "originally" because in the subsequent decade this photograph appeared with three different captions, one of which was downright eerie (figs. i.13 and i.14).

This slippage is symptomatic of an additional slant on the evidentiary merit of photographs. Photographs combine a felt experience of history—the prick of the real, the "having been there"—with an object lesson about the unknowability of the past.[57] A moment is recorded, but who recorded it, and how? What was cropped out? What occurred the day before, and the day after? These questions apply as much to a typed memorandum by the Department of Treasury as to a photograph by the US Army Signal Corps. But photographs teach this principle more evocatively than paperwork. Photographs of the zone beg for decoding. What exactly are we being asked to see in stacks of boxes of Argentine beef or mounds of Brazil nuts? The instrumental realism of these photographs—their air of impartiality, of logistical banality—taunts me to peer more closely. I speculate about

At the New York Foreign-Trade Zone. Relief packages for Norwegians—paid for and sent by relatives in the United States.

Repacking of Gift Parcels for Israël

Figures i.13 and i.14. When this image was first published in 1945, it carried the caption about Norwegians. But then the caption mutated as the image was reprinted. In 1947, Norwegians became "Europe," and in 1954, Europe morphed into, fascinatingly, "Israël," in a book by a delegation of Europeans who studied the FTZ system during a six-week junket through the United States. Thomas E. Lyons, "Foreign-Trade Zones' Post-Victory Challenge," *Foreign Commerce Weekly*, June 16, 1945; OEEC (Organisation for European Economic Co-operation), *Foreign Trade Zones in the U.S.A.* (Paris: OEEC, 1954).

how and why their scenes were arranged, mindful that all photographs are composed, as warehousemen have learned to appreciate (fig. i.15). Photographs of the zone want to be viewed as plainspoken and devoid of drama, as so tame as to be boring. Customs guards. Tariffs. Yawn. To my eyes, however, they are riveting in their quietude. The more they appear lifeless, the more I ask what they deaden. If capitalism thrives on coercion veiled by the promise of freedom—which it does—then how do visual representations of serene warehouses conceal the structural violence of the zone system?[58]

What stands out about the zone's aesthetic is its constancy. Even as the zone system has expanded in size and scope, the rhetoric surrounding it has not. This immutability merits attention. Historians deal with change over time, yet change is to be expected; that which does not change is the true enigma.[59] *Out of Stock* is structured to keep an eye on such patterns and regularities. I treat the zone as an object, an ever-elusive object of desire for capitalism and its architects. Rather than present a group of case studies about particular sites, I stay with the zone and take the measure of the general idea of it. The following five chapters trace its major iterations, from the warehouse and bonded warehouse, which incubated the zone concept in 1846, to the subzone, which revivified it in 1952. If you buy a new car, and it's not an import, chances are it was assembled in a subzone.

As a designation for a solitary building, the subzone has liberated the zone from geographical fixity, bolstering capitalists' quest for a space of free movement for commodity capital. At least, that's the spin. On the ground, the prospect of a space of free movement for commodity capital has proved hard to pin down. Commodity capital has never moved freely, not to mention that not all capitalists have wanted it to speed by. This is nowhere more evident than in the fact that those most responsible for the spread of the foreign-trade zone have been the warehousemen and their rentier brethren, the port managers—those invested in stalling commodity capital, not in expediting it. The history of the zone system is the history of how these self-styled "space specialists" have vied with each other to sign tenants to Zone 1, Zone 2, Zone 3, and, most recently, Zone 296, such that this utopia of frictionlessness has wound up fulfilling an early warning that it would provoke not free movement but "friction between different sections of the country."[60] It has validated the cynicism of a writer who, in 1926, cautioned against "this modern form of alchemy which it is alleged can breed golden calves on remote mud flats."[61] In the end, it has turned out to be less like a Shangri-la than like a weed-choked Olympic stadium, a municipally subsidized money pit that has failed to meet the hype. And

Take a Photo Tour of Your Warehouse (An Example)

On these two pages you will find an example of a photographic tour of our warehouse. I conformed to the limitations of the magazine in that I selected 27 photos in this sample. You might want more or less; it depends upon your situation. The important thing is to view the whole operation and not repeat unnecessarily. Also, publication requires that we reduce the photos — for your display, use 8–10 glossy prints.

Remember to caption the photos (type the caption on adhesive paper) because then the client can follow them on his own and ask questions as he sees fit. For our example, I displayed the photos in lines read left to right then down and left to right, etc. This should imitate the action of a viewer of your photos.

Finally, please consider these shots as examples only, not as a pattern or guideline. After all, I am sure you can do better for your own warehouse. Good luck!

4. *Our President ______(Name)______*

5. *Here's Who We Are*

6. *People Planning*

10. *______(Name)______, Customer Service Clerk*

11. *Serving a Customer's Need*

12. *Customer Service Clerk*

16. *______(Name)______, Warehouse Manager Giving Guidance*

17. *Greetings, Welcome to ______(Name)______ Warehouse*

18. *Looking Down a Main Aisle*

22. *Our Sanitation Patrol*

23. *Being Careful*

24. *Another Warehouse Area*

Figure i.15. The logistics revolution has compelled warehousemen to sell themselves as tacticians. In these spreads, men in suits far outnumber men in hardhats. Bruce Lederer, "Create a Photographic Tour of Your Warehouse," *Warehousing Review*, Fall 1982.

we need to excavate its origins for that reason, to take seriously capitalists' hopes about it. Only by scratching the surface can we reveal the lead that masquerades as gold. Only by showing the mismatch between fantasy and reality can we expose the counterfeit freedom that sustains the tyranny of capitalism.

Figure 1.1. The original caption reads, "Cases of Argentine corned beef piled up in the New York Foreign Trade Zone on Staten Island awaiting transshipment to the British Isles and the Empire. This 25,000 ton shipment is valued at $3,500,000." October 28, 1939. Acme News Photos.

CHAPTER ONE

Flow, or Fixity in Motion: The Warehouse

> Storage is subject to tidal movements of varying volume in the course of each year. Latitude, climate, seasons, social events, changes in style, customs, tastes, and manners all contribute to influence the demand for storing facilities. . . . There is what might be called a moving stock of goods earning an income for the establishment, but which remains in storage but a comparatively short time. On the other hand there is a permanent stock which remains on hand a comparatively long time. These two factors may be called, respectively, the *flow* and the *fund*. The flow corresponds to the transient guests at a hotel and the fund corresponds to the permanent guests of the hotel. It has been said that no hotel could be successful by relying wholly upon its permanent tenants for an income; that permanent guests serve to pay fixed charges, but transient guests must be relied upon to furnish the margin necessary for profits.
>
> —Department of Commerce and Labor, *Warehousing Industry in the United States* (1903)

"Circulation Reservoirs"

During the violent summer of 1877, a twenty-five-year-old journalist and self-described "rustic visitor" traveled to the nation's busiest seaport to research an essay for *Harper's*. As strikers jammed railroads and battled militias from Maryland to Illinois, Ernest Ingersoll wandered the docks of New York. He inspected the piers, marveled at the cargo, and scribbled notes about the ships and their attendants, chiefly the longshoremen ("among the most ignorant and brutal of men") and the "human wharf rats" ("whose only idea of home is a coil of rope or a recess under a warehouse, whose business is to steal for junkmen, whose ambition is to become pirates").[1]

Yet while this terrain impressed Ingersoll, it was indoors, in the "great caverns for the storage of goods," where the Michigan native found himself most captivated. "Cross the threshold and climb the stairways from one low-roofed loft to another," he beckoned, "and you wander among foreign fields and breathe the airs of every zone." Ingersoll drank in the scene. "Here are tier upon tier of hogsheads of sugar," he admired, "perspiring molasses with the memory of the Cuban sun." The rooms brimmed with "rows," "huge heaps," and "tall stacks" of organic matter. "Go upstairs now," Ingersoll urged his readers, "and look at the bales and casks stored to the roof-tree." Smell, taste, and "wipe your fingers on the clean matting bags of linseed sent all the way from Bombay for your convenience." Ingersoll savored the frisson of disorientation. "As you step out into the broad sunshine, and the heavy iron doors close behind you, you feel as though you were just landing after years of foreign travel, and you bear about with you for many hours the aroma of the tropics."

An accompanying engraving enhanced the drama of this florid travelogue (fig. 1.2). With a strong vertical axis, it drew viewers' eyes past the clerks and porters and along the center aisle into the chamber's "depths," an abyss of cosmopolitan anxieties and appetites. Where underwriters of fire insurance saw catastrophe in this grid of timber pillars and floorboards, overwriters like Ingersoll spied a portal to exotic lands. The edging of the engraving suggested a proscenium arch, theatrically telescoping the earth's manifold riches onto a city street. "Cross the threshold," the composition invited, and step onto far-away continents.

For those of us accustomed to tales of high-tech wizardry at Amazon fulfillment centers and Walmart distribution centers, Ingersoll is a fitting guide to the public perception of the warehouse in the period of its debut. He typifies the tendency that prevailed in the late nineteenth century (and that stubbornly persists) to regard the warehouse as akin to a museum. Sniffing and sampling and labeling, he was every inch the naturalist trained by Louis Agassiz at Harvard University in comparative zoology (and scientific racism).[2] Outside, streetcars rattled, elevators rumbled, and modernity hurtled forward; inside, time stood still, and accreted. "Upon these warehouse floors," he declared, "is written a history of our commerce."

Ingersoll's Edenic tomb is both so familiar and so wrong. Ingersoll was no warehouseman. Such an inert portrayal of cargo would have horrified an entrepreneur who preferred for a majority of the items under his roof to behave like "the transient guests at a hotel." No, a warehouseman would have nominated another homology: the reservoir. Like the warehouse, the reservoir was a space of circulation, and dialectically so: it was a space of *in-*

Figure 1.2. Engraving from "The Lading of a Ship," *Harper's New Monthly Magazine*, September 1877.

terrupted circulation. Unlike the human body—the more popular analogy for circulation—the reservoir was a holding bin. The human body failed to measure up as a medium of storage. Blood should not collect in pools.[3]

The links between the reservoir and the warehouse were as literal in the late nineteenth-century American city as they were metaphorical. They overlapped so much that they shared plumbing.[4] Water from reservoirs was pumped underground to warehouses, helping firemen douse flames and warehousemen lower insurance rates. In an early example, the manager of a Manhattan warehouse "effected one grand hydraulic insurance upon all the merchandise" when he arranged for "the Croton water to be introduced in a large pipe upon every floor of the building." So fierce was the water pressure that there was no commodity "with a combustibility too rapid for the Croton to quench."[5] The source of the "Croton water" was the Croton Aqueduct (the largest one in the world when it was completed in 1842), via a reservoir at the intersection of Fifth Avenue and Forty-Second Street. Adjacent to brownstones, this reservoir—a stone megalith that mimicked an Egyptian pyramid—even resembled a warehouse (fig. 1.3).

Nevertheless, few spoke of it as an aquatic "storehouse." Warehousemen were correct to refer to warehouses as "reservoirs" because the French word *reservoir* meant "storehouse." But fluidity was associated with reservoirs

Figure 1.3. *Looking Down 5th Avenue Aqueduct*. Thomas G. Pratt / Museum of the City of New York. X2010.11.4607.

and not warehouses in the vernacular of capitalism during the Gilded Age. As surpluses in the sphere of production triggered chronic crises in the sphere of distribution, a new cadre of statisticians monitored "reservoirs of goods." By 1903, this usage was so conventional that the US Department of Commerce and Labor characterized the nation's nascent warehousing industry as "a nexus of reservoirs, accumulating stocks in seasons of maximum supply and feeding the demand of tributary sections of the country as the periodical requirements of the community arise."[6] A warehouse was a spatio-temporal apparatus for modulating flows of capital.

It may seem needlessly antiquarian to trot out this etymology, since the purpose of a warehouse may seem manifestly self-evident: ware + house. Warehousemen, though, felt hampered by this common sense. Born after the Civil War, after the transportation revolution, they found themselves occupying a new category within the social division of labor. The warehouse was no storehouse, they came to believe, as they shaped it and it shaped them. It was something new altogether, much like the commodities exchanges it attended. Until the years after World War I they struggled to distinguish warehousing from storing.

"Struggled," moreover, is the perfect verb to capture what was happening in this realm, even though struggle was muted if not markedly absent in representations of the warehouse. In written descriptions and visual portraits, goods in storage appeared motionless, as if boulders in the currents of capitalism. Take the photograph from a warehouse at the nation's first foreign-trade zone (fig. 1.1): its crisp lines demarcate less a quantity than a quality of stock, with the rows of boxes and crates arrayed so rigidly that they might as well be bolted to the floor. Yet as an astute observer of capitalism, Karl Marx, once noted, "This apparent stagnation" was in fact "a form of the flow itself."[7] And struggle was a constant in that dynamic. This chapter chronicles the nineteenth-century rise of the warehouse—what Marx called a "circulation reservoir"—and then audits how it added up.[8] I profile the warehouseman as a merchant of flow, demonstrating how he siphoned the flow of commodities and profited off of blockages, so long as he absorbed the flow of "handling labor" that puddled at his feet.

"Storage Is Civilization"

Any inventory of the warehouse in the United States must begin by stressing its historical novelty. Only a decade before the Civil War did it emerge in mercantile centers as a stand-alone business, and only during the Gilded Age did it register as a destination on the cognitive maps of city denizens. This periodization is itself an argument, since warehousing is too often called "one of the oldest businesses in the world."[9] To grasp what was sui generis about the warehouse, first we need to set aside this canard about its primeval stature.

The claim that the warehouse is as old as humankind has been rooted in the fact that human settlements have always depended on caloric reserves. Indeed by this logic "storage is civilization," as said an ad in *Distribution & Warehousing* in 1922 (fig. 1.4).[10] "Primitive man ate his food where he killed or plucked it," the ad notes. "Only when he stored a surplus . . . did he find freedom from hunger for a long enough time to devote himself to the thought and arts that raised him above the brutes." A meal of fresh-caught rabbit was a mark of savagery, a meal of smoked salmon a badge of cultivation. The gravitas of this parable was visualized by a lack of visuals: the text was styled like a royal scroll decreeing the warehouseman's transhistorical stewardship of human prosperity.

But this timeline was no more than a jingle. Warehousing was decades young in 1922, and it was not reducible to storing. What was truly informative about this ad was that it testified to the existence of a bona fide

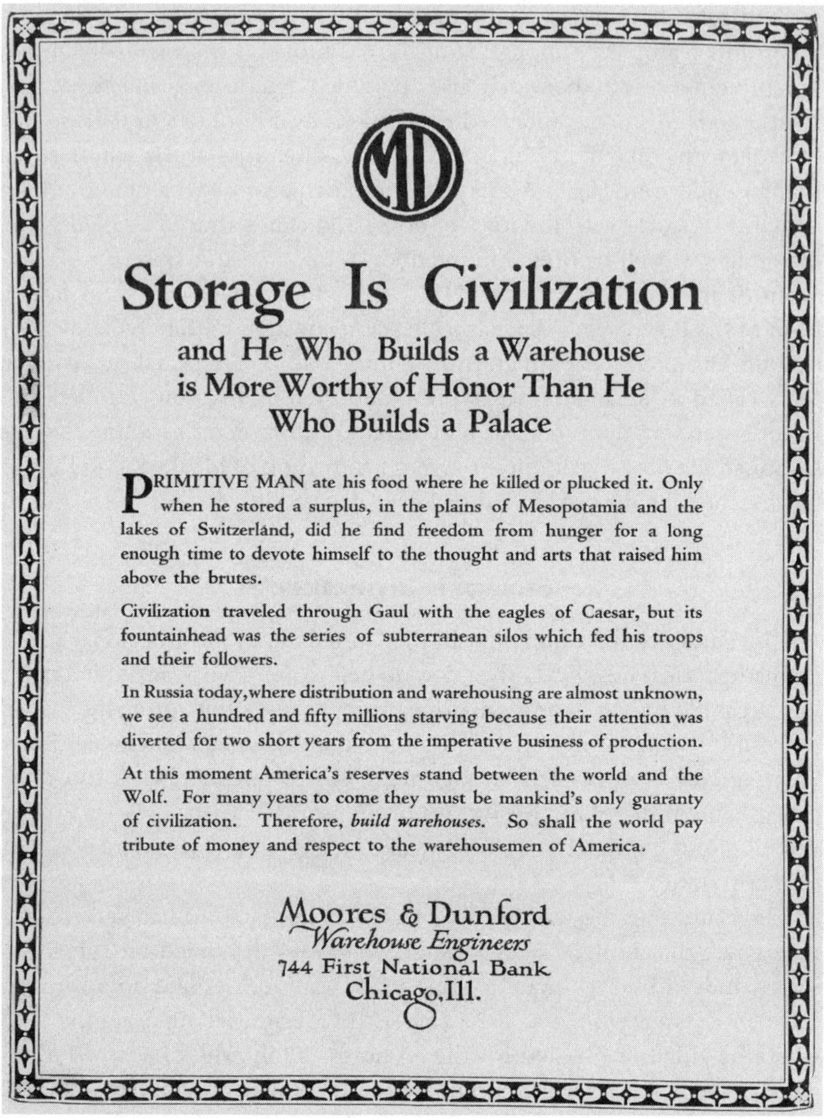

Figure 1.4. Advertisement from *Distribution & Warehousing*, April 1922.

industry, implying that the warehouse had achieved sufficient critical mass to warrant an origin story. Three years later, this reach was confirmed by the publication of the foremost treatise on warehousing, *Warehousing: Trade Customs and Practices, Financial and Legal Aspects*. Armchair expert H. A. Haring's 787-page volume revealed not only the scope and intricacy of the political economy of "warehousing" but also the maturation of what Haring called the industry's "self-consciousness."[11]

The rareness of Haring's study is meaningful for our purposes. To reconstruct the rise of the warehouse, we have to historicize how warehousemen historicized themselves—a job left to them because scholars virtually ignored them. In 1900, when the American Warehousemen's Association canvassed several leading libraries for holdings on warehousing, the Boston Public Library topped the list, "with three volumes, one of these a French work, another a copy of the law, and the other an essay on warehousing bearing the date 1829."[12] With such paltry offerings, warehousemen had to write themselves into the record under their own bylines and via commission. A gem of this archive is a seven-part "History of the Warehouse" that ran in *Distribution & Warehousing* from 1922 to 1924. Authored by a Manhattan-based historian for hire named H. H. Manchester, whose forte was "historical copy" for advertising, the series stands out for both its wealth of information and its assertion of selfhood on the part of the warehouseman.[13]

Manchester's oeuvre covered a variety of spatial forms: the garden, the safety deposit vault, the warehouse.[14] We might think of his method as archaeological. In excavating a site, he alternated between its physical trappings and its intellectual moorings—between the landscape of the garden and the idea of the garden, the architecture of the warehouse and the idea of the warehouse. These essays were erudite. Manchester researched them extensively, often mentioning "the records," and peppering sentences with phrases like "we find notice of."

In this series, Manchester discusses two types of warehouses. The more prevalent is the depository: "a public place in which to deposit goods for safekeeping."[15] Preservation is the essence of the depository, and the reason why the warehouse is often deemed a stagnant vault. Drawings of the tombs in Egyptian pyramids prove for Manchester that "the story of the warehouse begins practically with the dawn of civilization."[16]

The second type of warehouse is the depot. More similar to a shelter than a charnel house, the depot safeguards goods in transit, stowing them prior to their transfer to other vehicles, whether from ship to rail or rail to wagon. Hence the name for the first generation of warehouse businesses: "The [family or place] Storage and Transfer Company." Manchester finds depots throughout the annals of commerce, though he stresses that they proliferated during the Middle Ages and early modern period as the Italian and Hanseatic merchant empires extended as far as "the ends of what may be called the tentacles of civilization, carrying the manufactured products of Europe into distant lands, and drawing from them the raw products or merchandise peculiar to that district."[17]

Manchester's depository/depot binary captures quite lucidly two of the core aims of warehousing, but he omits a third, vexing term: *factory*. Before denoting a wool mill or clock manufactory, "factory" referred to a trading post, or what Manchester would term a depot. Merchants—"factors"—established factories to broker deals.[18] In English, etymologically, these factories first surfaced on the West African coast, where British factors purchased captives with "fetishes" and detained them in seaside "factories," prior to shipping them across the Atlantic in floating warehouses.[19] These factories fused circulation and production, converting the storage of human beings into "the harvest of raw material and the manufacture of goods," in the words of the cultural theorist Saidiya Hartman. "The very word 'factory,'" Hartman notes, "documents the indissoluble link between England's industrial revolution and the birth of human commodities."[20] Writing when survivors of slavery were still alive, Manchester whitewashed the warehouse by segregating it from the slave trade.

As a result of this sort of erasure, "warehousing" has come to be understood as unconcerned with people, not because warehouses have not hosted people, but because commerce has been presumed to stop short of trafficking in people: one of the most resilient reconstructions of capitalism after 1865 has been to redraw this line around what is saleable, what is available to commodify as property. Thus when activists have referred to mass incarceration as "human warehousing"—a motif of protest literature since the 1960s—the term has reverberated jarringly because, allegedly, "warehousing" has not touched the "human."[21] Like "child labor" for Progressive Era reformers, "human warehousing" has served as a monstrous compound to mark a social boundary.

Within this schema, to return to Manchester's typology, there were two basic reasons for the advent of warehousing: the quest for subsistence, or hunger; and the quest for accumulation, or greed. And hunger preceded greed, by an order of thousands of years. In the cradle of civilization, Manchester contends, warehousing sustained the commons. Its role was, as the saying goes, "to save for the time of plenty until the time of need."[22] What eventually repurposed warehousing into an industry—whether of depositories or depots—was the subsumption of storage to the profit motive. This shift is what is dodged by figure 1.4. While we can dig up artifacts of the practice of warehousing from as far back as the pharaohs, we cannot identify the enterprise of warehousing until much more recently.

Karl Marx, whose unfinished manuscript for the second volume of *Das Kapital* stands as one of the great unsung studies of warehousing, emphasized this insight in the 1860s. Writing about storage, Marx looked back to antiquity to refute "the incredible opinion" of Adam Smith "that the formation of a stock is a phenomenon peculiar to capitalist production."[23] As a corrective to Smith, Marx insisted on a profound historical break. Primitives, like capitalists, stocked food. The difference was that primitives stored for use, while capitalists stored for exchange. H. A. Haring, six decades later, inadvertently parroted Marx: "'Warehousing' is more than mere preserving. 'Warehousing' implies *storage*, but 'warehousing' connotes the additional element of trade and profit: 'warehousing' is storing for the purpose of commercial gain."[24]

Those whose workshops and fields filled nineteenth-century warehouses likewise perceived this divergence, often disapprovingly. Artisans and farmers rivaled Marx as theoreticians of warehousing. Many reasoned not only from their pockets but also from a moral critique of hoarding, a perspective found in Luke 12:18, the Parable of the Rich Fool. Some were interested in collectivizing food and tools, as in the bishop's storehouses set up by the Mormons in the 1830s.[25] Others were intent on eliminating middlemen, as in the proposal for a common warehouse in Philadelphia in 1806, which presaged the sundry warehousing bids of the Populists in the 1880s and 1890s.[26] For the Populists, the warehouse was to be communally owned, government-regulated, and a resource for producer and consumer—a cornerstone of the "cooperative commonwealth." Warehousing was to be a means of production, not a production in and of itself.[27]

This strain of thought endured well beyond the demise of the Populists; it turned up in the academic discipline of cultural anthropology, for instance, which found in rituals of communal storage a key facet of so-called "primitive economics."[28] Manchester himself codified it—and racialized it—in one of the storyboards with which he illustrated his articles. *When America Was Young* depicts the range of storage techniques in colonial and early America (fig. 1.5). At its center is a scene of precapitalist warehousing, "a sixteenth century picture of an Indian village with warehouses and huts." In erecting these structures, "the object was, of course, preservation or storage for the sake of future consumption, rather than for purposes of trade."[29] These were depositories as well as depots, but no one profited from them. "For this reason," Manchester continues, "while the Indians

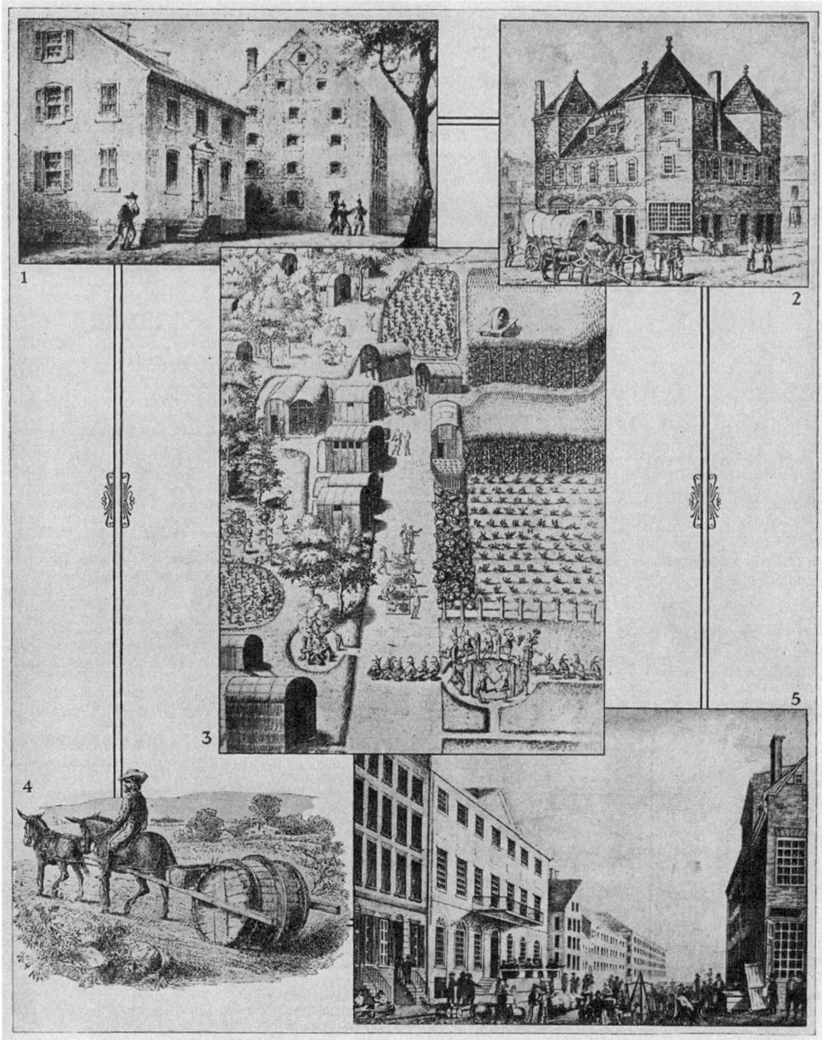

Figure 1.5. *When America Was Young*. Collage from "History of the Warehouse, Part V," *Distribution & Warehousing*, April 1923. The original caption reads: "1-The Rhinelander sugar warehouse, used as a prison during the Revolutionary War; New York City. 2-The old triangular warehouse, Boston, built in 1680. 3-A sixteenth century picture of an Indian village with warehouses and huts. 4-Hauling a hogshead of tobacco to the warehouse in Colonial days. 5-Coffee house slip, New York City, with buildings including warehouses, eighteenth century."

must be credited with storehouses, the first warehouses within the present United States were probably introduced by the whites" (warehouses "introduced by the whites"—an aspect of the imposition of private property and what Marx referred to as "primitive accumulation"). Manchester charts this progression in the collage. On the top are portraits of two iconic buildings, in New York and in Boston; on the bottom are views of for-profit warehousing of two staple commodities, tobacco and coffee.

After separating the Indians' subsistence storehouse from the whites' commercial warehouse, Manchester specifies one final break in the realm of the latter: ownership. Initially, the owner of the commercial warehouse was a man—a merchant—for whom storage was one phase of selling goods.[30] Later, he was a warehouseman who bothered not at all with selling goods and instead babysat them for a fee. Manchester's perimeter images show merchants' warehouses, not warehousemen's warehouses. These merchants arrived in the New World as delegates of trading companies, and then they spun off as forwarding agents and commission merchants. Their warehouses supported wholesaling and doubled as storefronts, with storage upstairs or in back. Take the senior partner of the Jenkins and Company Tea Warehouse in Philadelphia, who—per an 1852 advertisement—"resided seven years in China, engaged in the tea trade" (fig. 1.6). Jenkins, archetypically speaking, was not a warehouseman; he was a tea dealer who sold out of a facility he called a warehouse. Jenkins dealt in tea, not in square footage.

The transition from Jenkins to post-Jenkins took many decades to register. The life of Walter Loomis Newberry, a benefactor of Chicago's Newberry Library, is an illustration. Manchester spotlights Newberry in the penultimate article of his series, about the degree to which "warehouses marked step after step in the march westward."[31] By 1825, due to canals, all the cities of the Great West—Chicago, Buffalo, Detroit, Cleveland, and St. Louis—boasted warehouses. Newberry backed one such building with George W. Dole in Chicago in 1833, for grain. Manchester terms Newberry & Dole "a storage and forwarding business," and the term seems to have fit, since Newberry & Dole ran a depot for grain owned by others. Even so, Newberry never identified as a "warehouseman." He was like the Pierreponts, the Woodruffs, and the Robinsons, men who invested millions of dollars in the "the gray walls of the granite storehouses by the docks," in the words of Walt Whitman.[32] These men were still listed as "merchants" in the 1850 and 1860 censuses, by which time they were dealing primarily in real estate and only secondarily in tea or salt.

By 1877, then, when Ernest Ingersoll wandered the docks, it was recognized that regardless of the charms one might discover inside a warehouse,

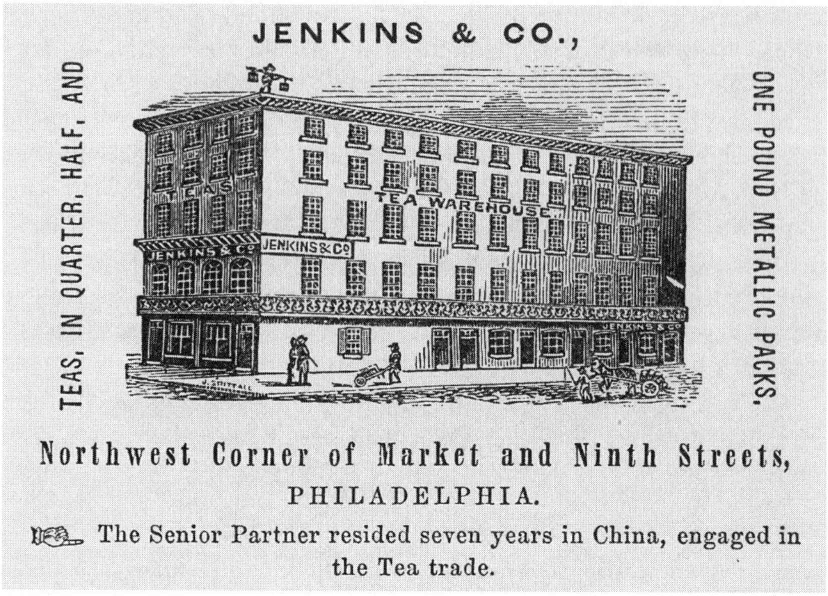

Figure 1.6. Advertisement from R. A. Smith, *Philadelphia as It Is* (Philadelphia: Lindsay and Blakiston, 1852).

the proprietor was wholly detached from them. That same year an inventor from Massachusetts filed a patent for a "toy warehouse" that reflected this logistical posture (fig. 1.7). Children who played with the contraption were captivated not by teas or spices but by "an idea of commercial articles and packages and the methods ordinarily employed in handling them." And if they aspired to greatness, they imagined themselves not the muscles but the brains of this operation: "A miniature set of books could be added to the counting-room," the application notes, "and children could keep an account of the merchandise received and delivered."[33]

This embryonic division between merchant and warehouseman would soon correspond to the dichotomy between "private" and "public" warehouses. A merchant, after all, would continue to store commodities in house, whether on site or at another property. Such a facility was a *private* warehouse. A *public* warehouse, conversely, was a business whose product was storage space. It was public in that it was open to all customers; "public," to the ire of Populists, did not signal government involvement. While public warehouses cropped up as early as the late 1840s, not until 1882 did the New York Building Department issue permits for "warehouses."[34]

The trailblazer among public warehouses was the Atlantic Dock Com-

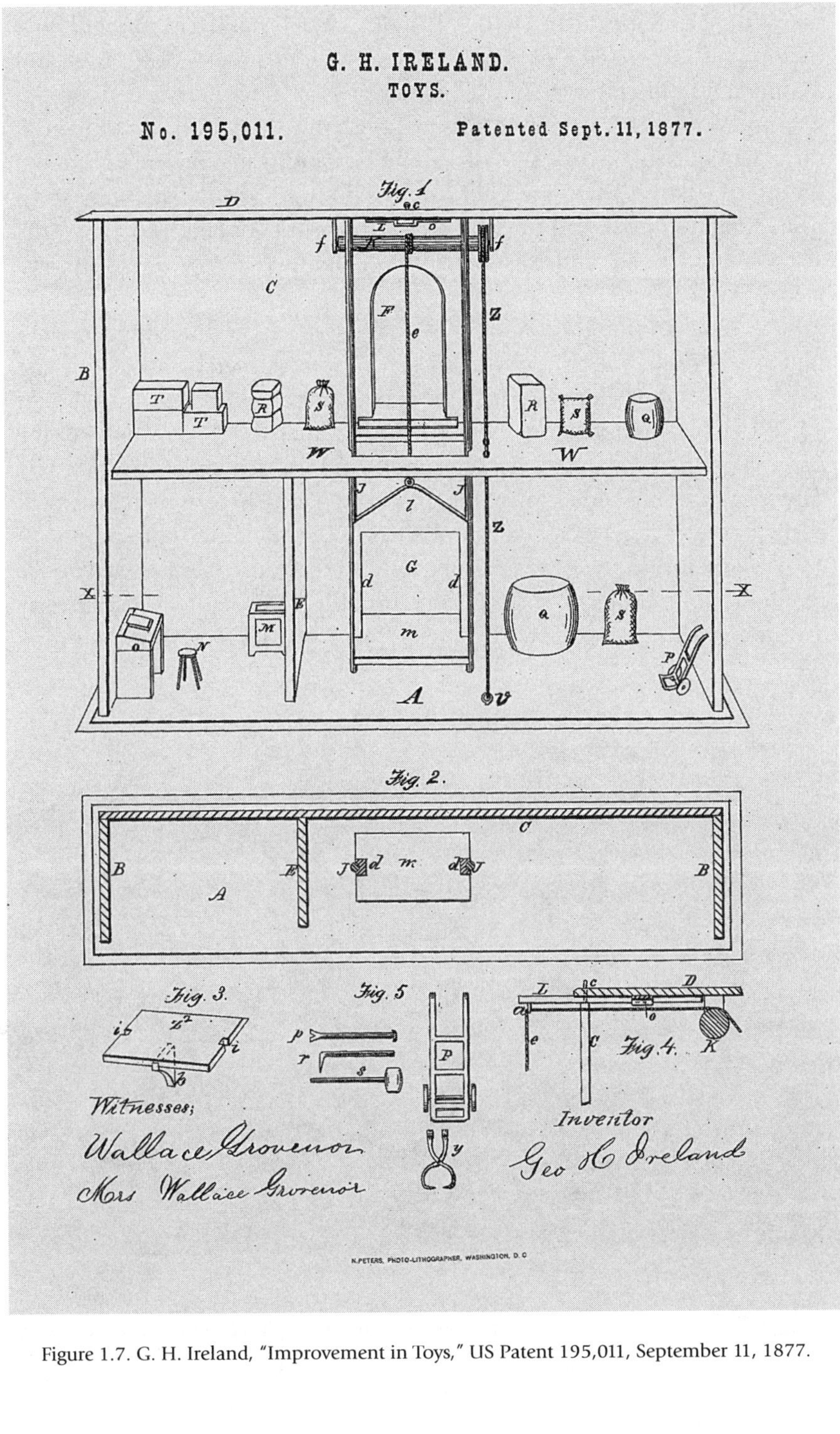

Figure 1.7. G. H. Ireland, "Improvement in Toys," US Patent 195,011, September 11, 1877.

pany (ADC), chartered in 1840.[35] The ADC was located in Brooklyn on a barren half-mile stretch of New York harbor across from Wall Street and Manhattan's old and overcrowded finger piers.[36] (By century's end, Brooklyn, not Manhattan, would be synonymous with warehousing.) Known as the Atlantic Basin, it consisted of warehouses and grain elevators mounted on top of wharves that jutted out into the dredged harbor, shielding ships from rough weather and uneven tides. Unlike the Jenkins and Company Tea Warehouse, an undertaking of this magnitude merited a bird's-eye view (fig. 1.8).

The ADC is the culmination of Manchester's centuries-long epic: a nineteenth-century public warehouse for general merchandise. But the ADC was just the beginning. By ending before the Gilded Age, Manchester neglected the specialization of warehousing after the Civil War.[37] As the national market expanded, the depository and the depot were followed by subtypes that responded to nuances in how goods were moving—two in particular were much-remarked curiosities of the late nineteenth century.

An early foil to the general-merchandise warehouse was the warehouse for household goods. The Civil War prompted this subtype because, as a warehouseman reminisced in 1916, "Many houses were broken up by

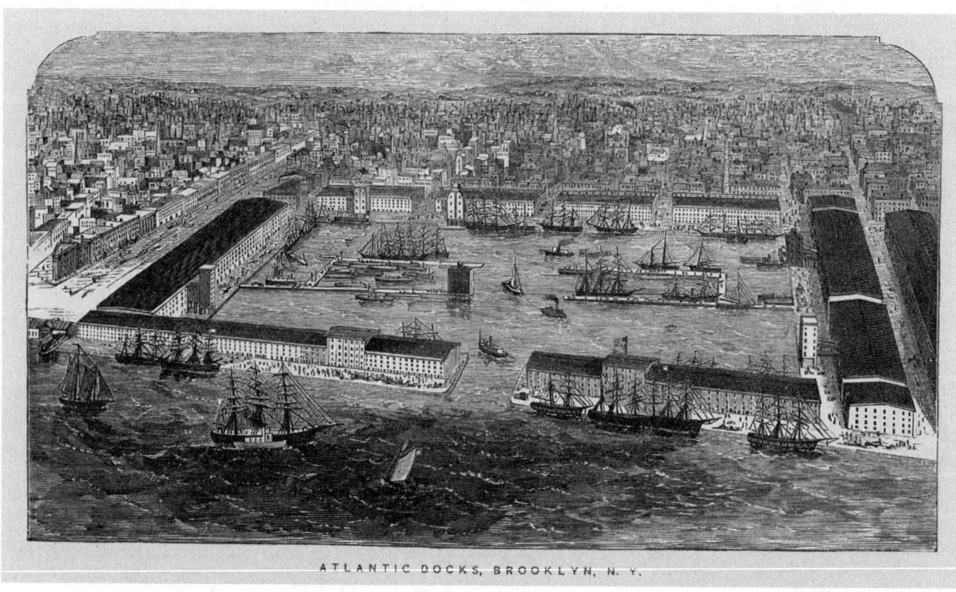

Figure 1.8. The water beyond the basin is choppy, but within it is calm. Engraving from Henry Reed Stiles, *A History of the City of Brooklyn*, vol. 3 (Brooklyn, 1870).

the fathers, husbands, and sons being called to the front."[38] During the Gilded Age, it spurred urbanization as it assisted the "large floating population," both the elites who traveled abroad in the summers and the masses who downsized from communal manors to single-family apartments.[39] It simulated a hotel, with as many as "1,000 private rooms in a six-story building"—some for paintings, others for fragile bric-a-brac.[40] As its stature grew, it acquired a reputation as a warren of domestic intrigue, "a place where family skeletons come into sight"; by the 1920s, it was known as a pit stop on a woman's trip to divorce court.[41] Notably, it stood apart from the general-merchandise warehouse by harboring "sentimental storage." As a modality of singularization rather than commoditization, the household-goods warehouse sheltered pianos, broken rocking chairs, and other mementos, like "a room of furniture left by a mother to her son, with the death-bed request that he never sell anything that had been hers."[42]

The other subtype garnered less warmhearted coverage. The first cold-storage warehouse opened in New York City in 1865, with fish on ice.[43] This technology revolutionized eating in America, and for that it was as much reviled as celebrated.[44] Cold-storage warehousing drew controversy in the early 1900s, as progressive reformers attacked the safety and morality of frozen "fresh" foods, and as "preserved assets" underwrote speculation on commodity futures. Newspapers fed the distrust. These gigantic refrigerators—vital nodes in the transcontinental networks of refrigerated railcars—showcased warehousing's triumph over the dangers of time and space, uniting "congealed edibles from every quarter of the globe" with frozen black bears.[45]

With specialization came a trend toward professionalization, especially among designers of warehouses. This shift mirrored that from merchant-warehouseman to warehouseman. Originally, warehouses were constructed by architects like James Bogardus, who collaborated with merchants in the 1850s.[46] As subtypes began to call for expertise, though, a new breed of builder—the warehouse engineer—joined the all-purpose architect. Moores & Dunford, the firm behind "Storage Is Civilization" (fig. 1.4), is a prime example: Charles H. Moores and S. H. Dunford met as employees of a firm that designed a variety of industrial buildings, and then they broke away to specialize in warehouse construction.[47]

By the time Moores & Dunford started filing patents for warehouse implements, in 1925, they could expect to find backers in a national confederation of warehousemen. The American Warehousemen's Association (AWA) was founded in Chicago in 1891.[48] Its inaugural roster was dominated by companies along the Chicago–New York rail corridors, with a smattering west of the Rockies and south of the Mason-Dixon.[49] By the 1920s, the membership had swelled to many hundreds of companies from across the country, whose "storage executives" met in posh resorts for multiday conferences and black-tie dinners. The industry was so robust that—as *Distribution & Warehousing* reported in a waggish feature in 1922—the membership also included "Mrs. Warehouseman," approximately fifty "women warehouse 'men.'"[50] In sum, by 1922, when Manchester issued his series of articles, the warehouse was, if not ancient, at least individuated enough and sufficiently capitalized that people believed it had a history that needed to be written.

"Bankers of Merchandise"

The mission of the AWA was to assert the rights and responsibilities of the warehouseman. From the start, in the 1890s, the association stressed the latter in its messaging, accenting security and stability. The warehouseman was a custodian of commodity capital: he facilitated movement when he prevented movement. He safeguarded the goods consigned to him, caring for them as they sat as stock, suspended between production and consumption. He shielded them against the elements, natural and social: decay, deterioration, fire, theft, strikes, and insurgency.[51] He braved the hazards of storage—helping his clients brave the hazards of the market—and he charged accordingly.

Still, if storage was such a boon, then why bother to hire the warehouseman? Why not do it yourself in a private warehouse? Commodities in storage constituted dead stock. Why lose money to storage fees? "The last thing a manufacturer really desires to do is to store anything," H. A. Haring reminded his readers in his 787-page treatise. "Storage, with him, is thought of as an evil, to be shunned wherever possible."[52] Haring subsequently confronted this barrier in a column for *Distribution & Warehousing*, counseling warehousemen to think of advertising as pedagogy and themselves as "teachers-of-warehousing."[53] Warehousing is tricky to peddle, Haring grants, because it is a new service. A new service requires changing of "business systems," and for manufacturers, ceding physical control of inventory posed a seismic such change, "about as fundamental as for the family to give up their detached home, store three-fourths of their belongings in a furniture warehouse, and live in three rooms and a kitchenette."[54] Manufacturers needed an attitude adjustment, Haring advised; warehousemen needed to foster new "habits" of storage.

Haring penned these columns in the late 1920s. By then there were a number of inducements for a manufacturer to offload warehousing. Distribution headed the list. In the prosperous years after World War I, in a market of national and international dimensions, it was strategic to deploy "spot stocks" in multiple locations.[55] Liquidity was next. Public warehouses eased the burden of fixed capital: not every manufacturer was flush enough to construct private warehouses; renting was cheaper than owning. Risk was also a buzzword: for food manufacturers, the cost of a public warehouse or a jobber who leased a public warehouse was mitigated by the upside of being able to let someone else worry about spoilage.[56] And one rationale preceded them all. It was the oldest in the AWA playbook: the warehouse receipt.

This was no ordinary sales ticket, and it was paramount in how warehousemen thought about the warehouse's utility as a circulation reservoir. The warehouse receipt was a contract that the warehouseman gave to a customer upon consignment of merchandise. It laid out promises and disclaimers, and it certified the warehousemen's insurance coverage. But it did not disappear into a desk drawer. The warehouse receipt doubled as currency, bartered for other receipts and for loans of coin—it converted dead stock into "live storage." It had done so for centuries.[57] In colonial Virginia, it was the primary source of paper money, in the guise of a "tobacco note."[58] Warehousemen hyped this lineage. "Choose your warehouseman as you would choose your banker," they urged in advertisements, fashioning themselves "Bankers of Merchandise."[59]

The warehouse receipt evolved in two stages as a paper technology of capitalism, and the transition corresponded to a mutation of the commodity form. In storehouses of the Middle Ages, the receipt designated unique units of merchandise, attributing ownership to those twenty pelts or that crate of herring. It was also transferable, for other commodities or credit: as Marx observed about the swapping of receipts, "Circulation of commodities can take place without their physical movement."[60] This type of receipt was prevalent in the United States up through the mid-nineteenth century. An Illinois farm family shipping a sack of wheat via canal could retrieve that same sack of wheat from a warehouse in Manhattan several weeks later and in the interim tender its warehouse receipt as an advance for food and supplies from a furnishing merchant.[61]

But lots were cumbersome to coordinate, as railroads opened up commodity frontiers and as shipments proliferated. So a new machine, the grain elevator, hastened the replacement of sacks with carloads. Thus was the second type of warehouse receipt—the general warehouse receipt—introduced at the grain elevator, which debuted in Buffalo, New York, in

1842 and at the Atlantic Basin in 1846.[62] The grain elevator was a tall, narrow warehouse with steam-powered vertical belts that carried grain in uncovered pails. Here the farm family contributed each sack of grain to a common stock (a quasi stock exchange) and in return received a general warehouse receipt, for a specific share of the common stock rather than a specific lot of grain. The grain was now fungible.[63]

The general warehouse receipt was an epochal invention.[64] (Vladimir Lenin once commented, "Grain is the currency of currencies.")[65] In the late 1860s, thanks to groundbreaking grain elevators in the US heartland, brokers in the pit of the Chicago Board of Trade stopped hawking warehouse receipts and started gambling on their worth.[66] In these inaugural futures markets nothing changed hands: brokers "contemplated delivery" while betting on prices.[67] Downplayed in the historical literature, however, is the essential role of the warehouse, the fortifications of storage. The warehouse subtended the pit. Without the street address on the warehouse receipt, the commodities vended in the pit carried no demonstrable, objective value—no exchange value. H. A. Haring nailed it: "Warehoused commodities are the physical basis for the whole fabric of trading and speculation," he wrote in 1925. "The warehouse is the foundation stone for the exchanges."[68] The fictitiousness of the "futures contract" depended on the facticity of the warehouse, on the legally binding pledge of the things themselves physically fixed in place. "Commerce" was treated by legal scholars as "transportation of the tangible," and the tangible had to reside somewhere, somehow secured.[69] All that was solid did not melt into air.

What sealed the deal was the visual epistemology of this connection between the warehouse and the pit. The new traffic in warehouse receipts intersected with the new traffic in photographs. "Form is henceforth divorced from matter," declared Oliver Wendell Holmes Sr. in 1859 as he praised the stereograph, another medium of "universal currency" fabricated in the mid-nineteenth century: "Matter in large masses must always be fixed and dear; form is cheap and transportable."[70] Quite literally, following Holmes, the immobility of the "matter" locked inside the warehouse enabled the mobility of the "form" of the warehouse receipt. The warehouse receipt was like a photograph of the warehouse interior (e.g., fig. 1.1), and as it bounced from ledger to ledger it materialized the dematerialization of the pit.[71]

The warehouse receipt generated flow from stasis. Of course, this stasis was a trick of the eye, an inability to perceive that stocks never stopped fluctuating. One kernel of grain replaced another in the elevator bin. One box of Argentine beef got trucked out from the foreign-trade zone, and another shipped in. "The immobile, independent existence of this world of commodities, of things, is only illusory," Marx wrote at the height of the railroad age. "The station is always full, but always full of different travelers."[72] Nevertheless, to the extent that travelers paused because their production time was protracted (like nuts and liquors and other agricultural commodities) or because their shelf life was out of sync with consumers' proclivities (like roadsters assembled in January), the warehouse buttressed a second circuit of capital along which their alter egos—their receipts—journeyed.[73]

Safe passage, in turn, was ensured by those pieces of paper. As the AWA well knew, the warehouseman needed to be trustworthy for the warehouse receipt to be bankable. He needed to enlist the cooperation of bankers, and if he specialized in agricultural storage, he needed to convince farmers to believe in him.[74] The AWA standardized and modernized the warehouse receipt, and after twenty-odd years of lobbying Congress, it celebrated the Warehouse Act of 1916, which instituted a federal licensing program for warehouses.[75] This legislation confirmed that, as one banker wrote, "one cannot make himself a warehouseman simply by calling himself one or by placing a sign to that effect upon his building."[76] The receipt was guaranteed if the warehouseman was government certified.

Or was it? Although many a receipt was crowned with drawings of buildings, what a receipt signified was a quality of inertia and impermeability, not a quantity of bricks and mortar. This point was vividly illustrated in "field warehousing," a method by which the warehouse itself—like the receipt—took flight. Sanctioned in 1854 for the on-site storage of "coal, mahogany, and other woods and lumber," field warehousing cabined off commodities too cumbersome or flimsy to move.[77] A warehouseman, hired by a farmer or a manufacturer to construct storage "in the field," leased land from that client, erected fencing on it around a stock of commodities and "signposted" that stock as off-limits. Afterward he forwarded a warehouse receipt to a bank, which routed it to a "commodity loan" department to appraise its value before granting a loan.[78] From isolated instances on plantations and farms in the South and West in the 1880s, the exercise grew into a standard procedure for dealing with dips in demand. Gold in gold mines, sugar in sugar refineries, rare stamps, Model Ts—all were field warehoused. Each winter in Detroit, warehousemen rented sheds and exhibition halls on county fairgrounds to park automobiles until spring, issuing warehouse receipts that companies like Ford and General Motors converted into fiscal fuel.[79]

During World War II, field warehousing gained traction, as business magazines plugged it as a "trick" for accessing credit (fig. 1.9).[80] In 1944

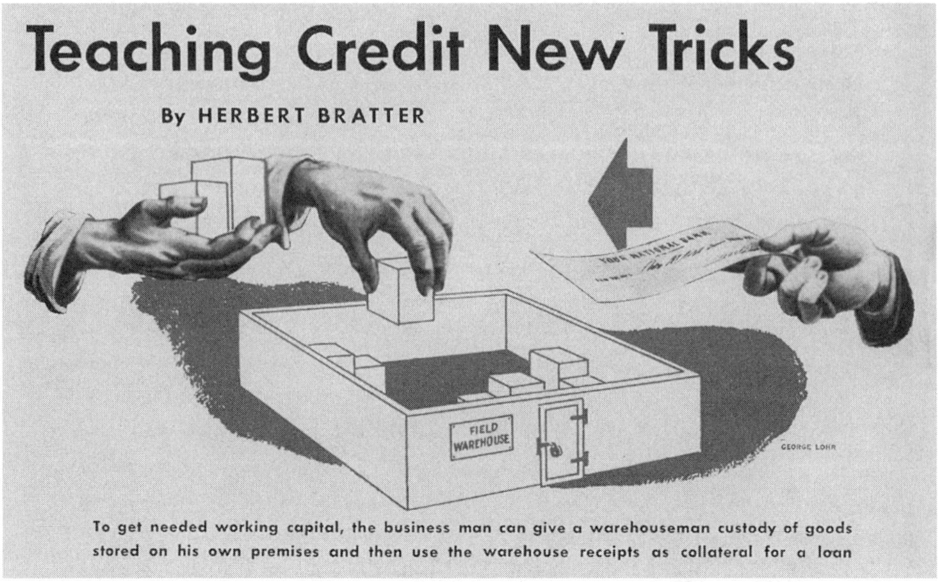

Figure 1.9. Illustration from "Teaching Credit New Tricks," *Nation's Business*, April 1944.

American Express acted on the trend and launched a division for field warehousing with the provocative slogan "Inventory in Action."[81] But this experiment became a cautionary tale about the magic of finance. Two decades in, American Express learned that warehousing was best left to warehousemen when a client fleeced some of Wall Street's biggest investment banks in "The Great Salad Oil Swindle" of 1963, rattling the stock market. American Express inspectors had discovered the true status of 136 vegetable oil tanks owned by Anthony "Tino" De Angelis—a kingpin who relied on multimillion-dollar loans backed by American Express warehouse receipts. Rigged with dummy bottoms, the tanks along New York Harbor in Bayonne, New Jersey, were filled with seawater and nearly empty of oil.[82]

"The Warehouseman's Dollar"

While the warehouse receipt helps us to position the warehouse in the longue durée of the history of capitalism, it was not determinative in warehousing's renovation into an autonomous sector. It was a nice hook to lure customers, but it was not what padded the warehouseman's wallet. This lesson began to dawn on him in the early twentieth century, as the AWA wrestled with the constraints of a business model that seemed to be stuck in square footage. AWA members were realizing that, as landlords, they were providing an array of "services" unrelated to building maintenance. The secret to success in warehousing was figuring out how to package those extras.

The problem with square footage, as the warehouseman recognized, was that there was only so much to go around. Warehouse space was not variable capital; it could not be endlessly exploited, no matter how intricately the warehouseman divided it—and divide and subdivide he did. "Aisle space," "working space," "waste space," "idle space": by the 1920s, AWA manuals taxonomized each square inch of the warehouse, horizontally and vertically.[83] These distinctions helped the warehouseman to assign costs. A client directly used X amount of working space, and this lot was indirectly supported by Y amounts of aisle, waste, and idle space. Still, the endless subdivision of space could not enlarge the total volume. The warehouseman's growth curve was finite.

Another difficulty was that warehouse space was cemented in place. Warehousemen could not jack up rents, lest their clients abandon them for warehouses down the river or across the ocean. Such menaces were plausible in the age of telegraphy and steam, as distances became more relative than absolute. By the turn of the twentieth century, warehouses in Havana and Matanzas were duplicates of warehouses in New York. Why stow and refine raw sugar in Brooklyn when you could do so with equal ease in Cuba, and for lower wages?

Creating a monopoly proved no match for this new elasticity of geography. In 1888, facing competition from Cuba and elsewhere, Brooklyn's old guard scrambled to retain clients by organizing a trust.[84] The *Brooklyn Eagle* warned that the trust would attract unions and repel customers and, to be sure, within six months, the Knights of Labor were canvassing for the Democratic ticket in Brooklyn and posting circulars that singled out the ploy: "Workingmen! Read this! Who owns the Warehouse Trust? Republicans."[85] Rates skyrocketed, and holdings plummeted. By December the trust's warehouses were vacant, even of rats.[86]

So how was a warehouseman to raise his bottom line? Efficiency. In 1895, Irving T. Bush, the heir of an oil-refinery fortune, unveiled the first of 123 warehouses and eight piers along the South Brooklyn waterfront, a few miles from Red Hook, the Warehouse Trust's turf.[87] "Bush Terminal" was where, in the phrase of *American Magazine*, "factory, warehouse, freight car and steamship all could meet and kiss one another."[88] Bush's insight was to play cupid in this romance, to combat "the endless lost motion" and "waste expense" that hindered trade in New York City. "The ships were on one shore, the railroads on another," he wrote in his memoir, "and the factories were scattered about the city on any old street without any relation to either kind of transportation."[89] A terminal would thrust Gotham into the machine age.

By mingling the roles of landlord and freight forwarder, Bush seized an advantage in the warehousing industry's long-standing beef with the railroads. During the late nineteenth century, the latter encroached on the former by allowing cargo to be stashed at railroad freight depots at no charge. In 1897, the AWA filed a complaint with the Interstate Commerce Commission (ICC), and the ICC obliged with a ruling that prohibited the railroads from granting more than four days of such "free time" (a phrase that indexed how the burgeoning transport industries were reformatting time as well as space). The ICC stipulated that storage was a for-profit endeavor, and the province of warehousemen.[90] Not satisfied, Bush—an early member of the AWA and later a two-term president of the New York State Chamber of Commerce—recognized that a warehouse was little more than expensive fixed capital if it hosted storage alone. At Bush Terminal, he upped the ante by creating his own railroad trunk line and by integrating distribution with production. So his rates ranged more than those of his predecessors. He charged for storage time, but also he factored in a new variable: handling time.

The term *handling* was one of capitalism's keywords during this period—the first era of globalization. "Handling," the antithesis of "crafting," referred to manual labor, too, but in the external care of commodities rather than in their internal transformation. An artisan "crafted" a set of iron tools, and then a shipper "handled" them to market. While crafting involved a change of form, handling involved movement, a change of location: transmission instead of transformation. By this logic, the warehouseman was one type of "handler merchant."[91] And supposedly the manufacturer was not.

Yet "manufacturing," too, was the inverse—or at least not the equivalent—of "crafting." "Manufacturing" ran on machines that powered the division of labor, and the division of labor was a spatial phenomenon, inserting acts of transmission into acts of transformation, within the factory and around the globe. The division of labor necessitated "handling" during, not only after, production. This hybridity became apparent by the 1920s in the supply chains of the vertically integrated multinational corporations, as manufacturers shipped materials across oceans to finish products, and it was correspondingly true of the inner workings of the temples of mass production. To cite one canonical case, "Schmidt," Frederick Winslow Taylor's trained gorilla in *The Principles of Scientific Management*, worked as a "pig-iron handler" at Bethlehem Steel.[92]

Henry Ford recruited engineers like Taylor to choreograph the eight hundred to one thousand "truckmen, pushers, and shovers" he employed at Highland Park.[93] "One of the principal problems," as the authors of a 1915 overview of the Ford Motor Company commented, "is that of transportation within the factory walls."[94] *Throughput* was the term, and it measured two aspects of circulation: the speed at which supplies moved within the factory walls and the speed at which finished products moved from the factory to the market. The two were related; the faster materials moved on the line, the faster they moved out the gates. "If transportation were perfect and an even flow of materials could be assured," Ford wrote in 1924, "it would not be necessary to carry any stock whatsoever."[95] Remnants of efforts to achieve this equilibrium are ubiquitous in the records of the Ford Motor Company, from memoranda by the superintendent of stock to photographs on how to mail supplies. In most of the visual aids, hands—cropped from their limbs—attach to cargo, reminding us that boxes do not move themselves (fig. 1.10). Unlike "throughput," which is a diachronic

Figure 1.10. At Ford an entire division was devoted to superintending the logistics of supplying the assembly line. Photographs and short films were commissioned to train workers in how best to care for goods in transit, in order to minimize damage, theft, and waste of man-hours (even when those man-hours involved manicured nails). From the collections of The Henry Ford.

calculation of velocity, "handling" is a synchronic narrative of how hands navigate the factory. Handling is the labor of throughput.

Ford's preoccupation with handling suffused the architecture of his factories. His architect, Albert Kahn, mapped out a "routine diagram" for each project, in order to ensure "that the paths of the material through the works do not cross at any point, as this involves the risk of congestion." This exercise would identify "the shortest path of the material through the works, with the least amount of handling & re-handling."[96] While engineers worried about timing tasks to the second, Kahn strove to dictate footsteps. Handling was a drag on the assembly line.

And this was where the public warehouse came in, the warehouseman hoped—in between factories, if not inside them, "to do everything that a manufacturer wants to have done except sell the goods," according to an AWA member in 1902.[97] The predicament for the warehouseman was how to price his handling. As a "handler merchant," he needed to make visible the labor of handling, using dollars and cents. The AWA issued a thick guidebook to that end in 1923. "The warehouseman's problem of existence," the AWA declared in *Warehousing General Merchandise,* was that he failed to docket handling costs. This blind spot was a serious weakness. "What applies to manufacturers dealing in tangible commodities applies with equal if not greater force to warehousemen dealing in intangible services."[98]

Warehousing General Merchandise evaluates an immense range of commodities, with a fixation on paperwork, which evidently propped up the warehouse. Paperwork was a prominent topic at AWA meetings in the early 1920s. Warehousemen, the mantra went, needed to homogenize their approaches to bookkeeping, for the industry was stunted by inconsistencies in paperwork. Manufacturers—who wanted to take advantage of far-flung warehouses for spot stocks—regularly complained about this problem.[99] *Warehousing General Merchandise* was written with the conviction that a warehouse receipt was on par with a ship or a railcar as a means of communication.[100] For the industry to thrive, information needed to move between depots as expediently as cargo.

So how did the warehouseman crunch the numbers? *Warehousing General Merchandise* answers this question with a tutorial—with sample paperwork—on flow. Overall, rates were quoted by the "lot," and handling was just one component of the quote. The other components were more straightforward. First, there were the costs associated with rent and administration, what the AWA termed "overhead," or "that portion of salaries, etc., which would continue if goods remained in store without moving," like maintenance fees for graves in a cemetery. These included real estate taxes, fire insurance, and assorted building expenses, as well as operations expenses like clerks' and managers' salaries, advertising, and watchmen's wages.[101]

Second, there were costs related to the characteristics of the commodities in the lot, correlating with commodities' use values. These were recorded on a "Lot Cost Form," and they encompassed the weight, mass, relative homogeneity of the lot (whether it contained "bulk" or "assorted" merchandise), as well as quirks of physiognomies (fig. 1.11). In the days before containerization, a warehouseman needed to know his apples from his oranges. *Warehousing General Merchandise* devoted 280 pages to the unique traits of thousands of types of merchandise, underlining propensities for spoilage or contamination—peaches could bruise, and glass could shatter.

To compute the daily rate for a given lot, apart from handling, the warehouseman averaged the first category of overhead costs into a unit of square footage (say, twenty cents per square foot for any commodity) and multiplied that number both by the lot's "space consumption" and by the AWA's recommended rate for that particular commodity. Silk might require less room than rubber, but it was more delicate and consequently more expensive to store.[102]

Only after he assessed the "nature of the lot" did the warehouseman reckon with the labor performed on it, or the left column on the Lot Cost Form: the "man-hour costs." A relic of the "cost accounting" movement of the turn of the twentieth century, the man-hour was an analog of the square foot: a standard unit of measure—the AWA embraced it as "a uniform basis of reporting" with which to compare practices in regions "where wages are different."[103] The warehouseman tracked man-hours on his weekly "Payroll Analysis" form, and interestingly, he divided them into a hierarchy of "productive" and "non-productive" man-hours (fig. 1.12). To a manufacturer like Ford, every single minute on this form was "handling" and therefore "non-productive"; for a warehouseman, only a fraction of man-hours fell into that column. Why? If the warehouseman could charge a task to a particular commodity, then he deemed it productive labor, not handling.

"Productive labor," as the AWA counseled, "being measurable without difficulty, can easily be ascertained in dollars and cents for each commodity or each lot."[104] Unloading and trucking a case of cheese from a railcar, weighing it, and if it smelled odd, sampling it ("handling" from the standpoint of the cheese manufacturer)—together these "intangible services" were directed at a particular commodity, and thus were billable by the "man-hour." The "man" in question was a figure of abstract labor, stripped of individual capacities. All that the warehouseman cared about was how

LOT COST FORM

Commodity *Vegetables, Preserved*

Type of P'kg. *Case*

Gross Wt. of P'kg. *70*

Lot or File No. *82519*

STORED IN

Bulk ☐

Ass't ☒

I.P.D. ☐

INWARD COSTS

	Date	No. P'kgs	Total Wt.	MAN-HOUR COSTS				NATURE OF LOT		REMARKS
					Unld'g Cars	Sill to Pile		No. P'kgs	Size of Unit	
	2/10/20	800	56000		9.60	22.40		500	L. U.	
								200	1/3 L. U.-L. U.	
								100	1/10 L. U.-1/3 L. U.	
	Totals	800	56000		9.60	22.40		800		

OUTWARD COSTS

	Date	No. P'kgs	Total Wt.	Man-Hour Costs			Size of Unit	Date	No. P'kgs	Total Wt.	Man-Hour Costs			Size of Unit
				Pile to Sill	Load'g Cars						Pile to Sill	Load'g Cars		
	2/20/20	25	1750	.60			-1/10							
	2/28	20	1400	60			-1/10							
	3/4	40	2800	95			-1/10							
	3/9	50	3500	1.10			1/10							
	3/15	25	1750	70			-1/10							
	3/22	50	3500	1.00			1/10							
	3/26	100	7000	1.85			1/10							
	3/31	35	2450	90			-1/10							
	4/2	25	1750	65			-1/10							
	4/6	30	2100	80			-1/10							
	4/9	75	5250	1.80			1/10							
	4/12	50	3500	1.30			1/10							
	4/16	165	11550	2.85			1/3							
	4/17	50	3500	1.20			1/10							
	4/22	60	4200	1.30			1/10							
	Totals	800	56000	17.60										

Figures 1.11, 1.12, and 1.13. Sample paperwork from American Warehousemen's Association, *Warehousing General Merchandise* (Pittsburgh: American Warehousemen's Association, 1923).

PAYROLL ANALYSIS For Week Ending *Feby 28* 192*0*

		PRODUCTIVE								NON-PRODUCTIVE				
		Receiving & Delivering		Car Service		Weighing	Sampling	Extra Serv.		Handling	Car Serv.	Undist.		Daily Total
Date	Foreman	Canned Goods	Misc.	Canned Goods	Misc.									
23		*Holiday*								103.52	46.80	107 08		257 40
24	Ryan		48.24							3.24				
	Green	10.49	39.95				1 04							
	Johnson			12.18	20.00	4.78		12.48			2.04			
	Bray	4.30	23.12									2.24		
	Dick	23.70	34.75		12.00							2.85		
	TOTALS	120.00	583.13	93.15	210.50	42.00	11.20	67.50		110.50	52.52	139.50		1430 00

Figure 1.12.

much labor power had been devoted to the cheese, or as the AWA put it, "the actual amount of time and money spent in handling the goods, no other factors being considered."

Unpacking the meaning of handling recasts the Lot Cost Form as a page straight out of *Das Kapital*. While marginalist political economists rejected the man-hour and posited the commodity as a bundle of consumer utilities, the AWA retained the labor theory of value to mind the till.[105] The warehouseman's great accomplishment was to deduce how to commodify tasks that industrial capitalists suffered as the costs of doing business (what Marx called "the *faux frais* of production").[106] A warehouseman attracted customers with opportunities for stretching time—storing, collateralizing. He then made money by billing them by the man-hour.

The warehouseman fretted that he could not recoup each man-hour on his Payroll Analysis. But at least he could monitor the "unproductive" hours with a time card (fig. 1.13). The AWA took pains to "translate" this hypothetical sample, which follows a foreman and his crew through one nine-hour day in February 1920. "From 7 to 7:15 A.M.," it details, "Ryan and 12 men were making room" (i.e., cleaning and organizing). "From 7:15 to 9:45 the same gang received 96 packages from trucks. The lot No. 7701 form indicates to the bookkeeper the merchandise handled and for whose account."[107] And so it continues.

FOREMAN Ryan **DATE** Feb. 16, 1920

Rec'd From	Del. To	No. of Pkgs.	Lot or File No. or Service	No. Men R	C	S	D	W	EX	Clock Record F	Clock Record B	Elapsed Time	
			Making Room						12	7 15	7 00		15
Truck		96	7701	2						9.45	7 15	2	30
Truck		25	7678	12						10.25	9 45		40
Truck		9	7694	12						10.45	10.25		20
Truck		20	7657	10						11 15	10.45		30
			Moving						10	11 35	11.15		20
	Car		6875		3		6	1		12.00	11 35		25
	Car		6875		3		5	1		2.25	1 00	1	25
	Car		7420		4		4	1		3 00	2.25		35
	Car		7420		4		5	1		5 00	3 00	2	00
			TOTAL TIME									9	00

Figure 1.13.

"Foreman Ryan" jotted down these snippets himself, consulting "an inexpensive watch" supplied to him by the warehouseman. "These should be returned each night and regulated before they are delivered to the foreman in the morning," the AWA cautioned, but they should not be so conspicuous as to foster an atmosphere of surveillance, which could lead to strikes and congressional inquiries. Make sure to rally "the men" to regard the time card with pride and to see it as an expression of their value, the AWA directed.[108] The time card should be to a warehouse worker what the car was to an autoworker: a testament to the fruits of his labors.

Nonetheless, the purpose of foreman Ryan's time card was to exhibit the unavoidable deadweight in his boss's budget. Here, for instance, two of the ten entries listed no lot numbers: fifteen minutes of "making room" in the morning and twenty minutes of "moving" before lunch. These entries added up to thirty-five man-minutes of lost time for the warehouseman. "Even when the men are engaged in such work as sweeping, re-tiering, and consolidating, their work is performed merely to facilitate the handling of future business and is not applicable to any particular commodity," the AWA encyclopedia instructed. "It is, therefore, part of the non-productive labor."[109] Cleaning and organizing were as nonproductive as they were indispensable.

Even more essential, though, was the crew's showing up. Like the manufacturer who needed stocks of commodities, the warehousemen needed stocks of workers. "It is obvious that, in order that goods be handled when wanted, these men must be always on hand," the AWA continued. "And it follows that the cost of keeping them on hand is directly a cost of handling the goods, and therefore that the unemployed time is wholly a handling cost."[110] The warehouseman docketed hours of nonproductive handling labor as overhead, as he did with machinery, rent, and administration. He incorporated these hours into his fee per square foot. While he could not shrink them appreciably, he scrutinized them, to gauge how to set his rates. If he failed to stay on top of them, then nonproductive "inside handling" would grab ever more of "the Warehouseman's Dollar" (fig. 1.14).

What was remarkable was how much the warehouseman curtailed this bloat, considering his station in the occupational hierarchy. Nonproductivity was the condition of the merchant capitalist. Merchants merely transferred ownership of commodities; they did not enhance their values. The warehouseman was a merchant capitalist, selling storage space and services. Or was he? Was Irving Bush a merchant capitalist, and were his services inherently nonproductive?[111] By the early twentieth century, "merchant" was a residual term, eclipsed by "retailer" and varieties of "whole-

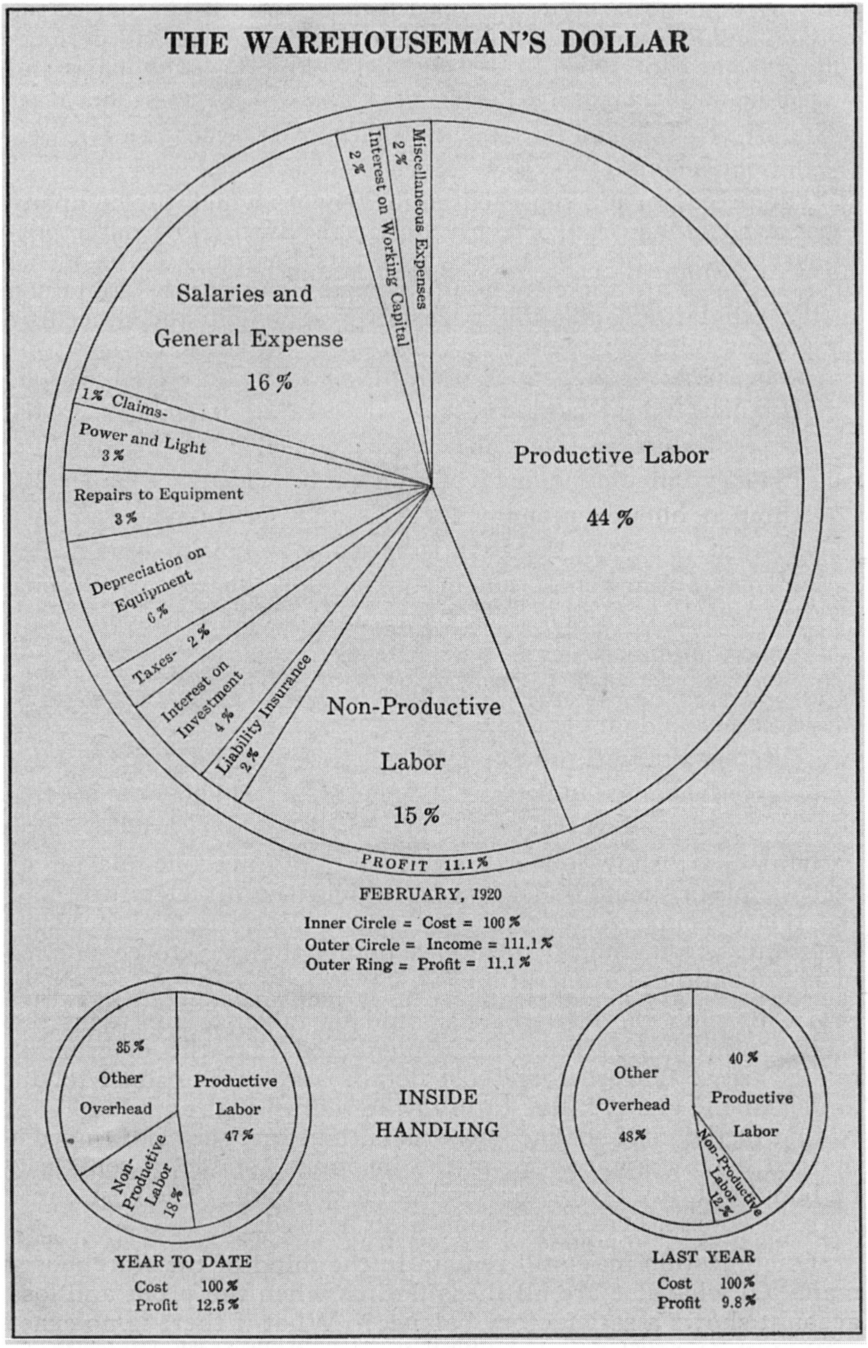

Figure 1.14. Pie chart from American Warehousemen's Association, *Warehousing General Merchandise* (Pittsburgh: American Warehousemen's Association, 1923).

saler." Often warehousemen opted for a third term, identifying as "distributors." Yet it was tough for them to determine what exactly that moniker meant. An AWA member attempted a succinct definition in 1922: "Distribution is everything that happens to commodities between Production and Consumption."[112] But where did production stop and distribution start? Where—or when—was the warehouse?

As Marx suggested—and as operators of foreign-trade zones would puzzle over during the rollout of the zone system, in the 1930s and 1940s—these spheres of production and distribution often blurred together. In one sense, railroads and other transport industries were "an independent branch of production." They laid tracks and constructed ships (transport *industries*). In another sense, however, they bridged production and distribution, ferrying commodities in what was tantamount to "the continuation of a production process *within* the circulation process and *for* the circulation process," given that a Model T or a bar of soap was worthless if it never left the factory. To heighten the confusion, they could double as spaces of production for vibrant matter, covering production processes "whose productive character is thus merely hidden by the circulation form."[113] In storage, grapes fermented. Nuts dried and shrank in weight.

These disjunctures between what Marx called "working time" (the length of a factory shift) and "circulation time" (the gap between production and sale) or "production time" (the chemical or physiological gestation of a commodity) were the warehouseman's bread and butter. If the railroad and other vectors of displacement "annihilated space and time"—which was to say *consumed* time—then the warehouse, which intersected these vectors, *saved* time.[114] It was a receptacle for "waiting time," in the words of Gilded Age political economist Henry George ("the Marx of populism," by one estimation), who urged admiration for this function of "the much-abused 'middleman.'"[115] A merchant or manufacturer could use a warehouse to hold supplies, seek shelter from a stormy market, expose nuts to oxygen, and bank commodities as collateral, and the warehouseman could invoice him for the amenity. The warehouse was a "circulation reservoir," Marx summarized, filled by production and emptied by consumption. Or as a Chamber of Commerce leader told an AWA audience in 1922, "You are the reservoir, the railroads are the passages from the reservoirs to the consumer."[116] In maintaining the reservoir the warehouseman could count as productive what other capitalists were compelled to write off as nonproductive. Straddling the border between production and circulation, the warehouseman was in the business of "the production of distribution."[117]

"Palletization"

If bookkeeping was one way for the warehouseman to cut the percentage of his dollar lost to nonproductive "inside handling," then mechanizing was the other. A warehouse in the black was a warehouse stacked with expensive materials-handling gear. This, at least, is the maxim that rings from AWA publications and the industry's trade magazines and from the files of the foreign-trade zone in Staten Island, New York. Binders and folders in the records of Zone 1 abound with pull sheets for gear. For that's what the foreign-trade zone was, before it was anything else: not a tax haven, not an extraterritorial encasement of the world market, but a warehouse.[118] Gear was a key to its vaunted frictionlessness.

The warehouseman came to tools much later than one might expect, considering that handling was his stock in trade. Manufacturers hailed advances in the new field of "materials handling" around the turn of the twentieth century, galvanized by engineers like Frederick Winslow Taylor. By contrast, warehousemen mostly watched from the sidelines until after World War I, aware of skids, lift trucks, and conveyors, but skeptical of their practicality in the storage of general merchandise. Such gadgets were suited to the mass production of sameness, but were they any match for the motley contents of a warehouse?

Leaders of the AWA had long thought so. They convened a committee on the topic of "labor-saving devices" in 1896.[119] Over the years this delegation chimed in with tips on how to arrange eclectic assortments of objects, frequently concentrating on how to streamline handling—in other words, to slash man-hours. They sought not to reprogram workers' bodies with ergonomics or time-motion studies but to eliminate workers' bodies in toto. They counted on the human motor to be outperformed by forces of nature, which worked for "free" and without complaint. ("Nature never goes on strike.")[120] A gizmo named the "lowerator" became popular in the 1920s, for instance, "because the energy to transport the goods did not incur any costs."[121] The star of this discourse was the "gravity-operated" conveyor belt. Usually photographed with no workers beside it, backlit by windows as it floated below a ceiling, it was a ghostly presence in warehousing manuals (fig. 1.15).[122]

Warehouse workers were wary of these upgrades. "It occasionally happens," conceded a consultant in 1922, that materials-handling equipment "is confronted by an attitude of indifference, perhaps even positive hostility, on the part of the laborer."[123] The managerial consensus was that this resistance was "a matter of pride"—an atavistic attachment to the brawn demanded by "the old style trucks"—and not a harbinger of class

Figure 1.15. Photograph from H. B. Twyford, *Storing: Its Economic Aspects and Proper Methods* (New York: D. Van Nostrand, 1918).

struggle.[124] One employee jammed an electric tiering machine with dust and grit; after the foreman fixed it and fired the saboteur, the man who took over was said to be delighted that the machine lightened his load. This was the sort of yarn with which warehousemen praised their acquisitions as "humanitarian." They avowed that materials-handling equipment eased toil and saved lives.[125] Which was undoubtedly correct. But insofar as it was sparking conflict over who pulled the levers of power in the workplace, and at a moment when unions were recruiting warehouse workers, consultants counseled warehousemen to watch their words.[126] Rather than "labor-saving," materials-handling equipment was "labor-promoting," or as one magazine extolled it during the Depression, "labor-serving."[127]

Not surprisingly, ads for materials-handling equipment belied this spin by representing workers as servants to machines. Frequently workers appeared only as limbs, as in an ad in which an outstretched hand swoops in like the winged arm of a Greek goddess, activating the animal spirits of lift trucks (fig. 1.16). And when workers were fully drawn, ads either

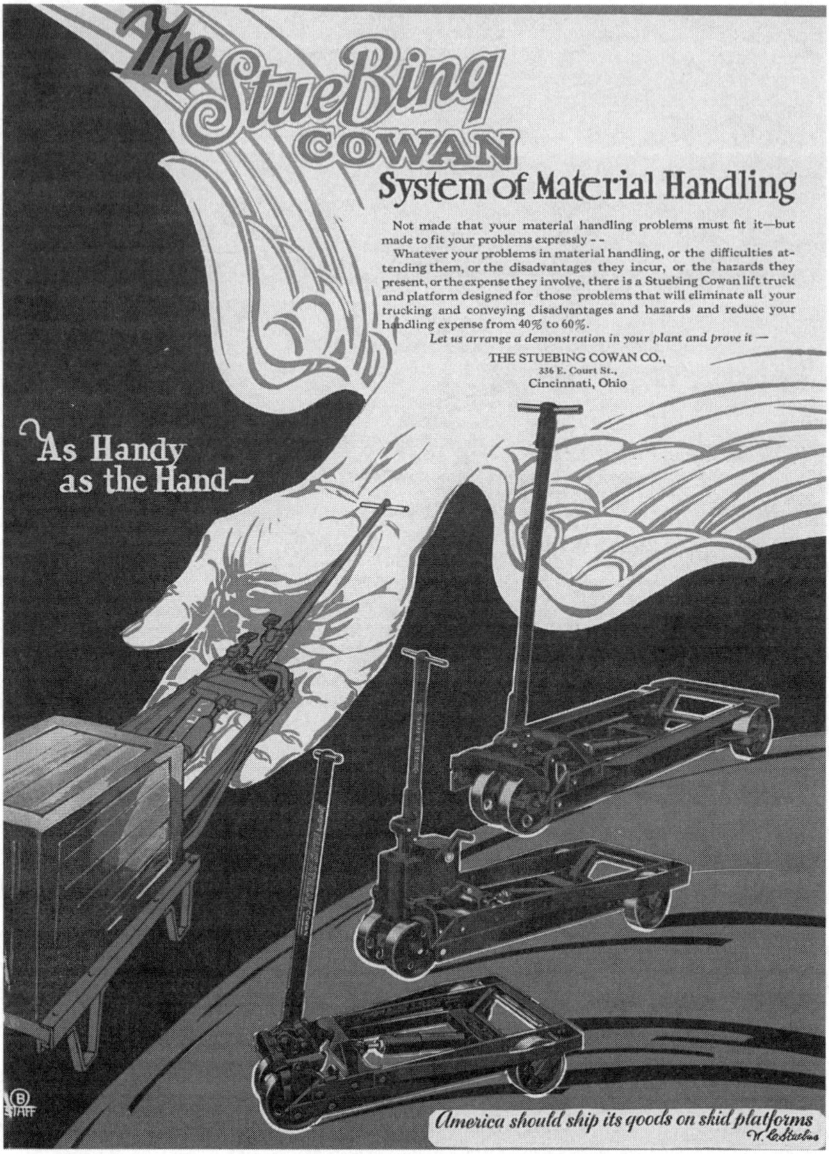

Figure 1.16. Advertisement from *Materials Handling and Distribution,* June 1929.

shrunk or belittled them. In 1929 a series of ads for chain hoists featured watercolors dramatizing the ineptitude of manual labor in remote—that is, barbaric—corners of the world: a "Mexican peon" or "human truck horse," a "plodding" "Volga boatman," and an unlabeled black-skinned brute in a loin cloth with an ivory tusk balanced on his shoulders (fig. 1.17). The musculature of the common man was here a mark of backwardness.

Skids. Lowerators. Conveyors. Lift trucks. Tiering and piling machines. These heroes of materials handling pervaded the warehousing literature. Beginning in the late 1930s, however, one humble device loomed largest because it linked them all: the pallet. "First used by the Egyptians to carry bricks," *Fortune* claimed in 1948, echoing the adage that "storage is civilization," the pallet was a tray on which objects could be stacked and under which a fork lift could catch hold.[128] The pallet opened up to productive use what warehousemen had written off as the "unproductive space" seven feet above the floor; now workers could load more and lift higher than ever before (fig. 1.18).[129] Warehousemen had long debated how high was too high—at what point would shelves teeter or workers tumble from ladders? The pallet solved such conundrums. And it was the linchpin in the warehouseman's control of the labor process: "making one big load out of many small ones," it standardized the anatomy of cargo and rendered moot the skill entailed in break-bulk handling.[130] "Palletization" paid dividends.[131] "It makes filling orders easier; it reduces congestion, checks pilfering," reported *Fortune*. "More important: in cutting down manual handling"—the passion of any right-thinking, *Fortune*-reading warehouseman—"it decreases damage as much as 90 percent."

Palletization caught on during World War II, when battalions of warehousemen assisted the military in arming and feeding the troops and educating the natives (fig. 1.19).[132] Such collaboration between warehousemen and generals was not novel. Logistics was one of the arts of war. Warehousemen had participated in depot operations during both world wars, and ever since the Civil War warehouses had been requisitioned as stockades, whether for matériel or captives. The nexus of warehousing and war making merits a book unto itself, although it is not the last word on the warehouse with respect to Washington, DC. Other federal authorities have grappled with warehousing for banal reasons quite separate from the exigencies of battle.

After World War II, to wit, palletization spread as a civilian weapon against a lurking threat to American abundance. The fledgling consumers' republic was threatened by the myriad tolls extracted along the paths from farms and factories to department stores and supermarkets. Fear of parasitic middlemen was as deep rooted as animosity toward the railroads

Figure 1.17. The man's feet are drawn to be as large as his head. Advertisement from *Materials Handling and Distribution*, July 1929. Other installments in this series featured a "human horse" in Turkey (June 1929), a "Volga Boatman" (August 1929), and a "Mexican Peon, a human truck horse" (September 1929).

Figure 1.18. The original caption announces the "three-dimensional cube concept of space." General Services Administration, Federal Supply Service, *Warehouse Operations Handbook* (Washington, DC: Government Printing Office, 1953).

(thanks to the farmers aligned with the Populists). But by the 1920s this distrust had acquired a scientific tone, from economists.[133] A 1939 study by the Twentieth Century Fund—a think tank bankrolled by the owner of Filene's Department Store—found that "it cost the country about 50 per cent more to get goods distributed than it did to get the same goods produced."[134] The authors illustrated this statistic with a diagram that looked like a plumbing system whose pipes were choked by billions of dollars of outlays to distributors (fig. 1.20). The stream of commerce was clogging in warehouses and other "facilitating agencies."

Tellingly, this diagram—as a warehouseman might have objected—is not a map. Its horizontal orientation bears a resemblance to the shape of the United States, but there is no actual reference to the friction of space, the hassle of moving goods across physical and legal geographies. The diagram is not the territory. What needs to be appreciated is that warehousemen, as landlords, valorized locations and services pegged to discrete locations. That's why they pocketed a portion of these capital flows. The warehouse was infrastructural. By the 1920s, it was a fixture of the landscape. No one could judge it superfluous.

Figure 1.19. Storage is empire. "Storage, in its ordinary meaning," opens the introduction to the manual that features this illustration, "is passive: supplies lying idle in a warehouse. Storage, in the Army meaning, is active: supplies moving through a vital stage in their forward journey from factory to fighting front." US Army, *Depot Operations: Storage* (1943).

And some saw it as downright inspirational. Despite how it sparked frustration in the scrum of the market, in the halls of academia and government—the realm of those who thought about not individual niches but the "national economy"—it modeled the virtue of conservation. Inventories were coming to be regarded as vital, together with the groundwork for keeping them. Instead of castigating the warehouse as a graveyard for dead stock or relegating it to the past, those who were investigating how to allocate the country's resources were welcoming the warehouse. Secretary of Agriculture Henry Wallace championed it with the idea of the "ever-normal granary," a vision of buffer stocks of farm crops sequestered in federally administered grain elevators.[135] Then the economist Benjamin

Graham elaborated this scheme for a wider spectrum of commodities in the aptly titled *Storage and Stability*. As a defense against "the problems of depression," Graham wrote (e.g., overproduction and "defects of our monetary and credit system"), "the concept of storage is unique in that it lies at the intersection of these two lines of difficulty, offering at once a synthesis and solution of both."[136] One year later, no less than the British economist John Maynard Keynes—the great interpreter of flow—argued that Great Britain should tackle underconsumption and the scourge of price fluctuations with a Wallace-esque program for the excess output of the British colonies, or "Empire producers": Keynes described himself as sold on "the policy of holding liquid stocks of raw materials as a natural evolution of the policy of holding liquid stocks of gold outside the banking system."[137]

This enthusiasm was not without historical context. The epigraph to this chapter was written by bureaucrats in the Department of Commerce and Labor in 1903. And the data they used were collected by bureaucrats in the US Treasury Department. For as it happens there already was a federally sponsored warehousing system. It was authorized in 1846, and the push for a zone system was a response to its limits.

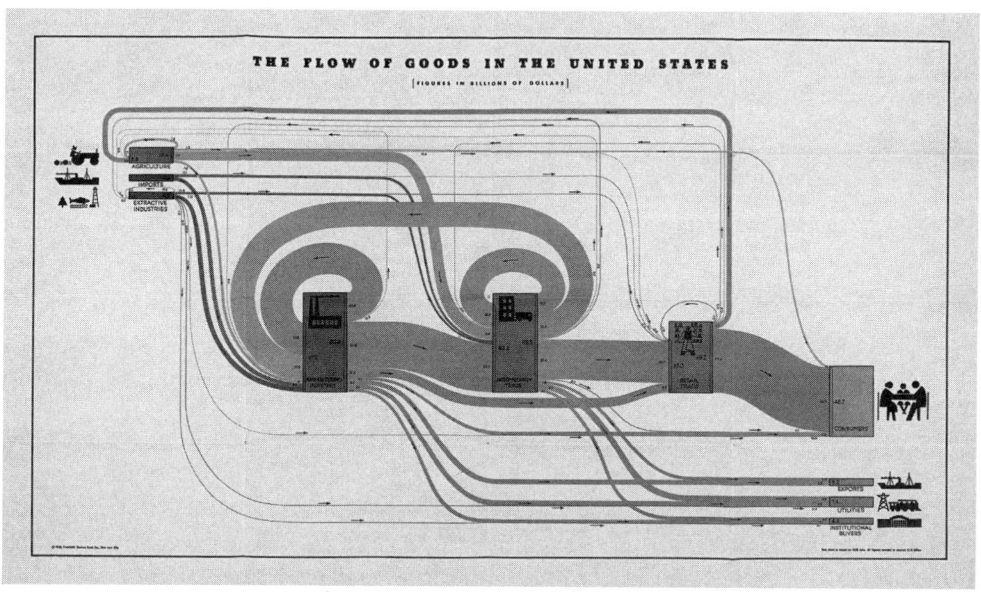

Figure 1.20. Measuring 35.5 × 20 in., this diagram was printed in color and included with the book, tucked into a pocket on the back cover. Reproduced by permission of The Century Foundation, Inc., from Paul W. Stewart and J. Frederic Dewhurst, *Does Distribution Cost Too Much?* (New York: Twentieth Century Fund, 1939).

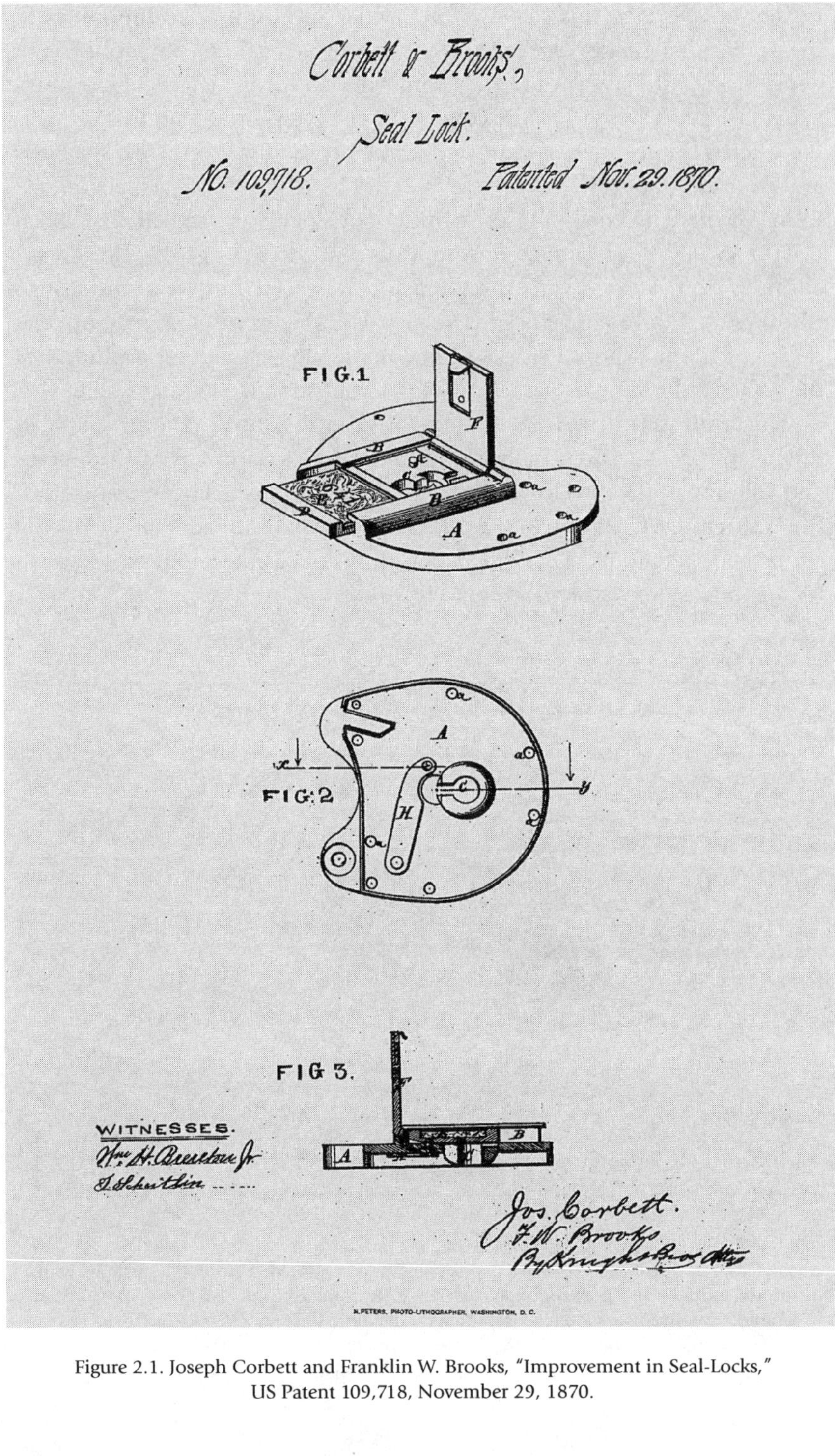

Figure 2.1. Joseph Corbett and Franklin W. Brooks, "Improvement in Seal-Locks," US Patent 109,718, November 29, 1870.

CHAPTER TWO

Security and Securitization: The Bonded Warehouse

> Casimir Périer said one day, while viewing the art collection of an illustrious enthusiast . . . "All these paintings are very pretty—but they're dormant capital." . . . Today . . . [the] sale of the curiosities and paintings . . . has proven in round figures that works of genius possess a value . . . a little more secure than bonded warehouses.
>
> —Charles Blanc, as quoted in Walter Benjamin, *Passagen-Werk*

"A Departure from the General System of the Government"

In late 1852, "at the northern extremity of the City of New York," beside the Croton Reservoir in mid-Manhattan, workmen raised the columns of a grand structure, soon to rival the orientalist artificial lake beside it in both aesthetic panache and technical audacity.[1] Modeled on the renowned London exhibition of the same name, the Crystal Palace would host "The Exhibition of the Industry of All Nations." It would be the debut performance of the United States on the world stage of capitalism. Backstage, meanwhile, it would be more than a neighbor to the Croton Reservoir. It too would be a kind of warehouse (fig. 2.2).

Bourgeois uplift was the exhibition's objective. Patrons were to be enlightened by exposure to goods from around the globe—from reapers and guns to silks and reptiles. Such spectacles were to effect another makeover as well, that of "quadrupling the value of property in the vicinity."[2] Tickets were to be sold to all comers. This was to be no parlor affair: "Here will be collected crowds of all classes," the exhibition's directors wrote, "but the great and crowning feature of the enterprise is that it will offer amusement and recreation to the working classes such as they can find nowhere else, that it will make a Palace of the People."[3] Walt Whitman, a frequent visitor,

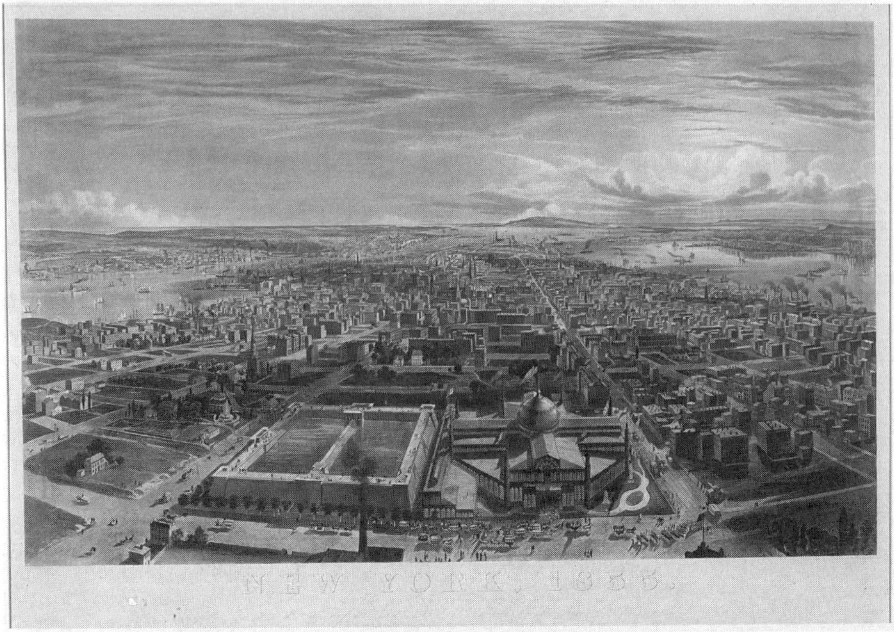

Figure 2.2. A tale of two warehouses: the Croton Reservoir on the left and the Crystal Palace on the right. "From the Latting Observatory," New York, 1855. New York Public Library.

later offered a less consumer-centered take on the exhibition's powers of aggregation: "Not only all the world of works, trade, products / But all the workmen of the world here to be represented."[4]

During 1853 and 1854, the crowds gathered, more than 6,000 ticket holders a day. Although many effused about the displays, quite a few—like seventeen-year-old Sam Clemens, a country boy from Hannibal, Missouri—suggested the building itself made the biggest impression. Clemens rhapsodized over it as "a perfect fairy palace—beautiful beyond description."[5] A cavernous shed of iron and glass, welded together from parts fabricated offsite, the Crystal Palace was proclaimed to be "the largest and most effective in its interior effect in the United States" (fig. 2.3).[6] "Walls, properly speaking, the building has not, being enclosed with glass sustained by iron pillars," the *Sun* reported. "This vast mass of crystal occupies 45,000 square feet. The cast iron weighs 1,200 tons, the wrought 200."[7]

What Clemens did not muse about was the less phantasmagorical reason for these enchanting materials: traffic. The Crystal Palace was a gilded depot, and along with its British prototype it has earned recognition from cultural historians—like Walter Benjamin and Sigfried Giedion—for prefiguring the Fordist architecture of commodity circulation. The iron was the magic. "In iron, an artificial building material makes its appearance for the first time," Benjamin concluded in 1935. "Iron is avoided in residential buildings and used in arcades, exhibition halls, stations—buildings serving transitory purposes."[8]

While iron would elevate public warehouses as stand-alone enterprises starting at this moment, it was not because of iron that the Crystal Palace joined their ranks. It was because of the building's legal blueprint. The US Treasury Department had categorized the Crystal Palace as a "bonded warehouse," a type conceived decades before other niche types, like cold-storage and household goods warehouses. As a bonded warehouse, the building occupied an unusual position in mid-Manhattan, for the procedure it manifested amounted to temporary suspension of federal taxes. When a foreign object subject to tariffs arrived at the New York Custom House, to be installed in the exhibition, its owner posted a bond for twice its value, and then it was admitted free of duty, and carried to the Crystal Palace. The bond—a contract indicated by a signature in a ledger—constituted a

Figure 2.3. The building—an immense terminal—is the main attraction in this engraving. *Interior of Crystal Palace,* 1853. Alamy.

promise to make good on the duties. What next happened varied: if the object was withdrawn from the exhibition to be sold to a patron, the bond would be dissolved when the duties were paid; if it was withdrawn for export, then the bond would be dissolved, and no duties would be incurred; if the object was damaged or stolen, then the bond would be called due. The exhibition's directors, merchants like August Belmont ("a band of speculators and showmen," according to the *Sunday Atlas*), had deemed such an arrangement "essential."[9] Without it, foreign merchants and manufacturers might opt not to participate.

The prospect of such a calamity spoke to how the spatial form of the bonded warehouse corresponded to other instruments of the "global condition" of the mid-nineteenth century.[10] How was the bonded warehouse similar to the exhibition hall and the railroad station? And as a public warehouse, what was its function? How was it like the Croton Reservoir? Core aspects of the bonded warehouse were refracted in the Crystal Palace. One was indicated by the swarms of southerners in attendance.[11] The politician almost single-handedly responsible for the importation of the model of the bonded warehouse from Great Britain was a southerner, the former US treasury secretary and ex-slaveholder Robert J. Walker, whose esteem for New York City as a capital of capital, as he told in his memoir, was as deep as his affection for the "faithful colored women " who raised his children.[12] Walker was convinced that the bonded warehouse would strengthen commercial and financial linkages between the economic geographies of the North and the South by widening the ambit of imports.

Another dimension was suggested by the ambitions of an enterprise whose goal was to entice "All Nations." Walker believed that the bonded warehouse would prime cities like New York and New Orleans for the world market. By modulating the space-time of the tariff so as to optimize circulation without monkeying with tariff policy—the tariff, protectionist and free trader agreed, was an indispensable source of national revenue—the bonded warehouse was a workhorse for urban expansionism. Its reach was discernable in a map that the Treasury Department issued in 1883. Outlining the borders of customs districts (with dots for cities that counted as ports of entry), the map projected imperial outposts over vast distances: in 1883, territories from Washington to Arizona were not yet incorporated as states, but they were included on the customs map, each ready to host a bonded warehouse (fig. 2.4).

And how would cargoes be propelled to those edges of empire untroubled by the tariff? The solution to this dilemma was approved by Congress in 1870, the year—to gauge how profound was this achievement, and how

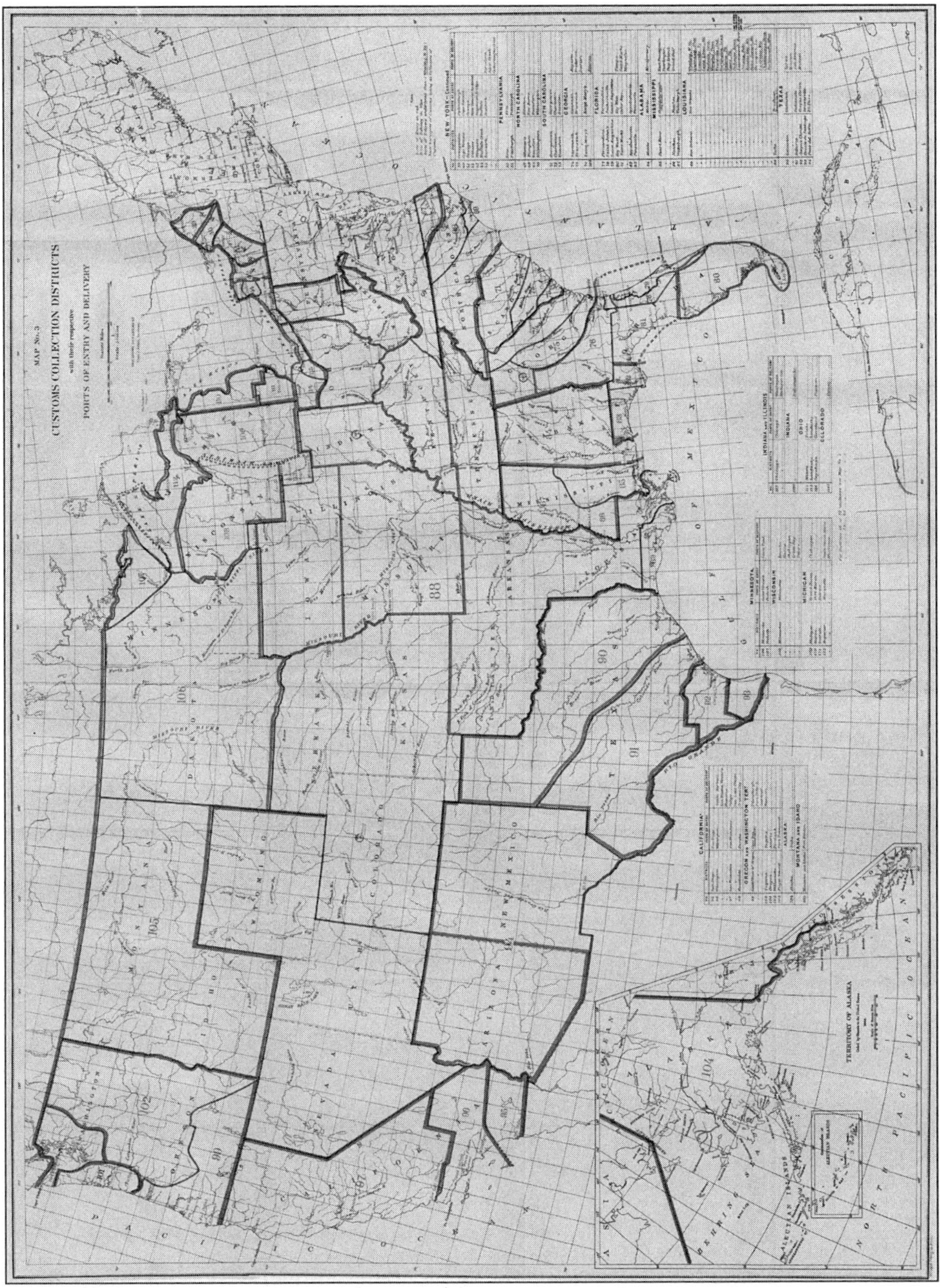

Figure 2.4. Incidentally, this map was issued the same year that the railroads organized the time zones. *Customs Collections Districts with Their Respective Ports of Entry and Delivery*, US Treasury Department, 1883.

it challenges the received wisdom that the tariff conflicted with global capitalism—when the average customs duty peaked at 44.9%.[13] It was a law that provided for "bonded transport," and it was emblematic of the most effervescent way in which the "principle" of the bonded warehouse, in the words of one of the exhibition's directors, allowed for "a departure from the general system of the government."[14] The essence of the bonded warehouse was not the building but the lock that sealed the warehouse doors, a patent for which is shown in figure 2.1. And that lock was portable, as evoked by how it floats in white space on the patent drawing.[15] It fit a wide variety of objects. Immobile or mobile, whether a warehouse or a "warehouse on wheels," like cargoes from Germany destined for Arizona, and inanimate or animate, whether "dormant capital," like a painting, or "thinking property," like a slave: anything or anyone could be bonded so long as government agents gave a stamp of approval.

Such multiplicity of applications reflected the two faces of the bonded warehouse. It locked certain things in, but it also opened certain things up. It restricted the circulation of one form of capital—commodity capital—to make possible the circulation of another—finance capital, or credit. It secured to securitize. Put another way, to invert the comparison from the French art critic Charles Blanc in 1858, a commodity shut inside a bonded warehouse was like an old master hanging in a collector's estate: dormant, yet not remotely at rest.[16]

"A Warehousing System"

Bonded warehouses were almost as newfangled as halls of iron and glass when the Crystal Palace opened in 1853. Congress had authorized them less than ten years earlier, in the little-known but groundbreaking Warehousing Act of 1846, which provided for "a warehousing system" to be overseen by the Treasury Department.[17] The warehousing system was a bold undertaking both because of the high stakes of tariff politics and because few such bureaucratic "systems" preceded it. The federal prison system, to cite a different mode of warehousing, would not be established until 1891.[18] Existing systems, like the "factory system" (as the textile mills in New England were referred to by the 1830s), were private and local, not public and federal; no mill owner answered to an entity of the stature of the US Customs Service. The systematicness of the warehousing system entailed an unparalleled degree of federal involvement in the management of interstate and—in the geographical imaginary of the act—"universal commerce."[19]

Statist regulation of storage dated to the colonial period. The Warehousing Act was not unprecedented, not in the circum-Atlantic world and not even in North America. In the colony of Virginia, planters had entrusted their tobacco leaves to storehouses at Norfolk and other seaports. The tobacco was to be inspected, graded, and packaged before shipment, per regulations. These storehouses were treated as public utilities. Common law pegged them as public in recognition that planters had no choice but to use them.[20] This logic undergirded another system that grew up alongside warehousing: the hotel system. Taverns and inns—sites of storage for bodies in passage—fell under the purview of colonial courts due to common law that provided for protection of travelers. By the late 1860s and the dawn of the first civil rights era, taverns and inns were vehicles for federal enforcement of the Fourteenth Amendment precisely because they were regarded as public accommodations.[21] It was in "buildings serving transitory purposes," as Walter Benjamin put it, where the federal government was first able to flex its visible hand.

The buildings covered by the Warehousing Act served a tangible and an intangible purpose, the flow of commodity capital and the flow of finance capital. Indeed the latter was the immediate impetus for the act. The warehousing system was instituted as an update of the "credit system," which the first Congress had set up at the customhouse to reconcile two imperatives. On the one hand, the infant nation needed money.[22] On the other hand, tariffs could just as well starve the republic as feed it, in that the more merchants were forced to tie up funds in duties, the less they were able to continue to cut deals and to afford duties. To prevent the revenue stream from drying up, Congress had installed a spigot at the customhouse: the "credit system." As detailed in the Tariff of 1799, this system let merchants reschedule payment of duties. They could retrieve their imported silks and spirits from the wharves and then devote months to finding buyers, later paying duties out of the proceeds rather than surrendering cash up front. The only catch was that they needed to post bonds at the customhouse, with sureties, promising to honor the duties. A bond was a kind of contract, with terms spelled out by Congress:

> Know all men by these presents, that we (here insert the name of the importer or consignee, or if by an agent the name of such agent, and of the importers or consignees and the sureties, their place of abode and occupation) are held and firmly bound unto the United States of America, in the sum of _____ to be paid to the said United States; for payment whereof, we bind ourselves, our heirs, executors and administrators, jointly and severally,

> firmly by these presents; sealed with our seals; dated this _____ day of _____ in the _____ year of the independence of the said United States, and in the year of our Lord, one thousand _____.
>
> The condition of this obligation is such, that if the above bounden (here insert the principal or agent for such principal and the sureties) or either of them, or either of their heirs, executors or administrators, shall, and do, on or before the _____ day of _____ next, well and truly pay or cause to be paid, unto the collector of the customs for the district of _____ for the time being, the sum of _____ or the amount of the duties to be ascertained as due, and arising on certain goods, wares and merchandise, entered by the above bounden (insert the name of the importer or consignee, or agent for such importer or consignee) as imported in the _____ master from _____ as per entry, dated _____ then the above obligation to be void, otherwise to remain in full force and virtue.[23]

As conveyed in this boilerplate, the bond served at once as carrot and stick. It allowed the importer, the "bounden," to borrow time, but if by the date named in the second paragraph he failed to "well and truly pay or cause to be paid" the duties he owed, then the collector could sue him (or his sureties or heirs) for the value of the bond, which was usually priced at double the value of the duties. In sum, the bond was akin to a no-interest, high-penalty credit card issued by the Treasury Department, subsidizing a merchant's risk.[24]

The trouble was that, as a rule, the customhouse was an object of distrust. Early on it was notorious for ad-hoc collection of duties, until the Napoleonic Wars prompted the White House to clamp down.[25] And even after merchants and the merchant-friendly customhouse started to play by the books, manufacturers complained of "reckless importation," citing storehouses and auction houses brimming with foreign goods that undersold domestic goods. Credit, or "fictitious capitals," as a group of protectionists contended in an 1828 pamphlet, bred "fictitious values"—"extravagance," "daring speculations," "inordinate importations, glutted markets, individual bankruptcy, and general embarrassment." As a cure, these manufacturers demanded that the federal government force merchants who waited to pay duties to relinquish their imports to government storekeepers. This was the first serious call for a warehousing system to help the nation metabolize its consumption of foreign trade. "The regulations we recommend bear the same relationship to the present credits," the manufacturers wrote, "which good nourishing food does to ardent spirits. We would feed, nourish, and invigorate commerce, but not stimulate it to intoxication."[26]

This recipe was never followed, and instead, five years later, with the Tariff of 1833, the Whig-dominated Congress took a drastic step, doubling tariff rates and abolishing the credit system. Congress stipulated that as of June 30, 1842—a decade hence—the Treasury Department would operate under a "cash system." Merchants would hear one edict at the customhouse: pay your duties, pronto.[27] No longer would they lean on Uncle Sam as they canvassed for buyers. Critics warned that, for those flush with gold and silver, such a turnaround would pose no difficulty, but that for those hedging their accounts, it would mean the difference between solvency and ruin. The critics were proved correct. As Democrats railed in 1846, during the Warehousing Act debate, the cash system had worked well for "large capitalists," whereas it entailed "an unreasonable extraction" from "men of moderate means," forcing them either to scrounge for bank loans or to discount their wares to pony up at the customhouse. Worse still, Democrats added, because this "extraordinary and violent transition" from credit to cash had coincided with a doubling of rates in the "Black Tariff" of 1842, the balance between common merchant and well-heeled capitalist was now even more skewed. The customhouse was in a credit crunch.[28]

The person who saw a fix in warehousing took charge of the Treasury Department in 1845. Robert Jackson Walker's upbringing suited him to the task of brokering between the era's fractions of capital: antitariff agriculture and protariff industry; antitariff South and protariff North; antitariff Democrat and protariff Whig. Born in Pennsylvania, where his father was a judge, he was tutored in the values of Philadelphia's manufacturers at the University of Pennsylvania (where he met his future wife, Mary Bache, granddaughter of Benjamin Franklin). But he took a Jacksonian turn, and in 1826 he headed south to make his fortune. He settled in Natchez, Mississippi, where, as a biographer wrote, "money-making was a mania and everybody had a hand in speculations, large or small."[29] "To this opportunity Walker responded without inhibitions," another biographer astringently added, "and soon he created an empire of plantations and slaves founded on credit."[30] Walker's dominion grew when he entered Congress as a senator in 1836. For the next eight years, the "Wizard of Mississippi" waved his wand for racial capitalism, campaigning for expansion of the slave system into Texas and Mexico and conniving with bankers in New York City.[31]

Walker was a soldier for free trade, and when President James K. Polk appointed him secretary of the treasury, he attacked the Black Tariff. His first report to Congress caused such a stir across the Atlantic that the British Parliament ordered several thousand copies to be distributed among its members.[32] Tariffs, Walker wrote, should plummet. As for the cash system, it should continue, with the enhancement of a warehousing system to aid cash-strapped merchants, to give them a chance to stash their merchandise in order to defer payment. Merchants should not be able to speculate as in the past, selling their merchandise before settling with the collector on the duties, but neither should they be forced to cough up duties prematurely. Commodity capital in the chambers of the customhouse would yield finance capital in the hands of the merchant, in the sense that this temporary waiver of duties would inflate the merchant's liquidity. The reason to embrace such an adjustment was twofold, Walker wrote. "It will greatly increase our revenue, by augmenting our imports, together with our exports," and it would span the continent, "from warehouse to warehouse—from the East to the lakes, and to Pittsburg, Cincinnati, and Louisville—from New Orleans to Natchez, Vicksburg, Memphis, and St. Louis, thus carrying our foreign commerce into the interior, with all the advantage of augmented business and cheaper supplies throughout the country."[33] Walker's fleet of warehouses would fortify the home market, agricultural and industrial, South and North.

Notice which regions and cities Walker highlighted. This dual citizen of Pennsylvania and Mississippi was straddling nineteenth-century America's greatest political divide, appeasing both sides of the Mason-Dixon. For the merchant class in the North, a warehousing system would be a conduit to virgin lands as railroads crept further west. And for the planter class in the South, it would be a wedge against the North. The combined and uneven development of the nation's foreign commerce was a staple of the political ideology of slavery.[34] The tariff conspired with the hegemony of ports in the North to keep the South in chains, or so believed the likes of John C. Calhoun, such that a central component of the clamor for "free trade" was a call for "direct trade." Pushed by the proslavery geographer Matthew F. Maury, "direct trade," supposedly, would liberate southern planters from northern jobbers.[35] With the ability to tout bonded warehouses, and thus to cater to ships from Liverpool and Hamburg (ships that would normally dock in New York), southern ports would flourish.

And those ports would not be the sole beneficiaries of the warehousing system. The campaign for "direct trade" was echoed in another part of the continent. As Maury knew, boosters in the South had allies in the West. The two regions—"the producing States," as Maury complimented them—were unable "to fetch and carry for themselves," thanks to a common enemy: the city of New York.[36] Ever since the debut of the Erie Canal in 1825, the Empire City had stood as the nation's chief port. So merchants in ports like Charleston were aligning with merchants in upstart "frontier cities" like St. Louis to dethrone the merchants of New York.[37] Their jealousy was about location, not about sector. Whether raw cotton was being exported or wool cloth was being imported, the question was who would pocket the profits from the logistics of circulation—the jobber in New York or his rivals in New Orleans or Chicago?

Southerners in league with Calhoun and Maury expressed no qualms about looking to the federal government for backing, despite the South's reputation for isolationism and antistatism. Southerners served in sizable numbers in the federal government during the antebellum era and even spearheaded federal and foreign policy. And they took a keen interest in the national market. They were not autarkic as a region. They simply distinguished between types of commerce in delineating their relationship to Washington, DC. Federal oversight of the domestic slave trade? Absolutely not, argued Walker before the Supreme Court in 1841. But federal oversight of commodity circulation in a way that benefitted southerners? Yes, please.[38] The warehousing system, an innovation in commercial and financial policy that was authored by an ex-slaveholder, was motivated by southern visions of imperial expansion.

The southern investment in the Warehousing Act thus reminds us to reckon with the materiality and territoriality of finance. The mode of production in the South—slave labor—was articulated with that in the North—wage labor—via the mediation of money. Money greased the wheels of commerce as they crossed state lines.[39] And, as implied by that idiom, *wheels of commerce*, the mediation of money itself depended on a physical and legal infrastructure. Warehouses were "instruments of exchange" in the same sense as banks and stock markets.[40] Robert Walker understood this principle. As treasury secretary, he saw a web of bonded warehouses-cum-credit clearinghouses as a way to draw finance capital into the plantation complex.

Walker drew inspiration for this money magnet from a mercantile wonderland across the pond. It was an assemblage that through in-person tours and intercontinental deals had captivated many Americans, from the foes of the cash system in Philadelphia in the 1820s to writers from Nashville to Boston in the 1830s and early 1840s: the warehousing system of Great Britain, which had debuted in London and Liverpool in 1803, expanding to all British ports in 1833.[41] The system—inspired by the Netherlands, where duty-free warehousing was invented—was introduced by Sir Robert Walpole in 1733 but failed to win favor.[42] It was later revived by economists, such as Josiah Tucker, and notably, Adam Smith, the former customs clerk.[43] Similar models could be found in other parts of Europe. For example, the *entrepôts fictifs*—literally, "fictitious warehouses"—in France and Belgium were pedestrian enough by the 1850s that they entered the consciousness of art critics like Charles Blanc.[44]

Discussion of the bill linked to Walker's report was perfunctory, considering how the warehousing system promised to revolutionize the nation's collection regime. (Politicians were likely distracted by the minutiae of the massive Tariff Act of 1846, also conceived by Walker, coincidentally.) What the conversation lacked in intensity, however, it made up for in prescience. One riddle preoccupied the bill's nitpickers, and it cropped up repeatedly for at least the next century. It concerned the "foreign importer" and the question of how boosting foreign commerce was not tantamount to suppressing domestic industry. As John Quincy Adams phrased it in 1834, "how a warehousing system, with long credits and auction sales, will operate upon the competition between your domestic manufacturer, mechanic, artisan, and the foreign importer of merchandise from abroad."[45] What would prevent "the foreign importer" from using bonded warehouses not as way stations for goods to be reexported to foreign markets, as in the case of Great Britain, but as beachheads for goods to be dumped on US soil? Had Walker inadvertently fueled this fear in 1845, when he promised that bonded warehouses would funnel "cheap supplies" to farmers in the South and West?

The standard answer to this concern was that the Warehousing Act was not about the tariff. No one was trying to dismantle the tariff in trying to build the bonded warehouse (or so said Maury and his comrades). The warehousing system was designed simply to help ensure that the tariff did not "shackle" commerce.[46] To "unchain" commerce was for the greater good of North and South, as part of a larger effort to elevate the nation to its proper status as empire, as the rightful successor to Great Britain. Americans should leap for such a goal no matter their position on the tariff, Walker urged in 1846:

> In Liverpool and its suburbs the number of bonded warehouses is estimated at five hundred, and in London and other parts of the British empire at many thousands. These immense structures, stretching along their fine docks and mighty basins, a single warehouse often covering many acres of ground, and storing throughout the year assorted cargoes of several hundred million dollars in value, invite to these marts the merchant and commerce of the world. Indeed, this is one of the great means by which England has built up her vast commerce; and for a long series of years her whole people, whether for or

> against protection, acknowledge the important benefits of this system. Here the advantages would ultimately be still greater, inasmuch as our chief commercial cities are already nearer than those of Europe to the center of the territory, population, and commerce of the world, and are destined, at no distant day, to be brought still nearer, when the waters of the Atlantic and Pacific shall be united at the Mexican isthmus, which, combined with our possessions on the Pacific, would revolutionize in our favor the commerce of the world, and more rapidly advance our greatness, wealth, and power, than any event that has occurred since the adoption of the Constitution.[47]

"Whether for or against protection"—this line was to appear again and again in the history of the bonded warehouse and of the foreign-trade zone. If you wanted an empire, the thinking went, then you needed to figure out how best to engineer circulation. What this axiom ignored, though, was the difference between a continent and an island. The United States was not surrounded by ocean, like England. Presumably plenty of cargo would go into the United States and would not go back out, drifting into the domestic market, threatening domestic producers. Walker sketched an image of global command vis-à-vis "the waters of the Atlantic and Pacific." But how exactly this empire of the seas was to hold sway over the vast continental empire he did not indicate. Numbers told a less encouraging, if equally vague, story. In 1847, the first year of Walker's new tariff and warehousing systems, British imports rose by 62% in volume.[48] How many were deposited in bonded warehouses and eventually reexported, never meddling in the home market? No one knew.[49]

"From Warehouse to Warehouse"

From its inception, the warehousing system extended from sea to prairie, from lake to mountain. As much as New York City was its busiest hub—and in a sense its raison d'être—the network was cross-regional, uniting North and South. Imports traveled from one node to the next, with duties charged only at the final destination, if at all. To illustrate, in his 1846 report, Walker appended customs documents from the British ship *Roscoe*, charting its duty-free journey through the United States. When *Roscoe* docked in New York on September 2, 1846, William Wilson and Stephen Stevenson deposited its cargo into a bonded warehouse. Two weeks later, they removed one case of cambric dimity—a fine cotton cloth—and gave bond to honor the sixty dollars in duties while they forwarded the case to St. Louis. On October 14, George Brown deposited the case in a bonded warehouse in St. Louis. On November 1, Joseph Franklin removed the case and gave bond to forward it to New Orleans, where, on December 1, James Holmes deposited the case in a bonded warehouse. Finally, on December 22, M. Busto removed the case to export it to Havana. Over nearly four months and 1,800 miles, the slave-cultivated cotton circled back through the South, now as cloth, and then left without triggering duties, generating profits in commission fees for the myriad merchants in its path.[50]

For this legal trajectory to be possible, one condition needed to be met. Each of these cities had to be either a "port of entry" or a "port of delivery." These two terms were as frequently summoned as they were seldom defined during politicians' deliberations on the warehousing system.[51] A port of entry anchored a "customs district," and a port of delivery, or several of them, "attached" to that district (vessels stopped at ports of entry before discharging cargo at ports of delivery; ports of entry doubled as ports of delivery but not vice versa). At a port of entry, the Customs Service hung its shingle, merchants signed bonds and handed over duties in a customhouse, and, ceremoniously, commodities crossed national borders. Only after a meticulous ritual of identification at a port of entry did a case of cambric dimity morph from foreign to domestic; it could sit for weeks on a pier at St. Louis, an "interior" port of entry, 1,278 miles up the Mississippi River, and not until a clerk recorded it could it be "landed."[52] These rites of passage on the shores of rivers and lakes instantiated the tributaries of US customs territory. The customs border was not so much a riparian line drawn by latitudinal and longitudinal coordinates as a process enacted in a sequence of spatially circumscribed transactions.

By the same token, to say that the customs border fluctuated is not to say that it rested on a solid foundation, as if the nation-state sat fully realized beneath it. To the contrary, in the United States, the customs border materialized before the nation-state. It came with the colony, in that it aided far-flung settlers in their coordination of funds, funds used to wage wars of conquest and to occupy land stolen from indigenous nations.[53] In the United States, the customs border was imperial. It was inherited from the British Empire, which boasted the same archipelago of customs districts (manned by clerks such as Adam Smith and John Stuart Mill). Some of the inaugural American customhouses were leftovers from the British, and the customs bond was, as the historian Gautham Rao writes, "the inner connective tissue of the British imperial customs laws."[54] Senator Walker was engaging in nation building and empire building, simultaneously, when he was harnessing the customs bond to tie St. Louis to New Orleans and New Orleans to Liverpool.

City building, meanwhile, fell to the citizenry. Early in its first session, in July 1789, Congress designated 52 ports of entry and an additional 111 ports of delivery; the resulting roster was an enduring cause for competition among cities.[55] It is a commonplace to emphasize how nineteenth-century city boosters vied for position with railroad companies, how the placement of tracks and the calibration of freight rates tended to make or break a city's prospects. "The railroad had the power to reorient the economic geography of the country," historian Walter Johnson writes, "to realign the connections between country and city as easily as a player moved a pawn across a chessboard."[56] Equally crucial, though, was whether a city qualified as a port of entry, an international portal. If not, the train might pass it by. Was it wise to bankroll a trunk line to a site where it was impossible to land imports without aggravation at a prior stop? This seemingly trivial label had global ramifications for local economies, arbitrarily privileging certain coastal districts as harbors of the world market and relegating others as backwaters, which was why merchants petitioned Congress throughout the nineteenth century to anoint their cities as ports of entry (and not as second-tier ports of delivery). They wrote from Cincinnati in 1817, St. Louis in 1825, Zanesville, Ohio, in 1835, indignant about delays and fees incurred at New Orleans, the port of entry from which foreign commodities commonly traveled into the Great West. "Memorial of a Number of Citizens of Chicago, Illinois," one such petition was titled in 1840, "Praying to have that place constituted a port of entry." Congress answered this prayer in 1846.[57]

Why limit the list? Why not "land" imports anywhere and everywhere? Manpower. As the map expanded, the Treasury Department needed its agents in the field to monitor every single bill of lading, to ensure that the nation lost not a cent of revenue. Whereas for state and local governments the aim was to spur foreign trade, for the Treasury, the breadwinner of the federal government, the goal was to police it. And because greater monitoring came at greater cost, in allocations for salaries and for construction of customhouses, not every bend in the river could become a legal port, and not every hamlet could host a bonded warehouse. As the secretary of the treasury wrote to the collector of customs in Ellsworth, Maine, in 1868, about an adjacent community, "Hancock being neither a port of entry nor delivery, it is not considered as a legal port, and consequently no warehouse, under Customs, can be established there."[58] In the absence of a decree from the Treasury Department, no amount of seagulls or seashells could make Hancock a "legal port."

For the top brass of the Treasury Department to weigh in on whether to construct a building on the northeasterly coast of Maine was just one example of their watchdog function. After a place's status as a legal port was confirmed, Treasury officials issued a slew of directives, all in the name of security. Architectural matters dominated, but plenty of other issues filled the Treasury letter books as well. For instance, each building had to be bonded (along with the goods it held), and officials ordered many warehousemen to revise their bonds with extra information. In 1868, the assistant secretary of the treasury told the collector in Georgetown, South Carolina, to investigate how Mary B. Marbury knew the bondholder for whom she was serving as a surety, given that wives were not normally accepted in that role. That same year, he also pestered the collectors to solicit certified lists of "the name and residence of each clerk, foreman, and laborer" from each bonded warehouse on a monthly basis.[59]

The Treasury Department cared more about this data in 1868 than in earlier years, since the warehousing system had mushroomed in size. The roster was larger because in 1854, in the middle of a period of reduced tariffs, Congress had voted to privatize the system, extending the franchise to the fledgling warehousing industry.[60] A poster released by the warehouse superintendent in New York a decade later indexed the impact of this change. It identified no fewer than fifty-two bonded warehouses for "general storage" in Manhattan and Brooklyn, as well as twenty for "spirits and wine." The poster's authorship and no-nonsense style testified to warehousing's public-utility status, at the same time that the text linked each location to a private entity or "proprietor" (fig. 2.5). A receipt for a bonded warehouse in Selma, Alabama, from 1867, captures this same dynamic in the design of its letterhead: the phrase *United States Bonded Warehouse,* in a sans serif font, contrasts starkly with the name of the proprietor, *O. F. Harrell & Co., General Commission Merchants* (etcetera), in a jumble of serif fonts (fig. 2.6). The federal government still regulated the system but, increasingly, private citizens owned the buildings, with the two parties sharing custody of the goods under deposit. Privatization had always been Walker's intent—easing the fiscal burden of investment in fixed capital without narrowing the purview of his office as he certified more buildings, since privatization entailed regulation—and it spurred growth after 1854. By the beginning of the Civil War, in fact, the warehousing system was so extensive that the Confederate States of America made provisions for its own.[61] Naturally, if ironically, the Confederacy was going to need a tariff system for revenue, like the neighboring one it rejected, and it too was going to want a release valve.

WAREHOUSES FOR GENERAL STORAGE OF BONDED GOODS.

NORTH RIVER.

LOCATION.		PROPRIETORS.
Jersey City Store,	Store.	E. Cunard,
Hoboken Store,	"	Oelrichs & Co., & Kunhardt & Co.,
371 Washington Street,	"	Humphrey & Co.,
56 and 58 Greenwich Street,	"	Humphrey & Co.,
24 Trinity Place,	"	L. F. Randolph,
71 Greenwich Street,	"	William Jackson & Son,
55 Greenwich Street,	"	Philip Livingston,
30 and 31 West, and 54 Washington Streets,	"	Blaxome & Co.,
4 West, and 6 Washington Streets,	"	Peck & Schuyler,
5 West, and 8 Washington Streets,	"	Charles Zast,
3 West, and 4 Washington Streets,	"	Jackson & Woodruff,
114 and 116 Washington Street,	"	John B. Hobby & Co.,
69 Greenwich Street,	"	Wm. A. McKee & Co.,
84 and 86 Washington Street,	"	John Phillips & Co.,

EAST RIVER, N. Y.

LOCATION.		PROPRIETORS.
286 Water Street,	Store.	Louis P. Merle,
298 Water Street,	"	Philip Livingston,
278 and 280 South Street,	"	M. S. Driggs & Co.,
221 South Street,	"	E. N. Lawrence,
745 and 750 Water Street,	"	E. N. Lawrence,
236 and 237 South Street,	"	Snyder & Sons,
557, 559 and 561 Water Street,	"	Hugh Miller & Sons,
271, 272, 273 and 274 South Street,	"	Miller & Conger,
61, 63 and 65 Cliff Street,	"	O. W. F. Randolph,
206 and 210 South, and 401, 403, 405 and 407 Water Street,	"	John J. Hicks,

EAST RIVER, N. Y.

LOCATION.		PROPRIETORS.
6, 8 and 10 Bridge Street,	Store.	Charles Squire, Jun.,
5 and 7 Stone, and 22 Marketfield Streets,	"	W. B. Peck,
37 and 39 Stone Street,	"	Gomez, Wallis & Co.,
63 and 65 Stone Street,	"	Westray, Gibbs & Hardcastle,
9, 11 and 13 Stone Street,	"	McMurray & Tate,
48 South Street,	"	Olyphant's Son & Co.,
5 Whitehall Street,	"	W. E. Harwood,
50, 52, 54, 56 and 58 New Street,	"	Thomas T. Ely,
Store in rear of 84 South Street,	"	Franklin & Lawrence,
88 Water and 124 Pearl Street,	"	Townsend, Clinch & Dike,
123 Maiden Lane,	"	Ward & Co.,
54 and 55 South Street,	"	Howland & Aspinwall,
74 Broad Street,	"	Wellington & Cox,
145 and 147 Front Street,	"	Covert & Acker,

BROOKLYN.

LOCATION.		PROPRIETORS.
Ford's Stores, 1, 4, 6, 7 and 8,		Hobart Ford,
Pierrepont Stores, 2, 3 and 4,		James K. Ford,
1, 2, 3 and 6 "Wheeler's Wall Street Stores," and Yard,		T. M. Wheeler,
Thompson's Stores, A, B and C,		George W. Thompson,
Ludovici's Store, A,		Louis Ludovici,
De Forrest's Store, A,		Frederick L. De Forrest,
Wetmore's Bonded Yard, cor. John & Adams Sts.,		David W. Wetmore,
Thorn's Store, N. S.,		David W. Wetmore,
Woodruff & Robinson's Bonded Stores and Yards near foot of Congress Street, Brooklyn, viz:—Stores, A, 4, and O, M. and N, as "Class 3;" and B, D, L and J., as "Class 4,"		Woodruff & Robinson,
36 and 38 Commercial Wharf,		Durkee, Hough & Co.,
Mora's Stores, 38, 40, 46, 50, 52 & 60 North Pier, Atlantic Dk.		Mora Brothers, Navarro & Co.,
Wheeler's Stores, 54, 56, 64 & 68 South Pier, Atlantic Dock,		T. M. Wheeler,
32, 43 and 45 Commercial Wharf,		Woodruff & Robinson,
Schenck's Store and Yard, foot of Joralemon St., as "Class 4,"		Jackson & Woodruff,

WAREHOUSES FOR THE STORAGE OF GOODS FOR THE PROPRIETOR ONLY.

LOCATION.		PROPRIETORS.
Naylor's Warehouse, corner Jefferson and Water Streets, N. Y.,	Store.	Naylor & Co.,
31 and 35 Burling Slip,	"	A. A. Low & Bros.,
47 and 49 Liberty Street,	Store.	Lanman & Kemp,

BONDED CELLARS FOR SPIRITS AND WINE ONLY.

BEING THE IMPORTATIONS OF THE PROPRIETORS.

LOCATION.		PROPRIETORS.
10 Beaver, and 49 New Street,	Cellar.	Edward Blackburn & Co.,
55, 62 and 64 Water Street,	"	V. Barsalou,
85, 91 and 93 Front Street,	"	John Caswell & Co.,
5 Beaver Street,	"	M. H. & D. Cashman,
7 Beaver Street,	"	A. H. Simonin,
75 Pearl Street,	"	Giro & Francia,
74, 90, 98 and 104 Front Street,	"	Ives, Beecher & Co.,
121 and 123 Front Street,	"	P. W. Engs & Sons,
47 Stone Street,	"	Schneider & Heidlauff,
49 Broad Street, and No. 1 Lord's Court, and 113 Broadway,	"	Reid, Vanderhorst & Co.,
45 Water Street,	"	Herman Bætjer,
32 Broadway,	Cellar.	Henry Leger,
45 Beaver Street,	"	John Osborn,
23 Beaver Street,	"	Renauld & Francois,
18 Beaver Street,	"	Udolpho Wolfe,
25 Beaver Street,	"	James McCormick & Co.,
46 Beaver Street,	"	Robert Stewart & Co.,
No. 7 Whitehall Street,	"	Charles A. Duvivier,
81 Pearl Street,	"	Theodore Stehn,
67 Beaver Street,	"	John W. Culbert,

SPECIAL WAREHOUSES FOR UNCLAIMED GOODS.

For the district on the Hudson River above the foot of Barclay Street, the Bonded Warehouse, 371 Washington Street, New-York.
For the district on the Hudson River below the foot of Barclay Street, the Bonded Warehouse, 56 and 58 Greenwich Street, New-York.
For the district on the East River below Wall Street, the Bonded Warehouse, 6, 8 and 10 Bridge St.
For Cunard Line of Steamers, Jersey City Store, at Jersey City.
For Hamburgh and Bremen Lines of Steamers, Hoboken Store, at Hoboken.

For the district on the East River, between Wall St. and Pier 55, the Bonded Warehouse, 286 Water St. New-York.
For the upper district on the East River, Pier 55 and all above, the Bonded Warehouse, 745 and 750 Water Street, New-York.
For the Brooklyn District, late U. S. Stores, now Wheeler's Stores, South Pier, Atlantic Dock, and Wheeler's Wall Street Stores, Brooklyn, will be used except that discretion will be exercised by ordering goods in bulk, and heavy articles, into bonded premises, near the wharf where such goods are to be landed, when expenses of lighterage and cartage can be saved thereby.

CUSTOM HOUSE, NEW-YORK,
MAY 15th, 1864.

Warehouse Superintendent's Office in the Custom House,
on First Floor, Corner of Wall and Hanover Streets.

Figure 2.5. Poster by the Warehouse Superintendent's Office in the Custom House of New York, May 15, 1864.

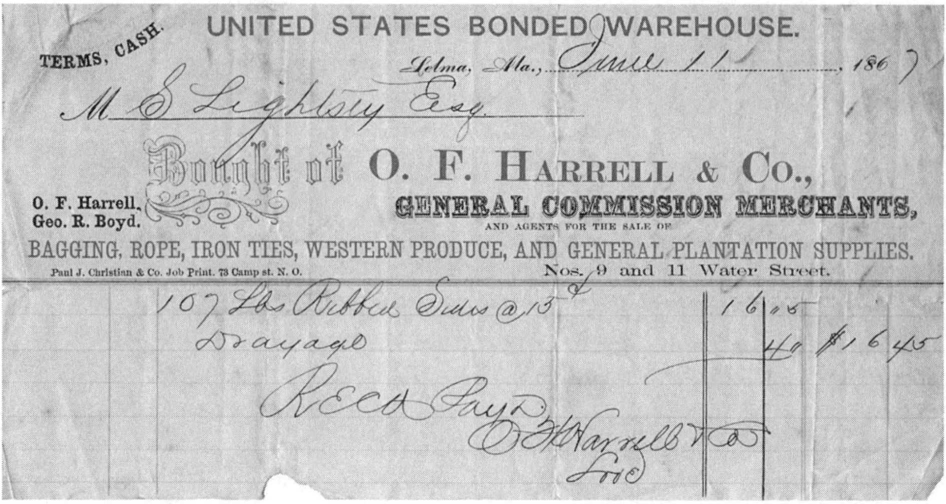

TERMS, CASH.

UNITED STATES BONDED WAREHOUSE.

Selma, Ala., June 11 1867

M S Lightsey Esq.

Bought of O. F. HARRELL & Co.,

O. F. Harrell, Geo. R. Boyd.

GENERAL COMMISSION MERCHANTS,

AND AGENTS FOR THE SALE OF

BAGGING, ROPE, IRON TIES, WESTERN PRODUCE, AND GENERAL PLANTATION SUPPLIES.

Paul J. Christian & Co. Job Print. 73 Camp st. N. O.

Nos. 9 and 11 Water Street.

107 Lbs Ribbed Sides @ 15¢ 16 05

Drayage 40 $16 45

Rec'd Payt O F Harrell & Co

Figure 2.6. Receipt for 107 lbs. of Swiss ribbon, from a US Bonded Warehouse in Selma, Alabama, June 11, 1867.

After the war, protectionism flared up, and it nipped at bonded warehouses. Echoing the 1830s warnings of John Quincy Adams and others, manufacturers and their allies raised concerns about the warehousing system. They claimed it baited foreigners to send massive quantities of goods to US shores, to stash them duty-free, and then to unload them onto US streets when desirable. "If Congress were acting for the benefit of the foreign manufacturers it could devise no expedient equal to this for power," an editorialist in Philadelphia wrote in 1867. "As to being a benefit to the regular, solid, and substantial import trade of the country, it is sheer nonsense to say so. The genuine American importer has no worse enemy than this warehousing system. His profits on his imports are perpetually liable to be swept away by the surplus of goods in warehouse being compelled to find a market before going out of demand."[62] According to this reasoning, as a New York writer put it, the foreign importer exploited the warehousing system "to swindle the Government of its revenue, and undermine the business of the legitimate importer": "The business of introducing foreign goods thus passes into the hands of mere commercial parasites, or smugglers, who pay hardly any duties, no rent, or interest, or taxes, have no property or interests in this country, and when they have made their fortunes here, mainly by destroying our own industry, and robbing our government, they return to their own country to congratulate themselves over the national stupidity of the American people in failing to protect their own industrial interests."[63] This writer was drawing on the language of congressional hearings, where invective spewed with Shakespearean flair about a "reservoir" of warehoused imports:

> Under the warehousing system a reservoir of goods is accumulated, to be poured upon the market at the first sign of improved prices in our domestic products. They are held by their foreign keepers
>
> like greyhounds in the leash,
> Straining upon the start,
>
> to be let loose upon our home manufacturers, whose fate it is to be hunted like hares in their own thickets. If there is a rise in prices in New York, the first advantage is taken by the foreign agent, who lies in wait in the ambush which the confiding government has built for his sally point.[64]

The warehousing system incensed protectionists because they felt it undercut the rationale for tariffs. (These men were not buying that bonded warehouses gave succor to all Americans.) They adduced that, no matter how high tariffs climbed, imports would stream in, harbored in bonded warehouses, and that, consequently, merchants—mainly foreigners, "commercial parasites"—could hedge the political and economic vagaries of the national market. Merchants could mitigate an unfriendly tariff schedule by waiting it out, for rates were constantly changing. They could dodge a financial panic by shipping goods back to Europe, "rather than pay the duty on them or incur the risk of not being able to sell them," as some did in 1857.[65] If their time elapsed (they were granted up to three years of storage), they could withdraw their goods and sell them, capitalizing on the respite from customs duties. The protectionists' barbs were warranted. "The figures themselves" offered "eloquent" proof. In 1881, $9.5 million worth of goods were removed from bonded warehouses for reexport, versus $149 million for import—that is, to be dumped on the market.[66]

A further enlargement of the warehousing system might have seemed ludicrous in the face of such attacks. Yet it was during this contentious period that Congress made a second major adjustment, broadening the system to encompass whiskey distilleries. This change deserves an asterisk because it heralded the bonding of all manner of domestic commodities subject to excise, such as tobacco, oleomargarine, and other types of alcohol. It came about because of the balancing act in tax policy. To sustain the Union forces, Congress imposed a tax on whiskey in 1862, the first since the Whiskey Rebellion (aside from a short-term tax during the War of 1812). Distillers pressured politicians for relief, and Congress obliged in 1866, granting warehousemen the right to store whiskey barrels under bond, and licensing distillers to bond their warehouses.[67] This latter endorsement altered the countryside in states like Kentucky and Tennessee. "Whiskey warehouses" cropped up in droves, hybrids of pastoralism and industrialism.[68]

The whiskey warehouse offered a case study in the temporality of the bonded warehouse. Time was important to the production of whiskey in two key ways. First, whiskey was a by-product of another commodity—grain—which meant that whiskey was a receptacle for surplus grain. Grain farmers borrowed time in glutted grain markets by producing whiskey. The corn in the "corn crib," worthless if sold as corn, was redeemed as mash for bourbon. Many agricultural commodities moved along this same spectrum of waste. "Distillation of brandies from fruit enables the producer to utilize material which may fail to find profitable markets otherwise," as the senator and ex-Confederate colonel Zebulon Vance of North Carolina observed. "It enables the vine grower to obtain profit from inferior goods which are not equal in quality to standard articles, and also to derive some benefit from such waste substances as are left over after expressing grape-juice from skins, seeds, and other residuum of the wine-press."[69] Second, whiskey was a commodity that matured over time, typically four to eight years before bottling. This span made whiskey an ideal commodity for deferral of excise taxes.

The whiskey warehouse turned out to be so effective for distillers that it provoked envy and resentment among farmers on the other end of the commodity chain. In 1889, the Farmers' Alliance cited the "murderous" whiskey warehousing system in its plan for "subtreasuries," which it envisioned as government-owned warehouses wherein farmers could deposit seasonal crops in exchange for greenbacks.[70] These commodity banks would help farmers survive during the lag between harvesting and retailing, or what Karl Marx theorized as the interregnum between production time and circulation time. "Some say the farmer is asking too much, but this is what the government gives to the whiskey men," parried the protemperance firebrand Rebecca Latimer Felton, noting that the price of whiskey depended in part on the number of years it cured in barrels. "They get more. Whiskey is worth $3 a gallon the minute it is put in the bonded warehouse, because the age gives it value by anticipation. The whiskey is worth only 50 cents a gallon before."[71]

Felton's notion of "value by anticipation"—the idea that the price of a gallon of whiskey multiplied "the minute" it entered a bonded warehouse—spoke to the branding clout of the federal government. When the Treasury Department approved templates for a warehouse receipt and a packaging label and allowed those documents to state "bottled in bond," it vouched that the distiller had not tampered with the goods. This federal seal of approval was affixed with the Bottled in Bond Act of 1897. Still, the validation relied on trust, with occasional spot checks, and that was a glitch. A receipt, a label—these were mere wisps of paper and susceptible to falsification. Rumors of swindling dogged the warehousing system, especially around bulk commodities without distinguishing features, like whiskey and sugar. In the 1930s, as the repeal of Prohibition saw the return of whiskey warehouse receipts, newspapers across the country reported rackets. The most elaborate made headlines in 1943, when Chicago mobster John "Jake the Barber" Factor was sentenced to ten years in federal prison for floating over a million dollars in fake receipts. Factor's fake receipts were premised on faux bottling plants and aided by deceptive ads. This indiscretion capped off Factor's wide-ranging career as a fabricator of fictitious capital. As one newspaper recounted, "Florida real estate, British securities, whiskey warehouse receipts—it was all the same to 'Jake the Barber.'"[72]

Jake the Barber was an extreme specimen of warehouse fraud, like Tino De Angelis and his empty tanks of vegetable oil. Nonetheless, such transgressions fed a growing anxiety about warehousing as it lodged itself in all aspects of the national economy, from production to distribution to finance. And this unease was directed foremost at bonded warehouses, for which the federal government was liable. By the eve of World War II, the security of the warehousing system was a source of insecurity. The wariness stemmed not only from the sense that bonded warehouses seemed to entice thieves and to incite invasions of imports. It also suggested that they threatened to expose cracks in the foundations of capitalism. The scariness of the second charge made the refutation of the first all the more pressing. For bonded warehousemen and their friends in government, the soundest response had long been to buttress the buildings themselves.

"Appearance of the Warehouse Idea"

Advocates of the warehousing system had vowed to preempt misdeeds like Jake the Barber's. Treasury Secretary Robert Walker had struggled to design a system of such strength and stability that the world's merchants would have faith in it. The Warehousing Act of 1846 had been his initial overture. Walker then commenced sweeping studies of both the customs regime in the United States and the warehousing systems in Europe. Working himself to the point of illness, Walker gathered and analyzed reams of data, some of which he obtained from three deputies he had dispatched to research Europe's facilities firsthand. Finally, in February 1849, he conveyed his findings to Congress in a report of 341 pages.[73] Surveying best practices in the architecture of warehousing, Walker's report underlined three doctrines. Over the next century, they shaped the emergence of warehousing writ large.

The first doctrine was concentration. Walker's report contained hundreds of pages of detailed descriptions of "docks," not strictly of warehouses. Docks clustered warehouses into waterfront battalions, furnishing unimpeded access between ships and warehouses, and eliminating the need to haul goods through the streets and alleys of a commercial district. Developed in England in the late eighteenth century—notably in Liverpool, at the Albert Dock, which Walker considered "the most perfect in every respect"—docks jutted out into rivers and bays, forming artificial, enclosed rectangular basins of brick and stone, which shielded ships against choppy waters. This setup also helped thwart pilfering and sabotage by dockworkers.[74] Docks epitomized a city's mastery of time and space, aestheticizing—as the historian Tamara Plakins Thornton writes—"emerging capitalist values: security, regularity, precision, impersonality."[75] Walker applauded the merchants in New York City who had recently organized the first such docks in the United States, in Brooklyn in the guise of the Atlantic Dock Company (fig. 1.8), and he called for their exertions to be replicated elsewhere in Gotham and in every other port of entry.

A key trait of the sublimely rational facade of the British docks was indestructibility. This quality had one goal: fire prevention, which was Walker's second doctrine. Fireproofing meant, for Walker, "entirely fire-proof," "free from all combustible materials," and he insisted that architects of bonded warehouses meet his guidelines. These centered on "arches of stone or brick" and iron—the miracle material of the mid-nineteenth century—"for roofs and rafters, for joists, for doors, for window frames, and shutters, slabs for flooring, and beams or pillars."[76] Where other capitalists revered gold as the bedrock of financial well-being, Walker prized iron. And iron paid off. Fire prevention pleased insurance companies. The lower the risk of fire, the lower the rates. Over the next few decades, insurance companies discounted policies for buildings that ditched wood for iron and adopted other elements of "mill construction," including low ceilings and small windows that contained flames by restricting airflow.[77]

Despite widespread embrace of these precautions, fires plagued warehouse companies and their reputations throughout the nineteenth century. Tales of disastrous, costly blazes earned frequent headlines, followed by vignettes suggesting that warehouse fires were as frightening for city residents as for merchants. One particularly "destructive conflagration" in 1869—at a bonded warehouse in Philadelphia that held thousands of barrels of Scotch whiskey—was memorialized on the cover of *Harper's Weekly* (fig. 2.7). Afterward, the fire marshal conducted public hearings to determine its cause. Hundreds of people gave sworn testimony, which was preserved in a remarkable book. In long, unbroken paragraphs—many spanning two pages, punctuated mostly with commas and semicolons—witnesses identify themselves by street address and vocation and describe where they were and what they were doing when the explosion startled them. "We were just sitting down to eat supper at home, when we heard a noise; we thought it was something like a horse and wagon running away," one related. And then, invariably, witnesses recount fleeing for their lives, scrambling to find children and loved ones, and hurrying through dust clouds, with "barrels tumbling down the street" and "blazing whiskey running down the gutters towards the river." A recommendation at the end of the hearings foretold the future of warehouses in urban landscapes: "Our large warehousing establishments ought to be located away from the crowded thoroughfares of trade and habitation. Caution, safety, and wise economy all demand this."[78]

Finally, the inadvertently inflammatory practice of sequestering barrels of whiskey and other dutiable goods in separate buildings resulted from Walker's third doctrine, one so commonsensical that he devoted little attention to it in his report. The thinking on the issue extended back to Sir Robert Walpole's original proposition for bonded warehouses in 1733. This doctrine was segregation, militaristically imposed. Walker prescribed precise regulations to barricade bonded warehouses—outside and within—from mixture with "free" (nonbonded) goods. Windows on a building for bonded goods were to be outfitted with iron shutters, and no more than one door was permitted. That door was to open for customers only during the daytime, and at all other times it was to be bolted shut with a special lock certified by the Treasury Department. The two keys to that lock were to be held respectively by the owner of the warehouse and the government-appointed storekeeper, whose salary was to be paid by the warehouseman and whose role was to mind the till, backed by a crew of watchmen after hours.[79] A bonded warehouse was to be a fortress.

These parameters informed early advertisements for bonded storage, such as in a directory published in 1892 by the American Warehousemen's

HARPER'S WEEKLY
A JOURNAL OF CIVILIZATION

Vol. XIII.—No. 660.] NEW YORK, SATURDAY, AUGUST 21, 1869. [SINGLE COPIES, TEN CENTS. $4.00 PER YEAR IN ADVANCE.

Entered according to Act of Congress, in the Year 1869, by Harper & Brothers, in the Clerk's Office of the District Court of the United States, for the Southern District of New York.

GREAT WHISKY CONFLAGRATION IN PHILADELPHIA, ON THE NIGHT OF AUGUST 4, 1869.—SKETCHED BY THEO. R. DAVIS.—[SEE PAGE 530.]

Figure 2.7. *Great Whisky Conflagration in Philadelphia on the Night of August 4, 1869,* sketched by Theo R. Davis. *Harper's Weekly,* August 21, 1869.

Association (AWA). In the entries for businesses that leased storage for free and bonded goods, buildings with decorative facades were pictured next to buildings with comparatively little personality.[80] These advertisements demonstrated how late nineteenth-century bonded warehouses were styled in more severe and utilitarian terms than general merchandise warehouses. They also marked a moment when such a juxtaposition was still plausible. Gradually, general merchandise warehouses would come to mimic the style of bonded warehouses: windows would recede as electricity replaced natural light, and safety precautions would trump ornamental flourishes. By the 1920s, this remodeling was complete. When the architectural historian Talbot Hamlin addressed the topic of warehousing in his definitive survey, *The American Spirit in Architecture*, he chose not one of the many-windowed filigreed buildings that are now lofts and boutiques in cities like Portland but rather a household storage warehouse, erected in Boston in 1883 (fig. 2.8).[81] With a photograph shot at an upward angle to heighten the sense of an armory or citadel, Hamlin commended the building for its "simplicity" and "truth to function," judging it a fine articulation of "the warehouse idea in big, strong, rather bleak, and generally well-proportioned forms." Most revealing is his caption, "Appearance of the warehouse idea," situating the building as a genealogical marker as well as an aesthetic icon.[82]

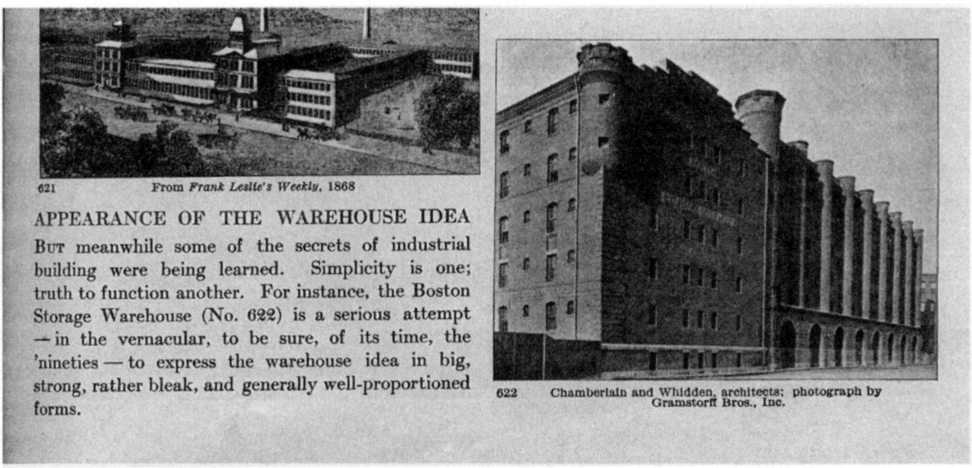

621 From *Frank Leslie's Weekly*, 1868

APPEARANCE OF THE WAREHOUSE IDEA

BUT meanwhile some of the secrets of industrial building were being learned. Simplicity is one; truth to function another. For instance, the Boston Storage Warehouse (No. 622) is a serious attempt — in the vernacular, to be sure, of its time, the 'nineties — to express the warehouse idea in big, strong, rather bleak, and generally well-proportioned forms.

622 Chamberlain and Whidden, architects; photograph by Gramstorff Bros., Inc.

Figure 2.8. The "idea" of the warehouse takes shape. From Talbot Faulkner Hamlin, *The American Spirit in Architecture* (New Haven, CT: Yale University Press, 1926).

"A Peripatetic System of Warehouses"

The architectonic gravitas of the bonded warehouse, the sheer bulk of it, would seem to suggest that the implementation of the customs bond required geographic fixity. But actually the mechanism hinged on legal fixity. What propped up the bonded warehouse was Walker's blueprint for security precautions, not a minimum quantity of iron or ferroconcrete. And in 1870—in an event as momentous and as underappreciated as the passage of the Warehousing Act of 1846—that blueprint proved to be adaptable, when Congress initiated "a radical change in the customs regulations of the country."[83] In an effort to expedite shipping from the seacoasts of the East to the gateway cities in the Great West, Congress voted that cargo could move straight to ports of final destination without appraisal at ports of first arrival, on railroad routes that were specially bonded for the purpose, like buildings. This shift splintered the national border and, as a result, reconfigured the jurisdiction of the Treasury Department, which now had to stake out what one disapproving senator derided as "a peripatetic system of warehouses."[84]

Bonding of railroad routes was even thinkable because it enhanced earlier stipulations for "transit in bond." Already it had been standard protocol to place imports under bond to move them short distances from ports of entry to ports of delivery. If a ship was headed to Smithfield, Virginia, a port of delivery and a small town on the Pagan River, then first it stopped thirty miles away at Norfolk, the port of entry to which Smithfield was annexed, where its cargo was appraised. After a bond was posted for the remainder of the journey, the ship proceeded to Smithfield, where duties were paid and the bond was canceled. Congress provided for this scenario in its first session, when it set up customs districts, and it reiterated the provision in the Warehousing Act of 1846, to help usher foreign commodities "from warehouse to warehouse."[85]

While merchants had milked this opportunity to attend to duties only once they claimed their imported goods at the port of final destination, they groused about the exertion involved. What they gained in deferring payment they all but lost in complying with the government's stringent oversight of in-bond transport. At Norfolk, using the same example, customs agents detained ships for days and weeks as they sifted through crates and sacks to scrutinize cargoes. Bottlenecks, damages, and the usual brokers' fees exacted a heavy price for the convenience of duty deferral. The predicament became particularly acute in the nation's busiest port. By

1868, merchants in Chicago were struggling with "three to five months' delays in the New York Custom House."[86]

Congress responded to this problem in two stages. First, it remapped how imports traversed the United States en route to Canada and Mexico. The US-Canada border was so loopy that, as one senator later put it, "Canada comes down by the lakes and by the State of Michigan on both sides, with its huge elbow into our territory."[87] For the Great Western Railroad or the Grand Trunk Railroad, it was faster to send imports from Niagara to Chicago or Detroit across Canada's "elbow" than to channel them exclusively through the United States—faster, that is, so long as customs officials in both countries cooperated. The "transit trade," as it was dubbed, was of necessity a bilateral affair, sanctioned by reciprocity treaties: if one side of the border had been malleable while the other had been rigid, then traffic would have stalled.[88] For its part, Congress made such a shortcut feasible because it granted the Treasury Department the authority to waive the imports back into the United States without pausing them for inspection: a consular seal was affixed to the crates containing the goods at the port of first arrival, and from there to the port of final destination it remained unbroken. Merchants' lore was that this ruse began informally around 1848, premised on the way that draymen ferried goods under bond in horse-drawn carts between shipside and warehouse.[89] Then Congress formalized it in 1866, employing the "as if" locution: imports could arrive in the United States, depart and move through foreign territory, and later reenter the United States "as if the transportation had taken place entirely within the limits of the United States."[90] With this legal fiction, Uncle Sam nudged Canada's elbow aside.

The second breakthrough—the "radical change in the customs regulations of the country"—occurred in 1870, when Congress entertained a proposal for "direct transportation." At issue was the principle that imports should be "immediately conveyed," "without breaking package," from ports of first arrival such as New York and Boston to ports of final destination such as Chicago and St. Louis—fast-track shipping should replace stops of three to five months. The crux of this proposal was that customs officers at seaports should issue bonds on cargoes that were headed inland on the basis of their bills of lading, in lieu of examining them piece by piece. As an editorialist in Cincinnati wrote in defense of the scheme, glibly conflating feet and miles, "It simply extends the law which applies to the draymen of New York City to the railroad companies which extend from New York to the West."[91]

Western merchants, hemorrhaging money to the eastern middlemen who shepherded their goods to the interior, pushed for this proposal. We are equipped to oversee our cargoes ourselves, they insisted, and our earnings would double if we could; as a matter of justice, Congress should arm us to compete. "We ask nothing but to be put upon a level," reasoned Senator Lyman Trumbull of Illinois. "The merchants who are selling goods by the tens of millions in the western cities ask nothing more than the merchant who sells his tens of millions in the city of New York. They ask to pay duties on the goods where they sell them."[92] It was not the tariff's unfairness that was at issue but the inequity of its enforcement. The merchants' issue was with means, not ends: logistics.

Eastern merchants scoffed at Trumbull. They and their mouthpieces in Congress cast this proposal as fanciful in the extreme. A Vermont senator mocked that an Ohio senator believed, apparently, "that this is a new method of turning the country inside out, and that by it he can make Cincinnati as near Paris (if that is where he gets his silk and champagne) as New York is."[93] To try to shrink the distance between Cincinnati and Paris would be "a dangerous experiment," easterners and their allies maintained.[94] "I think I have never seen a proposition made—and I speak now as a merchant—that was so vicious as this will prove to be in its practical operation," chided a senator from Michigan (weighing in less as a westerner than as a staunch protariff Republican). "Why, sir, it would be almost equivalent to putting your customhouses on wheels and carting goods all over the United States without any security whatever."[95] Customhouses on wheels—*quelle horreur!* That the railroad and the telegraph "annihilated space and time" was obvious; that the nation would follow suit was spectacularly implausible.[96] While a senator from Missouri asserted that postponed appraisal was routine in Europe, the senator from Vermont scoffed, "You cannot cross any frontier without having your trunk inspected."[97]

Unsurprisingly, given the frequency of customhouse scandals, fraud ranked at the top of the easterners' catalog of horrors.[98] They harped on how the Treasury Department adamantly opposed the proposal, with the secretary of the treasury predicting that it threatened "to enlarge the facilities for defrauding the revenue, by practically extending the line to be guarded over every principal route of transportation in the country."[99] The secretary contended that staffing would need to increase, at great public expense, to fortify "the line to be guarded," and that, regardless, more porosity would doubtless generate more vulnerability. He and his fellow critics suggested that New York City institute an independent arrangement for imports headed to the West. These critics understood westerners' frustrations, but they shunned the prospect of declining to screen cargoes the moment those cargoes were "landed" on US soil. Their mental maps of national territory pivoted on an impermeable, absolute—if ever-shifting—distinction between foreign and domestic.[100]

If those in favor of the proposal thought of space as more elastic and wanted to bend it to their advantage, they also, like their opponents, saw ample opportunity for funny business. But they alleged that the hazard lay in bolstering the Empire City, not in decentralizing oversight. For years, these western merchants and their allies had cited egregious examples of "abuse and extortion" at the port of New York: inefficiency, carelessness, graft, robbery.[101] They swore that a system of direct transportation would modernize customs administration and plug any leaks in the pipes. The government's revenue would be safer if steamship and railroad companies were assigned responsibility for the goods from the port of first arrival to the port of final destination. "I have the official proof to show that there is more danger of fraud and wrong-doing in carting goods from shipboard to warehouse in New York," said a senator from Ohio, "than there is in a great company like the Pennsylvania Central giving its bond for $1 million, receiving the goods in original packages from shipboard, and delivering them to the custom-house in Cincinnati."[102]

In the end, Congress approved the proposal, mollifying detractors with three main compromises. First, it limited the scope of "direct transportation."[103] Only cities with populations of 150,000 or more qualified as legitimate destinations—Chicago and St. Louis, but not Cairo, Illinois. Cairo had long faltered in its quest to be the "Metropolis of the West," and this legislation would not improve its chances.[104] Second, Congress saddled the system with several provisos. As in a bonded warehouse, goods under bond were to be sequestered, to be carried in padlocked boxcars and not to be mingled with "free" goods. And those boxcars were to be ticking clocks; they were to reach their destinations within specified periods (thirty days for distances less than one hundred miles, sixty days for less than five hundred miles, and so on). Finally, third, the custodians of the goods to be bonded—the transportation companies—were to file bonds as well. This stipulation was to be expressed territorially: entire routes, thousands of miles of rails, were to be bonded.[105] It was on these terms that American Express first enrolled in the warehousing system: in 1874, its subsidiary, Merchants Dispatch, became a bonded carrier.[106]

Bonded pathways helped capitalists colonize the Great West.[107] Now an outpost like Cincinnati could be promoted as an international entrepôt to merchants and manufacturers in Europe. Cargoes could sail the oceans, be stowed into railcars, and then be "landed" only once they rolled into Cincinnati. This revolution in political geography meant that some places gained ground because of topological instead of topographical position: for instance, a journalist noted that as Cincinnati and Memphis and St. Louis drew deliveries in bond, without appraisal at New Orleans, New Orleans recorded markedly diminished receipts.[108] To be fair, the uptick in imports at these nodes was low. A mere 2.2% of the foreign merchandise unloaded at the Atlantic ports and New Orleans in 1883 was forwarded inland directly.[109] From certain vantage points, though, the jump was sizable, and a harbinger. A whopping 87.9% of the imports registered at the Chicago customhouse in 1883 arrived directly.[110] Chicago's receipts were paltry in comparison to New York's, but they were plentiful enough, in the opinion of Treasury's chief of the Bureau of Statistics, to wash away the unquestioned supremacy of the water's edge in the world market.

Predictably, the bonded railcar's railroading of geoeconomic prerogatives over geopolitical barriers sparked ever-greater demands for physical supervision of dutiable merchandise.[111] Equally foreseeable was that this outcry for governance became an occasion for entrepreneurship. Soon after Congress gave the green light to in-bond transport, the Treasury Department mandated that each corner of each bonded railcar be bolted shut with a government-approved seal lock and issued a call for candidates. Although dozens of firms submitted applications—flagging pending patents—one was favored from the start.[112] The American Seal Lock Company (ASLC), chartered for this project, presented an ingenious design: it included a plate of glass that shattered if the lock was tampered with and that was etched with unique markings, a "photographic *fac-simile*" which verified if it had been removed and replaced—perhaps the first such use of photography in workplace surveillance.[113] The ASLC won the bid. But the railroads soon protested, denouncing the ASLC seal lock for its cost and faulty construction. Bad publicity followed, and within a few years the Treasury Department signed off on alternative models, like that in fig. 2.1.

The railroads denounced the padlock—any padlock—in one further sense. They resented the awkwardness of requisitioning whole boxcars in order to segregate bonded from free. "They are prevented from carrying any other goods in a car containing bonded goods, though the latter may occupy never so small a space," a congressman from St. Louis upbraided the secretary of the treasury in 1871. "In consequence of this rule, they cannot afford to carry bonded goods at all, and the practical effect of the law is destroyed."[114] The secretary tried to redress this limitation by crafting rules for a proto-containerization jig. He urged the railroads to build iron boxes (3 × 3 × 5 ft.) "of such size that they can be conveniently placed within an ordinary box or freight car."[115] Fastened with seal locks, these minicontainers would enable the railroads to cram cars with bonded *and* free goods and also to shuffle bonded goods to different trains (to accommodate changes in gauge) without breaking bulk, or interference from the Customs Service. The railroads swiftly complied, and also tinkered with the boxcar itself: when they needed to impound multiple lots of bonded goods but not so many to warrant a separate boxcar, they lost time and money in the extra labor to attach padlocks to individual containers, so they devised a sliding partition door, which took a single padlock (fig. 2.9). Vocal about the smallest of inconveniences, the railroads won considerable leverage in determining precisely how the bonded railcar put fixity in motion. They succeeded in repositioning and rescaling the spatial form of the bonded warehouse without undermining the safekeeping it signified, setting it aflow like a chest of bullion in the hold of a ship, and all the while dragging the national border along with it.

"Lost by Abstraction"

The railroads succeeded in propelling the bonded warehouse without tarnishing its integrity only to the extent that its reliability was established in American public culture. Despite Treasury's directives, accusations persisted. Foes of direct transportation decried the boxcar's being manipulated illegally as well as legally—"dummy doors" were being crafted, for instance, to abet smuggling. These charges pointed to a weakness in the bonded warehouse: the lack of transparency in both its physical design and its juridical status meant that people distrusted it even as they fortified its stature. On one hand, newspapers ran regular blurbs about smuggling; on the other hand, the bonded warehouse was considered the epitome of a crypt.

In practice, the strength of the bonded warehouse depended on an administrative maneuver, not on a magnitude of iron. The customs bond was the conduit, and the customs bond was tenuous. As it spread across the nation, whether via a bonded railcar or bonded warehouse, nobody could guarantee that it was robustly enforced. The files of the Treasury Department are rife with allusions to flimsy arrangements. And these measures were enforced by bribable employees, compounding the problem. ("No lock in the world could prevent collusion among the men who hold the keys to it.")[116] As the historian Ben Kafka observes of paperwork, the more the bureaucratic apparatus enlarges, the more surveillance increases, but to

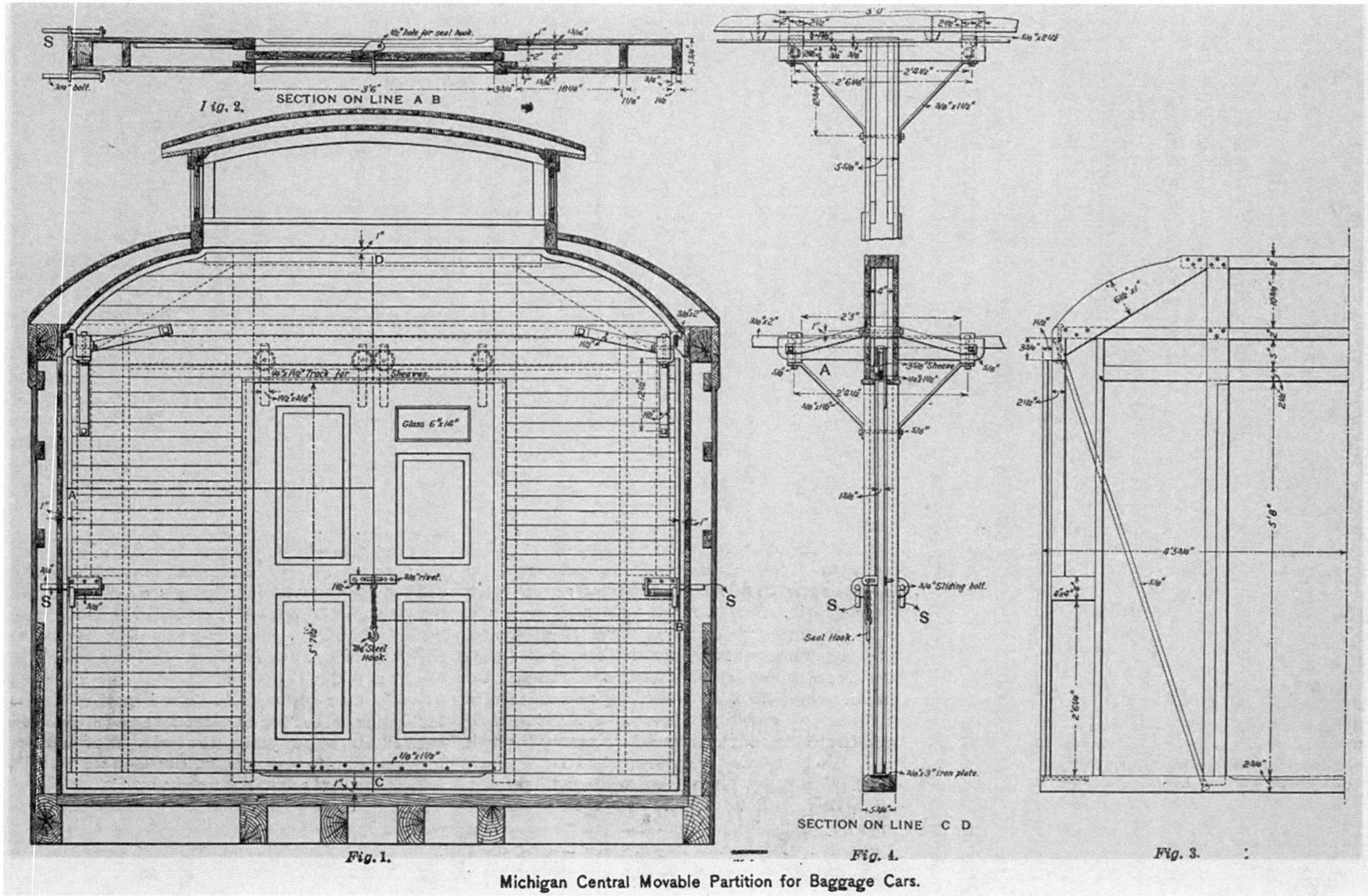

Figure 2.9. Drawing from the *Railroad Gazette*, January 24, 1896.

the extent that all such technologies begin and end with human labor, they are susceptible to inadvertent error and flagrant manipulation.[117]

That glitch in the feedback loop between circulation and surveillance—a problem of the circulation of information—is captured in an uncanny chapter in the history of the concept of abstraction. Throughout the nineteenth century, the word *abstraction* had two main meanings. The first, the one familiar to us, involved oversimplification or generalization (and in that guise, as it happens, it was a term of art in commentary on slavery—the "Southern Abstractionists" were said to be impractical dreamers, too purist to be persuasive).[118] The second, unfamiliar meaning involved removal. To abstract something was to separate it and take it away, either by intent or by mistake—when goods were not stolen outright from the bonded warehouse, they were "lost by abstraction," complained a Cincinnati congressman, in an evocative illustration of how warehousing converted use values into exchange values. "Whole pieces of staple goods, such as cannot be identified, disappear in the custom-house without remedy to the owner."[119] What's striking is that this meaning, over time, in the context of tariff (and immigration) debates, seemed to bleed into a connotation of theft, and in a way that took on shades of the first meaning—theft occurred by manipulation of identity, by illicit removal of something from a mass of somethings such that the act was easy to miss. It was this mode of abstraction that loomed over scandals involving bulk goods, as in the periodic hubbub over whiskey receipts, and as with Tino De Angelis's tanks of "vegetable oil."

To belabor the point, *abstract* is often presented as an antonym of *physical* or *tangible*—"concrete." In such usage, an "abstraction" is an immaterial idea, not a material object. But this neat schema forgets (or abstracts!) the older meaning of *abstraction* as removal or theft, removal or theft of value. When people in the archive of warehousing speak of "abstraction," they describe a tactile, sensuous process. A thing is missing. It has not dissolved or evaporated into an idea; it is simply elsewhere—misplaced. "Lost by abstraction" conveys a situation in which a thing is gone because its generic qualities make it difficult to track. In the warehouse that thing is one of many things, moving as one "cargo," and who can keep tabs on it? In this sense, then, in the context of commodity circulation, the abstract and the concrete can switch sides, such that the abstract is concrete, and the concrete is abstract.

The potential for this slippage was high when the commodity could talk. For the enslaved person in the slave market, as Walter Johnson has detailed, to abstract oneself, to conceal one's particularity in a performance of generality, was a survival tactic.[120] The opportunity for deception was doubled, moreover, when the enslaved person was in transit. Johnson speaks to this insight via the story of a fugitive slave, who, with a slave trader on the Mississippi frontier, played a captured slave as a part in a larger con game. The physical was fakeable, because the physical was an idea as much as a fact.[121] And the truth claim of physicality was ever more attenuated when a person or a thing was under bond, riven between two different geographies—owned in one location and possessed (by a custodian like a warehouseman or a railroad) in another.[122]

While ineluctably tied to the phenomenology of slavery, this confusion shadowed the warehousing system well after the formal abolition of slave labor, in efforts to manage Chinese contract labor. After Congress barred Chinese migrants from entering the United States in 1882, Chinese continued to enter, but often more as "human parcels" than as human subjects.[123] One route was illegal. By the end of the century, Chinese were regularly smuggled onto US soil in bonded freight cars, as in this scenario:

> On July 28, 1905, the inspector in charge at El Paso reported the capture at White Spur, Tex., of 13 Chinese, found in a sealed freight car. These men had been placed in a locked and sealed car, the end doors of which were left unfastened for ventilation, and were supplied with food and drink sufficient to last them until they could reach some interior part of the country, but through some mistake or miscarriage of the plans of those interested in handling the car, it was placed on a side track at White Spur and the presence of the Chinamen therein discovered.[124]

The bugbear of smuggling inspired lurid exposés in the press. "Found in a goods box," a drawing was captioned in a widely reprinted full-page article, startling the reader with a body in a crate.[125] In loosening the rules for foreign commerce in 1870, Congress had stretched "the line to be guarded," which now made it easier for people to cross that very line.

Another route for Chinese traffic, however, was entirely legal. Known as the "transit privilege," it came together in 1889, when the Treasury Department granted access to Chinese passing through the United States "in the course of a journey to or from other countries."[126] The one caveat was that these travelers were to be bonded and monitored by guards working for the railroads. Smuggling continued under this new regime, but partly through manipulation—abstraction—of permissible procedures rather than through outright trespass. Chinese rode the rails from San Francisco to El Paso or Brownsville in full view, crossed into Mexico, and then snuck back over the river. Or they purchased tickets to New Orleans, where they managed to switch papers with resident Chinese.[127] Although the migrants no longer hid in sealed freight cars, the transit privilege mirrored in-bond transport of commodities. "Recently Chinamen have been sent over from Prescott, in Canada, to Ogdensburg," reported a newspaper in upstate New York in 1893, "and shipped to New York through the State in bond—like merchandise."[128] It was not clear whether that last phrase was tacked on as a clarification or an indictment of the calculations that squared liberalism with racial capitalism in modern America, but for the Canadian novelist and journalist Sui Sin Far, the indignity was plain: "It is rather mortifying to have to travel in bond, like a Saratoga trunk, from Boston to Vancouver," she wrote, "but that's what these successful merchants are doing."[129]

"A Bonded Warehouse of 250 Acres"

Chinese laborers passed through the United States to travel to and from Mexico and Canada. They also entered the country under bond to participate in world's fairs exhibits sponsored by Chinese Americans. But even though the Treasury Department instituted a variety of precautions—collecting their photographs, barring them from leaving the fairgrounds, and requiring that they depart the country within thirty days of a fair's end—some managed to break off into the general population. At the 1898 Omaha Exposition, 860 Chinese who had been granted temporary entry to work at "The Chee Mee Village" were said to have disappeared.[130] Nonetheless, Congress formalized this arrangement in 1902, in anticipation of the Louisiana Purchase Exposition in St. Louis. In turn the Treasury Department clamped down on in-bond transport and all but erased any distinction between imported laborers and imported commodities.[131] When the first group of roughly two hundred Chinese arrived in San Francisco, as historian Mae Ngai writes, "the party was taken to St. Louis by train, confined in locked railway cars and accompanied by more than sixty U.S. soldiers and immigration officials."[132]

Such lavish law enforcement was common practice at the world's fairs by 1904. Much had changed since 1853. Whereas the administrators of the Crystal Palace made little effort to police the building's perimeter or its visitors, administrators of the Centennial International Exhibition of 1876 partnered with the Treasury Department to institute gatekeeping measures. Philadelphia's Fairmount Park, which a British observer likened to "an enclosure consolidated as a bonded warehouse of 250 acres," was a duty-free island, surrounded by a trench: 16,000 feet of fencing cordoned the main

Figure 2.10. *Flags in Field of Snow through Fence,* 1939. New York World's Fair, Manuscripts and Archives Division, New York Public Library.

complex, admitting visitors at 106 entrance gates of three types.[133] (Fencing would become a fixture of the world's fairs, as documented in promotional photographs [fig. 2.10]). In addition, hundreds of special agents were stationed along the paths from the wharves to the fairgrounds, where a Bureau of Installation recorded the foreign articles, and a Bureau of Transportation oversaw their unpacking in the exhibit halls. The carnivalesque required ostentatious security.[134]

Wage labor was dominant by the time the gates opened in Philadelphia. Farmhands were hitting the road, not least the nation's newly unchained "refugees." Crises were jolting the national economy, and resentments of foreign labor and foreign commodities were spiking. In this context, to be bonded was not about nationality, for now domestic goods like whiskey were eligible for bonding, and it was not about liberty, for now slavery was nominally abolished. Rather, it was about a fugitivity that now characterized the commodity form, a provisional capacity for interruption of capital's circuits and the nation-state's limits. To be bonded was to be both in limbo and in flux. The dialectic of the seal lock: movement through confinement.

Bonding connoted sovereignty, which must pretend to be strong even when it's weak. The seal lock represented the customs officer or storekeeper breathing over your shoulder. And the warehousing system, as a knowledge system, indicated the breadth of the nation-state's formatting of capital's circuits. It was an immense reach: by 1905, US bonded warehouses would be in thirty-nine states as well as Alaska, Hawaii, and Puerto Rico—and the treaty ports of China.[135] With every installment came more customs officers, more storekeepers. So even as Congress relaxed the regulations for bonded warehouses, people continued to perceive the buildings as restrictive. More and more could happen in them, yet they still seemed like iron cages. Commerce need not be shackled like this, people argued. There was an alternative. It was similar to the world's fair, but permanent. And people—led by a railroad magnate—began advocating for this idea in the 1890s: the free zone.

Figure 3.1. The original caption reads, "A free port has been established in New York City at Stapleton, Staten Island, for the benefit of foreign shippers wishing to rearrange cargoes not destined for sale in the United States, thereby not being subject to customs duties. Surrounded by wire fences, the port is to be guarded by customs officials." February 1, 1937. Acme News Photos.

CHAPTER THREE

Imperium in Imperio: The *Freihafen*, the *Zollverein*, and the Empire of Logistics

> Mr. Adams could not bring in his prospective bride from Greece. Immigration officials assured him that he couldn't. There was no way to meet the girl at Ellis Island on a neutral wedding ground—a "free port" in the harbor of matrimony—and marry her before she formally entered the United States. There was no provision for taking her to Omaha in bond, like an importation of books or machinery. But an unnamed official of the State Department had brains and a heart. He told Adams that he could bring the bride in by marrying her in Bermuda. That man deserves riches and fame above all his red-tape colleagues.
>
> —"An International Romance," *Baltimore Sun*, January 28, 1927[1]

Part I. The National Economy

Borders and Fences

In the wire-service photograph that opens this chapter, from 1937, two men are gripping tools, one crouched at the bottom of a chain-link fence and the other perched on a ladder. A third companion—whether coworker or coconspirator we cannot tell—is adjusting a strand of the barbed-wire rim, two sections of which are missing. Coats and caps touch the sky, black on gray. But these men are not the subject of the photograph, either compositionally or thematically. Dwarfing and bisecting them is the fence. What kind of a fence is it? Not a fence to enclose a pasture, that much we know: beneath it is dirt and cobblestone, and its height is excessive for cattle. Only in the wire-service caption do we learn that the fence is designed for a special purpose and that it does delineate an enclosure. It surrounds a free zone, an area in which goods in transit through the United States are exempt from customs duties and related regulations—an enclosure that shields the world market from the national politics of the tariff.

For capitalists of Henry Ford's generation who were anxious to speed up circulation within and beyond the factory, such an arrangement was an upgrade. As a port official put it in 1919, the free zone was to the bonded warehouse what a roadster was to a horse-drawn carriage.[2] It served the same core function but more swiftly, more cost-effectively, and most of all, more pleasurably. While the fence of the free zone and the lock of the bonded warehouse both bounded a special kind of space, they were symbolically opposites. The lock suggested inactivity; little could transpire in a bonded warehouse—finance capital could flow through only if commodity capital could sit undisturbed. The fence, conversely, teased the possibility of a laissez-faire bonanza behind a red velvet rope. To the extent that the free zone was more or less "the bonded warehouse on a grand scale," as its promoters maintained, it was the bonded warehouse of the world's-fair variety—the Centennial Exposition of 1876, not the Atlantic Docks.[3]

The fence itself was the object of an Atlantic crossing. Just as the bonded warehouse was adopted because it was admired as a crown jewel of the British Empire, the free zone was coveted as "a peculiarly German institution." Germany was said to have allowed something extraordinary in the port city of Hamburg. As one tourist from New York wrote in 1911, "The German customs officials had no more to say about what went on in the Hamburg Free Zone than they had to say about what went on in Long Island."[4] Americans praised how the German border accommodated and even generated circulation.[5] Hamburg's business-friendly reputation was so strong, in fact, that whiskey distillers were known to bypass bonded warehouses in the United States and to ship barrels from Kentucky to Hamburg to mature.[6]

Apart from a sign at the gate, the fence was the only physical marker of the free zone, which otherwise existed as a set of regulations. And it had the virtue of being easy to narrate. As former congressman and Chicago meatpacking scion William Kent described it in 1919, "In cattle parlance, they take a portion of the port and put around it a fence 'hog tight and bull high,' cutting it off from customs territory entirely."[7] The solidity of the fence helped overcome the ethereality of the free zone. As a paper border, a shadow of the equally intangible "tariff wall," the free zone posed a challenge for its promoters.[8] Grasping for other palpable evidence, Kent was left to direct his audience's attention "to the map of the free port of Copenhagen" (fig. 3.2). Drawn by US Army engineers, this document flattened the zone concept into the two-dimensional simplicity of black and white, yielding more questions than answers.

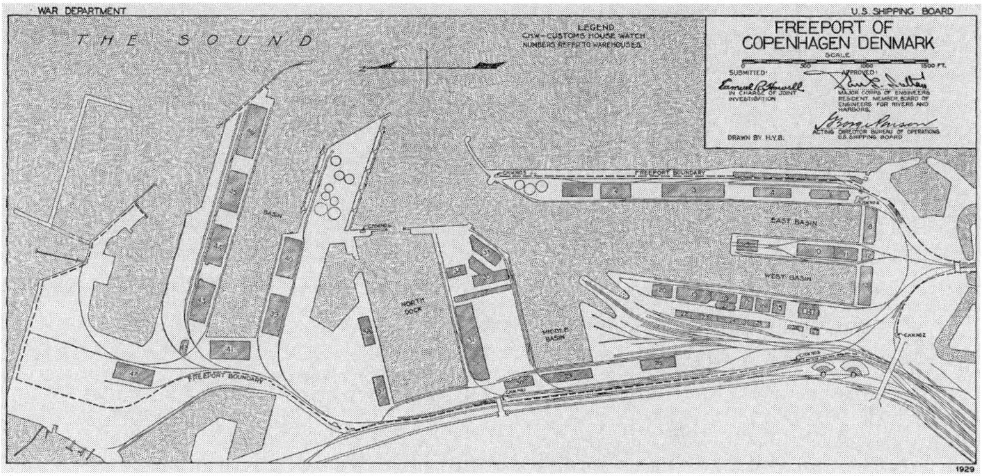

Figure 3.2. Faintly visible, the dashed line stands for the fence that surrounds the free zone. Map from US Army Corps of Engineers and US Shipping Board, *Foreign Trade Zones (or Free Ports)* (Washington, DC: Government Printing Office, 1929).

Namely, the map may have prompted Kent's audience to inquire into what exactly was at stake when the fence cordoned the port, "cutting it off from customs territory entirely." What was customs territory? What was gained by suspending it? These are two of the chief riddles of the free zone. It turns out that customs territory, a term almost wholly absent from histories of American capitalism, constituted the very foundation of modern nation-states. It was the realm of the home market, the jurisdiction subject to the police powers of the customs authorities. If one of the primary objectives of a nation-state was to distinguish its wealth from that of others, it did so within its customs territory—its *Zollverein*, in the German context.

It would be reasonable to infer, therefore, that when a parcel of land was removed from the customs territory, it was denationalized. But the outcome was not so binary. Although the free zone looked like an evacuation by the nation, like an abdication of power and like the opposite of colonization, it bore out the adage about the imperialism of free trade: "Refusals to annex are no proof of reluctance to control."[9] Indeed, the fence indexed an imperial formation. It indicated less a partitioning of onshore from offshore, national from global, than a nesting of the latter in the former—sovereignty within sovereignty, "*imperium in imperio*."[10]

To understand how the free zone instantiated imperialism it's helpful to think about how it related to a central tenet of imperial law: extraterritoriality. Traditionally, extraterritoriality sanctioned the extension of a sovereign's legal authority beyond its physical property. It meant that laws traveled like space suits, shielding diplomats and merchants and missionaries abroad from local rules. Often it was forcefully imposed—gunboat diplomacy—but sometimes it was strategically granted. This asymmetry of power was not the novelty of it, though. What defined extraterritoriality was the very premise of an exception wherein "normal" rules did not apply. A state of exception was not merely spatial but also civilizational. "Every claim to jurisdiction demands a narrative to justify it," legal historian Teemu Ruskola notes. Beginning with the Treaty of Wanghia in 1844, American law followed American citizens to China because "Chinese law" was considered an oxymoron.[11]

This nonsynchronicity was at play in the fabrication of the free zone, with a different orientation. The free zone was extraterritorial not in the sense that the sovereign's legal authority exceeded its physical property. When an American merchant committed a crime in an American free zone, American law applied to him, for he was in America. Or more precisely, his American rights were undisputed because he himself was irrelevant. The thrust of the free zone was that it recalibrated jurisdiction not for people but for goods. It was an economic space, not a political space—and its link to extraterritoriality lay in the plausibility of such a division. The free zone was not nonterritorial, in other words, as islands of capital are apt to be misapprehended.[12] It was monoterritorial, the territory of the commodity, not the citizen. We might regard it as the inverse of another German invention, the camp. In the same way that the camp withdrew people from economic society into a state space conceived purely as a prison, the free zone withdrew goods from political society into a state space conceived purely as a market.[13]

To flesh out this portrait of the free zone as an instrument of what a Honolulu newspaper called "de-Americanization," and to contemplate the strangeness of customs territory delinked from political territory, we need to consider that the zone concept emerged in the late nineteenth century at a moment of mass urbanization.[14] We need to pan out from the photograph of the fence. Over seven million people lived in New York City by 1937. But the free zone was closed to them. It was a gated community for capital, a state-sponsored, nonresidential space of "frictionless handling."[15] The freedom of this "free" zone was worlds apart from the freedom that labor sought nearby at Ellis Island. That was the joke of the *Baltimore Sun* column about the trials of Nikolas Adams and his betrothed stuck in Greece. The lovebirds had no recourse to dodge the immigration quotas via a "'free port' in the harbor of matrimony." It was axiomatic that there were no free zones for people.

"Portus Optimus": The Free Port

The notion of a duty-free district was well established in the United States by the time William Kent barnstormed for it, long expressed in the spatial form of the "free port."[16] Throughout the nineteenth century the free port was in the air, to be emulated in spirit if not in practice. Scan the map. Freeport, AL. Freeport, CA. Freeport, FL. Freeport, IA. Freeport, IL. Freeport, IN. Freeport, KS. Freeport, MD. Freeport, ME. Freeport, MI. Freeport, MN. Freeport, MS. Freeport, NE. Freeport, NH. Freeport, NY. Freeport, OH. Freeport, PA. Freeport, RI. Freeport, TX. Freeport, VA. Freeport, WA. Freeport, WV. And let us not forget the free port that almost was: New York City, whose Confederate-friendly merchant class plotted at the dawn of the Civil War to secede from the union as a "free city" or "free port."[17]

The essence of the free port was the open door. Whereas regular ports barred entrance to merchants from other kingdoms, or taxed them upon admission, free ports welcomed foreign traders and waived some or all duties and tolls. Boosters of the free zone have been wont to give it a venerable pedigree on the basis of this age-old precedent. "The first known free ports were the special stockades in the Greek ports of Challis and Piraeus," opens a typical study.[18] Ancient Greece: birthplace of the polis, the agora, and the free port. That genealogy could be loosely true, but the free port, properly speaking, emerged during the age of mercantilism, to spur interimperial trade. It was a "colonial free port."[19] Mercantilism forced trade into rigid patterns. The British Parliament, for instance, per the Acts of Trade and Navigation of the seventeenth century, prescribed how and where commodities from British colonies were to circulate: to other British colonies, via Britain, in British ships. The British Empire was to be self-contained, fueled by trade and piloted by London. When in the mid-eighteenth century British manufacturers began to seek customers beyond the colonies, Parliament passed the Free Port Acts, thereby expanding commerce without impairing mercantilism. "This was in no way a departure from the Acts of Navigation," in the words of Frances Armytage, a historian of the British free ports, "but was rather an elaboration of them."[20]

The first British free ports in the Caribbean confirmed that this new policy was not an overhaul of the old regime. In 1766, when Kingston, Jamaica, became one of three inaugural free ports (with the other two in

Dominica), the Caribbean was of growing importance to Britain, and it required close supervision. The goal of admitting other European merchants into Kingston was to assert authority over the contraband trade in the Caribbean and, secondarily, to lessen the impact of a post-1764 Sugar Act boycott by furnishing a new outlet for British manufactures. Better that British officials rather than smugglers decided how coffee from Saint-Domingue entered and exited Jamaica. This was not an experiment in multilateral trade liberalization, but rather an effort at imperial trade rationalization. Britain remained hegemonic.[21]

This sort of alteration of mercantilist space was not exclusive to the British Empire. The Dutch and the French had earlier founded free ports at Saint Eustatius in 1756 and Martinique and Guadeloupe in 1763, respectively, with more to follow. Even the empire most hostile to easing prohibitions on trade, Spain, issued a "Decree of Free Trade" in 1778 that relaxed restrictions between Spanish ports in the Americas and ports in Spain.[22] By 1800, every European imperial power counted at least one free port in the Caribbean.[23]

The free ports in the Americas have received scant attention, despite their ubiquity and their role in the slave trade (at times, more slaves moved through them than slave products).[24] Of course, they were not physically distinct spaces. They were isomorphic with port cities, not with discrete sections of ports; no gates bore signs heralding "The Free Port." And so they seem not to have generated unique depictions. Consider an 1852 engraving of the free port of Charlotte Amalie (fig. 3.3). It shows marketgoers in a quotidian public square framed by a series of awning-festooned buildings. The arches imply a crossroads, but the scene is unremarkable. Only a brief passage next to the engraving spells out that St. Thomas "is what is called a free port—nearly every description of goods being admitted at one uniform rate of duty, which is small, being little more than one per cent."[25]

The free port's elusiveness lies in a fundamental ambiguity: Was the free port a place or a strategy of space? The freedom of the free port could be spoken of and written of but not touched. It existed as an attribute of a port, not an actual material entity that people walked, smelled, painted on canvasses or evoked in travelogues. In the language of geography, it was not a form of absolute space, a fixed territory of measurable and definable proportions.[26] It was a form of relative space: the free port existed only in its relationship to other objects and events, as much a verb as a noun, a means rather than an end. On an imperial map, it was marked less by the dot of its location than by the lines emanating from the dot.[27] Which is not to say that it was not a feature of the map, however. To categorize the free port as

Figure 3.3. *Market Place, at St. Thomas, Gleason's Pictorial Drawing-Room Companion,* April 10, 1852.

a spatial form of "nonterritorial empire," as opposed to the settler and extractive colonies of "territorial empire," makes no sense, unless territory is to be understood exclusively in absolute terms. The free port *was* territorial, and in relative terms.

Certainly the British Empire's former subjects north of the Caribbean regarded the free port as a form of relative territory, a strategy of space. In the estimation of merchants in New York City and other US ports, the free port was a weapon as potent as a musket, one that fired two kinds of shots. First, it selectively obstructed access to trade. After the American Revolution, Britain's free ports were open to Spanish, French, and Dutch ships to varying degrees, but closed to American ships until 1822, stymieing American aspirations to dominate the traffic of the Caribbean.[28] Later, Britain's free ports snagged trade from ports that failed to tender comparable terms, grabbing reexport business for British shipping and commercial firms and carving out distribution paths for British manufactures. American politicians thus characterized the British free ports as aggressors. In

1826, a senator from Maryland pointed to Britain's extension of its bonded warehousing system to the free ports and urged the United States to follow suit: "The British Government are playing a great game," Samuel Smith warned. "They understand the subject, and unless met by a similar liberal policy, on the part of other nations, they will monopolize the commerce of the world."[29]

The free port was also said to factor into the vying for position between port cities within the same empire, even if, then as now, it was no guarantee of riches. Take the story of Perth Amboy, a British settlement in the colony of East Jersey that was treated as a free port for roughly forty years, decades before the arrival of free ports in the Caribbean. Nestled at the mouth of the Raritan River across from the southern tip of Staten Island, Perth Amboy was one of the chief ports of the North American coast during the eighteenth century. "The intended London of America," as a booster would memorialize it, it was envisioned as splendid for transshipment, closer than Manhattan to the Atlantic.[30] Its town seal advertised its maritime orientation: *Portus Optimus*, the seal read, *Best Harbor* in Latin, pledging a tranquil respite on calm waters. Not conveyed on the seal, but widely known, was Perth Amboy's other advantage: exemption from tariffs, most notably on human cargo.[31] Beginning in 1721, slaves were imported duty-free at Perth Amboy, where they were housed in barracks until they were sold to Jersey farmers, or, more controversially, moved to slave markets across the bay, as insinuated in a 1762 letter by a Manhattan merchant: "Our Duty is four pound a head from the West Indies, forty shillings from Africa. New Jersey pays none at all for which reason the Master might lay a mile or two below the Town & send up word."[32] In light of this avoidance of New York's slave tariff, Manhattanites repeatedly pressured the Provincial Council to bring New Jersey in line. Their distress was unwarranted, though. Perth Amboy never threatened other ports, in part because of the lack of diversity in its economy. By 1767, when the tariff was reinstated, homes in the area "swarmed with slaves," but the docks sat empty.[33]

By the early nineteenth century, free ports tended to be postcolonial. In the 1820s, a spate of free ports cropped up in the new republics of Latin America and the Caribbean: whereas before the status had been assigned by imperial officers, now it was asserted by legislators of independent nations. Colombia initiated this trend with free ports at Panama and Chagres in early 1822. Haiti followed a few months later with a free port at St. Mark. Mexico installed a free port at Tampico in 1829. Venezuela created one in Pampatar in 1829 and another in Maracaibo in 1832.[34] By the outset of the industrial revolution in the United States, an archipelago of free ports dotted the Americas, with some residually mercantilist, as in the British free ports, and others nascently liberal.

Given this proliferation, why was there not a single free port in the United States? The United States was a new republic, a postcolonial nation. It too emerged as an exercise in liberalism, and in defiance of mercantilism. It too was an emerging market, with loopholes in its customs apparatus to gin up foreign commerce—namely, the credit system and the drawback, later inspirations for the Warehousing Act of 1846. But its centralized authority was weak. During the nineteenth century, the United States never went so far as to set aside a port or cluster of ports as tax exempt—a project that would have been far bolder than the coast-to-coast warehousing system, which itself sparked static as it was implemented—because favoritism ran counter to the philosophy of federalism.

Federalism's limited capacity to empower the federal government to manage a national market entailed a quid pro quo that did not readily allow for exceptions. After the Revolution, prior to the ratification of the Constitution, the thirteen colonies had retained their economic borders. Perth Amboy, for instance, had announced a free port in 1784, since New Jersey had gained the prerogative to levy taxes, or, as in this case, not to levy taxes.[35] Then, five years later, Perth Amboy's free port was a dead letter. The Constitution shifted such choices from the states to the new national government. To ensure "a wide sweep for free trade throughout the whole American empire," as the historian Charles Beard explained, the Constitution vested the federal government with the exclusive power to tax foreign commerce and forbade states from impeding trade across state lines: states were not to be protectionist.[36] In return, and here was the rub, the federal government was not to dole out perks. Article One, Section Eight: "All duties, imposts, and excises shall be uniform throughout the United States." Article One, Section Nine: "No preference shall be given by any regulation of commerce or revenue to the ports of one state over those of another." These clauses were cited incessantly by early opponents of free ports—not out of patriotism but self-interest. As a senator from Pennsylvania argued in February 1833 during the nullification crisis, in dismay at the prospect of Charleston becoming a free port, "No merchant in Pennsylvania could bear up against such a system, and therefore must become bankrupt. He could not consent to pay the duty which is now properly levied on these goods, while, in a neighboring State, the goods came in free of charge. As a matter of necessity, as well as of sound constitutional duty, if a free port were connived in the State of South Carolina, you must make"—perish the thought—"every port free."[37]

Hovering over this rebuke, of course, was the larger significance of South Carolina's rebellion against the customhouse: Charleston's gambit was tantamount to a declaration of independence, exemplifying why the young nation was not yet ready for the free port. Before Pennsylvanians could abide one free port, much less a national system of free ports, the South (and the West) needed to fuse with the North into a national market—juridically, infrastructurally. In most respects that merger did not begin until after the Civil War.[38] Meanwhile, an external border had to be bolstered to foster this internal cohesion, or so Pennsylvanians and their ilk believed. The domestic economy would not thrive if the foreign economy was not held at bay; freedom on the inside required a fence on the outside.

"An American Zollverein*": The Customs Union*

One of the main backers of this project of a national economy was a German economist named Friedrich List. List is today best known as a mastermind of the German *Zollverein*, or customs union, which Prussian rulers had pioneered in 1818 and a swath of the German Confederation had adopted in 1834, and which paradoxically paved the way for the very negation of the *Zollverein*, the free zone. List had deemed the *Zollverein* a precondition for civil society. Before Germans could be expected to die for each other in battle, they needed to be able to mingle in the market. List was to capitalism what Alexis de Tocqueville was to democracy: a European translator of an American institution.[39] He arrived in the United States in 1825, in exile. On a multistate tour he conferred with key political figures, soon settling in Pennsylvania, where he fell in with Matthew Carey (father of Henry Carey) and other proponents of Henry Clay's American System.[40] Urged by Carey, List renovated and democratized the development model originally put forward by Alexander Hamilton into a robust case for protectionism. In a series of letters to the vice president of the Pennsylvania Society of Manufactures, published as a pamphlet in 1827, he skewered the oracle of the reigning theory of growth, Adam Smith. "He has entirely forgotten what the title of his book, *Wealth of Nations*, promised to treat," List wrote. Where were the nation-states in Smith's universe?

> If the whole globe were united by a union like the 24 States of North America, free trade would indeed be quite as natural and beneficial as it is now in this union. There would be no reason for separating the interest of a certain space of land, and of a certain number of human beings, from the interests of the whole globe and the whole race. There would be no national interest,

> no national law contrary to the freedom of the whole race, no restriction, no war. All would flow in its natural current. . . . An Englishman would as readily emigrate to Galicia and Hungary as now a New-Jerseyman emigrates to Missouri and Arkansas. No nation would have to fear for their independence, power and wealth, from the measures of other nations. This state of things may be very desirable. . . . But, sir, it is not the state of the actual world.[41]

Free trade between nation-states was a nice aspiration, but not in an "actual world" of thrones. It was folly for republics like the United States "not to fear for their independence" in the shadow of empires like Great Britain. To flourish, a nation-state needed to be self-sufficient, to harmonize agriculture, commerce, and industry "within the limits of the country."[42] List gathered these critiques into *The National System of Political Economy*, a study of the contradictory imperatives of capitalism and sovereignty, in which he made a case for the further enlargement of the *Zollverein*.[43]

The history of the *Zollverein* enters into the story of the free port's rebirth as the free zone not only because List figured large on both sides of the Atlantic in debates about economic order. The *Zollverein* was also the progenitor of the term *customs territory*—the retreat from which would define the free zone. Whenever Americans reported on the German Empire, invariably they brought up the *Zollverein*, as a common customs territory. They characterized "customs territory" as an administrative space devoid of customs barriers. As with territory of all types, that is, the term named an affiliation as much as a locale.[44] Customs territory was the lowest common denominator of political association. It was a necessary element of, but not a sufficient measure of, nationhood. And for that matter in some cases it was a mark of second-class citizenship. Like colonies such as Togo in 1889 and Puerto Rico in 1901, a state that was part of the customs territory could count as a member of an empire and not, or not fully, of a nation.[45]

"Customs territory," as such, was not a preoccupation within the United States until the moment of 1898. Instead it was the principle at the core of the *Zollverein*—an economic union separable from a political union—that drew attention. One early episode came on the eve of the Civil War when Senator Stephen Douglas suggested a way to redirect commerce between the North and the South in the event of a rift. Douglas began to call for an "American *Zollverein*" for unrestricted trade throughout the continent and Caribbean.[46] Splitting customs territory from political territory struck Douglas as a plausible second-order sectional compromise. The intent was to enlarge the home market without any corresponding extension of the rights or obligations of citizenship. Customhouses would be eliminated, a common currency would be created, and even a common system of weights and measures would be implemented.

Douglas had only glossed this plan before he died suddenly, but the idea lived on. Another Illinois Democrat, Congressman Richard Townshend, pushed it during the stagnant mid-1880s in the same acquisitive terms Douglas had used. "The Customs Union of America," Townshend said, "extends the line of protection beyond the borders of the United States and embraces all the southern nations." As in Douglas's version, Townshend's *Zollverein* was a limited liability partnership that uncoupled political from economic sovereignty:

> This proposition is not political in its character, but purely commercial. I do not believe it to be desirable or beneficial for us to make political conquest in any quarter. . . . The territory subject to our political power is already large enough. I would rather see our flag supplant that of England over the commerce of the seas than behold it the symbol of political sovereignty over the whole American continent. We ought not to wish to govern the Spanish-Americans, but to trade with them. They will be unfriendly whenever we approach them with a menace against their independence, but will receive us with open arms when we come with the arts of peace, to show them the way and to assist them in the development of their marvelous resources and the promotion of their prosperity.[47]

Townshend sought an American empire that was economic rather than political—that is, what might be thought of as nonterritorial. Yet such an understanding errs in regarding territory only in the guise of what Townshend calls "the territory subject to our political power." It overlooks that other kind of territory, that constituted "over the commerce of the seas." For the American *Zollverein* was to be no mere handshake between merchant princes; it was to remap the customs territory and thereby to install corridors to the US Custom House in locales well beyond the ambit of US citizenship.

Douglas and Townshend fancied the American *Zollverein* as a sphere of economic influence that would repel Europe and its proxies. As another congressman said a year later, "The trade of this western hemisphere [will] become ours against all comers."[48] People thought of the *Zollverein* as an update of the Monroe Doctrine. When Secretary of State James G. Blaine broached it in the summit that prefigured the Pan-American Union, in 1889, both Britain and France voiced alarm. In the judgment of *Le Temps*,

"This will amount to nothing less than to an economical reorganization of the New World, and the exclusion of Europe."[49] Latin Americans agreed. The Cuban leader José Martí urged his readers not to be pawns: "Why go as allies, at the height of youth, into the battle the United States is about to launch upon the rest of the world? Why must it fight its battles with Europe in the American republics, and rehearse its system of colonization on the territory of the free nations?"[50] Blaine was left stranded at the altar.

In lieu of an American *Zollverein*, the United States in the Gilded Age would continue to pursue reciprocity treaties. At face value, reciprocity treaties would seem to have been more innocuous than the *Zollverein*, allowing for greater autonomy. "Lucretia Mott thinks the marriage contract should partake more of the nature of a 'reciprocity treaty' than it does at present," the *Hartford Daily Courant* thus cheekily reported in 1866; if the *Zollverein* was an arranged marriage, the reciprocity treaty was a companionate marriage of adjoining bedrooms—an agreement between two sovereign powers to lower tariffs, with no transfer of customs territory.[51] The rhetorical presentation of these treaties banked on the currency of the United States as a force for liberty. "Reciprocity has always been capitalism's ideology of itself," as the cultural theorist Mary Louise Pratt has observed, and ever since the age of exploration it has starred in what Pratt calls the "anti-conquest" of Euroimperialism, sanitizing exploitation as equal exchange.[52] Frequently talk of "reciprocity" came with a wink, however, and approximated bullying: "Each party thereto strives to get, and believes it has got, the best of the other," criticized the Populist banker Wharton Barker.[53] Whereas Barker welcomed the *Zollverein* as a jovial paternalistic hug, the reciprocity treaty was a silver bullet—not a pooling of wealth among a family of nations but a duel between diplomatic hit men, in which the United States was holding the biggest gun.

From a Port to a "Customs Outland": The Free Zone

With the *Zollverein* failing to catch on, the men of the merchant class were primed to entertain other scenarios for how to massage protectionism. In the absence of a continental or hemispheric strategy, they were left with cities. At that scale they found a template that they believed would help them achieve much the same ends as a *Zollverein*, but inversely, and Germany turned out to be the source of it, too. In or about June 1888, on the Elbe River, a new form of territory was invented. Otto von Bismarck struck a deal with Hamburg's leaders, who had rejected the customs union when they unified with Germany in 1871. The former free city would henceforth belong to the *Zollverein* and assume its tariff structure, except that a parcel of land and water would remain outside of it: *Freihafen*, this enclave was named, or, the free zone.[54]

Almost as soon as it opened, American merchants, politicians, and scholars arrived to tour it. And what they saw they regarded as bracingly modern, although in a spirit of medieval modernity.[55] Innovative and audacious, the *Freihafen* nonetheless evoked for them a bygone precedent. Along with Bremen and Lübeck, Hamburg was one of a few surviving "free cities" of the Hanseatic League of the late Middle Ages, and its duty-free status was fabled. (In fact, the renegades who in 1861 plotted a "republic of New York" had cited Hamburg as an exemplar.)[56] This lineage took center stage in descriptions of the *Freihafen*, such that by the time Congress authorized the Foreign-Trade Zones Act, a person could not be faulted for believing the *Freihafen* was literally a surviving artifact of the Hanseatic League. "The free port is a thousand years old," a *Wall Street Journal* reporter recited the formula in 1945. "It found its most romantic expression in the Hanseatic League."[57]

How did these legends inform American understandings of free ports? The first and most salient overtone was of world commerce. The Hansards had been long-haul merchants, forming guilds because such travel entailed risks, physical and financial.[58] "Their object was mutual defense against piracy by sea, and pillage by land," according to a capsule history published in 1828 in the *Eastern Argus* of Maine, one of dozens that appeared in nineteenth-century US newspapers and magazines. "They were united by a league offensive and defensive, and with an intercommunity of citizenship and privilege."[59] This network—nowadays likened to the multinational corporation—drew together Hansa merchants from and to hundreds of central and peripheral sites throughout Europe.[60] As the *National Magazine* put it in 1860, "The Hansa merchants transacted most of the commerce of the Middle Ages—they were the Goldsmiths and Rothschilds of their day."[61]

By the turn of the twentieth century, the second connotation was of a "German" approach to world commerce, one that did not enlist the "Goldsmiths and Rothschilds." As the German Empire's economy matured in the decades before World War I, the Hanseatic League was prized in Germany as the antithesis of the vulgar commercialism of modern times—its hegemony having stemmed from seafaring skill and not usury or hucksterism. Phrased more bluntly, it was lauded for having barred Jews.[62] This trait of Aryan adventurousness continued to be claimed as patrimony during the Weimar Republic. In 1926, what would become Germany's premier

Figure 3.4. Lufthansa baggage label, 1930. Personal collection of Daniel Kusrow.

airline even selected the Hanseatic League as its namesake: Lufthansa, or Air Hansa.

Appropriately, then, a graphic on a Lufthansa baggage label from 1930 suggests the third and ultimate subtext of the free zone's ostensible heritage (fig. 3.4). Juxtaposing an ascending airplane with a Hansa ship towering above the horizon, it promises that sea power will yield air power, and that the Third Reich will dominate world commerce.[63] The label was a hieroglyphic for how the Hanseatic League had come to be defined. It was commercial, it was German, and it was imperial. And it was imperial through control of circulation rather than production. The Hansards traded the raw for the cooked, the East against the West—herring for wool cloth, lumber for armor. They "discovered" markets and reaped the rewards. It was in this light that the Trinidadian American sociologist Oliver Cox lingered on the Hanseatic League in *The Foundations of Capitalism*, published amid the upsurge of decolonization in 1959, concluding that "the crucial privileges of the Hansa cities was not the opportunity to trade among themselves, but rather primarily the right to participate in the exploitation of market opportunities in the 'backward countries.'" Cox, a socialist, added, "All feudal Europe and Asia were considered backward."[64]

The cornerstone of this market empire was a trading post or factory called the *Kontor*. The Hansards did not deputize natives as emissaries. Instead, they established offshore headquarters, fortifications in which they conducted business according to their own laws.[65] They lived in these compounds for years at a stretch, but the *Kontors* were not settlements, per se, like the Hansa towns. They were encampments devoted to minding the till and not to fraternizing. As the blue-blood historian Brooks Adams wrote in 1902 of the *Kontor* at Novgorod, "The merchants lived the lives of a garrison amidst savages."[66] The merchants journeyed alone and took vows of celibacy. Cloistered in their counting rooms and storehouses, they pushed paper and amassed fortunes. Of particular import to nineteenth-century chroniclers was the *Kontor* in London, "The Steelyard," for it was there, as Friedrich List wrote, that the English learned how to steer the ship. List and others held that the quintessential tools of the British Empire—the companies, the navigation laws—all derived from the example that the Hansards had set in monopolizing English commerce from within the Steelyard.[67]

Although the boosters who trekked from the United States to Hamburg's *Freihafen* beginning in the 1890s tended to rhapsodize about the Hanseatic League, generally, and not the *Kontor*, specifically, the latter was a more fitting model for what they had in mind. None of them sought to lodge free cities in the United States. What they wanted was a circumscribed platform to gain a foothold in the "colonial" trade, particularly in Latin America. And Hamburg's *Freihafen* offered just the thing. For the *Freihafen* was not a free city; to reiterate, it was the product of a compromise to dissolve the free city of Hamburg. If any facet of the Hanseatic League was recapitulated in the *Freihafen*, it was not the Hansa town. The *Freihafen* was the latter-day *Kontor*. The *Freihafen* was a foreign outpost. Literally, it was foreign to the German *Zollverein*: as a type of territory, according to an American geographer, it was "a 'Customs Outland' within the political boundary of a country."[68] This potentially unsettling arrangement was thought to be legitimate because it was created and administered by that country. Nation-states required *Kontors*, at home as much as abroad. Such was the common sense about free zones by the early twentieth century. The geographer Edwin J. Clapp best phrased it in 1922: "The foreign trading zone is a necessary tool of the seaport in a protectionist country if it desires to act as a middleman handling traffic moving between foreign lands."[69]

That the landscape of the free zone matched the *Kontor* more than the free city was communicated in English in a new use of the word *zone*. In 1888, "zone" referred mainly to bands or belts, whether in the sense of a borderland between two countries or of a girdle around a woman's waist. The former inflection was discernible in two well-known terms: the *zona libre* of the US-Mexico border, and the *zones franches* of the Franco-Swiss border, both of which denoted porous, duty-free stretches of land across many miles.[70] The zone of the "free zone" was much the opposite. It was fenced, overseen exclusively by the nation-state that hosted it, and usually less than a mile long. It was similar to a military base or a reservation in its regimentation of territory. While the *zona libre* and *zones franches* involved some degree of shared authority, this *Freihafen*-style zone was autocratic. One sovereign reigned, even as the free zone loomed in the bourgeois imaginary as verging on anarchic. It was a case of *imperium in imperio* in that it divided the sovereign within itself, like a wine cellar or a bomb shelter, not in the manner that the African American author and activist Sutton Griggs laid out in *Imperium in Imperio* (1899), a utopian novel about an African American nation within Texas.[71] The free zone was not a space of subversion. It separated the economic from the political, without forfeiting an inch of control.

At the ur-*Freihafen*, this legal fiction was concretely on display. The land area of the zone was blocked off from the rest of Hamburg by fencing, and the water area was policed by tangible and intangible contrivances. "On land," wrote Edwin J. Clapp, "the line is designated by high iron palings; along the river it is a floating palisade; where it crosses the river it is an imaginary line guarded at either end by customs men."[72] The harbor was strewn with battalions, such as a "floating customs inspection house," a hut built on pontoons with floodlights. Photographs and drawings of such features often accompanied text about the *Freihafen* (figs. 3.5 and 3.6). The emphasis on equipment implied that in the free zone the engineer replaced the bureaucrat and that barbed wire secured the nation's revenue more expeditiously than red tape. The *Freihafen* was a "customs outland," but it was by no means an undisciplined or lawless territory.

Figures 3.5 and 3.6. The original captions read: "Customs inspectors stop everyone coming from the free zone at the bridge leading across the canal which separates the free port from the customs area"; "Fence and customs guard enclosing the Freeport of Hamburg on the land side. The notice says *Zoll-Grenze*, i.e.—*Customs Boundary*." Photographs from Roy S. MacElwee, *Ports and Terminal Facilities* (New York: McGraw-Hill, 1925).

This arrangement yielded a business district without compare. Covering nine square miles, the zone consisted of warehouses and wharves that were erected in the 1880s at a cost of 30 million marks.[73] This price tag, though, was unexceptional. What was unusual was that the gates barred entry to all but commodities and their handlers. The free zone was a nonresidential space, wholly unlike the colonial free ports that had dotted the eighteenth-century Caribbean and that Europeans were continuing to instigate outside Europe (such as the free port that Germany would decree in Qingdao in 1899).[74] During construction, the city of Hamburg evicted 24,000 tenants from the harbor area and requisitioned 1,000 properties: no one was to live in the zone.[75] The streets of the *Freihafen* teemed with people—as many as 15,000 workers—but they were monitored by 1,700 guards.[76] The point of this restrictiveness was to minimize traffic: unconcerned about smuggling, customs officials could step aside to allow goods to move in and out around the clock and without inspection. It is striking how much commentaries on the *Freihafen* highlighted this duality of confining labor and liberating capital. "Goods which are voyaging across the seas, knocking everywhere against customs barriers," admired the French progressive economist Charles Gide in 1913, "find in these free ports little isles of liberty where they may rest, and they flock hither and thither from all quarters of the globe."[77] Little isles of liberty—for goods, not for people.

The magnitude of the *Freihafen* dazzled visitors and inspired a slew of imitators, starting with Denmark. Launched in 1891, Copenhagen's "free port" operated within more modest dimensions, just 150 acres, but under the same legal framework as Hamburg's. Its promotional booklet took a page straight from the *Freihafen*: "The port is for all practical purposes an international state within the state of Denmark."[78] Within the next decade, directors of other European ports took the cue by licensing bonded warehouses (in Belgium, France, the Netherlands, and Portugal) and by studying the zone question (in Spain and Sweden).[79] The end of World War I brought a wave of zone decrees. With Germany weakened, Scandinavians jockeyed to usurp the "Queen of the Baltic." Denmark ("No tide! No customs duties!") soon faced off with Sweden, which authorized three zones in 1919, while Norway and the new nation of Finland drafted legislation.[80] Elsewhere, during and after the war, news brought reports of scattered efforts in Italian port cities, some of which, like Genoa, had long operated as duty-free; numerous Spanish port cities, starting with Cadiz in 1916; Vladivostok, Russia; Saloniki and Piraeus, Greece; and a substantial number in Latin America.[81] What is crucial to appreciate about this stage in the free zone's evolution, the same period that witnessed passage of the Foreign-Trade Zones Act in the United States, is that the force behind all of these start-ups, from Copenhagen to Saloniki, was nationalism.[82] The free zone was geared to national uplift, and more unabashedly so than in the *Zollverein*. It was a way to draw in rather than to seek out—it was a cheap date, a roadside diner for enjoying intercourse with other countries without the onus of courtship.

Part II. The Warehouse of the World

"King Ford" and the Free Zone

The spatial form of the free zone, with its precedent in the Hanseatic League, piqued the curiosity of ever more Americans at the dawn of the twentieth century. Disagreements over how to reconcile protectionism with federalism initially presented obstacles to a zone system in the United States. Yet word spread as American companies kept abreast of the scores of new zones in Europe and Latin America. The Ford Motor Company's forays in this regard were paradigmatic. By 1924, Ford was cranking out Model Ts in the free zone of Trieste, to avoid Italy's steep tariff on automobiles. Ford assembled Italian and non-Italian parts into cars, trucks, and tractors and then loaded them onto trains bound for Eastern Europe. This venture came about after some skepticism in Italy: "Mr. Ford's request for free territory caused considerable amusement in certain circles here, where, it is said, he wanted to create a little kingdom of his own, called 'Fordonia,' and proclaim himself 'King Ford.'" This hyperbolic allegation was not entirely implausible, given Ford's subsequent adventures at "Fordlandia" in the Amazon, and it was a reminder that the free zone's hybrid territoriality was even thinkable because of the doctrine of extraterritoriality.[83]

Two dynamics in Ford's early patronage of such zones were emblematic of why zones would permeate the world. One was the extent to which Ford entered zones through partnerships with city governments. Unlike the *Zollverein* or reciprocity agreements, zones, though authorized at the national level, were instigated at the municipal level. Ford's files reflect the intensity of urban entrepreneurialism, as in the company's decision to erect an assembly plant in the *zona franca* that Barcelona launched in 1936. Ford had arrived in the city ten years earlier, cushioned by a duty-free arrangement of more modest scope. Designated as a *deposito franco*, Ford's operation was similar to a bonded warehouse for manufacturing, and it was a prominent presence in the city (fig. 3.7). Still, when Ford was ready for a larger building, employees of Ford Motor Ibérica scouted other cities in the region, compiling tables of data on costs per square foot. Barcelona's government swayed Ford to stick around and to lease space in the new *zona franca* only by ceding to the company's demands on the site plan and by waiving rent for the first five years.[84] Spain, as such, was not implicated in these negotiations; the city, not the nation, was the landlord.

The other way in which Ford was a forerunner was in how the com-

Figure 3.7. Photograph from an album titled "Ford Motor Iberica, Barcelona," ca. 1929. Benson Ford Research Center.

pany's geography of zones served a broader mandate to minimize the expense of storage. The battle that Ford waged against handling labor inside the factory was also fought across the "little empire" of Ford's "distributing system."[85] At that scale, for the Italian political theorist Antonio Gramsci, a signal feature of Fordism—and thus Americanism—was Ford's rejection of traditional middlemen in favor of "direct management of transport and distribution of the product."[86] No task was outsourced, not even the transoceanic shipment of parts, and all such steps were overseen by the superintendent of stock, whose office released instructional pamphlets and photographs on everything from how to label packages (fig. 1.10) to how to load railcars (fig. 3.8). This centralization of control tracked with aggressive homogenization of design. From one continent to the next, Ford relied on modularity. The branch plants were conceived as sets and were less architectural than infrastructural, like machines themselves—a typical blueprint was titled "Projected Layout of a Building for Producing 150 Cars & Trucks in 8 Hours." Storage was tracked as a ratio of each building's footprint. These numbers were vetted not on site in Barcelona or São Paolo or Antwerp, in response to local conditions, but in Dearborn, where Charles

Figure 3.8. *Ford Model A Body Panels Prepared for Shipment by Railroad Car,* April 1931. Benson Ford Research Center.

Sorensen and his deputies attended to the "little empire" as a whole as much as to any single colony within it.[87] It was in terms of this zeal to curtail storage that free zones held appeal for a multinational corporation like Ford. They blunted the impact of tariffs—Italian, Spanish—on inventories of imported parts.

The Bureau of Foreign and Domestic Commerce

Ford and other firms were assisted in these border-hopping ventures by a federal agency whose name reassured the public that the world market divided neatly and stably into national departments: the Bureau of Foreign and Domestic Commerce (BFDC). An arm of the US Department of Commerce, the BFDC's charge was to encourage trade, and this it did in the 1920s under the leadership of Julius Klein, a Harvard economist. Raised near the port of San Francisco as the child of (Aryan) German immigrants—"People who think that every Jew is a commercial genius and vice versa . . . have long believed Dr. Julius Klein a Jew," *Time* chided in a profile, noting that Klein was "a Republican Protestant" with "a notably broad forehead"—Klein had devoted much of his career to commodity circulation, and he set to work at the BFDC with gusto.[88] "Klein turned the BFDC into a bulging databank for businessmen," according to the historian William Leach, and in this library he included memoranda and correspondence on free zones.[89]

The BFDC files testify to the persistent illegibility of the zone phenomenon in its early years. Please inform us about the free zones of Norway and Sweden, wrote the Edes Manufacturing Company of Plymouth, Massachusetts, in June 1928; sorry, replied the BFDC New England district manager, we have no clue what came of the agitation for a free zone at Oslo, but maybe our man in Copenhagen knows, and enclosed is a report on Sweden—please mail it back to us when you are done. Two months passed, and at last Copenhagen supplied an answer: no zones in Norway.[90] "Please send us a list of free ports of the world," wrote the New Orleans office in a succinct request in December 1925; sorry, replied the chief of the BFDC Division of Foreign Tariffs, there is no such catalog, and we refuse to compile one given the diversity of free zones and hence the potential for error, but here is a memorandum on a few facilities.[91] And so on. For BFDC officials the free zone was a moving target, cropping up here and vanishing there, organized one way in Germany and another in Spain: fees varied, rules varied, amenities varied, and information about all of these issues was often difficult to come by. That said, the core idea of a customs outland never seemed to call for explanation.

Countless companies sought advice on how to sign up with free zones. Some were specific: General Motors (GM) needed access to Spanish zones in 1925; the White Motor Company had its eye on the Stockholm zone in 1927; and Goodyear asked for elaboration on Constantinople's zone in 1928.[92] Other firms envisioned a matrix: the Jordan Motor Car Company, for one, wrote in 1927 to raise the prospect of distributing through the zones of Barcelona, Bilbao, Copenhagen, Hamburg, and Stockholm.[93] The BFDC responded with utmost solicitousness. Julius Klein wrote to GM in 1926, "So far as it lies in our power our organization is always glad to serve in clearing the way for the admission of American products into foreign countries."[94]

The BFDC files provide a useful index of the activities that were pursued in free zones through the 1930s. Reexport of raw materials ranked highest. Before the war, 20% of Hamburg's traffic was estimated to arrive from foreign ports en route to other foreign ports.[95] In Bremen that same business had increased fivefold between 1889 and 1904 in the free zone, and in Copenhagen, in 1910, that tonnage was up 100% in the free zone versus 4% in the old harbor since 1900.[96] Firms liked the convenience of free zones—the vacation from red tape—in addition to the reduction in customs payments. Even firms that wound up importing most of their merchandise into Germany or into Denmark preferred the German and Danish zones for the ease of entrance, like Standard Oil in Hamburg's *Freihafen*.[97] This trait earned praise from the International Chamber of Commerce at its inaugural congress in 1921: "Free from all customs control"—such was the happy lot of tenants in free zones.[98] (And of bootleggers.)[99]

The secondary, but gradually more prevalent, use of the free zones in Europe was for distribution of manufactured goods. Distribution was capitalists' paramount task in the age of mass production: "Not the *overproduction* of merchandise but its *nondistribution* was the problem to which almost all business troubles could be traced," writes the historian Victoria de Grazia.[100] To apportion inventories appropriately was part of the art of distribution. Tariffs, on the rise during the interwar years, upped the ante. If it was inadvisable to leave goods to linger in storage as dead stock, it was all the more foolish to do so and to subject them to duties. Unless they could be deposited in a free zone—then it was wise, because the free zone allowed them to breach the tariff wall and to be positioned as spot stocks, ready for rapid deployment. "The stocks of merchandise must be kept, as it were, in immediate reserve," a manager of Sweden's free zones explained in 1921. "There must be full security for and unlimited freedom to dispose of them at any time and place, without control of customs or fiscal restrictions."[101] In sum, whether for the manufacturer or the reexporter with business overseas, free zones outside the United States were prized for maximizing flexibility in an age of growing inflexibility.

Walled Cities

What about the manufacturers and reexporters with no presence outside the United States? How were they to compete in the world market? Between the early 1890s and the late 1920s, between the end of one Great Depression and the start of another, Americans would wrangle over the prospect of a zone system. A series of bills would be introduced in Congress, and all would fail. Protectionism would doom them, but not because protectionism was inimical to an imperial approach to territoriality. Protectionism was not synonymous with isolationism. To the contrary, protectionism was an assertion of authority over territory, however that territory was demarcated, and it was expressed differently in the market for capital than in the market for labor.

Edward Rosewater, a German Jewish émigré and editor of the *Omaha Bee*, was said to be responsible for the first of these legislative campaigns.[102] In the summer of 1891, Rosewater toured Germany and chanced upon Hamburg's *Freihafen*. He became a lifelong advocate of the zone concept. As his son later recalled, Rosewater "saw at once possibilities in it for our country" and "carried back with him such reports and printed descriptions, explanations, rules and regulations as were available." Rosewater contacted politicians, adamant that the free zone was an improvement over the bonded warehouse. "The more he studied the plan and the exhibits of what had been accomplished by it," his son reminisced in 1932, "the more earnest became his belief in its advantages and feasibility for us."[103]

This optimism was infectious for men in real estate. Rosewater's message clicked with one listener in particular. In 1894, Austin Corbin, head of the Long Island Railroad, declared his intention to build a free zone near Montauk, at the far tip of Long Island, as part of a scheme to steer his railroad into the lucrative freight business.[104] Corbin's biography is worth highlighting because he is so emblematic of the zone booster. A robber baron who started out in banking, Corbin was an adventurer who liked walls. He fenced in his 21,000-acre game reserve in New Hampshire, where he hunted German wild boars and other imported beasts.[105] He offered to do the same for Yellowstone National Park.[106] Closer to home, he walled off his Coney Island resorts from Jewish patrons.[107] And for the free zone—on land fraudulently purchased from the Montaukett Indians—he anticipated "one of the prettiest cities within the walls there that there is anywhere."[108]

Corbin, a Democrat, cooked up this scheme with his friend Senator William E. Chandler of New Hampshire, a Republican. Between 1894 and 1896, Corbin and Chandler, with occasional input from Rosewater, conspired to launch a full-service free zone (technically, they sought to categorize it as part of the warehousing system, "on a grand scale"). It was to be a citadel, an outer port over one hundred miles from New York City, and it was to buttress both the city and the nation by bringing foreign materials to American shores in American ships, free of duty, to be handled by American dockworkers, and then to be assembled with American parts and tools by American laborers into American products for foreign markets.[109] This jingoism was more than a pledge of allegiance to American workers, however. It was a marketing gimmick—"When it comes to be talked about by people, I find it is a very attractive feature," Corbin stressed in a letter to Chandler, *"the big thing."*[110]

In essence, it was to be an export processing zone, the first proposed in the United States and an innovation of a greater order of historical magnitude than Hamburg's *Freihafen* because of how it was to privilege industry over commerce. The zone would "encourage home industry and home capital by permitting here the manufacture of goods that many American concerns are now engaged in manufacturing abroad."[111] Publicly, Corbin acknowledged that it was unclear if such a complex would be profitable "to prepare, open, and maintain."[112] And so he clarified that he and his partners would foot the bill. Privately, he elaborated to Chandler that while he was not expecting a subsidy, he was hoping that the government would kick him some transatlantic mail business.[113]

Chandler introduced a bill on behalf of Corbin and his partners in the spring of 1894.[114] It stalled in committee, where Republicans opted not to touch it, allergic to the slightest whiff of "free trade," and a second bill also petered out after Corbin died suddenly in 1896.[115] The project was too unorthodox and too bound up in the fractiousness of tariff policy to survive without Corbin's advocacy. But one notable change did result. In the Tariff of 1894, Congress authorized a "bonded manufacturing warehouse" in which foreign and domestic materials could be combined during production solely for export. This addition allowed for a narrow replica of Corbin's model but allayed fears of an adverse impact on the home market.

The zone concept had taken hold. Newspapers carried more and more coverage of Hamburg and other free zones outside the United States, and a decade later the proto–export processing zone was resurrected by another luminary of the eastern establishment, President Theodore Roosevelt's treasury secretary, Leslie M. Shaw. In 1907, amid gloom on Wall Street, Shaw, calling himself "a strong protectionist," made a couple of bold speeches. In January, before the New Hampshire Board of Trade, he called for transposing the legal architecture of the warehousing system from individual buildings to whole enclaves: "Within this bonded territory all kinds of factories could be built and in this zone all kinds of raw material could be entered without payment of duty." "This port should, of course,"—since in the free zone the territory of the commodity was quarantined from the territory of the citizen—"contain no dwellings." With that nod Shaw was also communicating that this compound was not a loophole for contract labor. He was adamant that he would let "free coal and every other element of manufacture except labor to be entered free." Permitted only for manufacturing for export, this zone, Shaw continued, would offset American wages by eliminating tariffs on imported components so that American products could be priced lower in foreign markets.[116]

Like every other zone booster before and after him, Shaw pressed on the zone's ineluctable historical "logic," the notion that it was a principle already implicit in protectionism that was merely waiting to be released from the forces of dim-witted reaction to realize its full potential. His appeal to pragmatism was noteworthy. This was the proposition of an elite banker, not a renegade Populist. Witness his bait and switch in a speech the next month before the Massachusetts Board of Trade:

> No one objects to a bonded tannery into which South American hides can be taken free of duty, provided the leather produced therefrom is exported. No one objects to a bonded shoe factory for the consumption of imported leather provided the shoes therefrom are exported. No one objects to a bonded mill for the consumption of cheap Canadian wheat provided the flour and all byproducts are exported. No one would object if a macaroni mill were bonded in which free Canadian flour should be consumed provided the macaroni produced therefrom was exported.
>
> But when the feasibility of including a tannery, a shoe shop, a flour mill, and a macaroni factory under a single bond is suggested in imitation of Germany, economic writers hold up their hands in horror and amazement and rack their imagination to find grounds for condemnation.[117]

A free zone was a simple question of synthesis, Shaw was saying, not a rupture with existing norms. Nothing to fear here! While Shaw fell short of converting skeptics, he succeeded in drawing renewed attention to the zone concept.[118] And in his reconciling of protectionism with expansionism he set the stage for a wider hearing, particularly in American cities. For, again, it was through cities and not nation-states that capital flowed.

Shaw's tone was of a piece with the managerial cult of progressivism. Whereas Austin Corbin had chased the free zone with the gold lust of a prospector on the frontier, now it was municipal organizations like chambers of commerce and port authorities that were rallying around it, nominally in a spirit of institution building as much as profit seeking. A trend was evident by around 1910, when John F. Fitzgerald (grandfather of President John F. Kennedy) pledged to back a free zone if elected mayor.[119] After his election, Boston's dock commissioners backed this plank by hiring an "expert" from Hamburg to consult with the city (another mark of progressives' arrival on the zone scene—genuflection to expertise).[120] Not to be outdone, the Merchants' Association of New York dispatched one of its members to Denmark, Germany, and the Netherlands to conduct research for what would be the first comparative study of the zone concept in the English-speaking world.[121] And Philadelphia was close behind.[122] By World War I, powerbrokers from coast to coast were weighing the merits of this domestication of extraterritoriality.

The Foreign-Trade Zone: "A Handmaiden of Protectionism"

Trade policy was the flip side of immigration policy in these conversations. Producing a flexible territory for capital was simultaneously a way of producing an inflexible territory for labor, and of reproducing a rigid hierarchy of racialized labor.[123] William Kent, a three-term congressman from California, would lead the charge in defending these twin agendas after World War I as the self-anointed "father" of a nationwide system of free zones.[124] A progressive, Kent favored the zone concept for the usual reasons: it would eradicate parasitic middlemen and sharpen efficiency at ports.[125] As a San Franciscan, too, he liked it because it would revive the US merchant marine and reinforce the US stake in the world market. To these rationales, Kent added a third, more illiberal dimension that was less commonly articulated, but still widely held. As a Social Darwinist who had opposed Chinese immigration, Kent put a racialist spin on debates between free trade and protectionism.[126] Swearing that he was not "a radical free trader," Kent argued—like Treasury Secretary Shaw before him—that it would be better to lift duties on parts and materials made by low-paid foreign workers than to import those workers themselves: "I reverse the emphasis placed on the importation of peoples and goods by the old stand-pat protectionists . . . who desired, and desire, a continuing influx of labor of any race or description, so as to produce cheaply for their tariff-enhanced benefit, and who at the same time demand the exclusion of foreign goods."[127] Similarly, Kent explained that it made more sense for Americans to import tea from countries where the "natives" were satisfied with "ten-cents-per-day wages" than to try to grow tea in North Carolina.[128] Kent's civilizationist twist on the classic theory of comparative advantage was not that Tar Heel soil was unsuited to tea cultivation. Rather, it was that tea cultivation was unsuited to Tar Heel labor standards. Kent divided the world socially as well as environmentally, as on the commodity maps taught in elementary schools. There were the people who harvested and extracted commodities, and there were the people who processed and distributed them. Capitalism worked best when it obeyed these natural laws. Technology was making it possible for people to switch roles, but Kent preferred for everyone to stay put. Commodities should move freely, not people.

Kent first became acquainted with the zone concept as a founding member of the US Tariff Commission, to which President Woodrow Wilson appointed him in 1916. With a progressivist charge "to take the tariff out of politics," the six-person commission informed policy with fact finding.[129] It looked at topics such as reciprocity treaties, the impact of war on trade, and the economics of commodities like sugar and wool. In August 1917, at Congress's behest, it began to examine the free zone, and over the next year it held hearings in San Francisco, New York, Philadelphia, New Orleans, and Galveston, while sending questionnaires to hundreds of merchants across the United States and reviewing laws and regulations in Europe. In late 1918, it issued a report of 115 pages, recommending that Congress authorize this spatial form.[130]

Seventeen bills to establish free zones were introduced in Congress in 1919, marking the beginning of a truly national review of the zone concept among the American plutocracy.[131] To stump for these bills, Kent teamed up with his former colleagues in Congress and with the port officials who made up the new National Free Zone Association. His chief opponent was Congressman Joseph W. Fordney, whom Kent regarded as a boorish dolt but who proved to be a savvy critic.[132] Fordney hailed from Saginaw, Michigan, where he had owned a lumber business, and he personified the patriotism of protectionism, casting such moral authority over the hearing that all who testified took pains to honor "American labor." "As a native son of Michigan, looking up to the chairman of your committee as the great old man of my native state, my father being a G. A. R. [member of the Grand Army of the Republic] and myself a member of the recent crowd that fought again," vowed one witness in a typical declaration, "my entire bias is toward protection, and if we are not going to have protection I would not be coming down to talk about this institution."[133] In Fordney's milieu, protectionism was sacrosanct. The drill for Kent and other cheerleaders for the free zone, then, was to frame it as "a handmaiden to protectionism."[134]

The two slants on protectionism that dominated the hearings diverged in their understandings of economic geography. Kent's wing assumed the plausibility of selective forays into the world market. Fordney's wing scorned such hopes, viewing the world market as interdependent. Kent's was internationalist, Fordney's was regionalist—the internationalist fantasized about isolation, while the regionalist recognized that the more the world market was integrated, the more that local markets were vulnerable. Fordney accepted why free zones were enticing to manufacturers on the seacoasts. But what was he to say to his fellow manufacturers in the interior? Was not the zone concept an alibi for elevating the seacoasts over the interior, and thus a violation of Congress's constitutional obligation not to favor one port over another? If manufacturers on the seacoasts were to open free zones, as Fordney asked of one witness, "would not that necessitate the transfer of steel mills to the free zone, sugar factories to the free zone, woolen mills to the free zone, cotton mills that import Egyptian cotton, magnesite, tungsten, graphite, zinc ore, everything processed in this country for which any portion of the product might be imported? Would it not necessitate the removal of all those industries from the interior to the seaboard? If not, is it not true they would be discriminated against?"[135] Au contraire, cried zone advocates. Any port of entry could host a free zone—even Saginaw! A Republican congressman from Cincinnati jumped in to help: "It does not necessarily mean a seaport, or a ship landing goods. It might be a railroad. Under this bill you could make Pittsburgh a free zone." "Yes, sir," agreed the witness, the author of the Merchants' Association's report. "Of course," he qualified, "that would be an unusual development." Fordney pressed back. *Unusual* was putting it mildly. The prospect of free zones in practically every large city was absurd, almost as ridiculous as "building a fence around the United States and calling it a free zone."[136]

Other prozone witnesses ducked this problem of spatial equilibrium by downplaying how much manufacturers stood to gain. Free zones facilitate foreign commerce, they said, not large-scale industry. "Take the Ford assembling plant for automobiles," pointed out a San Francisco port commissioner. "Do you expect to see that in the free zones? Not at all. The mere price of the land, the rent of the land involved in the free-zone area makes it absolutely financially impossible for these manufacturing plants to be established in the free zone."[137] A big widget maker from Pittsburgh was not likely to choose to relocate to a free zone in Philadelphia, but neither was a big widget maker who was already in Philadelphia. Indeed, another witness explained, "manufacturing" as such was something of a misnomer: "The word 'manufacturing' had to be included [in the law], because if you were going to do any assembling or putting together of parts of an article, no matter how trifling, that would be manufacturing, and unless that was provided for, you might find yourself handicapped."[138] While Kent and his colleagues hoped for far more than "trifling" assembling in free zones, they tried to neutralize Fordney's quibbles by feigning disinterest in the likes of Ford. Free zones were best suited to reexport and other types of commercial activity.

By shifting the focus from making goods to dealing in them, however, Kent's cadre invited another accusation: free zones would facilitate dumping. Even if it was commerce and not industry that would delimit the zone concept, was it realistic to expect that such commerce would be confined to transshipment and reexport? Would not at least some portion of goods entered into free zones wind up imported into the United States? Granted, duties would apply. But given that duties would apply to those goods if they were imported the old-fashioned way, would not their owners decide to import them through the free zones in order to defer the duties temporarily? And why would they bother? The reason was irrefutable, as Henry Ford might have answered (citing his company's experience in Trieste and Barcelona and Stockholm and so on): spot stocks. "Our cutlery manufacturers will compete with the cutlery manufacturers of Solingen and Sheffield, not in Solingen and Sheffield, but at the American free port," railed a leader of the American Protective Tariff League. "The difference is in having the stock ready, already here in the American free port. You go out to the American manufacturer and you ask him how soon he can deliver certain goods. The same goods happen to be lying in the free port, and they compete with the American producer, right here under the American flag."[139] Demonstrating a strong grasp of distribution methods, this witness raised the very same complaint that Philadelphians had lodged the previous century against the warehousing system.

This witness's sensitivity to the free zone's intensifying of time-space compression was shared all the way down the supply chain. For there were the parts makers to think of, too. "You must remember this," testified a manager from the bridge-building firm John A. Roebling's Sons. "What is one man's raw material is another man's finished product, and when we were buying steel in Europe we were depriving some Pittsburgh manufacturer of that business." By this measure, free zones would bring Europe's steel mills that much closer to Pittsburgh's steel mills. And bear in mind that most merchants know no loyalty to the nationalities of commodities, this witness said: "If I were a merchant or broker, I would not care where my goods were made or who made them. I would simply be interested in the profit, and I would just as leave, speaking from the standpoint of profit, ship out of New York a ton of German-made goods from a stock on Staten Island as a ton of American-made goods from Newark."[140]

Undeterred, proponents of the free zone fell back on the precedent of the bonded warehouse. The substance of the zone concept was already recognized in US customs law in the guise of the warehousing system, Kent and company contended. And that system was outmoded—too cumbersome, too expensive, too nineteenth century. The free zone, they said, "is an extension of the same principles for facilitating trade that we find in the bonded warehouse . . . to make it broader, larger, freer, easier and cheaper in operation, more frictionless."[141] The bonded warehouse is an important resource, they asserted, and it needs to be updated.

Noticeably absent from this homage to the warehousing system were those most knowledgeable about it, and perhaps most directly affected by the proposed legislation: the warehousemen. No leader of the American Warehousemen's Association (AWA) took the microphone, although one of them, Irving Bush, did submit a hostile letter in which he derided the zone concept as ill-suited to the nation's economic geography for much the same reasons raised by Fordney.[142] To this barb from Bush one of Kent's allies responded by guaranteeing that the free zone posed no threat to the warehousemen. In fact it would help them, for it had a magically magnetic quality: "Business seems to materialize out of the air. It is astonishing." Facilities like free zones, he promised, "are trade magnets, they are lodestones. They draw business to them." Bush's fears, he asserted, "are groundless."[143]

"Trade magnets": Kent himself could not have said it better. This was the notion he had tried to popularize, and in the plural—not one magnet, but many, united. Particularly in the wake of World War I, the United *States*, plural, needed to come together and to claim their rightful place, singular, at the crossroads of world commerce. The real battle, zone advocates held, was not between Pittsburgh and Philadelphia but between the Suez Canal and the Panama Canal. One member of the US Shipping Board conjured the image of a "butterfly" map with "the United States in the center of the world. . . . We are sitting in the middle with our hands stretched out on both sides and we just have this natural inward and outward motion" (fig. 3.9).[144] As Pittsburghians extended one hand, Philadelphians extended another; overseas empire resolved the contradictions of continental empire.

Ultimately this invocation of unity failed to persuade, and the zone bill never went to a vote in 1919. Fordney insisted that the constitutionality of it was the hitch—the potential for privileging one port over another.[145] But Kent diagnosed the tariff as the true culprit, writing that Fordney's "consti-

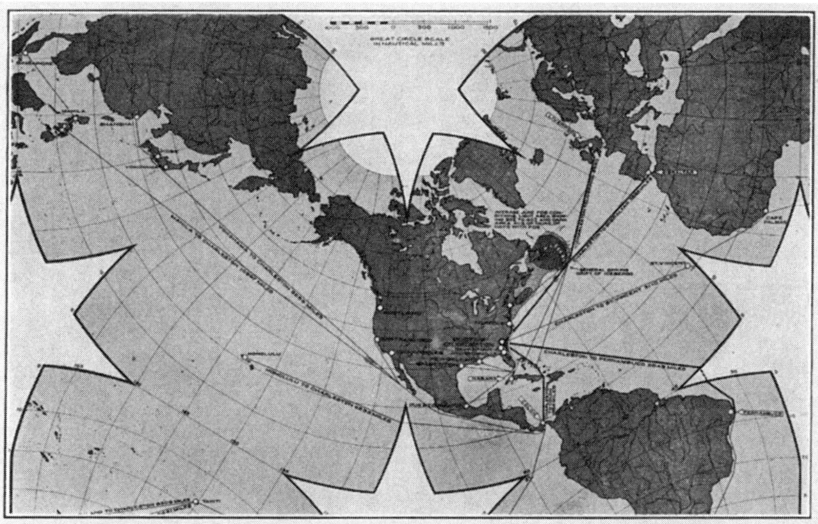

Figure 3.9. "Butterfly" map from Roy S. MacElwee, *Port Development* (New York: McGraw-Hill, 1925).

tutional objections, I am sure, are based wholly on his desire to not do anything with the tariff as long as the Republican Party hopes to make capital of it later."[146] Frustrated but fired up, Kent dipped into his own (substantial) bank account to help fund lobbying for further legislative attempts to establish a US free zone.[147] He and his colleagues did what they could to dissociate the zone concept from the tariff. They spoke of "foreign-trade zones" and not "free zones" or "free ports," a switch they had made in 1919 to avoid "free trade."[148] ("Free ports smacked of free trade," the *New York Tribune* editorialized approvingly. "A good idea got a bad name and unjustly suffered the consequences.")[149] And they axed manufacturing as an activity permitted in the free zones, swapping it for a variety of forms of "manipulating." These gambles were unsuccessful, and instead the warehousemen were rewarded in the Fordney-McCumber Tariff of 1922 with a provision for a new class of "manipulating" bonded warehouses, which were allowed for importing as well as for exporting.[150]

This latest add-on to the warehousing system was a flop. Scarcely anyone used "manipulating" bonded warehouses, and fewer liked them, doctrinally. They only incited more clamor for free zones. Even Commerce Secretary Herbert Hoover—a friend of the AWA—conceded that "the privileges available are not sufficiently attractive to be used to any great extent."[151] Merchants wanted to be at liberty to do business as they pleased, not to be encumbered by government regulations. Savings on customs duties were much less valuable than frictionlessness, or savings of time.

So the march for free zones carried on during the 1920s, led increasingly by the directors of the port authorities. New Yorkers were at the helm, but plenty of other ports of entry were in line as well—Boston, Providence, Newark, Philadelphia, Baltimore, Newport News, Savannah, Miami, Mobile, Memphis, New Orleans, Chicago, St. Louis, Detroit, Buffalo, Cincinnati, Galveston, San Diego, Los Angeles, San Francisco, Oakland, Portland, Seattle, Tacoma, even Honolulu.[152] (No Pittsburgh.) Politicians connected with this network introduced yet more zone bills during each session of Congress.[153] A leader of the Merchants' Association of New York wrote in 1929, "Business houses, ship operators, importers, exporters, commercial organizations, etc., in practically every part of the United States are on record in favor of legislation permitting such zones in the United States."[154] The zone concept had arrived. No longer dismissed as fantastical, it seemed to many businessmen to be eminently reasonable. Now all that was needed to sell it was a massive new tariff act and a global depression.

The New Deal and the Neo-Hanseatic League

In this context, what mattered about the infamously "infamous" Smoot-Hawley Tariff of 1930 was not its economic impact but its outsized reputation.[155] Introduced in mid-1929 and passed six months after Black Tuesday, Smoot-Hawley ushered in nearly nine hundred new duties. It was a behemoth, an exercise in logrolling par excellence. Advocates of free zones tried to amend it with a provision for foreign-trade zones, with President Herbert Hoover's approval.[156] Although prepared to support the tariff hikes, they felt that the bill needed to prevent red tape from sealing shut the nation's ports. But they failed to mobilize sufficient support. And, as they warned, Smoot-Hawley came to be pilloried—whether accurately or not—as a catalyst of the autarky that idled global capitalism in the early 1930s.

Certainly that was how presidential candidate Franklin D. Roosevelt opportunistically portrayed Smoot-Hawley in 1932. While Roosevelt was a Democrat and a New Yorker of the merchant class, it was not as if he entered office as an ardent free trader. Only 54 of the 1,800 words in his inaugural address were about foreign policy, and during his first one hundred days he opted for economic nationalism, shielding agriculture and industry from foreign competition in the National Industrial Recovery Act and the Agricultural Adjustment Act.[157] It would take a southerner in his cabinet, Secretary of State Cordell Hull, who as a congressman from Tennessee had sat on Fordney's committee during the 1919 hearing, gunning for free zones, to prod Roosevelt toward trade liberalization.

Spearheaded by Hull, a bold amendment to Smoot-Hawley was proposed as "an emergency measure" in March 1934: the Reciprocal Trade Agreements Act (RTAA). "A full and permanent domestic recovery depends in part upon a revived and strengthened international trade," Roosevelt announced.[158] With the RTAA, the president was asking legislators to move aside and to give him latitude to negotiate bilateral trade agreements *without congressional ratification*. Smoot-Hawley would remain in effect, but the executive branch would modify it without public debate. Despite Republicans' allegations that the bill was "fascist in its philosophy," Congress granted this executive power, tempering it as provisional; every three years the RTAA would need to be renewed.[159] And renewed it was. From the hermetic offices of the executive branch, the administrators of the RTAA laid the groundwork for the American Century.

It was in this atmosphere of exception that the space of exception would at last have its day. And the politician who would secure it personified, like Roosevelt, a change of the guard. Up through Smoot-Hawley's enactment in 1930, progressive Republicans like William Kent had been out in front in the crusade for free zones. But by 1930 this formation had fallen into the rear; Kent himself had died in 1928.[160] Poised to take over was a Democratic congressman thirty-five years Kent's junior, a son of Jewish immigrants who came up during the Jazz Age, not the Progressive Era. Soon this upstart would name himself, not Kent, the father of the foreign-trade zone.

Whereas Kent exemplified the zone concept's medievalism, its capacity to help repel the barbarian invasions, Emanuel "Manny" Celler stood for its modernism. Celler believed in free movement. He joined Congress in 1923 to oppose the immigration quotas that Kent endorsed. His father had fled Germany in 1848, and as he certified in his memoir, "I came from a district of aliens. I knew them." He empathized with the huddled masses, and he wanted to welcome them ashore as rights-bearing, property-owning Americans. He despised the tariffs for the same reason he hated the immigration quotas—for stifling "freedoms," or what he called "assertions of independence."[161]

This emotional attachment to self-governance underlay Celler's fondness for the zone concept. He wanted Congress to finish the job begun in 1846 by Treasury Secretary Robert Walker and to depose Britain as "the Warehouse of the World." Celler indicted *Pax Britannica* on the House floor. "England is way ahead of us in the matter of transshipments. Half of the goods bought by the United States from England are not produced there at all," he vented (in the very same sort of critique that southerners had long made of New York). "Cotton from Egypt we buy in London. Tin from Bolivia we buy in London. Wool from Australia and hemp from the Philippines we buy in London. We buy East Indian spirits in English ports. This should all be reversed."[162] The New Deal was a test of maturity. The United States was a developing country no more. Celler's rhetoric reflected not only the anxiety that suffused the discourse of the New Deal but also the will to power. We must liberate ourselves from Britain once and for all, he was saying, and take command of how goods traverse the Western Hemisphere. The fact that, in that event, neighboring nation-states would merely shift their dependence from an old to a new hegemon, via the Panama Canal in lieu of the Suez Canal, did not sully this ambition. Independence for "us" meant dependence for others.

Celler broached the zone concept in 1931 and then again in 1933 and 1934.[163] In his proselytizing for it he stressed its practicality. The bonded warehouse is self-defeating in its restrictiveness, he maintained, echoing the mantra of the previous forty years. "The Government is so jealous of its revenues that it, in a way, looks upon a man who tries to do the very things that the Government seeks to encourage as though he were a malefactor, as though he were trying to cheat the Government," he testified at a hearing in March 1934 on a bill he sponsored. "In other words, there is always held over his head a policeman's club, as it were. He is constantly confronted with a uniform." Give the man some room to maneuver. "Let me put it more mildly by saying that there is a feeling of irksomeness, there is a feeling of lack of freedom on the part of those who try to do these very things, when you have somebody constantly watching over them, because you cannot do your work as well as you can when you are given a little freedom."[164] During this round of debate, "freedom" was the refrain.

This aspect of the pitch for the zone—freedom for capitalists from "somebody constantly watching over them"—was the only issue to provoke questions about the zone's extraterritoriality. And even then the concerns were procedural rather than categorical. For the most part, the zone's territorial status seemed to pose no quandary. Advocates and opponents alike seemed to envision a nation with bright-line borders and an adjacent enclave of the world market, oriented to the outside—onshore geopolitically, but offshore geoeconomically. "Anything that took place in the zone would be of no interest to the United States," testified an official from the Port of New York Authority, "and the only interest the United States would have would be when the goods approached the barrier for entrance into the United States."[165] The trick was how to normalize that process of admission into the home market. For example, how would customs guards know that the goods leaving the zone were the same goods that arrived in the zone? How would they prevent smuggling without monitoring deliveries to the zone?[166] Not to worry, the port official replied, this compound would be nothing like the freewheeling colonial free port of the late eighteenth century; this would be a replica of the fenced free zone of Hamburg: "The ship and the goods would be in a territory which is policed. They cannot get out, and they could be there just as well as they could be in England."[167] Geopolitically, what defined this *Kontor* was not the activity inside it but the show of force that surrounded it.

The Great Depression hung over the 1934 hearings, lending calls for experimentation an additional urgency. Many witnesses said the zone concept deserved at least an audition, for the economic crisis demanded new strategies (or old strategies reborn). Unlike in the nineteenth century, Listian protectionism was now perceived as harming rather than protecting American jobs. New Yorkers delivered this message the loudest, given that the nation's chief port was hardest hit by the slowdown in world trade. "We have 5,000 or more longshoremen out of work," the New York City docks commissioner testified. "The warehouses are less than half full."[168] With Mayor Fiorello La Guardia estimating that a free zone would generate 25,000 jobs, another port official spun the legislation as a way for the public sector to lean on the private sector with "practically no cost to the federal government." "Here is a great step that the government can take for the stimulation of foreign trade," he said during the Senate hearing, "with a very minimum of cost to 'Uncle Sam.'"[169] All that Congress needed to do was to give the green light.

But would New York City be the sole city to benefit? What about Pittsburgh? The ghost of Fordney was no fright for Celler. Brushing aside the zone concept's supposed unconstitutionality, Celler gestured to the breadlines and reminded his fellow congressman that, in theory, any and every city could participate. He supplied a list of the ports of entry in existence as of 1934: a total of 281.[170] Furthermore, he pointed out, new ports of entry could be established by executive order. Celler never bothered to stipulate that a zone system would not pit Pittsburgh against Philadelphia. He invoked the crisis to suggest that it would be folly not to give such a system a shot. (For good measure, he also supplied a list of the free zones in existence and under consideration outside the United States—to underscore that Pittsburgh's struggle was as much global as local.)

The topic of manufacturing also lingered from Fordney's era, even though by now it was off the table, officially if not unambiguously. Politicians on both sides puzzled over how exactly manufacturing was precluded from the foreign-trade zone. After all, they asked, what is "assembling" if not an integral phase of manufacturing? A Republican congressman chided, "You have a condition here which is very indefinable."[171] Those angling for industry in the zones lobbied their colleagues not to get hung up on the semantics. "Manufacturing is manipulating and/or refining," remarked a Democratic congressman from Newport News, Virginia, sponsor of three previous bills. "What's in a name?"[172] Translation: if we can manipulate, we can manufacture. Celler navigated these murky waters by looking backward to the Hanseatic roots/routes of the zone concept. Think of London, he repeated. Manufacturing is barred—for now.[173]

"London," in the end, won the day. London, as an apotheosis of empire, summarized the argument for the foreign-trade zone in 1934. London—"the world's clearing house"—represented the political economy of the neo-Hanseatic League that Celler and other congressman from the seacoasts envisioned for their cities.[174] Celler encapsulated this mode of circulation on the day of the House vote with a case study, as if lecturing schoolchildren:

> Suppose you are importing laces and embroideries, and fancy goods from Europe, and you want to distribute them in South America, and let us assume that the South American trade is of such a nature that you have got to have a peculiar shape of package, that you can throw over the pack of a mule, or even a llama, an evenly balanced package. You would be surprised to know how much the success of South American trade depends upon such a small thing as the size and shape of the package.
>
> Now, suppose this embroidery and these fancy goods when they come from Europe are in square boxes, which are unsuitable for the South American trade. You cannot put one of them on the back of a mule. The customs regulation will not let you touch that box, or reopen it or repack it or change the shape of the package, without going through so much red tape that it just makes it unprofitable to conduct the operation at all.
>
> Now, under this free-zone proposition, you can bring in all of those goods to this free zone, take them out of their packages, put them into the kind of package you want, and send it down to South America.[175]

This hypothetical was an allegory for Celler's new deal for the seaports: the United States as a traffic hub for its good neighbors in Latin America. And he cannily chose not shoes or cars or another symbol of "American-made goods" but a luxury item that was forever branded as an import: lace.

Repackaging European lace for mules down south, with no engines or turbines required—where was the danger to Pittsburgh or Saginaw in that?

Celler's bill went to a vote in the House on May 29, 1934, and the tally broke down along the usual lines for tariff policy—mostly.[176] It won by 254 to 95, a ratio quite similar to the vote for the RTAA earlier that same day. Predictably, the yeas were Democratic, by a margin of 8–1, while the nays were Republican, by a margin of 3–1. The agricultural, Democratic South voted overwhelmingly in favor, and the agricultural, Democratic West voted largely in opposition. These were the typical patterns for tariff policy. But if Celler was to be believed, and apparently, to some, he was, the free zone was not a matter of tariff policy. Thirty Republicans did support it. Take Philadelphia, for instance. Out of an all-Republican delegation, three voted in favor, two voted in opposition, and one abstained. And what of Pittsburgh? Although one Democrat sat out the vote, the other Democrat voted in favor, as did the one Republican. Ever-incendiary tariff policy was traditionally dictated by geographies of production, and now Celler had managed to ground it in geographies of circulation.

Affairs in the other chamber were far less climactic. The Senate had already passed a companion bill sponsored by Royal S. Copeland of New York on a voice vote after five minutes of discussion.[177] When the House then sent over Celler's bill, the Senate sought to amend it to allow manufacturing, along with a few other provisions. But it conceded these points during a conference on the two bills, and in mid-June—one week after the RTAA was sent to the Oval Office—a final bill much like Celler's original one reached President Roosevelt's desk. As Roosevelt signed it, he chatted with reporters about another bill he had signed, allocating money for highways.[178] The Foreign-Trade Zones Act was also about highways, in a sense, and the culmination of nearly a century's worth of agitation, instigated first by Treasury Secretary Robert J. Walker with the Warehousing Act of 1846, then by New Yorkers in 1861, and then again by New Yorkers in 1894, and on until 1934. It might have merited a comment. It was a wild card, though, and so perhaps it was better kept off the record.

The Imperialism of Reexport

The United States has conventionally been called an "empire for liberty." The dissonance in this phrase—first attributed to the American revolutionary and slaveowner Thomas Jefferson—has typecast the United States as a quasi empire, or a Janus-faced empire, even an empire in hiding. Projections of this empire have been said to fall into two categories, formal and informal, with the former dwarfed by the latter. On the one hand we have the sprinkling of colonial possessions, from Guam to Puerto Rico (a sprinkling that is really more like a blotch, when we account for the continental empire of manifest destiny, as well as the 2,000 overseas military bases acquired to defend it by 1945), and on the other hand we have the web of supranational and nongovernmental entities headquartered in the United States, like the United Nations and the Red Cross (humanitarianism being the modus operandi of the empire for liberty).[179] But a third category intersects with and conjoins the other two. It is the empire of logistics, mediating between the formal and the informal. It is the counting room. It is the warehouse. It is an empire of connection rather than possession, and it is territorial, clearly, although with a light footprint, one that hops instead of tramples.[180]

Numerous scholars have wrestled with the incongruities of American empire and spotlighted these gradations of rule. I am indebted to their shared insistence that we see the "coloniality" of liberalism as a "dialectical" "inscription" of "degrees of imperial sovereignty" and not as "a brute binary division" between inside and outside.[181] Nevertheless, the archive of the free zone also pushes us beyond these theorists' preoccupation with sovereignty. The empire of logistics is unique in that it is an economic realm from which the political has been expunged. It is not a terrain on which citizen and alien are counterposed. It is the home of the commodity

Figure 3.10. Candidates for the seal of the FTZ Board, 1935. FTZ Board.

exclusively, the things themselves. It is the fantasy of frictionless accumulation. It is "customs territory."

What the empire of logistics shares with statecraft directed at citizens and aliens is the technology of the enclosure. In the free zone, the "policeman's club" that Manny Celler so resented was not dispensed with. It was relegated to the sidelines, to the fence, which, like the policeman's club, served a dual function: corralling unruly bodies when necessary, and in the meantime directing traffic. The free zone began and ended with the fence. This uncomfortable truth was self-evident for the people tasked with implementing the zone concept in the United States. One year after President Roosevelt signed the Foreign-Trade Zones Act, an artist came up with seven options for the logo or "seal" of the Foreign-Trade Zones Board. Five of them featured the fence, hands-down the most prominent motif of this new exercise in trade liberalization (figure 3.10).

A final point about the free zone and the empire of logistics is hinted at in the seal that the board ultimately settled on, which highlights "a ship in full sail on waves of the sea."[182] The zone system was supposed to orient the United States to the oceans. It was a ploy to mimic what the sociologist Giovanni Arrighi terms "entrepôt capitalism," of which Great Britain had been the standard bearer, "the principle of commercial and financial intermediation—the principle," Arrighi writes, "of buying in order to resell, of taking in order to send out, of being supplied by the whole world in order to be able to supply the whole world again."[183] The entrepôt was the middleman's city, and before it was the "transactional city" and the "global city," before it was annexed by banks and law firms, it was the port city where European lace was repackaged for South American mules.[184] It was the city of "trans"-shipment and "re"-export, or what we might call the labors of connection rather than possession. But there was a cloud on the horizon when the first port city to respond to the Foreign-Trade Zones Act, New York City, set to work in 1935. In the judgment of a contingent of businessmen and academics, that city was of a bygone era. The entrepôt was dead.

Figure 4.1. This silk-screen poster is one of three created to announce the debut of Zone 1 (another is shown in figure i.4). Harry Herzog for the WPA Federal Art Project, 1937.

CHAPTER FOUR

What We Talk about When We Talk about Manufacturing: The Foreign-Trade Zone

> Flocks of hitherto shiftless pigeons that used to loaf around the eaves of downtown skyscrapers have been put to work sorting raw ergot from rye grain at a government-owned warehouse on Staten Island, it was learned yesterday. Ergot is an important drug that in its raw form is derived from parasite-ridden kernels of rye grain. Before the war the sorting was done by the peasants who produced the grain. Now it arrives here unsorted. Officials of the foreign-trade zone warehouse learned recently that if they spread out the grain on a table and left a big window open, hundreds of pigeons would fly across the bay from Manhattan skyscrapers to the warehouse. The pigeons eat the good grain and spit out that containing the ergot.
>
> —"City's Pigeons Work at Drug-Sorting Job," *New York Times*, October 21, 1941

"A New Form of Business"

George Orwell would have loathed the term *foreign-trade zone*. The thud of those four syllables would have guaranteed his blank stare and a yawn. What was a foreign-trade zone, exactly? Was it *for* foreign trade, or was *it* foreign? Why the hyphen? Orwell would have noted that the term confused people because of how it was rooted in the doublespeak of political compromise. "Foreign-trade," supposedly, translated as "different from 'free trade'" and "zone" as "different from 'port.'" ("We call it a 'foreign-trade zone' to take the curse off the word *free* in free port.")[1] Most people knew what it was only insofar as they knew what it was not, and that was by design. As Orwell wrote in 1947, "Such phraseology is needed if one wants to name things without calling up mental pictures of them."[2]

This cognitive blankness nearly killed the career of the foreign-trade zone. Befuddlement was bad for business. Zone operators were not legislators, beholden to northern shoemakers or southern tobacco farmers. They swore no allegiances in the battle behind the name, the age-old fight between the ideals of "free trade" and "protectionism." They needed tenants. They cared about freight rates and square footage. Tariffs mattered to them for the practical reason that traffic slowed in the presence of the US Customs Service. As their tenants lobbied on Capitol Hill to slash duties, zone operators worried about the brick and mortar of trade policy. From their standpoint—that of rentier capital—the foreign-trade zone was not a "customs outland" on par with Hamburg's *Freihafen*. It was a piece of real estate.

These beleaguered zone operators were initially a small bunch, whether directors of port authorities or owners of port-based firms that subcontracted with port authorities. Their set was slow to embrace the zone concept because it was untested. During the period when it was implemented—from 1934, when Congress passed the Foreign-Trade Zones Act, to 1950, when Congress amended the act—it was regarded as an "experiment."[3] Considering that it entailed a raft of start-up costs, those who could ill afford to let piers rot seemed justified in their hesitation.

Skepticism boiled down to four main questions. One, what distinguished the zone system from the warehousing system? To invest Depression-era public funds in a zone system was wasteful, if, as some insisted, "a foreign-trade zone is but a more convenient form of bonded warehouse."[4] And two, even if it was an upgrade, was it premised on an antiquated theory? A zone would serve as an entrepôt for cargo en route from one foreign nation to another—ergot from Yugoslavia to Brazil. Yet apparently the entrepôt's days were numbered because goods were moving from production to consumption, without intermediary transshipment.[5] Moreover, three, if the entrepôt was not outmoded, would it succeed in the United States? Duty-free transshipment suited regions with nation-states in close proximity, like Europe. Ports in the United States functioned "under very different conditions."[6] Finally, four, the Foreign-Trade Zones Act included a limitation: a ban on manufacturing. Was the zone experiment "destined as a still-born child," as a German critic indelicately warned in 1937, doomed by one fatal flaw?[7]

This last concern at first seemed incidental. It did not rise to the fore until the first cluster of foreign-trade zones were up and running (or sputtering). Only once zone operators were aware of the extent to which this experiment was hard to sell to customers did they fixate on its parameters. Manufacturing, in other words, came to preoccupy zone operators not because the Ford Motor Company was knocking on the door—that wouldn't happen for decades—but because zone operators needed a way to attract tenants, tenants who were denizens of seaports, importers and exporters and freight forwarders and small-batch firms. So in order to get the hang of what the zone operators were talking about when they were talking about "manufacturing," we need to follow their own dawning appreciation of how to finesse the zone concept. We need to start with them at square one, literally, as they were pouring concrete and erecting fences and mailing fliers.

Then we can grasp not only how the ban was oppressive—zone operators bemoaned it persistently enough that Congress lifted it in 1950—but also how it was generative. Like a law defining marriage as heterosexual, it prodded people to expand the realm of the possible and to redefine the practice under restriction. To sidestep the ban, zone operators and their political backers construed the zone concept as "a new form of business."[8] They saw seaports as processing sites, platforms for American workers to prepare foreign commodities for foreign markets, without undermining American manufacturers. Such an arrangement was plausible because "processing" was not tantamount to "manufacturing," according to the Foreign-Trade Zones Act, and neither were its cognates—"assembling," "manipulating," "refining," and the like. Zone operators became fluent in this vocabulary, adept at wielding it in squabbles with the US Customs Service over whether this or that activity constituted "manufacturing." They pushed for American seaports to host "everything but."[9]

As zone operators recognized, this scenario was thinkable because the Great Depression was laying the foundation for the global assembly line. Most narratives of the global assembly line feature the runaway shop—a factory that flees unions by shutting down in one state and moving south to another, where it "manufactures" widgets as before, except now in the calm of an air-conditioned "open shop," before, abruptly, it abandons the United States for Central America and beyond.[10] Such an account of wholesale displacement adds up on the streets of the present-day Rust Belt, but it shortchanges how capital flight has hinged on the disaggregation of the factory as much as its relocation, with manufacturing broken into stages of production distributed across supply chains. "Distributed production," as the global assembly line is euphemized in business schools, has disassembled the Fordist social contract.

The legal and cultural dimensions of this butcher job are on full display in the foreign-trade zone. Legally, zone operators built the foreign-trade zone in tussles with the Customs Service; culturally, they invigorated Congress's Orwellian phraseology with "mental pictures" of what they called "live storage." This aesthetic was dissonant in the thirties in celebrating machines over men, as in the poster of a ship's crane and cargo net, with no hands in sight (fig. 4.1). What was a foreign-trade zone? In the plain English of historian David F. Noble, it was progress without people, a work camp for "shiftless pigeons," or as the *New York Times* later described it, a waterfront laboratory for the discovery of "a new cheap and rapid method of processing."[11]

"A Kind of Shangri-la for the Canny and Thrifty Trader"

Before it took shape on the ground, the foreign-trade zone came to life on paper. The most frequently cited profile was from the regulations for the zone system, published in 1935:

> A zone is an isolated, enclosed, and policed area, under the supervision of a designated board of Federal officials, operated as a public utility by a corporation, in or adjacent to a port of entry, without resident population, furnished with the necessary facilities for lading and unlading, for storing goods, and for reshipping them by land and water; an area into which goods may be brought, stored, and subjected to certain specified manipulation operations. If reshipped to foreign points the goods may leave the restricted trade zone without payment of duties and without intervention of customs officials, except under certain conditions. Such products cannot, of course, leave the trade zone for domestic use or consumption without full compliance with existing customs laws. Goods may not be manufactured or exhibited in such an area. The area is subject equally with adjacent regions to all the laws relating to public health, vessel inspection, Postal Service, immigration, and to the supervision of Federal agencies having jurisdiction in ports of entry, including customs, to a limited extent.[12]

"Isolated, enclosed, and policed," the zone is first positioned as an enclave, segregated from the polity, "without resident population." It is at the border of the customs territory (a term that is implied in this passage—if not stated outright—and that is invoked elsewhere in the regulations), "in or adjacent to a port of entry," oriented to the world market. "Goods" from abroad can be brought in for storage and "manipulation operations"—no manufacturing or exhibiting—and brought back out, with minimal obstruction by the Customs Service. "Of course," if goods are shifted into the customs territory, the Customs Service expects "full compliance."

From the perspective of a newspaper reporter, this innovation in customs law was rather ho-hum: foreign goods subject to tariffs entered a zone, they underwent various "manipulations," and then they left for foreign lands without incurring duties. The bottom line was so flat that it begged for embellishment. Rye grain from the Balkans went to Zone 1 to be culled for ergot, and pigeons flew to the task! "That would sound like publicity from a pigeon lobbyist except that the Commerce Department swears it's the gospel truth," wrote a reporter for United Press International.[13] Newspapers throughout the country picked up these morsels, sometimes extending the joke. "Burlington and other pigeon-infested cities will be pleased to ship birds in flocks to Manhattan in case a shortage develops," quipped a columnist in Iowa.[14] The incongruity of banal commodities stuck on an atoll of regulatory indeterminacy never failed to amuse reporters, as in this case from Los Angeles: "Currently posing an international trade problem are 19 camels received by the zone June 20 from an Australian firm. The dromedaries were shipped here for the Shrine convention. Due, however, to quarantine safeguards against foot-and-mouth disease, the animals must undergo a 15-day isolation period before being released, hence they didn't get to kneel for the Nobles. The San Diego Zoo is purchasing two of the displaced beasts. The remaining 17 are for the present creatures without a country."[15] "Creatures without a country" were the stars of "an international trade problem." Even though what happened in the foreign-trade zone entailed, essentially, warehousing, the oddity of exemption from customs territory inspired the press to find comic relief in customs law.

Literature written by administrators of the zone system gave off the opposite vibe. Planning documents outlined a spatial form that was simultaneously abstract and concrete, materialized and serialized, dialectically so—what the philosopher Henri Lefebvre has termed a "concrete abstraction."[16] That each zone was concrete was unmistakable. A list in the regulations stipulated fifteen types of "physical facilities required in the operation of a zone," from sewer mains to fuel lines, and a paragraph detailed the barbed-wire fence mandated to protect surrounding customs territory, from the gauge of the wire to the height of the posts.[17] With these accoutrements each zone made a tangible footprint, spanning on average thirty acres (ninety-two in New York City) and one or two finger piers. Yet each zone was also abstract, a blueprint for circulation of commodity capital and finance capital. As illustrated in a diagram for Zone 1 that explains the "legal movement of merchandise by classification in the foreign trade zone"—a diagram that lays out zone activities in a grid without any reference to physical geography—each zone was interchangeable (fig. 4.2). Akin to an embassy or a McDonald's, a foreign-trade zone franchised a general protocol in a specific place.

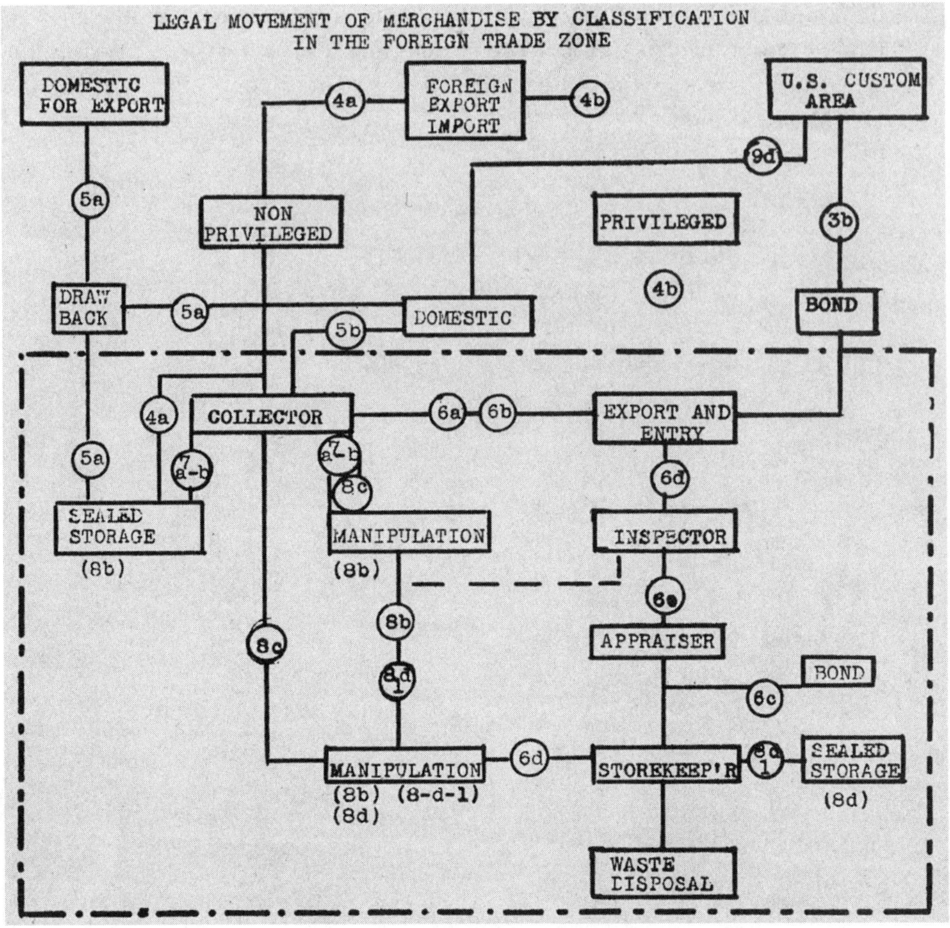

Figure 4.2. WPA Engineers, "Legal Movement of Merchandise by Classification in the Foreign Trade Zone," November 1, 1945, reproduced from John McKenzie, *Administration of the Foreign-Trade Zone in New York City* (New York, 1940).

Even as the regulations nailed down the fence, however, no rule spelled out the foreign-trade zone's relationship to customs territory. The concreteness of the fence crumbled into the abstraction of the state. This ambiguity led to fights between zone operators and bureaucrats whose regulatory arms touched zone operations. Everyone agreed that the zone was on US soil, but where was it under the law? Zone advocates never wavered on the principle that no federal or state agency that oversaw commerce held jurisdiction over the zone. "The foreign-trade zone for all intents and purposes is foreign territory," insisted Congressman Manny Celler in 1946.

"To attempt to put ceilings on goods in the zone would be like putting ceilings on goods in Mexico or British South Africa or in some other foreign place."[18] Here Celler focused on jurisdiction, the position of the territory. More often he dealt with situs—the position of the property, or where in the world goods were when they were in the zone. When copper from Chile was carted from a bonded warehouse to a foreign-trade zone, was it in the United States? Arguing that its owners should be allowed to cancel the bond because, in transferring copper to the zone, they "exported" it, Celler reasoned that "there can be no question that goods can be and in fact are severed from the mass of things belonging to this country"—the legal standard in determining situs—"while physically within the zone area."[19] Whether in terms of the status of the territory or of the things themselves, the zone concept opened room for maneuvering between the soil and the law, between the concrete and the abstract.

Zone operators had a word for the zone's absent presence: *extraterritoriality*. In public speeches or in interviews, they invoked this doctrine (often with the antiquated "exterritoriality") to confirm the zone's legal bona fides.[20] No doubt they liked it because, paired with allusions to the Hanseatic League, it lent an aura of manifest destiny and, by extension, impunity. Extraterritoriality, as discussed in chapter 3, was an orientalist discourse of incommensurability. It estranged place from space, alienating land from its immediate physical surroundings. When zone operators spoke of the zone as extraterritorial, the adjective signified what the philosopher Michel Foucault has called a "heterotopia," with the zone circumscribed by little more than the fact of its difference.[21]

The foreign-trade zone was otherworldly, an Arcadia. Journalists played up the poetics. A brief list of popular translations of zone-style extraterritoriality during the 1940s and 1950s includes

A waiting room for foreign goods shipped to this country
A no-man's land of international trade
A comfort station on a highway for ocean-going trade
A kind of Shangri-la for the canny and thrifty trader
A haven where goods may be held in a suspended status
A commercial waiting room
A tiny "free city"
A halfway house of trade
A sort of hospitable fenced-off vestibule in or adjoining the customs port
A sort of sanctuary where foreign goods may enter the United States
and be stored duty-free

An Ellis Island for merchandise
An oasis within a customs-protected country, but segregated from customs supervision
A little neutral, stockaded area where a shipper can put down his load, catch his breath, and decide what to do next[22]

None of these locales corresponded to coordinates on a map. Rather, they expressed a geographic imaginary of blank spots in a national economy—itself a fantastical object of post–World War II technopolitics.[23] In the aftermath of a global depression that had shuttered "vestibules" and fortified tariff walls, these analogies treated the liminality of the warehouse—once a cause for suspicion—as a virtue. As the president of the New Orleans Board of Port Commissioners enthused in 1947, the foreign-trade zone siphoned "the world market to the front door of the small businessman."[24]

Left to these analogies alone, the zone concept still might have eluded general readers. Frequently, though, an article included photographs, which asserted the foreign-trade zone's "exterritoriality" with a handful of visual cues. Most palpable were two markers of the zone's presence at street level, the sign and the fence. Any exterior photograph of any zone was guaranteed to include one, if not both. The sign resembled a billboard, and it captioned the image—elevated by wood posts in Zone 1 in New York City (fig. 4.3), stretched across a roof in Zone 2 in New Orleans (fig. 4.4), and mounted above the entrance to a shed in Zone 3 in San Francisco (fig. 4.5). The fence then enhanced this *mise-en-scène* by accenting the "foreign" in the sign. Whereas the sign distanced the zone from the rest of the port, the fence "stockaded" the zone from the city. As the *Washington Post* tagged the scene from Zone 1, "U.S. customs agents police the 'frontier.'"[25] And when an aerial view was supplied, the faintness of the fence was compensated for with a line of white tape, as in a shot of Zone 4 in Los Angeles (fig. 4.6). But the fence was not depicted as impenetrable, not for the stream of commerce. As allegorized in a photograph of the mayor of Los Angeles and the US secretary of commerce at the dedication ceremony for Zone 4, the chain links were "trade links": they channeled capital more than they blocked it (fig. 4.7). From this angle, another staple of zone photography—the customs guard—was reduced to a stage prop. In an image from Zone 1, his function is more to convey the immensity of the shed than to vouch that Uncle Sam's revenue is safe from smugglers (fig. 4.8).

The lone guard was a metaphor for the foreign-trade zone's emplacement. "Extraterritoriality" was shorthand for a reallocation of control. That is, the chance to save money on duties was just one of the zone's selling

Figure 4.3. The original caption reads, "'Frontiers': Since the Foreign Trade Zone is regarded technically as foreign soil, U.S. customs men are on guard at the gate. Goods inside the zone are duty-free only because they are for transshipment to another country." Ca. January 1940. Acme News Photos.

Figure 4.4. Zone 2 in New Orleans, Louisiana, ca. 1948. Geer Studio.

Figure 4.5. Local business leaders gathered for the dedication ceremony of Zone 3 in San Francisco, 1948. *San Francisco News-Call Bulletin* newspaper photograph archive, BANC PIC 1959.010, pt.2, box 194, 141338.07:C-5. © The Regents of the University of California, The Bancroft Library, University of California, Berkeley.

Figure 4.6. Zone 5 in Los Angeles, marked out with white tape, ca. 1950. US Information Agency, National Archives and Records Administration, College Park, Maryland.

Figure 4.7. US Secretary of Commerce Charles W. Sawyer and Mayor Fletcher Bowron welded "trade links" to complete the construction of Zone 4 in Los Angeles, September 15, 1949. Los Angeles Times Staff. Copyright © 1949. *Los Angeles Times*. Used with permission.

Figure 4.8. A customs guard stands alone in a warehouse at Zone 1, ca. 1945–55. Collection of Historic Richmond Town.

points. Another was the control it afforded. Control meant that tenants decided when duties were assessed, whether upon entering or exiting the zone, which gave them options. Control also meant that tenants could untether cargo that was "encumbered by some government regulation," as an engineer brainstormed in a report on "potential Free Port business," cargo like camels subject to inspection for foot-and-mouth disease.[26] As a 1948 master's thesis on the zone system put it, "Merchandise in a zone maintains maximum flexibility."[27] The fence marked out a space of time in which capitalists had leverage over how capital crossed state lines. The prefix *extra* in "extraterritoriality" suggested freedom from state power: "extra" as in beyond or outside territory. But the zone was not a lawless domain. It was not nonterritorial. In a zone, all US laws applied (at least federal laws).[28] The fence sanctioned an alternative matrix of customs procedures, not a Hobbesian free-for-all (fig. 4.2).

Control was what distinguished a foreign-trade zone and what set it apart from a bonded warehouse. By 1934, the nearly century-old warehousing system consisted of eight distinct "classes" of bonded warehouses, dictated by more than sixty pages of regulations. Doing business in them was a headache. "Just getting permission to examine a bale means a lot of trouble, and if the goods are inferior when [a merchant] finally gets them, he has lost valuable time," a customs broker explained. "He may have already paid a draft on the goods, or gone to any number of other kinds of expense." By contrast, the broker continued, "In a free port he could examine the bale as soon as it was unloaded and then make arrangements to return it immediately if it was not up to standard."[29] Within a bonded warehouse, a merchant's every twitch was surveilled. Within a zone, he was at liberty to manage his bales largely as he pleased, as if they were still at sea. "The chief difference," as one scholar summarized in 1937, "is that with the foreign-trade zone the customs guards are outside looking in," whereas in the bonded warehouse, "they are inside looking on."[30]

"There's a Lot of Red Tape to Eliminating Red Tape"

The conversation about what was and was not "manufacturing" was provoked by zone operators as they tried to realize the putative freedoms of extraterritoriality for their tenants. Control was a situation, a social relation. In order for a zone tenant to gain control, someone else needed to lose it. And that someone—the administrative state—was not about to give it up. What the zone tenant was able to shrug off, in terms of the hassles of navigating rules, the zone operator had to shoulder. A specter haunted

Shangri-la: the specter of bureaucracy. Using a foreign-trade zone was a way around bureaucracy, but running one was another story. And this downside was evident well before a single tenant was enrolled.

The mere act of launching a foreign-trade zone took years of effort, no matter how eager the zone operator. The first hurdle was to apply to the federal government for authorization. As soon as Mayor Fiorello La Guardia learned via telegram that President Roosevelt had signed the act, he dispatched a crew of clerks and engineers to conduct the requisite research on behalf of New York City. From mid-1934 to mid-1935, over ninety people prepared a dossier, surveying an exhaustive list of fiscal and technical topics. "With the maps, plans and the hundreds of pages of typewritten matter, aggregating some forty-five pounds in weight," they later wrote, "every significant feature of the proposed zone was covered in detail."[31] Once permission was granted, more paperwork ensued. It was not until early 1937 that Zone 1 opened for business. Other cities experienced similar delays, long after opening day. "We're still fumbling around finding out who has to sign what papers," a manager at Zone 3 in San Francisco confessed to a reporter. "We're eliminating red tape here, but there's a lot of red tape to eliminating red tape."[32]

The wielder of all that red tape was the Foreign-Trade Zones Board—a small unit headquartered in what was the country's biggest office building, the US Department of Commerce.[33] The FTZ Board relied on an "executive secretary" and his staff of five or so assistants, typists, and analysts, with no regional offices or representatives.[34] Thomas E. Lyons inaugurated the post. Like a number of the white men associated with the zone system under the Roosevelt administration, he hailed from Dixie—a region where schoolchildren learned about foreign trade via "King Cotton" and what Lyons referred to as "the War between the States."[35] A midcareer veteran of the Bureau of Foreign and Domestic Commerce, the board's parent agency, where he had served as chief of the packing and handling section of the transportation division, Lyons directed the zone system until he retired in 1955.[36] Occasionally the Oval Office weighed in, as when a few businessmen in Poughkeepsie, New York, asked native son President Roosevelt for help with a zone. By and large, however, Lyons worked autonomously and without scrutiny from above.[37] Although nominally the FTZ Board boasted three cabinet-level directors—the secretaries of commerce, treasury, and war—they delegated decisions over daily affairs to the executive secretary.

Delegation of federal authority was so much the norm, in fact, that the zone system was barely a national initiative. The FTZ Board issued regulations and vetted would-be zones, and afterward it passed the reins to the "grantee." This detachment is reflected in an organizational chart for Zone 1, with the federal apparatus looming over the local apparatus—in this case, the city of New York—but with no line fusing the two (fig. 4.9). If a city or some other public entity (such as a state agency) sought a zone, it applied to the FTZ Board, which then held a public hearing in front of the "examiners committee" (bureaucrats who substituted for the cabinet secretaries). Otherwise, the grantee flew solo. To roll out the zone, the mayor turned not to the FTZ Board, but rather to the scores of architects, engineers, and number crunchers under his employ.

The only hands-on assistance that the FTZ Board offered the grantees involved publicity. In addition to sponsoring features in journals like *Foreign Commerce Weekly*, the FTZ Board maintained a clearinghouse of information, sharing reports and other materials. Lyons also acted as the system's ambassador, canvassing on its behalf within the United States and in the wider world of commerce. He gave speeches to commercial groups, arranged tours for technocrats (such as a delegation of port officials from Egypt in 1948), and in general, shilled for business. He visited twenty-six cities in Latin America in 1946, after he spent several weeks in Panama advising on how to set up a zone at Colón (see chapter 5).[38]

The absence of a federal role in daily zone operations suited grantees perfectly well. No one wanted Lyons second-guessing how to shape up stevedores or deciding which lift truck to order. But what did trouble grantees about the FTZ Board was that its largesse went no further than Lyons's efforts at promotion. By law, the FTZ Board provided no support of the kind that mattered most: dollars. It was empowered to designate zones, not to fund them. The Foreign-Trade Zones Act made no provision for loans along the lines of, say, the Export-Import Bank, another invention of 1934 to foster foreign commerce. The zone system was a jobs program in the guise of a trade policy—"More trade means more jobs," Congressman Celler had stressed in pushing for the legislation—and with its urban spin on New Deal cooperative federalism, it anticipated the Great Society, when the federal government would bypass state governments and partner with cities and neighborhoods. The only difference was that, in this case, no money changed hands.[39]

Congress had structured the zone system in this manner because the federal government could not be responsible for funding every seaport, and it could not be reproached for playing favorites. Constitutionally speaking, participation in the zone system needed to be equal access (despite Roosevelt's stated wish for a maximum of four zones). And that led to still another problem: cannibalization. "Should the number of free ports become at all considerable," the initial interim director of the FTZ Board

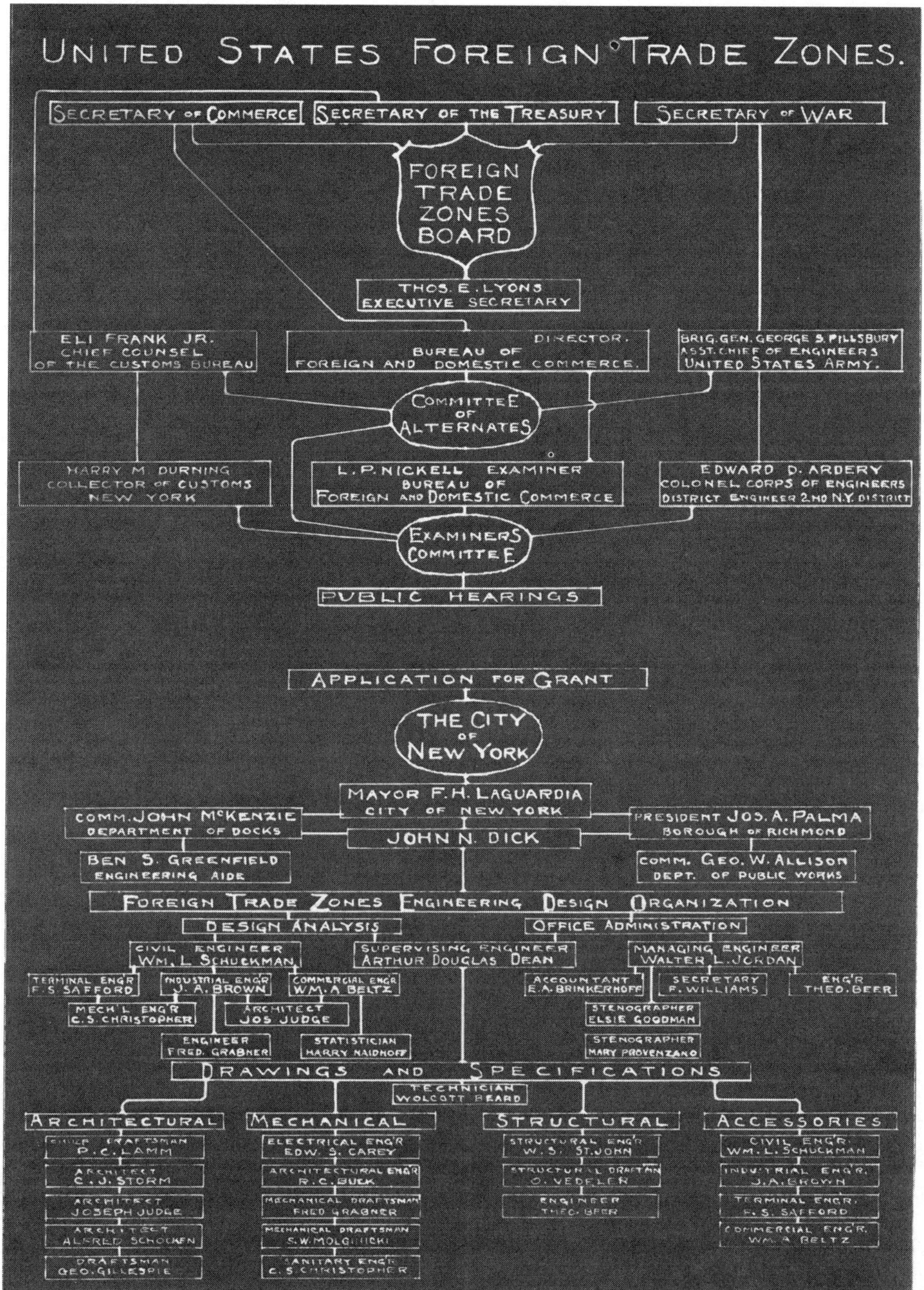

Figure 4.9. WPA Engineers, Organizational chart of the FTZ Board, November 17, 1935. The paper is blue because it was printed with India ink. File sharing remained very low-tech during the 1930s (this method dated to the 1870s). In publicizing the FTZ system Tom Lyons mailed original copies of reports and illustrations and asked for them to be returned by special delivery. Collection of Historic Richmond Town.

warned, "the division of available business among them would seriously endanger the possibility of profit for any."[40] The sanguine Tom Lyons rarely acknowledged that risk, instead implying that Baltimore was competing with Hamburg, not Philadelphia, and that the proverbial tides of foreign commerce would rise high enough to lift all boats. But port authorities worried about glut.

Port authorities regarded themselves as entrepreneurs, viewing piers and warehouses as spatial products. "We treat Seattle's harbor like a big business," the thinking went, "and it is run like any business enterprise."[41] The port of Seattle even leased office space 2,000 miles away in the prestigious Conway Building in Chicago, where an "eastern representative" tried to woo railroad companies to shift routes from San Francisco to Puget Sound.[42] Once zones were up and running, operators obsessed over fluctuations in commodity traffic like jealous husbands. "This business might have come to Mobile" was a typical refrain, as Mobile's operator complained about a shipment of 5,083 tons of Mexican garbanzo beans reported to have landed in New York City.[43] Given these national feuds, one can imagine the intensity of local rivalries. The San Francisco Bay merited a zone, but where? The city wanted it. Oakland wanted it. Richmond wanted it. San Francisco elites expressed concern about "an over-supply of harbors" and "an under-supply of commerce," due to a tendency during the 1920s "to develop a harbor out of every damp spot in California." The Bay Area could support no more than one zone.[44] The same tension pervaded discussions in New York City. Jamaica Bay in Brooklyn and Queens; Stapleton in Staten Island; Elizabeth and Jersey City in New Jersey—all clamored for a zone.[45] The FTZ Board would make the final call, and few would be pleased.

Competition came not only from prospective grantees but also from other elements of the port complex—namely, the warehousemen. Often speaking in the guise of the American Warehousemen's Association (AWA)—which was "pretty strongly organized," with no rival organization and hundreds of members—the warehousemen saw the foreign-trade zone as encroaching on their turf.[46] In letters and in hearings, from Philadelphia to New Orleans to Seattle, they argued that it was bad policy to open new warehouses when so many existing warehouses were vacant. (The government calculated that existing warehouses were 63%–67% full in New York City, but, in truth, as an AWA leader noted in 1935, only 45%–50% of "revenue-producing space" was occupied—for a warehouseman, one square foot was not necessarily equal to the next.)[47] The federal government should protect mature businesses, an AWA member wrote to the US secretary of commerce that same year, not coddle newborns in "an already demoralized market."[48] In response, the FTZ Board reasoned, again, that a zone guaranteed an increase in overall tonnage in a port. The warehousemen guffawed.

The warehousemen raised these grievances because they saw a foreign-trade zone as basically a freight terminal or a gussied-up bonded warehouse. They resented that municipal funds supported it and assailed the very notion of government-sponsored warehousing, insisting that a "costly experiment" should be funded by private capital. Early on, warehousemen like Brooklyn's Irving Bush led the New York State Chamber of Commerce in opposition to the zone concept.[49] After Zone 1 started running, what seemed to anger the chamber members was that the port authority paid most of the bills yet gave away part of the profits. In 1937, New York City paved the way for this arrangement, when it contracted out the management of Zone 1 to a private firm. "Private capital, ingenuity and enterprise is needed to make the Free Port a success," Congressman Celler explained.[50] Allegedly, the Docks Department lacked the "expertise" to keep Zone 1 afloat. The Chamber of Commerce—prodded by Bush and "the bonded warehouse Poobahs"—attacked this decision, calling it "a substantial and unwarranted subsidy."[51] The AWA even sued the city government because of it. On paper, the lawsuit flopped, but in the court of public opinion, it caused a stir, generating further hassles for the zone system.[52]

Gradually, the AWA tried to incorporate the invasion rather than obstruct it. During the war, members of the AWA's special committee on foreign-trade zones started pushing for national legislation. Writing to Congressman Celler and other politicians, they demanded a provision for "foreign trade warehouses"—bonded warehouses without the red tape—and secured the introduction of a bill in 1949.[53] But it turned out that the local fix was already under way, unprompted by Congress or the FTZ Board. First, port officials in New Orleans set a precedent in 1947, when they allowed warehousemen to lease space in Zone 2.[54] That same year, the Texas State Legislature gave the green light to a warehouse company to administer—not simply to operate—Zone 6 at an airport in San Antonio, with no municipal oversight.[55] The Scobey Fireproof Storage Company, founded in 1907, expected to cash in on the transshipment of beef flown in from Argentina, now that, in the guise of Zone 6, the company's cold-storage facility was equipped with an additional tool for freezing assets.

"Putting White Elephants to Work"

Despite the AWA's grumblings, and before the oppressiveness of bureaucracy was felt, the nation's ports hummed with interest in the zone system. Soon after the passage of the Foreign-Trade Zones Act in mid-1934, port officials from myriad cities—as dissimilar as Miami, Pittsburgh, and Stockton, California—inquired with the FTZ Board.[56] Some had pursued the zone concept during and after World War I, while others had caught the bug more recently, and they spurred each other on. These men (and they were men, to a person) wrote not only to Lyons but also to each other, gossiping and swapping tips, even sharing names of specialists from the United States and abroad. The same consultant who helped the Alabama State Docks Commission prepare an application for Mobile in 1937 also helped California's Board of State Harbor Commissioners resubmit its application for San Francisco a few months later.[57] Eager to become the first port on the Atlantic with a zone, the Boston Port Authority commissioned a study from the director of Copenhagen's free port. He found that, geographically, Boston was ill-suited to the transshipment trade.[58]

As the infatuation dimmed, few plans went past first base. After weighing advice and scrutinizing the fine print, most businessmen concluded that the foreign-trade zone was too speculative—"a big IF" and "perhaps rather an expensive luxury"—to warrant the price.[59] Many wondered about the viability of the entrepôt model. And every port official feared a money pit, given the need for substantial investment in fixed capital. The FTZ Board made no effort to ease these jitters. Quite the opposite: it stoked them, with Secretary of Commerce Daniel Roper having cautioned that each zone "must be self-supporting."[60]

Nevertheless, for one city, the foreign-trade zone was a fait accompli, and in its episodic travails we can see why zone operators began chafing against the law's restrictiveness around manufacturing. In the words of Congressman Celler, "it seems almost axiomatic" that New York should host a zone, in light of "the importance and preeminence of New York as a port."[61] The city's leaders were undeterred by the fiscal commitment because they were crunching a separate set of numbers. Mayor La Guardia wanted to recoup the cost of bricklayers past by reviving a cluster of dormant docks. On Staten Island, twelve piers—erected by Mayor John F. Hylan during World War I, for the not insubstantial sum of $30 million—were sitting empty. As Congressman Celler confided in President Roosevelt, La Guardia was "anxious" to resurrect these piers—"Hylan's Folly," as they were known.[62] Backing him were some of the city's most prominent watchdogs. No less than Nicholas Murray Butler, president of Columbia University and confidant of US presidents, plugged the possibility in 1932. (Butler was a longtime acquaintance of the zone concept—purportedly he had known Edward Rosewater, the German émigré who tried to drum up interest in Hamburg's *Freihafen* in 1894.)[63] When the FTZ Board held a hearing on New York's application in November 1935, Butler was head of the Citizen's Budget Commission, and he sent a colleague to testify to the wisdom of "putting idle but potentially valuable facilities to productive use."[64] John McKenzie of the Docks Department then made a final pitch: locating the zone on Staten Island would enable the city to cash in on the zone immediately rather than a year or more after construction.[65]

The menace of useless infrastructure spoke to an old dilemma. "Putting White Elephants to Work," to quote a headline about Hylan's piers, was no easy matter.[66] White elephants, which the *New York Times* characterized as "something requiring much care and expense and yielding little profit," usually resulting from "frenzied municipal finance,"[67] cluttered American cities. In Philadelphia, businessmen talked about a foreign-trade zone for Hog Island, the city's World War I–era "white elephant."[68] Rehabbing old docks may have struck some observers as counter to the New Deal ethos—old, not new—but the project was as emblematic of the New Deal as La-Guardia Airport in that New York City wound up relying on staff from the Works Project Administration (fig. 4.10). Mayor La Guardia's timing was ideal: he had docks at the ready, and he had federal workers on deck to renovate them.[69]

Still, in keeping with the mixed reputation of the zone system—and with the disconnect between the frictionless fantasy and the sclerotic reality—almost nothing went according to plan. In 1934, Staten Island's borough president, Joseph Palma, had vowed that the piers could be ready "tomorrow."[70] Dredging proceeded slowly, and the fencing of the zone, bafflingly, took seven months to complete.[71] The *Staten Island Advance* mocked the meager results of Palma's grandiose forecasts, with front-page, close-up photographs of potholes and knee-high weeds. The *Advance* condemned the Docks Department's ineptitude, calling the zone "a Sargasso Sea of inaction." "With the exception of a fence, flood light, plans, and dredging of the berths between piers," it reported two months shy of the department's much-delayed opening in February 1937, "NOTHING HAS BEEN DONE."[72]

No dignitaries showed up on the first day. "The opening is a rather dreary, make-believe affair," the *Advance* wrote, "a mere conforming to technicalities to evade withdrawal of the Department of Commerce franchise."[73] And after just eight days of operations, they were again hobbled, this time by the installation of fireproofing sprinklers, which suffered from "destructive tendencies," going off at random and soaking merchandise.[74] The *Advance* cataloged the zone's mishaps, noting each leaky pipe and missing shingle. The boundary fence was off by 4.5 acres. The railroad tracks were malfunc-

Figure 4.10. The WPA Federal Works Project dispatched men to Staten Island to help with the launch of Zone 1, ca. 1936. Courtesy of *Staten Island Advance*.

tioning. Worst of all, the shipments were not coming. Three months after opening day, the sheds were harboring "(1) case of eyebrow tweezers from Japan in solitary grandeur."[75] Zone 1's debut was a drawn-out fiasco, which gave the *Advance*'s cartoonist no shortage of material (fig. 4.11).

Mayor La Guardia seemed to have erred in his hopes for the hinterland of Staten Island. In 1935, the borough was peripheral to the metropole. Horses still grazed widely. In the hierarchy of the harbor, it was the place from which you did little but gaze at Manhattan.[76] Accordingly, in 1934, when the FTZ Board had held hearings on Zone 1's application, much of the testimony had addressed whether Staten Island was up to snuff. The Docks Department swore to its potential, as if an entrepôt could be willed into existence. Docks Commissioner John McKenzie went so far as to frame the island's geography as an advantage: "The zone is capable of being completely isolated"—for policing—"and yet has adequate railroad, highway, bridge and ferry connections with the rest of the harbor and of the continent."[77] "Adequate" was not exactly a ringing endorsement. Even neutral observers doubted the island's potential. "You can invest $50 million in

Staten Island," testified an ally of warehouseman Irving Bush, "and it won't bring it one foot nearer the center of activity."[78] "Staten Island, in short, is somewhat out of the way," the Federal Writers' Project summarized in 1938, contradicting maps issued by the Docks Department that showed arrows converging on Staten Island from all corners, as if it were a geographical pivot of the harbor. "Traffic lanes point in other directions."[79]

Staten Island's inaccessibility was soon plain. Most cargo arrived there not on ocean liners—as illustrated in the WPA posters for the zone—but rather on "lighters" and trucks.[80] "Lighters" were small, transitional harbor vessels that "lightened" ships by ferrying portions of their cargoes to other docks.[81] Although lighters moved under bond, extending the suspension of duties, they drew the Customs Service. In this sense, using lighters

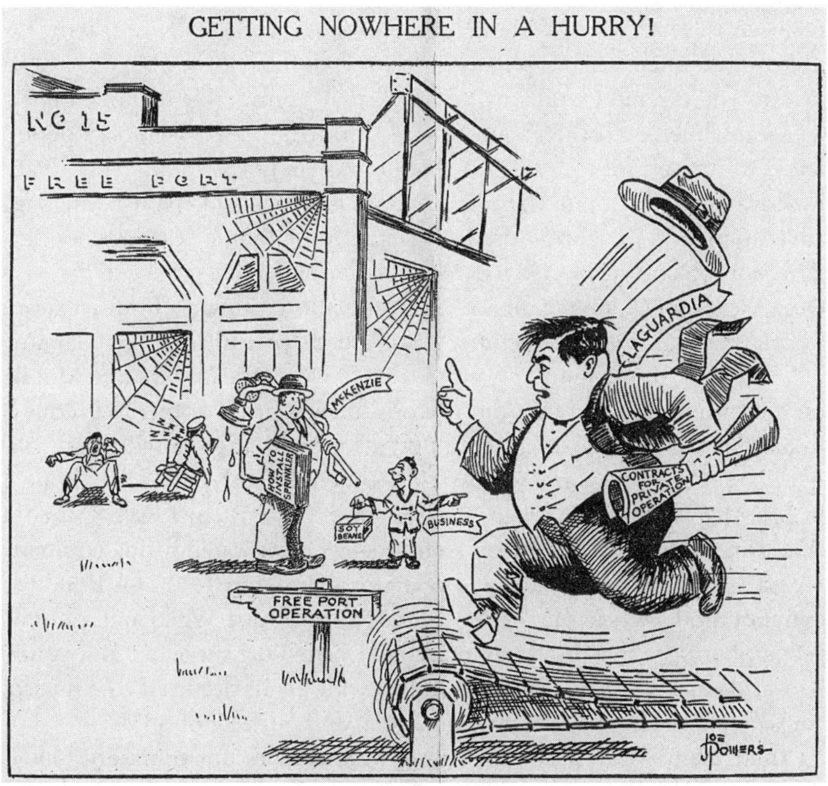

Figure 4.11. J. Powers, *Getting Nowhere in a Hurry!*, *Staten Island Advance*, May 15, 1937. With a slew of visual stereotypes, this cartoon indicts Zone 1's administrators via caricatures of, from left to right, the lazy workers, the inept bureaucrat, the coolie, and the fat-cat mayor. Courtesy of *Staten Island Advance*.

undermined the basic rationale for using zones. The same held for bonded trucks, when portions of shipments arrived at the zone via roads from other piers. Yet Staten Island was too far removed to draw ships away from Manhattan and Brooklyn. The first ship to dock at Zone 1 did not drop anchor until October 1937, nine months after opening day.[82]

By the end of Zone 1's first year, pundits were asking if the city's taxpayers were being swindled. As the *New York Sun* put it, "Unless the experimental free zone idea succeeds beyond the wildest hopes of the Mayor and his advisers—and there are even those close to the Mayor who insist that no stimulant, however heady, will ever bring the Staten Island white elephant to life—the taxpayer of the city of New York stands a better-than-even chance of being saddled forever with the biggest single loss the city has ever sustained."[83] The sunk costs of renovating the piers and the surrounding property—all of which the city's Board of Estimate had approved and financed through a mix of long-term corporate stocks and short-term tax notes—were substantial.[84] Not until 1940 would the city see a return on its investment in Zone 1, and a paltry one at that, considering the total bill.[85]

Meanwhile, the other zones created during this honeymoon period failed to turn a profit. Zone 2 in Mobile was supposed to attract the Pan-American trade, facilitated by an agent posted abroad and Spanish-language advertisements. The zone closed after little more than a year, when a new governor took office. Elected to streamline state affairs in rebuke of the New Deal, Governor Frank Dixon scoffed at the allure of riches from reexport, calculating that during its tenure, Zone 2 had "cost the State of Alabama $59,632.85 with the return of only $1.32."[86] New Orleans replaced Mobile on the roster in 1946, but it did not post its first profit until 1952. Zone 3 in San Francisco also struggled to find a foothold after its red-taped rollout in 1948. Zone 3—and the two that joined the system in 1949, Zone 4 in Los Angeles and Zone 5 in Seattle—posted consistent losses.[87] Zone 4 closed in 1956.[88] Zone 6 in San Antonio—where a warehousing company served as both administrator and operator—closed in 1953. By 1955, the entrepôt model was kaput, in the United States at least. When an economic geographer from the University of Omaha visited the surviving four zones, he was dismayed. "Does the difficulty lie with the device itself," he mused, "or with a basic incompatibility between it and our economy?"[89]

There are two plausible conclusions to infer from this summary. One is that the foreign-trade zone amounted to nothing more than pocket change in the US economy before the 1960s. The other is that if you are fixated on profit in the history of capitalism, maybe you are missing the action. Backers of the zone concept emphasized that they gauged its worth less in pennies than in ripple effects, beyond the business cycle. "The City cannot and should not look upon the Free Port as a source of revenue," averred an advisor to Mayor La Guardia. "The true advantages of the Free Port are indirect to the City, but direct to its citizens." He continued: "Without vision in judgment, we would not now enjoy Central Park, Riverside Drive, or the East River Drive. America is the largest trading nation in the world. New York is the largest maritime city in the world. The NY free port should be the largest and best equipped free trading zone in the world. These considerations should dictate a large and understanding point of view in establishing this enterprise and selecting its personnel."[90] This endorsement reads as performative, as if naming New York "the largest maritime city in the world" would make it so. This was the confidence of a booster, and it spoke to the basic reason why city officials bothered to bankroll the foreign-trade zone: advertising. The zone was a place that sold a place. As an early student of the subject wrote, "It occupies somewhat the same relationship to the port as does a restaurant in a department store."[91]

"Border-Line Manufacturing"

Not everyone could afford to lose money. To be clear, two entities were in charge of a foreign-trade zone at the municipal level: the grantee (the public officials responsible for port finances and on the hook with the FTZ Board) and the operator—the on-site manager, often a private subcontractor. While the grantee viewed the foreign-trade zone as a line item, the operator saw it as "a new form of business," the production of distribution. It gave him a means to squeeze value out of that parasite in the sphere of production, handling labor. The way that he came to think about how he sold the service of handling—handling as processing—is one of the most momentous aspects of the early years of the foreign-trade zone, shaping what would become the world's largest zone system and illuminating the intellectual history of the global assembly line.

Traditionally, handling connoted movement. Handling could mean a change of location, like a lift truck of steel rods handed off to a machinist in a Ford factory. Handling could also mean a change of ownership, like a railcar of Model Ts being handed off to a Ford dealer. Because such transfers involved changes that left the commodity untransformed, handling was a loathsome necessity for producers like Ford—a drain on profits, not an enhancement. Handling was the province of the foreign-trade zone, albeit with the perk of extraterritoriality. Zone 4 handled camels, camels under quarantine.

And therein lay the problem. Storage, even of headline-worthy camels, was not lucrative for a zone operator either. Zone 3, for instance, refused a shipment of calcium nitrate, noting that the zone was not "a storehouse for slow-moving domestic commodities."[92] Zone operators were angling for higher-paying tenants interested in higher-order handling jobs that required human hands—after all, they could not charge for the labor of a pigeon. They were hoping for tenants with cargoes in need of action more than suspended animation. As a result, by the late 1940s, they were conceiving of the zone in the spirit of an early booster who called it a station for "border-line manufacturing."[93] This phrase referred to the zone's territorial indeterminacy, but it was also an apt summary of how zone operators were nudging the zone from the category of a storehouse to that of a processing center.

This innovation came about in spite of the law, not encouraged by it. Textually, the Foreign-Trade Zones Act was explicit: no manufacturing. Congressman Manny Celler had crafted the legislation with this restriction so as to appease politicians from interior states whose districts were heavily industrial. Zones would revitalize American seaports, Celler had vouched, not encroach on American factories. They would dethrone the bankers of London and the shippers of Hamburg, not the candy makers of Chicago and the automakers of Detroit. After the act was passed, skeptics were directed to the first page of the FTZ Board regulations: "Goods may not be manufactured."

Celler and other zone boosters had swallowed this prohibition because the act had left wiggle room. Nine pages later, the regulations also ticked off the myriad ways that goods could be handled: "stored, broken up, repacked, assembled, distributed, sorted, graded, mixed with foreign or domestic merchandise, or otherwise manipulated."[94] Those last two words—"otherwise manipulated"—seemed to provide leeway for a healthy profit margin in the mold of an entrepôt. Under this language the zone operators were expected to be able to peddle a variety of services to zone tenants who had goods moving between storing and manufacturing, the warehouse and the factory.

Yet during the first decade of the zone system, zone operators time and again found themselves bewildered. Textual interpretation of government regulations tends to summon the inner Derridean in even the most literal of readers. Wordplay caused no end of trouble. What, precisely, separated "manufacturing" from "manipulating"? Demands for clarification came from all corners. "As the bill now reads, a certain amount of processing will be allowed but no manufacturing," an illustrative leather dealer wrote to the FTZ Board in 1935. "It would be a very good idea if Washington would clarify this phrase and state what processing means and how far we can go in processing before it is called manufacturing."[95] Over the next decade, newspapers repeated this sentiment. Some asked innocently enough, "Where does handling and processing stop and manufacturing begin?"[96] Others voiced distinct disapproval, as when the *Wall Street Journal* discussed "the annoyance and confusion which arise from the difficulty of drawing a line between manufacturing and 'manipulation.'"[97] Even native speakers stumbled. Touching base about the purview of "manufacturing" in a private meeting, Congressman Celler and Treasury Secretary John W. Snyder paused to check a dictionary.[98] Charts provided little enlightenment (fig. 4.12).

"Manufacturing"—that sacred cow of protectionism—was a keyword that everyone knew but no one could define. Vernacular descriptions of machine-age "manufacturing" centered on human labor. Take the example of the tongue-in-cheek press coverage of a skirmish in Baltimore between a resident and the health commissioner. "Is a beehive a factory? Because bees make honey, is their keeper a manufacturer?" So began an article about the disputed legality of the three beehives that a World War I veteran kept in his apartment—in a district zoned for residential use, not for manufacturing. The official served an eviction notice, but the *Baltimore Sun* and others lampooned him, because obviously, only people, not bees (or pigeons), can engage in manufacturing.[99] While what motivated the press coverage was bureaucratic overreach, what lent humor to it was the underlying belief that "manufacturing" involved human labor.

Such an assumption was not unreasonable: *manu factum*, production by hand. Yet this etymology elided the reality that "manufacturing" described less a physical activity than, as Andrew Ure noted back in 1835, a labor process that privileged machines. "Manufacture is a word which, in the vicissitude of language, has come to signify the reverse of its intrinsic meaning," Ure wrote in *The Philosophy of Manufactures*, "for now it denotes every extensive product of art which is made by machinery, with little or no aid of the human hand; so that the most perfect manufacture is that which dispenses entirely with *manual* labor."[100] Three decades later, Karl Marx went further to contend that "manufacturing" referred to the division of labor and prefigured what he called "large-scale industry," or what Americans later termed "mass production."[101] Fleshed out in terms of labor, this word was atavistic. River Rouge was a "manufacturing" facility like the A&P was a tea merchant.

Still, the term not only invoked a linguistic vestige of nineteenth-century

CHART OF SELECTED COMMODITIES AND PERMITTED MANIPULATIONS IN FOREIGN TRADE ZONE

	Beans	Brandy	Bulk Goods	Burlap	Canned Meats	Chemicals	Coffee	Cotton, Bales	Eggs	Jewelry	Leather	Nuts	Oils	Rugs	Spices	Stones	Tea	Textiles	Tobacco	Wine	Wool
Analyze		●	●		●	●							●							●	
Bag	●		●				●					●			●						
Bottle		●	●			●							●							●	
Can	●		●			●	●		●			●	●		●				●		
Clean	●		●				●	●		●	●	●		●	●	●	●	●	●		●
Combine			●			●	●			●		●	●		●		●		●		
Crate	●	●	●		●	●					●		●	●		●		●	●	●	
Cull	●		●							●		●			●				●		
Cut				●							●			●		●		●	●		
Destroy	●	●	●	●	●	●	●	●	●	●	●	●	●	●	●	●	●	●	●	●	●
Dry	●		●	●			●	●			●	●		●				●	●		●
Dye																		●			
Examine	●	●	●	●	●	●	●	●	●	●	●	●	●	●	●	●	●	●	●	●	●
Filter		●				●							●							●	
Fumigate	●		●	●				●			●	●		●	●			●	●		●
Gauge		●	●										●							●	
Grade	●		●			●	●	●	●	●	●	●	●	●	●	●			●	●	
Label		●	●	●	●	●				●	●	●	●	●	●	●		●	●	●	●
Mark	●		●	●	●	●	●	●	●	●	●			●	●		●	●	●		●
Mature		●	●									●	●						●	●	
Recooper		●			●	●	●	●		●			●		●		●		●	●	
Sample	●	●	●	●	●	●	●	●		●	●	●	●	●	●	●	●	●	●	●	●
Scour	●		●	●						●	●	●		●		●		●			●
Weigh	●		●	●	●	●	●	●		●		●			●	●	●	●	●		●

Figure 4.12. The process of manufacturing is reified into twenty-four discrete gerunds in this diagram on the grammar of nonmanufacturing in a foreign-trade zone. *Facts-Figures-Description-Information: Foreign Trade Zone No. 3* (San Francisco: California State Board of Harbor Commissioners, 1949).

producerism. There was another way to apply it: to classify commodities. In this usage, whether or not a commodity was "manufactured" depended less on what was done to it than on where and when it was handled. Context determined the status of a commodity, not some inherent quality. As Marx noted in *Capital*, a treatise that itself unfolds from the perspective of the commodity, "A product, though ready for immediate consumption, may nevertheless serve as raw material for a further product, as grapes do when they become the raw material for wine."[102] One person's raw was another person's cooked. Expressed in this manner—contingently rather than rigidly—"manufacturing" was embedded in time and space, in history and geography.

That's how an influential US Supreme Court decision parsed the meaning of "manufacturing" in 1898. The issue before the court in *Tide Water Oil v. United States* concerned boxes that were constructed in Bayonne, New Jersey, with parts imported from Canada and Europe. Were the boxes manufactured in Bayonne? The answer would determine Tide Water Oil's eligibility for a rebate on the duties on imported parts. The Supreme Court said no. Finding that the parts arrived in Bayonne almost entirely assembled, the court lingered on the multiplicity of phases and sites of production, characterizing the final commodity in Bayonne as "partially manufactured."[103] Such a conception of fragmented production struck a discordant note for 1898, the age of monopoly capital, when the industrial corporation was supposedly rooted in place, a vertically integrated leviathan.[104]

Tide Water Oil was one of a number of decisions that lawyers for zone operators came to know chapter and verse during the 1930s and 1940s. Customs law was perhaps the sole domain in nineteenth- and early twentieth-century business culture in which the meaning of "manufacturing" was explained, not assumed. Because tariff policy grew out of Hamiltonian efforts to protect infant industry, most tariffs targeted "manufactured" imports. The definition and demarcation of this threshold prompted frequent legal challenges. Customs law is a cache of commodity biographies, since, as in *Tide Water Oil,* customs law elaborated the meaning of "manufacturing" by starting with the commodity, not the labor process.[105]

Many of these cases concerned the Treasury Department's drawback policy. Dating to Hamilton's eleven-point plan for American manufacturing, the drawback policy was the nation's first effort to push production for the world market. If a firm used an imported commodity subject to duties when it manufactured for export, it was eligible for a refund of 99% of the duties, but only after exporting the finished product and filing reams of paperwork with the Treasury Department. When the Ford Motor Company enameled and baked hub caps and assembled them with wheels in Detroit and then exported them to Cologne, Germany, drawback was allowed (but not when flanges, tires, and tubes were added—"this was not a manufacture or production").[106] The drawback policy set a mixed precedent for zone lawyers. Whereas in an application for drawback the impetus was to dilate "manufacturing," now, in a request for permission to "manipulate" (i.e., "not manufacture") in a foreign-trade zone, one researcher wrote, "The shoe is on the other foot."[107] Even so, zone grantees hoped to shift the law in their favor. To them it seemed that, because of the drawback policy, lawyers at the Customs Bureau "leaned over backwards to call everything manufacturing."[108]

It was reasonable to expect customs lawyers to perform such acrobatics—narrowing the ambit of "manufacturing" in one instance, just to widen it in the next—only if "manufacturing" had no universal meaning. And, in customs law, this was true. The case that set out the doctrine that customs lawyers enforced—and continue to enforce—reached the Supreme Court in 1907. *Anheuser-Busch Brewing Association v. the United States* weighed in on whether corks imported from Spain were subsequently "manufactured" or merely manipulated in St. Louis, when they were cleaned and coated prior to being plugged into bottles of beer. If Anheuser-Busch exported those bottles of beer, was it entitled to drawback on the duties for the corks? No, the court unanimously ruled, calling attention to the bafflement around "manufacturing":

> The words of the statute are indeed so familiar in use and of meaning that they are confused by attempts at definition. Their first sense as used is fabrication or composition—a new article is produced of which the imported material constitutes an ingredient or part. When we go further than this in explanation we are involved in refinements, and in impracticable niceties. Manufacture implies a change, but every change is not manufacture, and yet every change in an article is the result of treatment, labor and manipulation. But something more is necessary. . . . There must be transformation; a new and different article must emerge, "having a distinctive name, character, or use."[109]

Anheuser-Busch Brewing Association established what came to be known as the "substantial transformation" test, according to which "manufacturing" referred to whatever labor process altered a commodity into "a new and different article," distinguished either by a new name, a new character, or a new use. Soon after the Foreign-Trade Zones Act became law, the Customs Bureau reiterated this formula in a memorandum on how to determine if an activity counts as "manufacturing": "(a) the name and condition of the merchandise used; (b) the kind of process or processes applied thereto; (c) the character of the change which results from the process or processes."[110] Customs lawyers decreed no bright-line rule, no single meaning of "manufacturing." The test would be meted out on a case-by-case basis.

Fortunately for zone tenants, almost all of whom were small-scale import-export firms, the buck stopped with the FTZ Board, not with the Customs Bureau. First, the customs collector at the zone decided whether a "contemplated manipulation" was allowable. If in doubt, he consulted the commissioner of customs; if the commissioner's decision was not to the tenant's liking, the FTZ Board heard appeals.[111] This sequence all but guaranteed conflict. Lawyers for zone operators and zone tenants bombarded the bureau with briefs, scheming with Tom Lyons, the board's executive secretary, and with Congressman Manny Celler. They litigated each case to the hilt, battling the Customs Bureau's intransigence. Could bulbs be screwed into flashlight cases in a zone? Customs: No, such an operation constituted manufacturing. Could wristbands be attached to watch heads in a zone? Customs: No, such an operation constituted manufacturing. Could sugar, shortening, salt, and flour be combined to package a baking mix in a zone? Customs: No, such an operation constituted manufacturing.[112] In appeal after appeal, zone lawyers rebutted these findings, not by professing what manufacturing *was*, but by asserting what it *was not*. They sought to curtail its meaning into oblivion. And in almost all cases the FTZ Board agreed, overruling the Customs Bureau.

These victories, however, exacted a heavy toll. Often an appeal halted business for months, not to mention the legal fees that such cases incurred.[113] In early 1947, the FTZ Board held a hearing to review the rules. In front of a packed room of the Commerce Department, textbooks were wielded as if it were the *Scopes* trial. While Manny Celler hauled out *Funk and Wagnall's New Standard Dictionary* (1944), one of the managers of Zone 1, Sterling St. John—who later made a career of zone consulting—offered both the board and the audience a tutorial in neoclassical economic theory. One wonders whether people took notes, read the newspaper, or dozed, as St. John read paragraph after paragraph from Edward R. A. Seligman's *Principles of Economics* (1905), E. L. Rhoades's *Introductory Readings in Marketing* (1927), Paul D. Converse's *Elements of Marketing* (1930), Walter E. Spahr's *The Economic Foundations of Business* (1932), and Henry H. Bakken and Marvin A. Schaars's *Economics of Cooperative Marketing* (1937). At a minimum it seems safe to assume that they left with the word *marketing* lodged in their ears. These treatises included much talk of "time utility," "place utility," and "form utility," all in contemplation of a basic point summed up by John D. Black in *Production Economics* (1926): "Whether a given operation will be called manufacturing or processing depends somewhat upon the simplicity of it and to what extent it changes the nature of the product, but more upon whether it is performed as an incident to marketing by some recognized middleman agency, such as a milk distributor, a jobbing house, or"—hello, foreign-trade zone—"a terminal warehouse."[114]

"Marketing" as a term gained currency after World War I, synthesizing most of the gerunds that approximated "manufacturing." It gestured to distribution in the conventional sense of delivering goods to market, and to "processing" as well, as per Black, and as a zone lawyer illustrated with a razor:

> Gentlemen, here is a piece of metal. We excel in this country in making metal products. Here is a plastic handle. . . . I take this into the zone and I want to assemble a cheap safety razor so I can sell it to some poor fellow in Peru, or Havana. What do I do in the zone? I just screw it on there, and now I have come out with a safety razor. A new name. This part was not a safety razor and this part was not. But putting the two together, I have a safety razor. Is that a manufacture? . . . I have a three-year-old son who uses this as a razor. Does he manufacture that every time he puts that on that?[115]

This zone lawyer indicated—with the disconcerting image of his toddler brandishing a safety razor—that marketing was essential to production but that it was somehow less complex. Marketing helped to form goods, but not to *trans*form them.

After the hearing, the FTZ Board released Order Number 15, announcing that a variety of manipulations fell safely within bounds of the law.[116] This outcome was indicative of how the zone concept corresponded to a reformatting of the labor process toward production across national boundaries. While it was the daily drill of the Customs Bureau to assess manipulations by classifying the commodities at stake, the FTZ Board, when assaying the zone system, ignored commodities and instead elicited testimony that ranked forms of labor. The upshot: manufacturing happened in factories, with skilled labor; marketing happened anywhere, with anyone. "You and I can put a flashlight bulb into a flashlight case without being a skilled man," an official from the Port Authority of New York said at the hearing, contrasting manufacturing with "a simple assembly operation where the primary components of the thing are already there."[117] Marketing boiled down to "simple assembly." Your three-year-old son could take part in marketing. So, too, could a flock of pigeons or a Hollywood actor in a suit and tie (fig. 4.13). Zone tenants posed no threat to American industry, because zones were not industrial. The foreign-trade zone was not a factory.

"I have never felt that manufacturing as such was necessary for the success of a foreign-trade zone as there are so many important manipula-

Figure 4.13. The film star Douglas Fairbanks Jr. "handles" a forklift at Zone 1 in Staten Island, ca. 1955. Courtesy of *Staten Island Advance*.

tions that are awaiting opportunity to be authorized," Tom Lyons wrote to Manny Celler in 1944. "However," Lyons added, in a telling afterthought, "if manufacturing were authorized it would facilitate the matter of zone administration."[118] At the time, Celler was drafting an amendment to the FTZ Act to permit manufacturing, which Congress would pass in 1950 amid the buoyancy of postwar prosperity. Celler agreed with Lyons, but his personal correspondence indicates that he was seeking the amendment only because he wanted to unburden zones of bureaucratic restraints. He wanted manufacturing, to be sure, and he believed that he had already provided for it in the FTZ Act. What he wanted, as Lyons suggested, was already in motion on the spatio-temporal "border-line" of manipulating.

"Electric Eyes Stand Guard"

"Every one of these manipulations," pledged a politician at a 1947 hearing, "means work and labor for people that reside on Staten Island and in the city of New York."[119] Publicly, politicians touted jobs as the primary benefit of the zone, and manipulating as their best generator. Still, Zone 1 was not bursting with employees, at least not in the zone's advertising materials, where crowds of men rarely surfaced. Look again at figure 4.1, a WPA poster from early 1937, when the national unemployment rate was around 14% and about to shoot up. Not a face in sight. What the poster celebrates is a sensibility unfazed by the plight of the common man. It boasts of a high-tech waterfront and a landscape dominated by massive machines. It lays out the math of the zone system: "frictionless handling" jettisoned human handling.

The number of people who punched the clock at each zone was never specified. Although annual reports to the FTZ Board tracked shipments of cargo, they included only a few sentences on "labor." In 1940, the Department of Docks for New York, the zone grantee, listed city employees devoted to Zone 1 as a distinct quantity (seventeen), but only estimated those hired by the zone operator: 50 full-time and 150 part-time employees for the whole gamut of "administrative, soliciting, and clerical forces, and labor for handling commodities." This last phrase referred to people engaged in manipulating cargo. People involved in moving cargo—or longshoremen—were singled out in a separate sentence, fluctuating from month to month, "e.g.: 450, 1000, 600, 300, 500, 400, 200, 200, 320, 256, 42, 0." As for the number employed directly by zone tenants—such as the Chinese immigrants staffing a tungsten refinery—that total, roughly seventy per month, "can only be approximated."[120]

Amid this haze of approximations, one type of employee stood out. He was the type of "nonproductive" employee who drained profits, and he was monitored to the person: the security guard. Manning the gates at all hours and even sometimes sleeping on site, the security guard personified the zone system (fig. 4.14). He milled around in his cap, tie, and brass-buttoned coat, chatting and watering flowers.[121] He lent the scene a ceremonial air, but he irked zone grantees because he embodied the worst kind of overhead. He not only contributed zilch to the valorization of commodities; he also resisted scientific management. He and his colleagues could not be shrunk to a skeletal crew, not by zone grantees or operators. He answered to officials at the Customs Service, who dictated the extent of his presence.

Zone grantees fumed because they, not the Customs Service, paid his entire salary. In one of the more ironic illustrations of how federalism undermined the zone system, leaders of the Treasury Department refused to split the bill, claiming that covering zones entailed costly adaptations. They punted to the grantees the full financial burden for defense of the US border. The grantees fought this arrangement, arguing that the Treasury

Figure 4.14. The gatehouse doubled as office space and sleeping quarters for Zone 1's most devoted employees: the customs guards, 1953. Herbert A. Flamm, Collection of Historic Richmond Town.

Department should charge strictly for "additional" labor, over and above whatever it funded at other parts of the port. Congressman Manny Celler backed them, applying pressure at the highest levels, all to no avail.[122] Over the years, the stalemate worsened, and the commissioner of customs predicted it would "choke" the zone system beyond rescue.[123] At Zone 1, 129 part-time guards patrolled the customs boundary in 1949, up from 9 in 1940.[124] At Zone 3, 53.6 cents of every dollar earned went to guards in 1951.[125] Such data drew a dystopian picture: a system built to cut customs red tape, "shackled" by customs guards.

This years-long debacle captures the friction in frictionlessness, and it relates to the first instance of automation in a foreign-trade zone. Back in 1935, engineers for Zone 1 needed to figure out how to fortify the water area between each of the finger piers, to thwart smugglers. They settled on "a new kind of fence," as it was touted, "which no one yet has been able to climb or evade."[126] The "electric eye" was the latest trend in laser equipment, the reason why doors swung open automatically at Pennsylvania Station. Whenever it sensed a disturbance of a laser beam, it set off an electrical current, activating a door, a bell, or an alarm. Deployed at the outer edges of the piers, it would project an infrared beam across the water. If a swimmer or boat interrupted it, a siren would sound. The device would guarantee security, promised an *ADT Transmitter* article, "Electric Eyes Stand Guard," "marking the customs boundary as definitely as though built of steel and concrete."[127]

Zone 1's engineers—employees of the WPA—had a little help with this venture. At first, they conferred with General Electric (GE), Westinghouse, and the Signaphone Corporation, but talks eventually stalled because skeptics at the WPA refused to commit sufficient resources.[128] Then the lead engineer hooked up with American District Telegraph (ADT), via a colleague on the FTZ Survey (the name for the initiative backed by the WPA to assist Mayor La Guardia in applying for a foreign-trade zone). ADT—an acronym now synonymous with the suburban lawn—was investigating similar alarm mechanisms and made its staff and equipment available to the FTZ Survey. Together, they adapted the electric eye to Zone 1's conditions, testing it across the roofs of midtown Manhattan's skyscrapers ("This work involved some stiff climbing," the lead engineer noted) and in the morning mist of the New Jersey wetlands. They built a contraption that housed the electric eye and that moved it up and down with the tides. The lead engineer later concluded that the project had hinged on ADT's assistance. "They granted me every facility of their research laboratory and allocated funds necessary to carry on the work," he wrote. "Any success," he stressed, "is in large part attributable to the active support I have received from ADT."[129]

That the electric eye could be deemed a "success" seems doubtful, though the gizmo did give fodder to journalists. On loan from GE for sixteen dollars a day, it often malfunctioned, twice slipping off its elevator and plunging into the water. "It sounds off a deafening siren at intervals," the *Staten Island Advance* reported; officials from the nearby Marine Hospital disliked that the noise "disturbs patients."[130] This snafu merited recognition from the bards at the *New Yorker*: "The idea was that if pirates attempted to creep up to the piers and steal freight, their boat would break the beam and sound an alarm," the item began. "Well, the alarm sounds day and night, keeping the special guards on the run, but it's never pirates." And the punch line: "You could probably guess what it is, easy enough. Sea gulls."[131]

In theory, the electric eye saved money. It dispensed with the need for guards to patrol the water, as in European free ports, where guards moved a physical barrier to admit each vessel. Zone operators cited this contrast with pride.[132] But none of them went so far as to compare the guards' wages with the costs of building, installing, renting, and maintaining the electric eye. Their praise suggested that they evaluated the contraption in less quantitative terms. "It removes the chance that a guard might let some craft slip by when he closed his eyes," the editors of the *Staten Island Advance* commended. "The electric eye, its sponsors point out, never sleeps."[133]

It also never strikes. The electric eye was the peerless worker, and it complemented other trappings of what zone operators termed "live storage." This eerie term bespoke how "the majority of cargoes in storage at the zone," as a brochure insisted, "are in no sense in dead storage but are actively making money for investors."[134] Whether thanks to pigeons or sea breezes, cargoes at the zone leveraged the warehouse's magic to "make money," all by themselves. Take the oft-cited story of the Brazil nuts. Deposited in a zone, nuts made money by sitting still. Taking the cure in the salty air, they shed water as they dried. By the time they were dressed to be reexported from the zone—or to be "imported" into the United States—they weighed less than when they first arrived and reveled in lower duties. (With the aid of the warehouse receipt, they also levitated as they dried, crossing the harbor to banks on Wall Street, where they collateralized loans.)[135] How was this alchemy depicted by the Department of Commerce in its *Foreign Commerce Weekly*? Not with a didactic series of images. Not with an image balanced between the piles of nuts and the people who handled them (fig. 4.15). And definitely not with an image foregrounded by laborers (fig. 4.16). The image of choice zooms in on the nuts (fig. 4.17). "Ambassadors of Good Will," it anoints them, vouching for the zone system's positive impact on relations with Brazil, and rendering the nuts as agents of history.

In a nutshell, this image encapsulated how the foreign-trade zone repackaged warehousing into a dreamscape of frictionless transactionality: a delivery system free of the deadweight loss of a soldiering wage earner or a rent-seeking state. Stored in a zone, cargoes themselves could serve as stores of value, via collateralization, and during that space of time, they could also rise in value merely by curing or ripening, without any human handling—a "natural" transformation whose logic opened up the possibilities for more hands-on interventions, like reconditioning, refining, and other varieties of manipulating. Extraterritoriality enhanced these fundamentals of warehousing. Apart from the tariff exemptions and the relaxations of customs controls, Brazil nuts could have behaved in the same fashion at Bush Terminal. Their storage-based metabolism was on display at Zone 1 because the zone system was a publicly financed endeavor. The zone system amplified tendencies inherent in warehousing.

And what's not to like about frictionlessness? Surely no "busy housewife" would spurn the aid of an electric eye. "Can Be Used to Open Doors

Figure 4.15. The original caption reads, "From Soup to Nuts: Merchandise of all descriptions and from all parts of the world is stored in the warehouse of New York City's foreign trade zones on Staten Island. Here is a huge supply of Brazil nuts waiting to be graded, cleaned, and packed. When ready for shipment this foreign merchandise may go to a third country for consumption without having paid United States import or export duties." December 23, 1939. Associated Press.

Figure 4.16. *Man and Women Working, Sacks/Baskets of Nuts*, May 13, 1953. Herbert A. Flamm, Collection of Historic Richmond Town.

Ambassadors of Good Will—Brazil Nuts.

Figure 4.17. The original caption analogizes the foreign-trade zone to an embassy. Photograph reprinted from Carter R. Bryan, "Like the Pea in the Shell Game," *Foreign Commerce Weekly*, February 21, 1942.

for a Person Who Is Using Both Hands to Carry Trays or Dishes."[136] "Now the All-Electric House Evolves."[137] Most journalistic allusions to the device underlined its potential for individual liberation. Yet "automation" was not a one-off substitution of a machine for a person, like cruise control on the interstate. It envisioned a critical mass of machines for "the automatic handling of parts between progressive production processes."[138] This notion of a network suggested a challenge to the political clout of American labor, but its implications would not crystallize for another generation.[139] Coined in 1936, the term *automation* was still novel enough to be spun as "labor-serving," not "labor-saving." ADT's "robot detective" would mimic US customs security guards, not replace them.[140] A good three decades before containerization would banish the longshoreman's hook, the electric eye at Zone 1 heralded a technocratic utopia. While reporters mocked the hiccups with seagulls, no one raised an eyebrow about the idea of job creation through job elimination.[141]

Figure 5.1. The original caption reads, "'Fish-eye' view of Union Carbide's petrochemical facilities at Peñuelas, Puerto Rico." The photograph is the cover image for Linda Liston, "Plant Your Plant at a Home Away from Home, at Home," *Industrial Development*, November/December 1967. Reprinted with permission from siteselection.com.

CHAPTER FIVE

"Plant Your Plant at a Home Away from Home, at Home": The Subzone

The question of whether foreign trade zones result in a net gain or loss in U.S. employment is not easily determined.

—"U.S. Foreign Trade Zones: Boon or Bane for Production, Jobs?" *Los Angeles Times*, April 18, 1982

Part I. The Greater United States

"Suspended Parallelograms of Chain-Link Fencing"

In the 1980s, the metropolis imploded.[1] Outside was inside, and the periphery was permeating the core: in a global city like New York, garment factories —symbols of capitalism of yore that were assumed to have left the United States for Asia—were showing up in Chinatown.[2] Places were losing their coherence (or what had felt like coherence to those prosperous enough to believe in it). As the geographer David Harvey observed in 1989, "Baltimore was essentially a one-beer town (locally brewed) in 1970," but then it was flooded by regional drafts from Milwaukee and Denver, followed by Belgian ales and English stouts.[3] "There is a Boston in L.A., a Lower Manhattan and a South Bronx, a São Paulo and a Singapore," wrote the geographer Edward Soja that same year.[4] "In a hidden sweatshop in downtown Los Angeles, Asian and Latino migrants produce automobile parts for a factory in Detroit," chimed in the anthropologist Roger Rouse in 1991. "As the parts leave the production line, they are stamped 'Made in Brazil.'"[5]

Harvey, in a book that quickly became an academic best seller, interpreted this dislocatedness as a fundamental trait of "the condition of postmodernity."[6] While such fragmentation was not new—it was a hallmark of modernity—what was novel about *postmodernity* was the intensity of disorientation, the speed and the scope of "disruptive spatiality."[7] The shrinking of distance by dint of satellites, semiconductor chips, shipping containers, and other technologies of global capitalism meant, counterintuitively, that differences between locales were heightened rather than flattened, even with all those beers on tap. "The less important the spatial barriers," Harvey theorized, "the greater the sensitivity of capital to the variations of place within space, and the greater the incentive for places to be differentiated in ways attractive to capital."[8] In a maxim that is taken for granted today but that was only dawning in the 1980s, Boston was now in competition with Singapore as much as with New York or Los Angeles.

Harvey saw in this economic volatility a crisis in "how we represent the world to ourselves," a crisis that had yielded the aesthetics of postmodernism. In relating cultural forms to economic forces he was dialoguing with the cultural theorist Fredric Jameson, who had declared postmodernism to be "the cultural logic of late capitalism."[9] Writing in 1984, Jameson had described the unprecedented reach of capital flows in the 1980s as akin to the mirrored, vertiginous, curvilinear walls of the Westin Bonaventure hotel in Los Angeles. The hotel presented a "spatial equivalent" of the psychic experience of global capitalism by allegorizing unevenness, not simply by mirroring or reflecting it; for as he wrote of the steel and stucco disjunctures of Frank Gehry's famous house in Santa Monica, California, postmodernity was characterized both by unevenness and by its unrepresentability (fig. 5.2): "The problem, then, which the Gehry house tries to think is the relationship between that abstract knowledge and conviction or belief about the superstate and the existential daily life of people in their traditional rooms and tract houses. There must be a relationship between those two realms or dimensions of reality, or else we are altogether within science fiction without realizing it. But the nature of that relationship eludes the mind. The building then tries to think through this spatial problem in spatial terms."[10] In Gehry's "deconstructivist" style, Jameson found a language of disconnection. A jumble of traditional and contemporary, refined and raw, square and trapezoidal, the house in its layers conjugates the political economy of the age of the microchip.[11]

Frank Gehry is often derided as the epitome of a "starchitect" whose bling buildings have spurred on gentrification (witness "the Bilbao effect").[12] His name signifies the redevelopment of the urban waterfront into a post-Fordist playground. Yet, as it happens, in 1978, as he wrapped up his house, Gehry also completed a project seldom cited in the canon: offices carved into a Toyota parts distribution warehouse. It took Gehry to a

Figure 5.2. Chain-link fencing encloses the yard and crowns the front porch of Frank Gehry's bungalow. The original caption reads, "Canadian-American architect Frank Gehry and his son, Alejandro, in the yard in front of his self-designed home, Santa Monica, California, January, 1980." Photo by Susan Wood / Getty Images.

new kind of harbor. Located in an industrial park in Glen Burnie, Maryland, seven miles from BWI Airport and eleven miles from Baltimore's marine terminals, the facility sat at the head of a stream of imports; beginning in the 1970s, Baltimore ranked as the principal port of entry on the East Coast for German and Japanese cars.[13] With this assignment, Gehry wound up at the edge of a metropolis and the center of a logistics cluster.

Gehry was selected by Frederick R. Weisman, owner of Mid-Atlantic Toyota Distributors and a Los Angeles–based art collector. Weisman adorned the offices with millions of dollars' worth of paintings, ranging from a portrait of himself by Andy Warhol to a series of eighteenth-century Japanese woodblock prints.[14] The inclusion of "Oriental" art was a tribute not only to Toyota but to Weisman's yen for the fruits of Japanese business acumen. "Mr. Weisman's goal is to make employees feel part of one big Toyota 'family,'" reported the *Baltimore Sun*. Even more crucial than the decorations in this respect are the offices themselves. There are none, technically speaking, or very few. Instead, large rooms painted in "the soft, clear pinks and blues of a Maryland sunrise" cascade one into the next like waves on a beach, fostering an openness that allows—or forces—workers to enjoy "constant contact with one another."[15]

Progressive Architecture proclaimed Weisman's choice of Gehry as "nothing short of inspired," but less for the pastels than for the floor plan that hosts this harmonious atmosphere (fig. 5.3).[16] Gehry upends the grid of the Fordist firm as if he's dumping out a wastebasket. Skylights and cutouts, "both regular and unexpected," filter "kaleidoscopic impressions of light and space." Beams, columns, and walls collide at oblique angles, unmoored from function, prompting confusion. What is a beam, a column, a wall? "At Mid-Atlantic, walls are constructed so that workers can see through them and around them," wrote a *Sun* reporter (who might have noted the upside for prying bosses). "Walls don't exist to create private areas."[17] Save for a picture window that "gives a contrasting view of the staggeringly proportioned storeroom for Toyota parts, everything from bumpers to dashboards," all of this visual noise is accentuated by the absence of a conversation between the second-floor offices and the ground-floor warehouse (the work of a general contractor, not Gehry). Both interiors are bounded by the "orthogonal severity" of the box, but while the latter hews to convention, the former mutates within its shell. Or, considering that Gehry employs "a repertoire of materials with strong industrial references," perhaps the dynamic between the two levels is better described as the ground floor jutting into the second, reprising how, in 1978, in Baltimore and Los Angeles and beyond, the Third World was erupting into the First. Cement blocks, plywood, corrugated metal, and exposed ducts sculpt the space. "Suspended parallelograms of chain-link fencing," a Gehry trademark, hang from the ceiling to delineate niches, vectors to the export-processing zones in Asia that likely produced those bumpers and dashboards stacked downstairs.[18]

Gehry's "axonometric" drawing is noteworthy for how crisply and comprehensively it conveys the distortedness of his design. At first glance it looks like a maze bisected by diagonals. The eye strains to navigate it because it depicts three-dimensional space on a two-dimensional surface: a hybrid of a bird's-eye view and a street view, it offers no shift in scale—the back wall is equivalent in height to the front. Like Gehry's house—and global capitalism—these spaces are unrepresentable in their totality; you cannot snap a decent picture of them.[19] Gehry's rupture of the cube would never register in the rigid perspectivalism of the generic warehouse photograph (fig. 1.1). It is a perfect corollary to the postmodern metamorphosis of the foreign-trade zone (fig. 5.1).

In that image, the helter-skelter of global capitalism is expressed in quite

Toyota

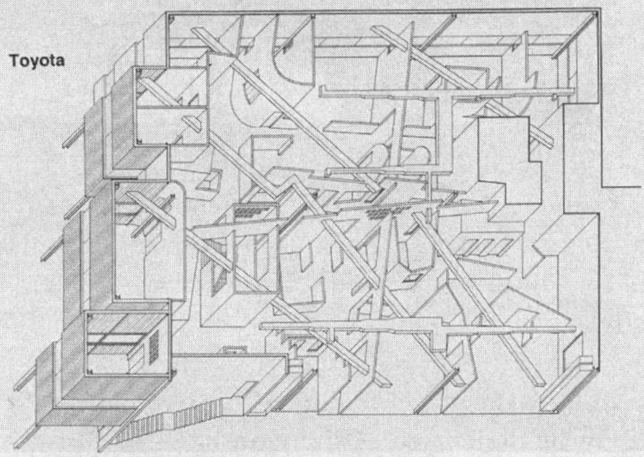

AXONOMETRIC—SECOND FLOOR OFFICES

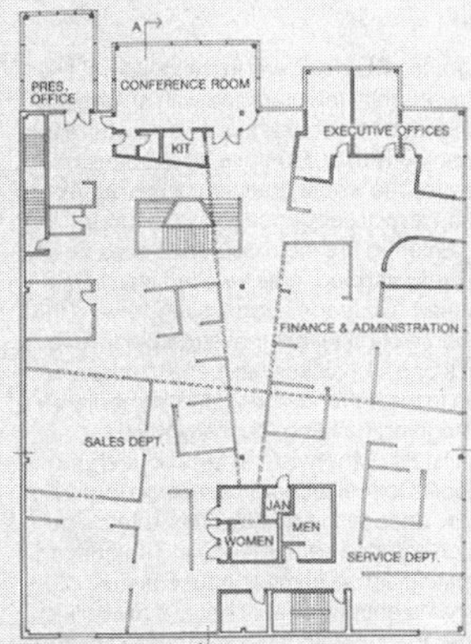

SECOND FLOOR

Conference room (above) has steel paneling. Offices (below) show complex spatial development.

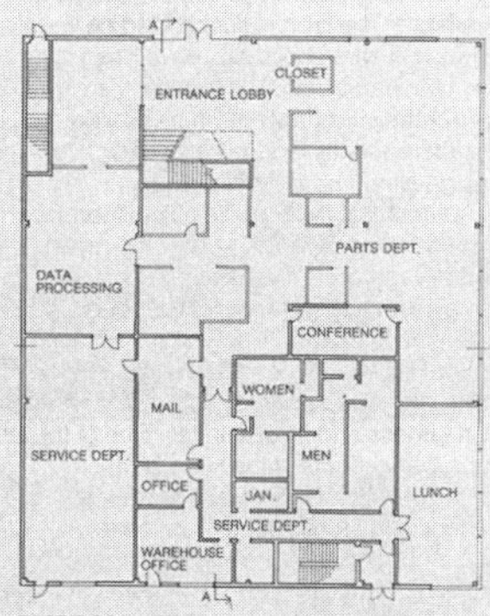

FIRST FLOOR

Data

Project: Mid-Atlantic Toyota Distributors Offices, Glen Burnie, Md.

Architects: Frank O. Gehry & Associates; Frank O. Gehry, C. Gregory Walsh, Frederick Fisher, design team.

Program: offices for import automobile distributorship, attached to warehouse facility.

Site: 7.7 acres in planned industrial community close to a large Eastern city.

Structural system: steel frame, columns, beams, open-web joists, concrete slab on grade.

Major materials: stucco over concrete block exterior walls, insulated double-skin wall, galvanized both surfaces at second-floor office bays. Painted drywall over metal studs interior walls, carpeted and VAT floors (see Building materials, p. 126).

Mechanical system: package roof units.

Consultants: Athans Enterprises, electrical.

General contractor: Dickerson-Heffner, Inc.

Client: Mid-Atlantic Toyota Distributors, Inc.

Costs: withheld at request of client.

Photography: Tim Street-Porter.

Figure 5.3. The axonometric and plan drawings from Frank Gehry's design for a Toyota distributor's offices near Baltimore, Maryland, with photographic views, from Martin Filler, "Perfectly Frank," *Progressive Architecture*, July 1979.

literal terms with the aid of a circular fish-eye lens. Shot in 1967 (almost certainly with a Nikon, which is to say, a Japanese camera), the photograph evokes the trippy swirls of a Jimi Hendrix album cover. And that psychedelia was warranted because at the end of the 1960s—on the cusp of the 1980s, as Jameson might say—the spatial form of the foreign-trade zone was in the throes of a radical permutation.[20] At the heart of the change was a new iteration called the *subzone*. Introduced in revised regulations issued by the Foreign-Trade Zones Board in 1952, after Congress lifted the bans on manufacturing and exhibiting in zones in 1950, the idea of the subzone was to delink the zone concept from the waterfront, to enable any existing operation in close proximity to be designated offshore-onshore. While a complex like Zone 1 on Staten Island would constitute a "general-purpose zone," a subzone might be a decades-old warehouse five miles away—with the requisite fencing and signage. The idea of the subzone elevated the geographic imaginary of the zone system to a new order of weirdness: now it was possible to step off US soil without lifting a single foot. The subzone manifested the emerging regime of flexible accumulation. "Plant Your Plant at a Home Away from Home, at Home," went the headline under the fish-eye photograph, with syntax worthy of Samuel Beckett. "It's something like having an overseas plant without leaving home."[21] The phrase *overseas plant* marks the subzone's divergence, too, in a vernacular equally redolent of the 1960s, the period that witnessed the coronation of the multinational corporation. Notably, the subject of the fish-eye photograph was not the usual shed or storeroom; it was a Union Carbide petrochemical refinery in Puerto Rico, Subzone 7A.

When it was debuted, the subzone drew little notice. It was a fix for a serious limitation of general-purpose zones: because they were sited in areas where land was at a premium, they were small. The subzone gave them a way to grow. Ten years passed before Union Carbide secured permission for 7A, the first subzone on record. Only five came on line during the following ten years. But then the roster doubled, and quadrupled. By the end of 1984, the Foreign-Trade Zones Board had approved 102 subzones, as appendages of the 113 general-purpose zones that cropped up between 1970 and 1985, from North Florida to Oregon. Although Brazil nuts and other "colonial goods" continued to move through the zones, it was thanks to two icons of the American Century that the system took off: oil and cars. By 1989, nearly every single auto plant was in a subzone—a prospect that had been unthinkable just two decades earlier. During a hearing in the US House of Representatives in 1948, an official from the Commerce Department had sworn that permitting "manufacturing" in zones would result in fewer tussles over semantics and not in actual manufacturing (whatever that was). His testimony is uncanny:

> I believe that the nature of a zone itself . . . would actually deter or discourage the establishment of a large manufacturing industry in the zone. . . . [T]he very fact they are in congested ports where land values are very, very high, makes it very unlikely that any manufacturing company would go into such an expensive locality, such a congested locality, because it would be for such a small percentage of their business. To illustrate the point, I cannot conceive of Mr. Ford wanting to establish his automobile factory in such a location.[22]

Lo and behold, the Ford Motor Company so desired in 1982, when it filed for Subzone 70C in Wayne, Michigan. Still more headline worthy was the statistic that all foreign automakers that opened plants in the United States starting in the late 1970s—"transplants," they were christened—opened them in subzones. To be clear, the subzone was not a prerequisite for Nissan's investment in Tennessee. Rather, it was a mediator for larger transitions in the international division of labor, as the fragmentation of production across borders put pressure on particular regions and particular sectors inside the United States, pitting Detroit against Nashville and makers of cars against makers of car parts. As a result, the subzone was a prime target for the anxieties that Harvey and Jameson diagnosed as symptoms of the condition of postmodernity. By 1989, the zone system was under siege, a metonym for unequal exchange. Who benefitted from it? Was it a net gain or a net loss? How was its impact to be measured? If the period was troubled by a struggle over how to represent global capitalism, it was also fractured by a battle over the very existence of a national economy.

"Exporting Jobs," or, "If We Do Not Buy from Other Countries, They Will Not Buy from Us"

Toward the end of World War II, Congressman Emanuel Celler started to take steps to revise the Foreign-Trade Zones Act to encompass "manufacturing" and "exhibiting." Celler had long considered such an amendment more a matter of streamlining than redefinition. He saw zones as commercial spaces in which importers and exporters would ready goods for market, not as industrial spaces in which manufacturers would set up shop; these were spaces of circulation, not spaces of production. Celler introduced the first bill to amend the act in 1945, and another in 1947, culminating in the hearing in 1948 during which it was said that "Mr. Ford" would never, ever produce cars in a zone. Most of the speakers that day testified to what was by then the commonsense about the act's constraints: the ban on "manufacturing" was not staving off foreign competition; it was forcing zone operators to chew up precious time in reasoning through "exasperating" and "ludicrous" quasi-theological distinctions between *manipulating* and *manufacturing*.[23] Liberate the zones and let them function as I intended them, Celler insisted, as replicas of Hamburg's full-service *Freihafen*, and they will flourish, and our port cities will prosper, and Mr. Ford will not budge from River Rouge.

When the bill failed in 1948, stymied as usual by isolationist protectionism, Celler enlisted a new ally.[24] Celler's recruit, Congressman Hale Boggs of New Orleans, brought fresh clout to the table. He represented the nation's second-largest port, home of Zone 2, and he embodied an aggrieved wing of the Democratic Party in speaking for the South, a region where party leaders resented tariffs nearly as much as they loathed unions. Celler and Boggs each introduced bills in 1949, and Boggs regularly updated his friends and constituents that his bill seemed assured to pass—until the companion bill in the Senate collided with Senator Joe McCarthy, who hijacked it in the name of God, country, and the fur farmers of Wisconsin. McCarthy attached a rider imposing a steep tariff on Russian furs and stalled the bill in committee. Partnering with Senator Hubert Humphrey from the neighboring fur state of Minnesota, McCarthy slammed Amtorg, the New York City–based firm that distributed Russian imports in the United States, for underselling American furs and funneling the proceeds into Soviet espionage.[25] McCarthy's claims, amazingly, were not baseless. Boggs heard them from his own voters, who harvested the most muskrat furs in the nation. "We depend solely on the sale of furs for our living," one implored him in a handwritten letter, "and unless we can get better prices, we will starve."[26] Boggs, however, never wavered from his conviction that the zone system should be detached from the pathos of trade policy. Even as longshoremen in New York City subsequently sparked a bicoastal protest by refusing to unload Russian furs, he and Celler held firm in their belief in the neutrality and efficacy of the zone concept.[27] Boggs found no hypocrisy in, on the one hand, pledging himself to economic nationalism and vowing to push the State Department to negotiate tariffs on Russian furs and, on the other, advocating for an infrastructure to subvert all such limits to capital.

As for the technical specifications of that infrastructure, there was one other quagmire that Boggs had to avoid: the American Warehousemen's Association (AWA) was, predictably, protesting that the zone system threatened bonded warehouses. Writing from New Orleans, New York City, Houston, and Chicago, AWA members were imploring Boggs and Celler to insert language in the bill for "foreign-trade warehouses," contending that zone status should not be monopolized by "one location in each port if additional zone areas are economically advantageous."[28] The notion was to let bonded warehouses operate less like vaults and more like free ports. Boggs depended on the AWA members on his home turf, and initially he acquiesced. But in the end he opted to sacrifice the provision. He needed to avoid blowback from bureaucrats in the Treasury Department, who, in contemplating "foreign-trade warehouses," were raising flags about the prospect of weakening "the underlying concept of foreign-trade zones as enclosed geographical areas which are operated as integral parts of port facilities."[29] According to precedent, a foreign-trade zone was a physical enclave at a port, not a legal status that any warehouse on any humdrum street could acquire.

If the grounding of the foreign-trade zone in a fenced, port-based compound was so pivotal to the concept's acceptance, then why did the invention of the "subzone" rouse not a peep of disgruntlement? Partly because no one expected it to amount to much, not to mention that it was bureaucrats and not politicians who were its architects. The subzone concept was unveiled when the FTZ Board issued new regulations in mid-1952; the act itself made no reference to it. The genesis of these regulations is hard to reconstruct at a granular level, as scant documentation remains. Nonetheless, it seems clear that the board viewed the subzone as a modest innovation. Its regulatory language defined it as simply a means to accommodate the occasional activity that demanded more square footage than the typical seaport availed:

> *400.304 Zones for Specialized Purposes.*
>
> The establishment of a zone, or a sub-zone in an area separate from an existing zone, for one or more of the specialized purposes of storing, manipulating, manufacturing, or exhibiting goods may be authorized if the Board finds that existing or authorized zones will not serve adequately the convenience of commerce with respect to the proposed purposes.[30]

Treasury officials harped on the narrowness of this mandate, agreeing that it was imperative to prevent subzones from proliferating willy-nilly, "on a fragmented basis," due to "the administrative problems that zone fragmentation might impose" on efforts to police the zone system.[31] They drew stark lines of authority between the subzone and the general-purpose zone, noting that a "special-purpose zone" is "not a *sub*-zone," to the extent that the latter term suggested semiautonomousness.[32] Celler echoed this interpretation in a letter to the board's director in 1955. "The choice of location and maintenance of such sub zones," he advised, "would have to be under absolute mastery of the zone proper."[33] Celler deemed the subzone a minor phenomenon, a footnote.

More broadly, meager protest surrounded the Boggs Amendment of 1950 and the subzone regulation of 1952 because the politics of trade were shifting. The epoch of the "American Century" (so named by media magnate Henry Luce in 1941), from the end of World War II to the beginning of the long 1970s, marked a turn to widespread support for trade liberalization, even among long-standing proponents of tariffs such as Republicans and unions.[34] Much had changed since the passage of the Foreign-Trade Zones Act in 1934, when midwestern and northeastern congressmen tried to kill the act. By 1950, the United States dominated the world market. Foreign trade continued to constitute a mere fraction of GDP—less than 10% for both exports and imports—but increasingly it was a rallying cry, heralded by Celler as "America's insurance for peace and prosperity."[35] Celler expressed the corporate outlook of the 1950s when he inveighed against "Fortress America" and counseled that exports relied on imports—"If we do not buy from other countries, they will not buy from us." Joseph Marrone, outgoing director of the FTZ Board cited this orthodoxy when he quoted none other than President Dwight D. Eisenhower, a Republican: "The whole free world needs capital; America is its largest source. In that light, the flow of capital abroad from our country must be stimulated and in such a manner that it results in investment by individuals or private enterprise rather than by government."[36] Marrone left the FTZ Board to head the new Office of Foreign Investment in the Department of Commerce, an outfit tasked with assisting US corporations in going offshore.[37] In this climate of postwar optimism, those who objected that buying from other countries was the same as "exporting jobs" to them—a spin that was common by the 1970s but in the air even in the 1930s—were chastised as ignorant of the realities, and rewards, of interdependence.[38]

Of course, not everyone drank the Kool-Aid. The Socialist Workers Party's *Militant* heard in those same lines from Eisenhower an imperial call for coordination: "That is the voice of the executive committee of the capitalist class, demanding that the particular interests of this or that manufacturer or section of the class be subordinated to the general interest of the class as a whole."[39] The *Militant*'s take on the newfound thirst for trade among Republicans focused on the dangers of domestic overproduction: "American imperialism will drown in its own capital if it does not succeed in opening up new fields for foreign investment." Tariffs that smacked of 1890s protectionism presented a "dangerous obstacle" to Celler's brand of buy-to-sell internationalism. The *Militant* asked, "How can Wall Street consistently demand that other countries lower their trade barriers to admit American goods on a competitive basis while McKinley's ramparts still stand?"

Socialists knew that, for those capitalists who clung to McKinley's ramparts, who refused to see beyond "particular interests," there was always anticommunism to rally around instead. If expansionism failed to entice these protariff stalwarts, then the Red Scare jolted them back into compliance. The corollary to Senator McCarthy's warning about Amtorg's profiteering off of Russian furs was the argument that Americans needed to contain the Soviet economy, to prevent it from turning American allies. An official in the Commerce Department invoked this reasoning when he described foreign-trade zones as boosting trade with Japan and thus as aiding in the mission "to keep the island nation on this side of the Iron Curtain."[40] The United States was spending oodles of dollars overseas during the American Century, from the Marshall Plan that was rebuilding industrial capacity in Japan and Germany to the public-private initiatives that were helping US corporations to exploit that capacity. The goal of this Cold War Keynesianism was not only to secure buyers for American exports but also to assert American control of global capitalism, and to do so less through boots on the ground than through financial networks.[41] As with the flight route of a junket that the director of the FTZ Board took to Latin America in 1946, to confer about plans for free zones in twenty-seven cities, the geographic imaginary of American empire after World War II entailed a logistical map of lines of communication rather than areas of occupation (fig. 5.4).

So the invention of the subzone rattled no cages both because it was a quiet affair, in the usual manner of administrative rule making, and because it occurred at a moment when the national mood was brightening toward foreign trade, buoyed by a structural imperative to reach more consumers and by an ideological push to outflank the Soviet Union. Whatever anxieties the manufacturers were feeling in 1950, the balance sheet seemed to warrant optimism overall, especially in comparison to 1934. Crucially, moreover, capitalism was expanding geographically inside as

Figure 5.4. The flight map of FTZ Board Director Tom Lyons's tour of Latin America, a trip triggered by Lyons's side job as a zone consultant to the Panamanian government. Thomas E. Lyons, *Report on Proposal to Create a Foreign-Trade Zone (or Free Port) in the Republic of Panama* (Washington, DC: FTZ Board, 1946).

well as outside the United States. It's difficult to overstate how much the map was growing, how many new cities and regions were emerging. Capital was decentralizing and suburbanizing, newly mobile via airports and highways. Diffusion was not without precedent, but after World War II this restructuring began to accelerate. To capture this general flux in a particular place, city boosters began to try to lure capital with the foreign-trade zone and its floating appendage, the subzone.

"The Once Quiet Foreign-Trade Zone Has Blossomed into a Full-Blown Controversy"

The radicalism of the subzone was slow to catch on in business circles, masked as it was by a veneer of practicality. Sizing up existing zones as "physically handicapped," officials at the FTZ Board had simply wanted for zone operators to be able to annex parcels of land outside the congested confines of the waterfront.[42] This tweak was more superficial than foundational: it remained faithful to the old pipe dream of the entrepôt, wherein the United States muscled in on the business of reexport and transshipment in order to make work at seaports both for stevedores and for customs brokers, freight forwarders, bankers, and the like. Yet the spatial form of the entrepôt was outmoded by the mid-twentieth century, amid decolonization and the advent of containerization and computerization. Not only were so-called colonial goods moving ever more directly to purchasers, skipping intermediate stops, but also there was a growing gulf between the transport of the cargo and the coordination of the sale; the bill of lading was no longer signed in a nineteenth-century counting room, steps from the stuff. Therefore while it remained stuck in the mold of the entrepôt, the subzone failed to draw customers.

Exacerbating the situation was the dysfunctionality of the zone system's administration. Infighting was rampant between Commerce and Treasury, the two departments in charge, with Defense in the wings. Commerce was full of Don Quixotes who hungered to conquer the world market. "Our jobs are wonderful," one wrote to a colleague, "in that they provide us so much latitude for dreaming up new ideas, and for devising means for lifting the zone requirements—found to be 'fitting' by our elders in the Customs—out of the mire."[43] Treasury, correspondingly, was dominated by bean counters who tried to redirect such stargazing with demands for "extracts of extracts," as a zone tenant vented of the oppressive paperwork ("Their clerical methods are open to question," carped the chief counsel of customs).[44] In particular, the two flanks continued to tussle over the cost of customs guards. The issue was so intractable that the FTZ Board seemed not to know how to spin it in meetings with peevish zone operators, other than to hedge that the goal was not for zones to rake in money. Zones held "considerable intangible value" as "promotional" gimmicks for local commerce.[45] Granted, on that score, as well, the FTZ Board seemed to be falling short. Even Treasury wonks grumbled that publicity about the zones begged for greater "sex appeal."[46] Throughout the 1950s, not a single new site, neither a general-purpose zone nor a subzone, joined the roster.

The spark that at last ignited an explosion came from an unlikely spot (or a predictable one, if you give adequate due to the role of overseas territories in the shaping of US history). Puerto Rico is where the subzone first fully crystallized out of the general-purpose zone. The island's link to the zone system dated back to the New Deal, when President Franklin D. Roosevelt queried in a two-sentence note to his staff, "How about a free port for San Juan, Puerto Rico? It sounds like a practical suggestion."[47] Roosevelt's men in the Caribbean did go ahead and muster up an application for the FTZ Board in 1934, but they soon rescinded it. Governor Rexford Tugwell doubted the island's appeal as an entrepôt. His deputy Abe Fortas expressed the conventional wisdom to Manny Celler in 1944: "The income from it would not be enough to cover the operating expenses, let alone yield a return on the investment."[48] Resistance waned only once it was clear that a foreign-trade zone could encompass more than simple shipping and handling. And, in fact, it was Puerto Rico that loomed in Celler's mind when he initiated the push for an amendment on "manufacturing" in the mid-1940s. Pittsburgh industrialist Leon Falk—who wanted to build a cotton mill "under the American flag and still utilize cheap foreign raw materials and meet cheap foreign goods in a competitive market"—nudged him to action.[49] Celler, after checking with Tugwell and other key players, drafted the bill that would eventually catalyze the Boggs Amendment of 1950.

A general-purpose zone opened in the port city of Mayagüez in 1960, bringing the total number of zones to five.[50] According to the FTZ Board, it joined the system as "the only general-purpose zone established primarily for industrial activities, rather than as a port warehouse."[51] Or, in the lingua franca of apostles of global capitalism like the United Nations Industrial Development Organization and the World Bank, Zone 7 was an "export-processing zone," the first in the Americas and the second on the planet.[52] Moreover, it was a realization of the late nineteenth-century ambition of Austin Corbin and other merchant princes for an enclave on US soil wherein American manufacturers could mix American labor with foreign parts to produce for foreign consumers. In Puerto Rico, though, it was merely the latest addition to the toolkit of Operation Bootstrap (PRIDCO), a joint effort by San Juan and Washington, DC, to leverage the island as "a sales processing center for United States corporations" (a former leader of PRIDCO even served as the first director of Zone 7).[53]

To appreciate what was fundamentally at stake in this new twist on the zone concept, it's helpful to return to the backroom lobbying that resulted in the Boggs Amendment. Why was a Pittsburgh industrialist instrumental in paving the way for Zone 7? Why did Falk pester Celler for a foreign-trade zone in the colony of Puerto Rico and not in the state of Pennsylvania? Falk was focused on a specific factor of production—labor: the scheme for a cotton mill, he wrote to Celler, hinged, "of course, on the assumption that labor in Puerto Rico would be willing to work for a reasonable wage and prefer doing that to receiving W.P.A. assistance."[54] Falk's tone figures workers in Puerto Rico as presumptively malleable, more so than unionized workers in Pittsburgh and surely thanks to their tenuous claims to the rights of citizenship. This calculus pervaded news reports on the launch of Zone 7—"Although Puerto Rican labor is not 'cheap' by Caribbean standards (minimum hourly rates of 91 cents compare with 11 cents in Jamaica), the largely non-unionized Puerto Ricans are happy to work for wages far below those prevailing in the U.S."[55] Here, the discourse of efficiency—the zone guaranteed frictionlessness because it eliminated red tape—was fused with that of coloniality, with the allure of a cocktail of exploitable workers and business-friendly colonial agencies. Two visual documents distilled this revised rhetoric. One was an advertisement about Zone 7 that PRIDCO ran in mainland newspapers: designed by David Ogilvy, it centered on a coupon (a gimmick that Ogilvy called the centerpiece of "the most effective advertisement" he had ever written).[56] The other is a kind of foil to the coupon, a color advertisement for Zone 7 that PRIDCO ran in the *New Yorker*, featuring a white woman and her "small fry" frolicking in the calm, azure waters of a Puerto Rican beach (fig. 5.5): the zone was a tax holiday for the whole family![57]

In historical perspective, then, Zone 7, as a general-purpose zone, stands out because it marked the beginning of the era of "export-processing" and the end of haggling over what constituted "manufacturing." Now a tenant could attach razor blades to plastic handles without second-guessing from a customs guard. But such so-called light manufacturing is about all that happened in the forty-two-acre industrial park in Mayagüez; if Zone 7 were the end of the story, Puerto Rico would not count for much in the annals of the zone concept. The true milestone came two years later, when PRIDCO opened the nation's first subzone. Subzone 7A was located forty miles away in Peñuelas, on the southern coast near Ponce. To repeat: *forty miles away*. Subzone 7A was an entirely separate facility, sharing nothing with the general-purpose zone in Mayagüez other than a number and a landlord. Equally significant, it hosted an already existing operation: a Union Carbide petrochemical refinery, the subject of figure 5.1. Subzone 7A announced that the spatial form of the subzone offered to manufacturers an unusual degree of—to invoke a then-emergent catchword—flexibility. As

Figure 5.5. *Puerto Rico is known for business incentives,* teases this advertisement by David Ogilvy for Zone 7. "But there are other dividends to count in this sea-breezy land," where the corporate executive's wife and "small fry" can enjoy "an outdoor life 12 months a year." *New Yorker,* September 8, 1962.

the grantee, PRIDCO had covered the fees for the FTZ Board application and for the barbed-wire fencing and would pay the salaries of the customs guards. As the tenant, conversely, Union Carbide had expended not a single dollar to move to Subzone 7A. Subzone 7A had moved to it.[58]

Before explaining why this happened, I want to linger briefly on the refinery itself, an operation that was representative of how the zone concept had been applied up to that point; until the late 1970s, processing of one commodity was far more the norm than assembling of multiple commodities. To clarify this distinction, consider the various ways we might diagram the geography of production.[59] If we opt to track sectors rather than occupations—say, to show how steel concentrated in the Midwest rather than how large numbers of welders worked there, though each statement would be true—then we need to specify one further variable: either one material (steel) is processed in stages, yielding many products and by-products (rebar, slag), or many materials (steel sheets, vinyl, and windshield wipers) are assembled into one product (a car). It was the first of these modalities that dominated both the warehousing system in the nineteenth century and the zone system well into the twentieth century. To the extent that "handling" happened, with or without human hands, value was extracted from the rites of passage in the life cycle of one commodity. Curing of tobacco. Grading of sugar. Aging of whiskey. And, in 1962, refining of oil. It was fitting that the inaugural subzone entailed processing and not assembling.

Oil, meanwhile, intersected with the zone system at a highly combustible moment in the negotiation of oil policy in the United States. Oil-producing states like Texas, Louisiana, and Oklahoma still called the shots in Washington, DC, but they faced mounting competition from foreign wells. In 1959, President Dwight D. Eisenhower protected the Southwest in the name of national security with the Mandatory Oil Import Program, which instituted annual quotas for oil imports, limiting foreign crude in ratios pegged to domestic crude, and varying by region. By 1962, though, instability was rising. In some cases, the disruption came from independent upstarts that were angling to encroach on Big Oil; in other cases, it came from established companies that were dealing in by-products of crude oil, not in gasoline or heating oil. In Puerto Rico, for instance, a petrochemical company, not a gasoline company, was using the refinery—and for naphtha, a derivative of crude oil and a feedstock for plastics. Union Carbide was blazing a trail by taking advantage of the subzone to import low-cost naphtha from Venezuela, a permissible maneuver because, for the time being, naphtha was covered by a tariff but not by a quota.

Not far behind Union Carbide were rivals such as Dow Chemical and Monsanto. After Subzone 7A went live, the chemical industry took notice, and companies began jockeying for position, with federal bureaucrats right on their heels. The metropole recapitulated the colony: in 1964, Union Carbide applied for another subzone in Taft, Louisiana, twenty miles from New Orleans; in 1966, Dow Chemical applied for a subzone in Bay County, Michigan (the first instance in which an application for a general-purpose zone was simply a Trojan horse for a subzone).[60] As questions were raised about whether these projects were capitalizing on a loophole in the oil quotas and whether, therefore, imported naphtha should be subject to the same limits as imported gasoline, officials at the Department of the Interior scrambled to mediate. Wavering on how to regulate distinct phases in the life cycle of a single commodity, Secretary Stewart L. Udall threw up his hands, wondering, "Where do you draw the line?"[61] (Udall settled on shoehorning naphtha into the quotas.) Customs officials next weighed in, vetting the equipment. Dow Chemical went back and forth with Treasury lawyers over how best to monitor the pipelines from Texas to Michigan and "to assure complete segregation and accountability for the naphthas from the moment they are unloaded."[62] Readers may recall Tino De Angelis, whose tanks of "vegetable oil" jolted the stock market in 1963. With a bulk commodity like naphtha, fraud was an ever-present hazard.

These petrochemical projects continued apace, until, in 1968, one suitor nearly ended the marriage between oil and the zone system. That proposal centered not on naphtha but on gasoline and heating oil, to the consternation of politicians from the South and Southwest—including, ironically, Congressman Hale Boggs. The drama started with an oil-industry consultant who brought the zone concept to the governor of Maine, Kenneth M. Curtis. Seizing on what would be the first refinery in New England—on the northernmost coast of Maine, in a town named Machias—Curtis drummed up support by citing "discrimination" against New Englanders, since they underwrote a good chunk of the nation's petroleum consumption—9%—but suffered additional delivery costs in the absence of regional production.[63] (As Maine Senator Ed Muskie declared, "The New England area is a captive of the fuel companies of America.")[64] Eager to court Curtis was Occidental Petroleum, helmed by the notorious Dr. Armand Hammer, "former president of a Moscow pencil factory," protégé of Lenin, and East–West powerbroker.[65] Hammer had struck a deal to import Libyan crude. If the refinery was designated a subzone, then any output that was exported would be exempt from the oil quotas.

Mere miles from the Canadian border, Machias was as remote as Mayagüez or Peñuelas. But despite its neocolonial relationship to the cities where "the Secret Government of Oil" was now plotting its future, it was not an overseas territory.[66] It was part of the continental United States, and as a result the scheme for a foreign-trade zone at the edge of its deep-water harbor was treated as a bellwether.[67] Nationally, environmentalists rallied against the proposal, judging it a death certificate for "the beauty of the whole of a noble heartland in the last completely unspoiled forested section of the Maine coast."[68] Locally, the vacation set—led by the New Deal economist and "summer resident" Gardiner Means, a PRIDCO consultant—convened a committee that called for antipollution regulations, "to make sure that the gains outweigh the sacrifice and that the sacrifice is kept to a minimum."[69] The most heated response, though, flared up in the South and Southwest, where politicians railed against "cheap foreign oil, produced by cheap labor" and linked arms against threats to "national security."[70] Hale Boggs starred in this parade of patriotism, flying to Maine in October 1968 for the packed hearing on the FTZ application.[71] Newspapers characterized Boggs's "incoherent," drunken outbursts as jabs in a brawl between good-ol'-boy shills for Big Oil and "patrician" scions of a downwardly mobile region.[72]

It is hard to overstate the histrionics of the press coverage on Machias. Time and again, reporters and columnists harped on the "veritable hurricane of publicity" that swirled around the conflict.[73] They ranked it as "one of the most highly-charged debates in the recent history of the petroleum industry," often accentuating the contrast between the outsized reputations of the combatants and the paltriness of the battleground.[74] "Machiasport is a small coastal community in Maine, almost on the Canadian border," as one article teased. "In 1968 it became the biggest economic story in New England."[75] Understandably, much of the voyeurism focused on the turmoil in the oil industry. Charges of attempted bribing and backroom bartering left commentators gawking at "one of the last great feuds of the Johnson administration."[76] Still, quite a few writers also paused to wonder at the bit of bureaucratese that was causing all of the trouble: *foreign-trade zone*. None had ever heard the phrase. "Now, seemingly overnight, the foreign trade zone is front-page news and the Foreign Trade Zones Board—a quiet, three-man organization working long hours for years to keep the program going—has been swamped with activity," marveled the *New York Times*, with the kicker: "The once-quiet foreign trade zone has blossomed into a full-blown controversy."[77] Or, as Peter Greenough quipped in the *Boston Globe*, "Funny thing about foreign trade zones. They have plodded along for years somewhat anonymously and not always too successfully," he began. "Suddenly they are under fire from all sides."[78]

"Not only the petroleum industry," Greenough continued, "but steel people are incensed at the idea." Greenough was astute to highlight this parallel. The zone concept was catching on among producers of another basic commodity, steel, and it was rankling the old guard in the Midwest. The anxiety for Big Steel was the same as for Big Oil: the zone system imperiled the domestic market's (artificial) equilibrium, exposing it to dumping of low-cost imports. Actually, this fear was all the more acute for the steel barons, because, unlike the oil executives, who were bothered mainly by the Mandatory Oil Import Program, with some going so far as to say that they were agnostic about the zone concept and were opposed strictly to the oil quotas, the steel executives were worrying about tariffs and were targeting the zone concept in isolation. So while Big Oil played politics against the traitorous Occidental—triumphing after six months, as appointees of the newly sworn-in President Richard Nixon discreetly scuttled the Machias proposal—Big Steel went to court. The adversary was Equitable-Higgins, a New Orleans shipyard. To build river barges for a Japanese firm, Equitable was aiming to use Japanese steel and was seeking a subzone to avoid a 7.5% tariff. In late 1968, Armco, a steel corporation in the Ohio valley, filed suit to torpedo Equitable's application.

In this case, more striking than the hullabaloo around Japanese steel was the pretext for Armco's lawsuit: the illegitimacy of the subzone. Where the Machias affair was momentous for drawing back the curtain on the political economy of oil, the Armco dispute directed attention to the legality of the zone system's newly "flexible" framework. Sidestepping the larger quagmire of the steel tariff, Armco's lawyers argued that the FTZ Board had exceeded and violated congressional intent in devising the subzone, which they characterized as "a perversion, distortion and frustration of the FTZ Act."[79] Never, they asserted, had Congress envisioned that the FTZ Act would vest in local port authorities (here, the Board of Commissioners of the Port of New Orleans) the ability to shape US customs territory like a piece of Swiss cheese, carving out holes at random; the subzone was an egregious example of overreach. Armco lost, both at trial and on appeal, but not because the judges scoffed at this critique. While they found the subzone to be consistent with congressional intent, they also recognized the merits of Armco's beef. What ultimately guided them was less their take on the FTZ Act than their opinion that "important questions of national policy are for Congress to consider and determine, not the courts."[80]

"National policy" is a phrase to single out, to capture the full significance of this juncture in the strange career of the foreign-trade zone. What kind of national policy was at issue? Steel policy? Oil policy? Foreign policy? Domestic policy? The answer was in flux. When FDR signed the FTZ Act—"during the Depression," as reporters were wont to emphasize—he and politicians like Manny Celler praised the zone concept as a legacy of European merchant capital. Roosevelt, the ex-assistant secretary of the navy whose family hailed from the nation's greatest port city, agreed with Celler and others that the United States should aspire to be more of a seafaring nation, forging ties outward as much as inward, commanding the ocean's highways of commerce. Locally, a robust commitment to foreign trade would boost business on and around the docks; globally, it would keep the country engaged with other countries rather than insulated. Good zones made good neighbors. But by 1968, in the twilight of the American Century, this atavistic notion of a Hamburg on the Hudson was fading, overshadowed by the urban crisis. Trade policy was now urban policy.

And it is telling that it was not Detroit or Newark but a fishing village on the outskirts of New England that propelled this re-vision of the zone concept into the public eye. Increasingly, rural and urban were understood as symbiotically linked and as similarly vulnerable. Thus as Occidental campaigned for a subzone in Machias, it enlisted no economists or geographers to lecture on the windfalls to be reaped from reexport and transshipment. Instead, it hired the management-consulting firm Arthur Little—which boasted expertise from decades of collaboration with PRIDCO on luring investment to Puerto Rico—to frame it as a lifeboat for an Other America. Arthur D. Little designed a large-format pamphlet, for instance, that paired pages with statistics on income and population—laid out with ample white space in a crisp, sans serif font, on par with the most elegant of corporate annual reports—with pages that juxtaposed modernist maps of Maine and New England with black-and-white landscape photographs of a rotting wood shack and a rusting pickup truck (figs. 5.6 and 5.7). On the center of the first page was a quote from *The People Left Behind*, a report issued in 1967 by the president's National Advisory Commission on Rural Poverty. The message was stark. Occidental needed to rescue Machias. The elite media echoed this line, figuring Machias and its environs as "one of the worst pockets of poverty on the East Coast," an assessment that banked on an implicit comparison to more infamous, urban "pockets of poverty"—as a vice president of Occidental joked about these supporters of his company's bid, "About the only thing they haven't said about Machiasport is that it's going to be operated by Negro ghetto dropouts."[81] Or as an editor for the *Washington Post* wrote in early 1969, in the racist

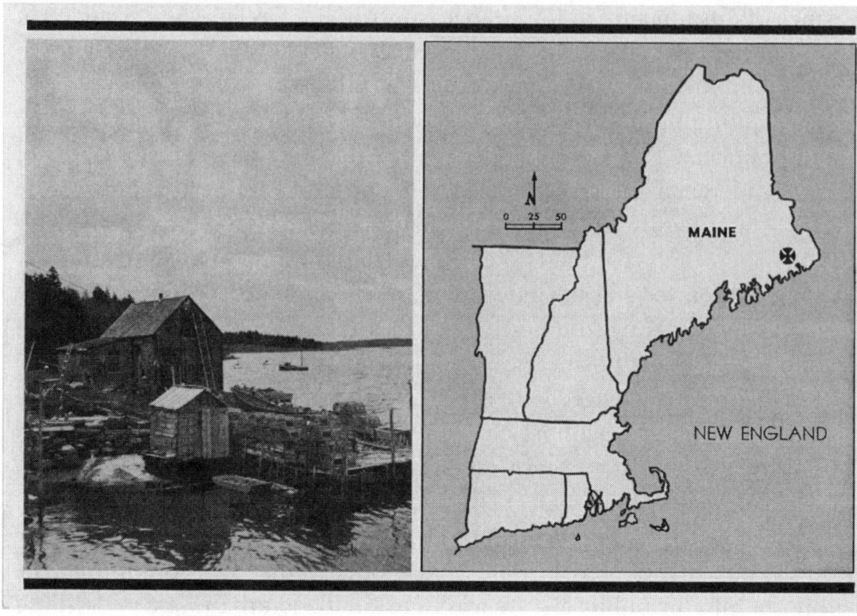

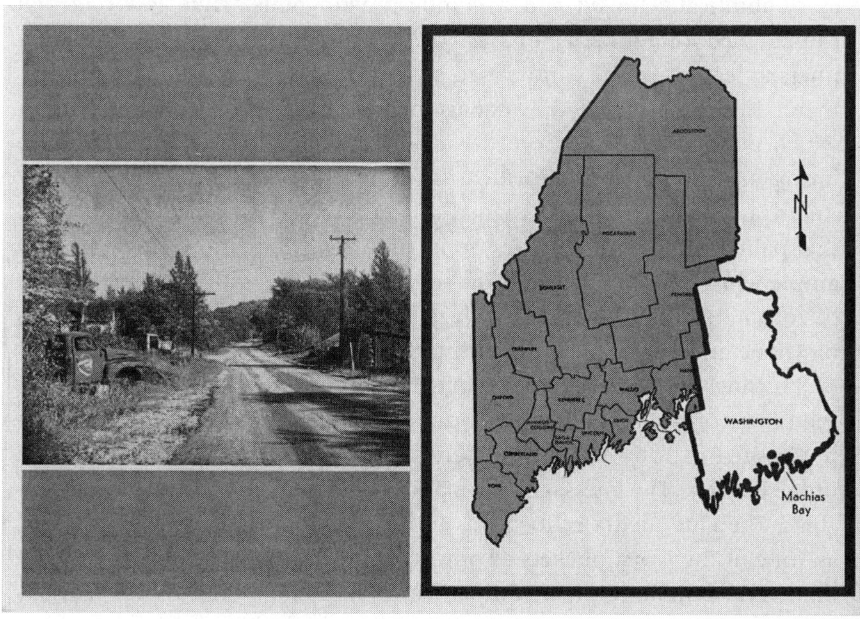

Figures 5.6 and 5.7. "Maine's Appalachia" is evoked in visual contrasts by Arthur D. Little on behalf of Occidental Petroleum and the governor of Maine in the pamphlet *Machias: An Industrial Project Proposal for Eastern Maine* (Maine Office Emergency Planning, 1968). FDR Library.

code of the North, poverty in Machias "is of a more genteel brand," "experienced silently, without protest or demonstration."[82] Pastoralism aside, this second description was apt. Machias residents were seeking aid, not plotting secession, and reportedly they gave no resistance to the incursion from Occidental, a corporation based in Los Angeles that was in cahoots with politicians based in Boston and Washington, DC; oil in "Maine's Appalachia" was the opposite of what oil was coming to mean in the decolonizing Third World, in nations like Libya.[83] For the destitute fishermen and their families, the subzone signified economic development not as an assertion of sovereignty but as—in the mocking appraisal of journalist Peter Greenough, a Mayflower descendant for whom a harbor was a scenic spot and not a livelihood—"a magical solution for unemployment."[84]

"A Reverse Marshall Plan for the South Bronx"

The phrase *economic development* was the rallying cry of the era, an era of secular stagnation, and it carried two meanings that collided in Machias. The first connoted a booster's efforts to entice capital to a frontier, to modernize it and help it "take off"—ergo all of those riverbanks of the mid-nineteenth century that Congress turned into ports of entry.[85] The second evoked the temporal counterpoint to such homesteading: it referred to an urban planner's struggles to resuscitate an "aging" city. Congressman Celler used this latter inflection when, in mid-1969, he prescribed the zone concept as a remedy for "blighted cities."[86] During the Depression, Celler had promoted the foreign-trade zone in a pioneering tone, for the benefit of an up-and-coming nation that was poised to grab a larger share of world commerce. Now that nation was ailing, and the best instrument to restore "healthy development" was the zone concept.

Often historians track how the urban crisis of the sixties and seventies unfolded in the context of broad theories and wide-ranging, multifaceted social policies: the underclass, the war on poverty. The zone concept gained prominence in that same conjuncture, but its delimited, molecular morphology set it apart. It was as much a "spatial product" as it was a policy or a program.[87] And so it invited replication, like more infamous feats of serial "revitalization"—shopping malls, convention centers.[88] Zone 1. Zone 2. Zone 3. Subzone 1A. Subzone 2A. Subzone 3A. This capacity for endless extension also meant that the zone concept enabled a way of seeing that articulated seemingly disparate spaces and scales of capital. Contemplating Subzone 7A in Peñuelas, Governor Hulett C. Smith of West Virginia declared, for example, "What's good for Puerto Rican poverty should work equally well in fighting the continental U.S. variety."[89] The foreign-trade zone mediated among "varieties" of poverty.

Applying for a zone and hanging a shingle was a first step, but then how was a zone operator to recruit tenants? Once upon a time, a state poached companies from other states, like Mississippi in the 1930s.[90] By the 1970s, the drill was to woo investors from beyond US borders. After decades of life support from the United States, Germany and Japan were on the rise as industrial powerhouses, and with the accelerating mobility of commodity capital in the age of the containership, combined with the devaluation of the dollar in 1973, the tides were turning, and the Other America was looking like a fertile field for foreign ventures. To enter this arena, governors and mayors fashioned themselves less as diplomats than as salesmen, innovating what would become a rite of passage for practitioners of local economic development: the trade mission.[91] Shunting aside the traditional rules of engagement, they ignored Washington, DC, and reached out on their own to foreign firms and governments, dangling the zone concept and similar perks. Virginia led the way, sending two delegations to Germany in the late sixties and stationing an employee of the Virginia Department of International Trade and Development in Brussels in 1969. "Such an expensive and bold move by a state agency," as a consultant later appraised it, wrote, was, arguably, expressive of the federalist structure of the US zone system.[92] It was eerie but not inaccurate or inappropriate when a governor enthused during a trade mission to Toronto in 1972 that "such a zone allows an area to operate practically like a country without a flag."[93]

Cities were even more cavalier than states, often in a spirit that was suggestive of a kind of nonaligned movement (fig. 5.8). In the face of the twin blows of capital flight and white flight, business-minded mayors from the darker cities found common cause with capitalists in the darker nations.[94] In 1977, African American officials in Camden—amid the downsized homes of Campbell Soup and RCA—initiated talks to become "the primary export-import base for products from Nigeria and the Ivory Coast of West Africa"; in 1979, an African American state senator from New York City called for "a reverse Marshall Plan for the South Bronx," traveling to Tokyo to pitch zone-based industrial parks for "labor-intensive manufacturing operations"; and in the early 1980s, Andrew Young, the first African American mayor of Atlanta, praised Zone 26 as he broke bread with foreign dignitaries abroad and at home, from Arab sheiks to Robert Mugabe of Zimbabwe: "The former United Nations ambassador, who has also led trade missions to the Caribbean and attended a recent trade conference in Tunisia, has stressed the importance of increased trade with less-developed

Figure 5.8. Hershey Richardson, president of local 858, the all-black local of the International Longshoremen's Association in Baltimore (local 829 was all white), greets the chairman of the Yokohama Chamber of Commerce during the three-week Maryland Far East Trade Mission to Japan. September 17, 1970, *The Sun*. Reprinted with permission from the Baltimore Sun Company.

nations. His message to former colonial nations, says deputy chief Atlanta administrative officer Henry Miller, is that rather than go through their former colonial capitals to trade with the U.S., they can deal with American cities such as Atlanta directly. 'This is a city that understands what the third world is trying to do,' Mr. Miller says."[95] In Atlanta—"Bandung, Georgia," we might shorthand this procapitalist postcolonial formation—the New South welcomed the Global South, with no hand-holding from Washington, DC.[96] The zone concept helped cities pursue do-it-yourself trade policies.

The only catch was that Zimbabwe and Tunisia were hardly prepared to engage with multiple venues across the Atlantic, which were themselves competing with one another. Much as "the Sultan of Atlanta" and other mayors linked arms and their staffs pooled resources in organizations like the National Council on Urban Economic Development—"a loose-knit group of like-minded big city development chiefs," founded in 1966—

the diplomacy among cities screened "an unchecked arms race," with the foreign-trade zone merely one item on a full menu of subsidies and tax breaks.[97] These "place wars" provoked studies of what came to be called the "growth machine." As the sociologist Harvey Molotch pointed out, elites shaped and wielded land "to gain the *preconditions* of growth"; as a result, the cabal of landowners and elected officials—the growth machine—was the "essence" of the city.[98] While both Molotch and David Harvey characterized this "boosterism" as a long-standing practice, Harvey further identified a seismic shift in the transition from Fordism to post-Fordism. Under "urban entrepreneurialism," speculation was trumping planning, and localities alone were absorbing the risks: every city was an island, a neo-Hanseatic *Kontor*, to their detriment.[99] Multinational corporations were the winners of this race run by cities, enjoying more rather than less mobility as a result of these attempts to root them in place. Zone 1, Zone 2, Zone 3—an atlas of public choice!

At this time, fittingly, an occupational sector was coalescing to broker leases between corporations and governments. By the mid-sixties, "site selection"—or, to borrow an insider locution, "industrial gamesmanship"—had emerged as a stand-alone profession.[100] (The atlas was a battle plan, and, for corporations, the goal was "site stockpiling.") In-house employees of corporations and governments were continuing to perform this labor of scouting, but now droves of Arthur D. Littles were on the scene as well (fig. 5.9). It was a gold rush, "one of the greatest growth industries of the nineteen-sixties," according to the *New York Times*: "An old hand in the development field could have as little as 10 years' experience, and the old days may be as recently as five years ago."[101] Legal expertise was of exceptional value, and two names came to stand out among the US zone crowd: Diamond and Miller. Walter Diamond, as he tells it in his modestly titled memoir *One of a Kind*, parlayed World War II–era stints with the Federal Reserve and at Bretton Woods into a role in dozens of zones onshore and offshore, aided by his wife, Dorothy, who cowrote his books and sat beside him in press photos, positioned below his shoulder. The Diamonds traveled far and wide to advise governments on the zone concept, and in 1973 the couple authored the first installment of what would become an annual compendium on tax havens.[102] Marshall V. Miller, a generation younger than the Diamonds, has left less of a paper trail but more of a legacy. In 1969, while a law student at the University of Virginia, Miller published an article about the US zone system. After graduating he helped to shepherd an application for a zone in his hometown of Kansas City, also cofounding, in 1972, the National Association of Foreign-Trade Zones.[103] Miller ex-

Figure 5.9. "George" and his forehead are at the ready in this advertisement for site-selection services from Burlington Northern—an echo of the importance of the railroad as a vehicle of capital flight and colonization in the nineteenth century. *Traffic Management*, October 1970.

emplifies the private-sector promoter of zones who has instigated them and who has mastered the intricacies of administering them but who has worked not a single day in governing them.

With such manpower propelling it, the US zone system started to motor. By the end of 1969, it was not much larger than in 1939, with nine zones. But by the end of 1979, fifty zones were open, and of those from the seventies, thirty-six—86%—dated to 1975 or later.[104] Suddenly the foreign-trade zone was a bona fide trend, and leading magazines were taking note, printing maps to illustrate how the zone concept was "sparking keen interest from California to Connecticut."[105] Commentators attributed this surge to the recession that peaked in 1974–75, as companies felt "the need for 'pinching pennies,'" as Marshall Miller said.[106] All the same, Miller and other zone boosters were careful not to oversell. FTZ Board chairman John Da Ponte elaborated, "'Don't look at the foreign-trade zone as a panacea, but as a symbolic feature, an indication that a community is trying to create a welcome for industry.'"[107] The foreign-trade zone was like aspirin—a pain reliever but not a cure. The true antidote for a stagnating city was a commitment to free enterprise. President Gerald R. Ford delivered this reminder when in 1975 he presided over a ribbon-cutting ceremony at the coronation of Zone 18 in San Jose, California. "On your own, with your own enterprise, your own initiative," Ford praised the zone's directors, "you have established an international business park that is expected to create millions and millions of dollars in new revenue for this area and provide as many as 12,000 jobs in the forthcoming years."[108] (Almost in recognition of the hot air inflating those numbers, newspapers dwelled on how Ford struggled with his scissors: "As about 750 business and civic leaders laughed lightly, Ford kept working the scissors until the stubborn tape was severed.")[109]

Although the idea of the subzone sparked curiosity during this period, few applications centered on it. Localities mentioned it as a perk—Chicago's private operator said to a reporter about the debut of Zone 22's general-purpose zone, "We could also add to this later and set up subtrade zones"—but virtually none filed for subzones right off the bat.[110] Instead, initially, applications called for industrial parks. Speculation was normalized, as cities like New Bedford, Massachusetts, advertised not for tenants but for real estate developers, ballyhooing the zone as if it were an attribute of the terrain, like a river or an interstate highway. This happened in all manner of locales. A seaport such as New Bedford could cite a history of foreign trade, but an interior city like Toledo, Ohio, could make an equally compelling case for the advantages of distributing via the St. Lawrence Seaway and the Great Lakes, given recent advances in containerization. In Toledo, the DeBartolos, shopping-mall magnates, spearheaded Zone 8 in 1960. Marveling at this promiscuous departure from FDR's original mandate of a zone on each coast, the *New York Times* concluded, "A new economic grouping, suggesting the Hanseatic League of the Middle Ages, is growing up among cities on the nation's 'fourth seacoast.'"[111] In 1979, the addition of an Indian reservation to the roster of zones—the Tohono O'odham Nation, in the desert of southern Arizona, near Tucson—was surely of greater gravitas on the question of territorial sovereignty, but it did not elicit the same analogy.[112]

The most hyped of these industrial parks of the seventies was Zone 15 in Kansas City. Inaugurated in 1973, it sparkled for a variety of reasons. It was the first general-purpose zone to consist of multiple sites, with two on the Missouri side and one on the Kansas side (so as not to corral tenants unnecessarily; as the zone's president noted, "Other FTZs are built like a zoo, with all the animals moving into the zoo if they want the benefits").[113] It was the brainchild of a group of businessmen, led by the law student Marshall V. Miller, who boasted—incorrectly—that it was the first zone to be privately run and to be liberated from government ineptitude (a warehousing company had nurtured the brief life of Zone 6 in San Antonio).[114] It was lauded as the second "inland" zone (it succeeded and soon outstripped Zone 14 in Little Rock, Arkansas, which had opened the previous year and was still awaiting tenants); "isolated in the vastness of the Farm Belt," it was a marker of Kansas City's maturation "from corn pone to cosmopolitan."[115] And it was characterized by an unmatched landscape, a "subterropolis": one of its three sites was "an underground industrial park" in a limestone cave. Spanning 2.8 million square feet, this annex offered "a unique cave-and-surface concept of material handling, manufacturing, display and distribution of international materials and products." Certainly no other zone could beat that tagline, nor the accompanying charges for roofing, flooring, heating, and air-conditioning: "zero."[116]

What was downplayed about these industrial parks was how much energy was drained in erecting them. Zone 26 in Atlanta, like its model, Zone 15 in Kansas City, took six years to come to fruition. Endless hurdles had to be jumped, by edict of the FTZ Board—from passage of enabling legislation at the state capitol to completion of a feasibility study to staffing, marketing, and so on. Delay was as much of a nuisance for Zone 26 as for Zone 15, even though Atlanta's was steered by an exemplary growth machine, a combination of private citizens and public authorities, rather than private citizens alone. Even the governor, George Busbee, known for his probusiness bent, barnstormed on behalf of the Georgia Chamber of Commerce's task force on foreign-trade zones. Busbee and company advocated for "the final piece of the puzzle to make Atlanta an international city," in defiance of the city's distance from the ocean.[117] "Satellites"—subzones—would follow, they vowed.[118] "Never mind the lack of a seaport," they assured reporters: "The key is highways."[119] Not to mention the international airport next door, as Congressman Newt Gingrich accentuated in a letter endorsing the zone.[120] Those six years paid off, then, as Zone 26 put Atlanta at the crossroads of commerce! Why else would El Salvador's military dictator, General Carlos Humberto Romero, have bothered to attend the dedication ceremony as its sole foreign dignitary? (Perhaps to provide "technical assistance": El Salvador's first export-processing zone had opened three years earlier, one of a spate of antirevolutionary zones in the "empire's workshop.")[121]

As for the "satellites" that were slated to orbit these industrial parks, they were under construction. The subzone was ascendant as the next big thing by the end of the decade. Five subzones were activated during the seventies, heralding a new receptivity for what the masterminds of Zone 1 on Staten Island in the thirties termed "border-line manufacturing." Only one of them had earmarks of the first generation of subzones: an oil refinery in Hawaii, which was authorized in 1970 with little fanfare, despite the brouhaha over Machias; because it supplied the US military with jet fuel, it was exempt from the oil quotas and therefore "largely free of controversy."[122] The other four, all of which opened between 1977 and 1979, focused not on refining but on assembling—not on separating a single commodity into multiple commodities but on combining multiple commodities into a single one. They also coincided with a recoding of the discourse of rescue, as the subzone, often as not, yielded not a new facility but a reborn old one, saving a community from a plant closure. Such was the justification for Subzone 24A, an Olivetti typewriter plant in Harrisburg, Pennsylvania (sited *ninety-two miles* from Zone 24 at the Wilkes-Barre / Scranton International Airport). As reported in *Nation's Business*, "The subzone exists for the sole purpose of keeping Olivetti in the typewriter assembly business in the United States, specifically at Harrisburg where it has 875 employees."[123]

The most renowned of these subzones of the seventies was in another corner of Pennsylvania. In 1977, Volkswagen became the first foreign automaker to mount its logo on a plant in the United States when it settled into a subzone in Westmoreland County, thirty-five miles south of Pittsburgh. Housed in an unfinished Chrysler plant, Subzone 33A—authorized at the same minute as Zone 33, near the Pittsburgh airport—enabled Volkswagen to pay a tariff of 2.6% on each finished Rabbit, Golf, and Jetta that rolled off the line and onto US customs territory, in lieu of tariffs of 6% and higher on imported components such as engines and transmissions. Volkswagen tapped Pennsylvania—not Buffalo or Cleveland—after "the greatest industrial courtship of all time," judged the *Wall Street Journal*.[124]

It was an uncommonly happy ending for the Rust Belt, a victory over "the growing muscle of the Sunbelt."[125] And in a broader frame, it was a rerouting of a circuit of capital. Three decades after the United States began sending funds to Germany, in aid and in investment, Germany sent funds back. There were murmurs about the geopolitical implications, but in the midst of stagflation, laid-off workers were relieved to see the abandoned plant be put to use: "Even if half of the plants in these zones are foreign owned, it is better to have them built in the United States than abroad because of the jobs they create, officials believe."[126] Money was money, whether a deutschmark or a dollar.

Part II. Offshore Onshore

"The Integrated Circuit"

When a growth machine in a city like Pittsburgh was unable to keep a manufacturer in town, where was that work headed? To the Sunbelt, yes, as a city like Phoenix beckoned with incentives, but, increasingly, to cities outside the United States.[127] I need to sketch this larger geography, variously known as "the global assembly line," "the new international division of labor," and, in a dialectical nod to a technology that both compelled and facilitated offshoring, "the integrated circuit."[128]

Two broad dynamics explain this realignment. One concerns the labor process. By the seventies, industrial production was breaking apart into tasks that were separable across oceans. If in Henry Ford's day a steering wheel was made hundreds of feet from a gear shaft, in Lee Iacocca's that distance might run into the thousands of miles. The deskilling that had fueled Fordism continued to power the domination of labor by capital, as these tasks became all the more simple and minute and their management all the more complex and elaborated, except that now a shipping container stood in for a lift truck—as capitalist production colonized the globe in the computer age, these social relations, as the geographer Doreen Massey theorized, "stretched across space."[129] Consequently, as three labor activists wrote in 1982, "The basic division of labor in the world-economy is increasingly not by product (*what* is produced) but by the degree of complexity of the production process."[130] The commodity maps of empire were being redrawn, as Honduras was now exporting underwear in addition to bananas, and South Korea was harvesting semiconductors rather than rice.

The other dynamic is the adoption of the zone concept by nations in the Global South. Export-processing zones (EPZs) purportedly gave "least developed countries" a shot at spurring employment and at transferring technological know-how from multinational corporations to local managers. These installations channeled the underwear and the semiconductors: they facilitated circulation, as in the entrepôts of yore, but now with the perk of intermediary enhancements. The first EPZ has been said to be the one at the Shannon Airport in Ireland that opened just before Zone 7 in Puerto Rico, but in retrospect it was more of a vanishing mediator than a wholly new spatial form, in that it was premised mainly on Ireland's position in transatlantic flight paths rather than wholly on its reserves of "cheap labor."[131] The true breakthrough happened in the US-controlled corridor of East Asia, in South Korea and Taiwan. Kaohsiung's EPZ was inaugurated in 1966, and it marked the arrival of the "labor-intensive" (translation: sweatshop) EPZ. From its gates the zone concept spread, on steroids: "Artificially inseminated and easily transplantable into any developing nation," reported the *Far Eastern Economic Review* in 1979, with a lurid photograph to match, "free trade zones have spread across the Third World like a test-tube baby boom." More than eighty EPZs had been "spawned" outside the United States and Europe since 1970.[132]

The midwife of these births is usually said to have been the United Nations Industrial Development Organization (UNIDO), but Americans unaffiliated with UNIDO were also present, in a variety of roles. Early on, leaders of the US zone system acted as tour guides for foreign envoys. Tom Lyons, the first director of the FTZ Board, demonstrated the alchemy of Brazil nuts at Zone 1, for example, to representatives from China.[133] In 1952, he hosted a six-week tour for a study group from the Organisation for European Economic Co-operation (OEEC).[134] Lyons also helped to conceive at least two zones, traveling to Panama and Liberia in 1946 and 1948, respectively.[135] (Panama's Colón Free Zone grew into a force in the Western Hemisphere as a distribution platform for US multinationals like Pfizer and Coca Cola: a French journalist memorably dubbed it "a sanitized concentration camp and commercial turntable for Latin America.")[136] Manny Celler, for his part, dispensed wisdom from Capitol Hill: in 1949, he wrote Indian ambassador Vijaya Lekahmi Pandit, enclosing a brochure and offering tips, and he corresponded with Israeli ambassador Eliahu Eilat about a zone in Haifa.[137] In the private sector, Walter Diamond served as a zone specialist in trips to, among others, Costa Rica in 1957, India in 1965, Iran in 1968, China in 1972, Guatemala in 1978, and the United Arab Emirates in the mid-1980s; his memoir is a hodgepodge of marvelous anecdotes, such as the revelation that authorities in Egypt implemented an IBM computer system at the Suez Free Zone that was originally built for Zone 35 in Philadelphia.[138] Overseas, the US State Department pushed the zone concept via embassies, as in East Pakistan.[139] Along with the US Army, which monitored political repression at EPZs as part of its counterinsurgency agenda, State kept tabs on the spread of EPZs, gathering data and filing reports.[140] And, needless to say, the private sector helped preach the gospel, in the guise of entities like the Egypt-US Business Council, whose "task force on free zones" was helmed by an executive of antiunion Texas Instruments.[141]

Stateside, these affinities with the wider world, and worldview, of EPZs were evident in personal relationships. A manager of Zone 15 in Kansas City, for instance, expressed his enthusiasm for how socialism had been stamped out in nations like Chile—which debuted a *zona franca* at Iquique in 1975—when he penned a fan letter to the conservative columnist William F. Buckley, bragging of his friendship with the military dictator Augusto Pinochet.[142] In more of an institutional sense, zone consultants migrated along the chain: Richard Bolin, the longest-serving president of the World Export Processing Zones Association, which was chartered at a meeting of UNIDO in 1978, gave input on Zone 7 in Puerto Rico on behalf of Arthur D. Little, and later issued newsletters about EPZs under the auspices of a nonprofit organization he founded, the Flagstaff Institute.[143] And sometimes such advisors themselves hailed from the Global South, such as Framroze Johangir Spencer, who graduated from Bombay University and worked for the Anglo-Iranian Oil Company in Abadan, Iran, before he hung a shingle in Houston, Texas, where he served as counsel to zones in the gulf states.[144]

In 1966, Spencer spent eight weeks in McAllen, Texas, conducting interviews for a three-hundred-page report for the FTZ Board on the suitability of a foreign-trade zone for the US-Mexico border.[145] If engineers like Spencer and Bolin embodied the transnational scope of American capitalism, then the industrial park that would open in McAllen—Zone 12—modeled it. Zone 12 was unique for being intended as a direct adjunct of a set of facilities outside the United States, anchoring a regional growth complex that fused but also transcended the territories of two nation-states. Paired with *maquiladoras* in Reynosa, Mexico, Zone 12 was a realization of the "twin plants" model: parts from Asia and elsewhere were shipped to and modified in McAllen, then trucked (via bonded carrier) twelve miles to Reynosa for assembly, and then either exported to Latin America or back to Zone 12, where they sat duty-free and temporarily stateless until they were imported into the United States, giving liquidity to manufacturers like Zenith Radio Corporation, which became a banner tenant of Zone 12 in 1978. As the sociologist Leslie Sklair wrote of Zone 12, "The zone works as a sort of geophysical credit card."[146] For all of its "geophysical" singularity, though, Zone 12 was no different from any other foreign-trade zone in its space-time mechanisms, or in its indebtedness to an urban growth machine. Businessmen in McAllen, recognizing opportunities in Mexico's *maquiladoras,* joined forces to crusade for Zone 12, shelling out their own funds to hire Spencer.[147] Their sacrifices were rewarded, and Zone 12's profile was elevated, when President Luis Echeverria of Mexico met with them in McAllen in a gesture of solidarity.[148]

Echeverria's visit was a sign of the tectonic changes under way along the border and a prequel of the earthquake to come for the US zone system. The initial tremors date to 1964, when Richard Bolin—now ensconced as general manager of Arthur D. Little of Mexico after his foray in Puerto Rico—started to plug the idea of "twin plants."[149] Enlisted by an urban growth machine in Ciudad Juárez, Bolin advocated for US corporations to provide employment in the north of Mexico, in the wake of the bracero program, which ended in 1964; officials in Mexico's Ministry of Industry and Commerce were willing to sign on to such a framework after one of them toured Hong Kong in 1965—the hope was to implement the zone concept to gain an edge over Hong Kong and Puerto Rico.[150] What these talks yielded was Mexico's Border Industrialization Program (BIP), which began in 1966 and was less a matter of zone-like bounded parcels than of a whole swath of territory under a regime of export processing. Cities from Tijuana to Matamoros were soon dotted with *maquiladoras,* a term that refers to the miller of corn or grain whom a farmer paid with a portion of the flour. "By analogy," as the historian Jefferson Cowie writes, "the Mexican plants assembled clothing and electronics for U.S. corporations and charged a fee in the form of wages in return for the service." Cowie cites a union leader in El Paso, Texas, who interpreted the BIP as "a Bracero Program in reverse": "Where we used to bring low-pay Mexican labor to our country," he said, "we now take the work to them."[151]

But this assessment does not consider the legal architecture of this milling of Mexican labor, which is an object of politics in itself. The very notion of a *maquiladora* demands our attention. Where did it come from? Which crises did it forestall? Which contradictions did it resolve?[152] These questions speak to the point that while the spatial form of the zone (if it is acknowledged at all) is often cast as a bureaucratic sideshow, to be skirted in hot pursuit of the headline act, it is, in reality, a sedimentation of decades of struggle.

Viewed in this light, the *maquiladoras* take on new valences, and we perceive how the BIP mirrored the US zone system. Mexico limited the BIP to assembling—prohibiting manufacturing—for the same reason that the US Congress did so with the US zone system during the New Deal: to shield domestic industry from low-cost imports. Legally, the *maquiladoras* were categorized as "in-bond" factories because—like US foreign-trade zones and their precedent, class 6 manufacturing bonded warehouses—they were cabined off from the rest of Mexican customs territory and thus required customs bonds to ward against fraud. And the keystone of the binational BIP was a provision of the US tariff schedule that likewise bore the imprint of Hamiltonian (or Listian) protectionism. Item 807.00 dictated that if components manufactured in the United States—say, TV antennae—were sent to another country for assembling into TVs, not for manufacturing in such a manner that they "lost their physical identity," then they could reenter the United States without incurring duties: in appraisals of the TVs, the value of the assembling labor would be dutiable, but not the value of the American-made components.[153] For a customs officer to carve a TV as if it were a hog was preposterous, but no more so than for a politician to gerrymander a voting district. The aim of 807.00 was to inject American-made components into foreign-made products. Far better that at least some portion of the foreign-label TV was manufactured by American workers, the thinking went, than none whatsoever.

While 807.00's language about assembling was "vague," as Cowie comments, it was also quite standard, in the long tradition of tariff law in the United States and abroad.[154] Distinguishing "assembling" (and "refining" and "manipulating" and all of those other gerunds that preoccupied operators of foreign-trade zones before 1950) from "manufacturing" was a way of hierarchizing labor. Tariff law policed those distinctions, enforcing the supposed naturalness of Ricardian comparative advantage, or what David Harvey derides as "the geography of 'common sense'"—Mexicans assembled, Americans manufactured.[155] Overall, therefore, the keyword *assembling* hints at the family resemblance between the BIP and the US zone system. Tellingly, officials at the US State Department had no doubt about this affinity: "The Mexicans in effect have made a Foreign Trade Zone out of the entire frontier area," one wrote in 1968. "They operate it in much the same way we operate foreign trade zones in a number of U.S. ports."[156]

The State Department was weighing in not only because of its general interest in trade and in transnational phenomena like EPZs but also because the BIP, in particular, was on the White House's radar. In the spring of 1966, President Johnson held formal talks about it with his counterpart in Mexico, President Díaz Ordaz, and later that year his ambassador to

Mexico floated a blueprint for how the United States might support it with "bi-national industrial free zone industrial parks." This tongue twister is fascinating for how it ratcheted up Richard Bolin's "twin plants." Whereas Bolin bridged the customs border with shared management (one corporation occupying two plants a short distance apart), this model submerged it with shared jurisdiction:

> Each park would be bisected by the international boundary line and the whole area surrounded by a fence.
> All ordinary jurisdiction continues as before on the respective sides: police, tax, labor, etc. The sole difference is that *customs jurisdiction* is withdrawn, so that each half is a free trade zone. This means that goods may enter free of all customs duty, quotas, or licenses.
> The operations would consist of twin plants in which the Mexican side would specialize in labor-intensive operations, such as assembly of electronic equipment or sewing of clothing from parts produced in the U.S.
> The U.S. would specialize in the more technological operations, such as quality control, finishing, maintenance of machinery, etc.[157]

This model never left the drawing board, but, in effect, it is what took shape at Zone 12 in McAllen. The White House (from Johnson to Nixon) did endorse Mexico's goals for border development; Mexico was needing to fill the gap left by the bracero program, and US corporations, aware of Hong Kong, were angling for that reserve army of "cheap labor." But the White House was treading carefully, because there were people to please on many fronts. Internationally, the White House needed to honor its "interdependence" with Mexico and to behave like a good neighbor and not hamper the BIP, lest Mexico "retaliate." Nationally, it needed to balance its cheerleading for corporate growth with its courting of labor unions. Regionally, it needed to heed the wishes of border merchants, who applauded the foot traffic that came with the *maquiladoras*: what was Sioux City's loss, when Zenith shut down in Iowa in 1978, was McAllen's gain.[158]

Of these disparate constituencies, labor unions proved the most nettlesome. The AFL-CIO lambasted the "shipping" of jobs "overseas"—although in this case the jobs were heading over the desert. Apart from inflaming a nativist critique of "cheap labor," the AFL-CIO was insisting on a kind of social contract between corporations and the communities that fed them, "a community responsibility" that extended beyond the walls of the plant. It was wrong—un-American—for corporations to split without paying the bill, as a leader of the Iowa Federation of Labor bellowed at a rally of the Zenith workers about to be laid off in Sioux City:

> If we have a democracy, and we participate in that democracy, then we have a right to change this society in the way that *we* want it to be run, not the way the private enterprisers want our ship to be run in this country. We have that right! And we have a right to say that that employer has a community responsibility, a responsibility that says that you don't go to the place where you can get the cheapest labor, or the best tax deal (and I'm not just classifying Zenith, because there's one hell of a lot of other employers that are doing the same thing that Zenith's doing, that they're doing to you here in the United States today), that when you invest in a community, it means to be a good citizen, it means to provide jobs for those people that live in that community.[159]

By the time of this gathering, in 1978, the AFL-CIO was deftly appropriating the rhetoric of urban entrepreneurialism and arguing that to "invest in a community" was to "invest in American workers." Long gone were the days of Roosevelt's "freedom from want"—by the age of "human capital," the social contract had been streamlined into a spreadsheet. And it was rife with fine print, with clauses and subclauses that confounded what you thought you had learned about foreign trade in high school. That's what had struck DeVier Pierson, advisor to President Johnson, when he pondered the BIP in 1968:

> With respect to the Mexican border situation, the real problem would seem to be that this U.S. investment in Mexico is for a questionable purpose—the export of virtually all of the products [from the *maquiladoras*] into the United States.
>
> This certainly isn't trade in the ordinary sense. Do we run a risk that more and more industries will leave this country to produce goods for export to the United States? If so, it is just going to be a matter of time before the AFL-CIO is firmly on the side of the protectionists.[160]

"Trade in the ordinary sense" this was not, and the AFL-CIO vehemently agreed. The AFL-CIO zeroed in on 807.00, calling for its repeal since it egged on "runaway plants." What pop out from the ensuing skirmish over 807.00 are the memoranda within the White House and the State Department, which reveal the significance of this moment for the very meaning of capital flight and not merely the morality of it. Cabinet officials dwelled on how they disagreed with labor activists about what constituted a "runaway" plant:

> "Runaway" plants have been seized on by the AFL-CIO as their main talking point in calling for Government action to prevent such transfers. The AFL-CIO has never offered any definition of what it means by "runaway" plants, but we are reasonably certain it is broader than the traditional one involving plants which close in one place and reopen in another to avoid union activity or high wages. We understand their idea of "runaways" includes, *inter alia,* plants which may eventually close in the United States after subsidiaries abroad have taken over former domestic operations. What the AFL-CIO really appears to be against, however, is U.S.-owned plants in the Mexican border area, by whatever name they may be called. Most of these plants are not "runaways" by any reasonable definition of that word.[161]

The White House wanted to restrict the epithet *runaway* to its Depression-era connotation, to the textile mill that ditched New England for the Piedmont of North Carolina, transferring every single piece of machinery. That was the thirties "runaway." The sixties "runaway" was a different phenomenon. It moved in stages. The White House understood, grudgingly, that the AFL-CIO thought of it as such, as a measured evacuation. The assembly line was not being repositioned; it was being elongated.

The diplomatic quandary for the White House, then, was how to respond to the AFL-CIO's accusations. For not only did the AFL-CIO have its definition of "runaway," but so too, presumably, did Mexico. Staffers at the State Department were inclined to extend an olive branch to the labor unions—publicly, at least—by issuing an antirunaway statement, or by asking Mexico to do so unilaterally, but they were wary of inadvertently heightening the tension. "A joint U.S.-Mexican statement of our common opposition to 'runaway' U.S. plants locating in the Mexican border area could lead to more trouble than it is worth. The AFL-CIO could ask us to explain the implicit definition of 'runaway plant' (or whatever other term we might use) and ask whether the Mexicans had the same understanding. Since our definition, the AFL-CIO's definition, and the Mexican definition will probably never coincide, an argument would not be helpful."[162] Ultimately, a milquetoast statement was prepared, phrased in basic terms to satisfy the masses. By referring to "runaways" without further elaboration, it would invoke the thirties definition, and thereby "would deal only with what the AFL-CIO *says* it is against, not what it is really against." It would have no teeth but would have "public relations value," to arm the AFL-CIO leadership to defend itself against its locals.[163] An empty gesture was the most that the State Department staffers could muster. The lesson here is that, as early as 1968, two decades before the "trade wars" of the eighties, offshoring was presumed an inevitability.

Once the "complaining" started to spill over into the pages of activist newsletters and academic journals, in the late seventies and early eighties, critics of offshoring attacked this type of caricature of the AFL-CIO by exposing how the work being done in EPZs was not "inside" other countries any more than it was "outside the United States." Indeed, for these writers—who were coming to regard the EPZ as a kind of metonym for the "global reach" of "late capitalism"—the EPZ in, for instance, Sri Lanka (a nation freed of the British Empire into the dominion of the World Bank), was neither outside nor inside; as the novelist and public intellectual A. Sivanandan quipped in 1980, the EPZ was "the colony within the new-colony," or as the economist Tsuchiya Takeo put it in 1978, "an alien territory within a national territory."[164]

Like the US foreign-trade zone, the EPZ was a space apart. In the former case this deviance tended to inspire little more than mild bemusement about the exotica of foreign trade, as in a blurb from New Orleans about "Japanese nationals" employed by Sears, "the Dock Board's single largest customer in the Foreign Trade Zone, that out-of-the-country territory at the foot of Napoleon Avenue" (fig. 5.10). In the latter case, however, it provoked investigations of superexploitation. The EPZ was in its own category because it was a space of lax regulations. Which is not to say it was lawless. To the contrary, it was held up as an island of "stability" in underdeveloped areas, thanks to its ties to authoritarian rule. In the Philippines, for example, where an EPZ was installed in Bataan in 1971, there was no doubt that the nation-state was the landlord. As Hong Kong's English-language *South China Morning Post* duly reported to its business-class readership, "Industries operating in the zone will receive better government attention than those set up elsewhere in the country."[165] After the Ford Motor Company opened a stamping plant in the EPZ in 1976, the military dictator Ferdinand Marcos liked to cite the new tenant as proof that his imposition of martial law in 1972 was key for "the investment climate needed to bring in foreign manufacturers and help his country prosper."[166] This firm grip was instrumental both in outfitting the EPZ with supplies—water, electricity, roads—and in keeping workers in line. By presidential decree, unions were banned and wages were well below the minimum in Manila. "With a largely single and female labor force housed in crowded barracks and paid at the rate of less than a dollar a day," Filipino academic and activist

Figure 5.10. The choice of this photograph of "Japanese nationals" to accompany a short article on the activity of Sears in Zone 2 is best framed by the global assembly line, images of which were dotting US newspapers and magazines at this time. "Trade Zone Fix-It," *Times-Picayune,* April 20, 1975. Reprinted with permission from the New Orleans Media Group.

Walden Bello concluded in 1981, "working conditions in the zone are straight out of the late 18th century."[167]

Bataan was extreme but by no means exceptional. Throughout the Global South, the EPZ was packaged as a bonanza of "cheap labor," and far more so than in the United States. Although the desperation of unskilled workers in places like Atlanta was a facet of the sales pitch for the US foreign-trade zone, it was never the unadulterated shark bait that it was for the EPZ. "Cheap labor," far and above enticements such as tax breaks and even land grants and other subsidies, underwrote the EPZ. "More blatant than these incentives is the way that governments seek to sell their own people in order to woo foreign capital," explained the journal *Race and Class* in 1980. "In the hands of the promoters of [EPZs] and the copywriters for glossy investment brochures, the labor itself is a commodity to be traded in non-human and purely commercial terms."[168] This flagrant dehumanization of labor was so endemic to the cultural and political economy of the EPZ that one of the most popular hieroglyphics for global capitalism in leftist writing of the eighties was the barbed-wire fence that caged the labor (fig. 5.11).[169]

The fence invited two opposing ways to construe the mess of wires that linked up the world system of zones by 1980, from Kansas City to Kaohsiung. Observers based in business schools and writing for and from the standpoint of capital crowed about the advent of an unprecedented trend in foreign trade, "neither 'export' nor 'import' in the traditional sense," as Peter Drucker laid it out in 1977: "production sharing."[170] Drucker, a conservative Austrian émigré and a darling of modern management theory, is storied for scolding business executives in 1962 that they ignored the

Figure 5.11. During the Reagan era, activists saw parallels between the camp and the zone via the fence. This photograph is uncaptioned in the essay where I found it, and it would seem to show a zone, given the quote below. But it is itself a reproduction of a contemporaneous photograph from *Caribbean Review*, and that photograph is of a Haitian refugee in a detention camp in Florida. The essay concludes, "We are facing the *implosion of Empire*—the beginning of an era in which the people of the United States will begin to see the democratic veils stripped away from the face of American power; they will begin to experience what has been the fate of the colony. The precise forms of this repression we cannot predict; but certainly the image of barbed wire fences around urban enterprise zones, such as have accompanied their Third World models—a kind of South Africanization of the United States—is a vision of the future which we would dismiss at our peril." Marlene Dixon, Susanne Jonas, and Ed McCaughan, "Reindustrialization and the Transnational Labor Force in the United States Today," *Contemporary Marxism* no. 5 (Summer 1982).

mysteries and exigencies of the distribution sector at their peril. "We know little more about distribution today than Napoleon's contemporaries knew about the interior of Africa," he warned in *Fortune*.[171] For Drucker, the twin plants model and the reassembly of the assembly line added up to "economic integration by stages of the production process." Now that corporations were finally taking seriously the possibilities of distribution, and now that "population dynamics" were generating "enormous and rapidly growing labor surpluses," capitalism was unifying the planet. Drucker perceived in the fence the "trade links" that politicians toasted to at Zone 4 in Los Angeles in 1949 (fig. 4.7). Rather than engaging in one-off exchanges of goods, nations were coming to rely on each other to facilitate transnational supply chains (albeit with everyone and everything in its place—some did the "technical" work, as Drucker wrote in 1962, and some did the "donkey work.")

Against the bonhomie of Drucker's accent on "integration," the new social scientists of labor and capital, many of them shaped by decolonization and still carrying the torch of Marxism into the long 1970s, saw a less sanguine theme in the trope of the fence: fragmentation. By their lights, it was not the links in the chain but the barbs on the wire that best described the new world order: the zone concept was the grounding of a new enclosure. Thus the authors of *The New International Division of Labor* detected in the EPZ fence the apotheosis of how the zone entrenched segregation. "The screening off of the free production zones from their surrounding underdeveloped environment, which is nonetheless the source of their labor-force," they wrote, "and their physical encirclement with fences and sometimes watch-towers—initially for customs' purposes but also for the control of employees—visibly reveals the enclave nature of the zones."[172] Unevenness, asymmetry—the EPZ fence, as the journalists Annette Fuentes and Barbara Ehrenreich deciphered it in 1981—meant "more freedom for business and less freedom for people."[173]

These divergent decodings of the fence were suggestive of how people wrestled with the legacy of the zone concept by the eighties. The challenge was to reconcile integration with fragmentation, for, literally and figuratively, both forces were at work. The fencing broke up and even obstructed flows of bodies and things, but at the same time, as in Frank Gehry's house in California or in his office for the Toyota parts warehouse in Maryland, it coordinated a larger whole. The task was to grasp the connections among those disconnections. If the US foreign-trade zone was not a clone of the EPZ, what was it? And was it the exception or the rule?

"Nissan in Tennessee"

During the eighties, the US zone system came under fire like never before, reproved for privileging one sector of that mythic entity the *national economy* over another. Appropriately, while the first explosion over the zone concept involved oil, two decades later—in the wake of the oil crisis—this latest round of attacks targeted oil guzzlers. Cars revved up idling disagreements about what it meant to "create" jobs and for a federal agency to collaborate with cities and states to do so.

Cars had traveled through the US zone system since the early sixties. Initially, zone operators tried to garage them. American demand for foreign sedans had jumped up during the fifties, in the luxury market, and so the managers of Zone 1 on Staten Island and Zone 2 in New Orleans had hustled to sell the foreign-trade zone as stateside duty-free storage for dealers of Mercedes Benzes and Fiats and the like (fig. 5.12). They reported minimal success: "Orders are piling up ten months ahead of deliveries with

Figure 5.12. In the context of the American Century, a line of Mercedes in a foreign-trade zone was no cause for alarm. *Times-Picayune*, September 23, 1963. Reprinted with permission from the New Orleans Media Group.

the result that as fast as the little things are unloaded from a steamer, a dealer is waiting at the head of the pier with delivery papers in his hands," the proprietor of Zone 1 wrote to a friend at the Commerce Department. "He pours some gas and drives it away. There is no need for storage."[174] Then, in 1963, a more lucrative opportunity presented itself, as Volkswagen shipped trucks to foreign-trade zones for conversion into "vacation campers." Workers employed by zone operators in Seattle and Toledo—that is, warehouse workers, not factory workers, to underline the blurring of the two categories—fabricated Volkswagen campmobiles "by cutting metal sections from side panels for window openings and installing domestic windows, flooring, wood paneling, cushions, ice chests, curtains, mirrors, coat hangers, etc." (fig. 5.13).[175]

These overhauls happened in general-purpose zones. Subzones became attractive to foreign automakers only in the late seventies, such as when Volkswagen bought the Chrysler plant near Pittsburgh to launch Subzone 33A. A few changes in global capitalism emboldened foreign automakers to set up shop in America. One was a shift in consumer preferences: the oil crisis was raising demand for small cars, and small cars were foreign cars, because Detroit was asleep at the wheel. Another, relatedly, was protectionism: as Henry Ford well understood in the 1920s, the best way around the tariff wall was the road to the branch plant, especially if—as for Ford in Barcelona—that plant was located in a free zone, into which parts and equipment could be imported duty-free. (What upped the ante in this regard was "the ability to label products assembled in a zone 'Made in U.S.A.,' even though the products are mostly or entirely of foreign origin.")[176] Most weighty, judging from media commentary, was the devaluation of the dollar. Nixon's break with the Bretton Woods system in 1971 primed the pump for "the new competitive position of American labor," relative to wages in Europe and Japan: by the late seventies, "American labor" equaled "cheap labor."[177]

Basically, by the late seventies, it was a no-brainer that foreign automakers should produce in the United States, and in subzones. As they migrated, every single one of them obtained authorization for a subzone: in 1977, Volkswagen in Pittsburgh in Subzone 33; in 1979, Honda in Cincinnati in Subzone 46B; in 1980, Kawasaki in Lincoln, Nebraska, in Subzone 59A; in 1982, Nissan in Nashville, Tennessee, in Subzone 78A; in 1983, Toyota in Long Beach, California, in Subzone 50A. And there were ripple effects for general-purpose zones. Those on the coasts at last drew the warehousing business that zone operators had bet on in the fifties. At the Port of Long Beach, Zone 50 thrived as "auto processors" filled the shoes of

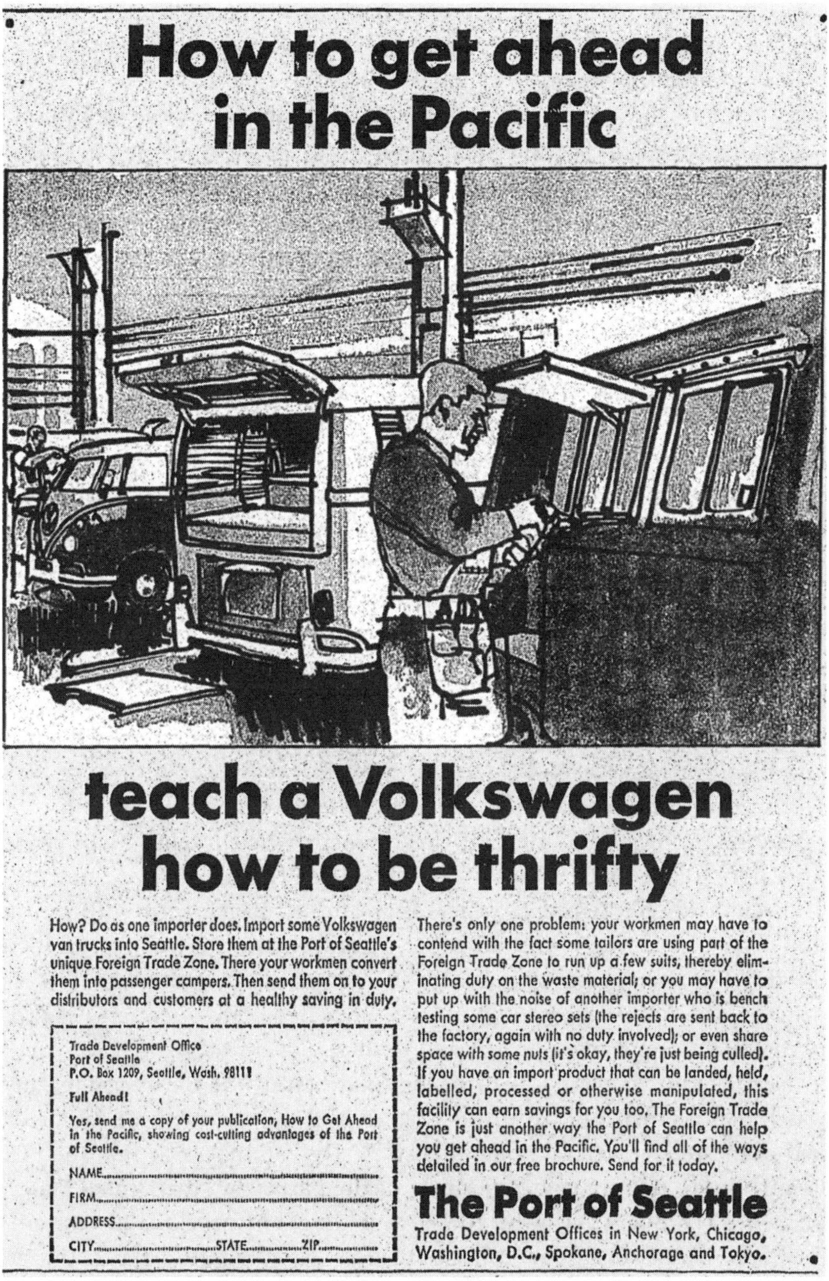

Figure 5.13. Advertisement from the Port of Seattle in *South China Morning Post,* October 29, 1969. Courtesy of the Port of Seattle.

stevedores (evacuated by containerization), servicing rows upon rows of Japanese imports with "tasks ranging from polishing and painting the vehicles to fine-tuning them."[178]

At each of these sites, it must be said, the subzone status was the icing on the cake. Foreign automakers wanted to be in a subzone, but none would have been content with the subzone à la carte; they expected a full serving of incentives. "Tax breaks, cut-rate loans, specially trained workers, new roads—all are in the bags of pitchmen trying to 'sell' California, Pennsylvania, New York and most other states to increasingly receptive Japanese automakers," reported the *Los Angeles Times* in 1978.[179] Administrators at the FTZ Board candidly conceded this calculus, in a departure from the grandiosity of forecasts in the forties and early fifties. Director John Da Ponte admitted that the economic benefits of foreign-trade zones "'probably aren't enough to stimulate new imports but may be enough to encourage companies to do work in the United States that would otherwise be done overseas.'"[180] Here Da Ponte unwittingly gives us insight into what was beginning to be understood as "job creation" in the sphere of industry: the clue is in the adverb *otherwise*. These were not new jobs; they were other people's jobs. And while Da Ponte spoke of the national economy, the reality was that the subzone mattered most in a kind of arbitrage between specific locales, all within the United States. "People are trying to use zones to promote every backwater town," zone boosters were lamenting by the late seventies. The race was on.[181]

There was one tweak to the zone concept that enhanced its worth considerably, however, and right at the moment when foreign automakers were poring over maps of North America. The FTZ Board altered how duties were assessed. Before, if a car was assembled in the zone with car radios from Taiwan and with all other parts from the United States, then the duty—a percentage—was based on the total cost of the car. Now, as of 1980, the duty was based on just the imported component and "a proportionate amount of the profit and domestic overhead and labor costs": if the car radio was one-fiftieth of the total cost of the car, then the duty was levied against the cost of the car radio plus one-fiftieth of the profit and domestic overhead and labor costs.[182] The rationale was that the FTZ Board should not encourage taxation of the parts from the United States, or, as the FTZ Board was wont to say, in the argot of neoclassical economics, of the "value added" by "American labor." For all its arcane and stultifying technicality, this revision was amazing for amounting to a rare—even downright verboten, in the Reagan era—acknowledgment that value was yoked to labor. And by removing duties on the price of work performed in the subzone, it rendered American labor all the more "cheap" within the context of the global factory.

This casts light on the historical geography of how the foreign automakers took up residence in the United States. Except for a brief and ill-fated foray in California, where Toyota attempted a partnership with General Motors, all of the new corporate citizens went to the South or adjacent to it, to subzones in—or, in and not in—states with laws and lawmakers hostile to unions. In the first few years: Ohio, Nebraska, Tennessee. In subsequent years: Kentucky, Alabama, Mississippi, Georgia, South Carolina. What is more, the foreign automakers were arriving at a time when the United Auto Workers (UAW) was already very much on the defensive, hobbled by the Big Three's decentralization from Detroit, a strategy crafted to dull the collective impact of strikes and protests at individual plants.[183] Given this disfranchisement of American labor, and global factors such as the tariff wall and the weak dollar, foreign automakers could forgo the EPZ and its draconian curtailment of workers' rights and instead settle among the ex-Confederates.[184]

To wit, Tennessee won the cheap-labor lottery in 1981 when Nissan selected farmland outside of Nashville for its first plant in the United States. Tennessee duked it out with Georgia for the coveted contract, marshaling a $315 million industrial bond at the county level to secure what was at the time "the largest single investment ever made in the United States by a Japanese firm."[185] Applications were filed forthwith for a general-purpose zone in Nashville and a subzone in Smyrna, to cover the importation of "engines, transmissions, drive trains, steering and electrical systems, instrumentation, suspensions, wheels, tires, chassis, body parts, and metal products," or approximately 60% of the materials in the plant's slated product, the Nissan truck.[186] Made in America (on paper if not on customs territory), the Nissan truck was made up of parts made elsewhere, otherwise. You could call it the original hybrid.

Governor Lamar Alexander led Tennessee's delegation, and he rhapsodized about new beginnings and interracial unions. "In April and May our dogwoods bloom at the same time your cherry trees bloom," he fawned to his Japanese counterparts at the groundbreaking ceremony.[187] Turning to spectators from closer to home, he waxed sentimental about the Hillbilly Highway. "Twenty years ago," he reflected, "Mel Tillis wrote a great country song, 'Detroit City,' about the thousands of Southerners who had to leave home to find jobs in the assembly plants and factories of the North. Now, thanks to Nissan, many members of the present generation can stay here and get those high-paying jobs, and some of the ones who had to go away before can come back home.'"[188] Nissan reciprocated the warm welcome later that year when it published a coffee-table book that documented this atmosphere of fellowship and harmony in full color. *Nissan in Tennessee* was a 127-page testament to, in the words of the cultural theorist Leslie Bow, "triumphant transnational corporate cooperation."[189]

The text was composed by John Egerton, an improbable author of blue-chip propaganda. Raised in Kentucky, Egerton was a white liberal in the mold of writers like William Styron and Lillian Smith. As a journalist, he tackled the cultural politics of racial formations in the South, problematizing the South as much as explicating it. This antiessentialist sensibility informed his ode to his homeland, *The Americanization of Dixie: The Southernization of America*, published in 1974 amid the fallout of the Second Reconstruction. Egerton's prophetic title gestured to the history of the South as a nation within a nation (or a colony within a nation, according to one strain of southern thought), not to the future of the South as a node of the Global South. Yet it was that future that had landed him the gig for Nissan. And so Egerton found himself in a pickle: how to bear witness to the traumas of racial capitalism and still get paid? He did testify to some extent. "A sprawling cotton plantation had flourished here long before the Civil War," he set the scene, circling back to the poetry of "plantation soil" when he recounted how a thousand demonstrators stormed the groundbreaking to chastise Nissan for contracting with a nonunion construction firm.[190]

But the sleek photography glossed over the main story. Like other Japanese industrial firms, Nissan adhered to "jointism," a team-centered approach to management and a refreshing break from the rigidities of Fordism, or so it seemed. Tennesseans clamored for the team uniforms: 2,000 out of 130,000 applicants counted themselves the lucky few. Referred to as "technicians," these recruits were expected to feel honored for the recognition and for the opportunity to contribute to what was billed as a joint endeavor. Throughout the plant, they were clustered into groups with shared tasks, as in the open floor plan of Frank Gehry's Toyota offices. Egerton dutifully praised this workplace culture as a leveling of hierarchy. "The company strived to eliminate the traditional barriers between management and labor," he wrote, alongside photographs of Americans and Japanese tinkering side by side, eating sushi together, "no time clocks to punch, no executive dining rooms in the plant, no reserved parking spaces" (fig. 5.14).[191] Labor activists, however, had a dissenting take—not labor activists involved with a union at the plant, because there was no union. Word spread via magazines like *Labor Notes*. Exposés detailed how "jointism" resulted in heightened, not diminished, stress: "technicians" were worked to the bone,

A coming-out party in trim and chassis for Nissan's first trial-run truck, February 1983

In February, the company announced that these first trucks for consumers would roll off the assembly line two months ahead of schedule An exact date—June 16, 1983—was targeted

"We're ahead of schedule," said Jerry Benefield, vice president for manufacturing, "because all of our people have done such a good job of building the plants, equipping them, supplying them with parts, and training the technicians. We're ready to make trucks equal to or better than the ones made by Nissan in Japan."

In its first few months of production, NMMC would be making trucks at a gradually accelerating pace calculated to reach 10,000 units a month by mid-1984. That number, or 120,000 a year, would represent full production capacity for one shift. Beyond that, additional shifts or expansion of the facility could be accomplished as demand for vehicles dictated.

By the June 16 launch date—863 days after the groundbreaking—Nissan would have spent $660 million

Dennis Little with Mike Kotake and Tom J. Satoh in Japan (left) and with Hidemasa Koga in the NMMC paint plant (below)

Dennis Little *came to Nissan with unusual qualifications. A native of upstate New York, he spent four years with the army in Japan, where he gained a working knowledge of the language, a Japanese wife, and a degree from Sophia University in Tokyo. Back in this country, he picked up a master's in public administration at Western Kentucky University and then went into industry. In November 1980, he heard about Nissan's plans in Smyrna:*

They didn't even have an office in Tennessee then, and I had to get a friend in Japan to find out where I could apply. They hired me as a recruiter in August 1981, but three months later I switched to training. That was the start of a whole new career for me. In Japan I served as a team leader and guide for NMMC trainees, and I also worked under Hidemasa Koga, a master *sensei* (mentor), to learn about dry sanding and body repair techniques in the paint plant. Mr. Koga is on the launch assistance team here with us now, helping me and the other supervisors in the paint plant to prepare our technicians for full production.

This is not a regular type of industrial corporation. There's much more latitude for individual contributions, more room to grow. Strong personal relationships are developing, and everybody takes a genuine pride in the quality of the product. It makes you want to see this thing fly—not only for the company's sake, but for the people involved. We're bringing three cultures together here—Tennessee, Japan, and the American automotive industry. It's very satisfying to see people learn to appreciate the best qualities of all three.

Figure 5.14. A page from a tribute to "jointism." John Egerton, *Nissan in Tennessee* (Smyrna, TN: Nissan Motor Manufacturing Corporation, 1983).

pushed at a tempo they likened to "8-hour aerobics."[192] The injuries they sustained from "jointism" gave tangible proof that it was as brutalizing in practice as it was egalitarian in principle.

"Jointism" inhabited the spatial form of the subzone, but not exclusively so. It flourished in Japan in the absence of a zone system. What was more of a direct outgrowth of Subzone 78A was the plant's security setup. From day one, foreign-trade zones were hyperpoliced because of requirements in the FTZ Act to ward against smuggling—ergo the barbed-wire fence, the customs guards. As the subzone rose to dominance, though, these requirements became less costly for zone operators and more onerous for zone workers. In 1986, the FTZ Board stopped forcing zone operators to reimburse the Treasury Department for on-site customs officials and instead instituted a regimen of periodic audits, facilitated by software. As a result, computers substituted for customs guards, and security was enacted through electric eyes that tracked workers' handling of each and every object. "It's like being inside a customs area in any international airport," Nissan's czar of "safety, medical and security" explained. He commended the "added benefits" of compliance with the FTZ Board's regulations; the strictures of the zone concept lent the plant "an atmosphere of federal law enforcement" to which he attributed "the low percentage of employee theft at Nissan" and "little trouble with drugs in the workplace."[193] While Nissan's "technicians" were not sleeping in bunkers or walking to work from nearby shantytowns, as was often true in the social landscape of the EPZ, they were enduring a comparable degree of surveillance.

Beyond critiquing the labor conditions of subzones, labor activists also pressed the question of how exactly subzones factored into the US economy writ large. Behind all of the hoopla over the jobs that came with the proliferation of subzones, a counternarrative was gaining credence. Rejecting what they regarded as a mythology of "job creation," labor activists were starting to argue that policy makers needed to think holistically. They measured the zone system in terms of supply chains rather than individual plants: trade policy that strengthened one segment of a chain, they theorized, often strained another segment. "There are those who suggest that the job benefits are illusory," wrote a reporter in 1982, "that jobs created inside the zones mean jobs lost elsewhere in the nation."[194] By the early eighties, labor activists saw a zero-sum equation in zone math, not a chart of infinite growth.

They were joined in their pessimism by a cranky contingent from the auto industry. Auto-parts companies were on the wrong side of the foreign-trade zone. Their problem was the inverse of what they faced in the 807 framework, where auto parts and TV parts and so forth were fabricated in the United States, assembled into autos and TVs outside the United States, and then brought back into the United States with duties waived on the value of the foreign labor. With the foreign-trade zone, auto parts and TV parts were fabricated offshore and then assembled into autos and TVs back onshore (or, again, technically, offshore onshore, in that the cars and TVs were assembled in subzones and then "imported" onto US customs territory). With 807, parts makers came out ahead; with the foreign-trade zone, they fell behind. And so as they decried the zone concept, they discredited the type of employment it privileged, too. This was not the muscular labor of the Fordist factory; this was the emasculated labor of the EPZ. Castigating auto-assembly plants as "screwdriver plants," they set the tone for jokes about the Gen-X guy who fumbled with an Allen wrench to construct an IKEA bookcase.[195]

Revealingly, the rejoinder to parts makers was phrased defensively, in a spirit of lesser-evilism more than Hamiltonianism: "If they buy car radios from Korea," went the reply from zone boosters, "isn't that better than producing whole cars in Korea?"[196] For that was the bind: you could influence whether "they" acquired car parts offshore or made whole cars offshore, but you could not keep them onshore altogether. "Manufacturing" had come to mean fabricating and assembling along global supply chains: production was internationalized and subordinated to circulation. While producerism in the nineteenth-century sense was salvageable in clusters of small-batch, specialty manufacturing (as in post-2008 firms capitalizing on nostalgia for artisanal labor, like Shinola in Detroit), mass production was a world system. This was the crux of how the eighties contrasted with the sixties in arguments about the zone concept. During the fight over Occidental's bid for Machias, a rhetoric of foreign/domestic was still conceivable, even if Big Oil had holdings in other countries; companies like Texaco and Gulf Oil still drilled in the United States, albeit less than the general public realized. Now, however, it was disingenuous for the Ford Motor Company to fret about threats from "foreign" imports. Who were "they," sourcing radios from Korea? "They" were Ford! Ford was a multinational corporation! "There's no such thing as a domestic industry. There's no such thing as a domestic market," as an executive for General Motors opined in 1980. "There's an international market and an international set of manufacturers."[197] By the eighties, therefore, the binary had shifted from foreign/domestic to parts/wholes, and the question was, in whose favor would the nation-state try to resolve capitalism's contradictions? The American parts maker, or the American assembler?

The American assembler prevailed, largely by deflecting this spat onto an interloper: the Japanese assembler. The "transplants," as the foreign multinationals with US assembly plants were known, caught most of the flak from the American parts makers. Granted, Japanese companies like Nissan were relying on a high percentage of imported parts. "They come in and establish what amounts to colonies in the United States with their own suppliers," accused Congresswoman Marcy Kaptur.[198] Some even in effect camouflaged parts as American-made, as a vice president of the Ohio-based Champion Spark Plug Company insinuated to the director of the FTZ Board in 1984, in protest of Nissan's application to expand its operations at Subzone 78A: "Many of their *so-called* domestic suppliers are actually Japanese-owned 'little sister' companies who put up plants here when existing U.S. production facilities are under-utilized."[199] But the old specter of "Asiatic" capital also made for an easy target, framed somewhat opposite

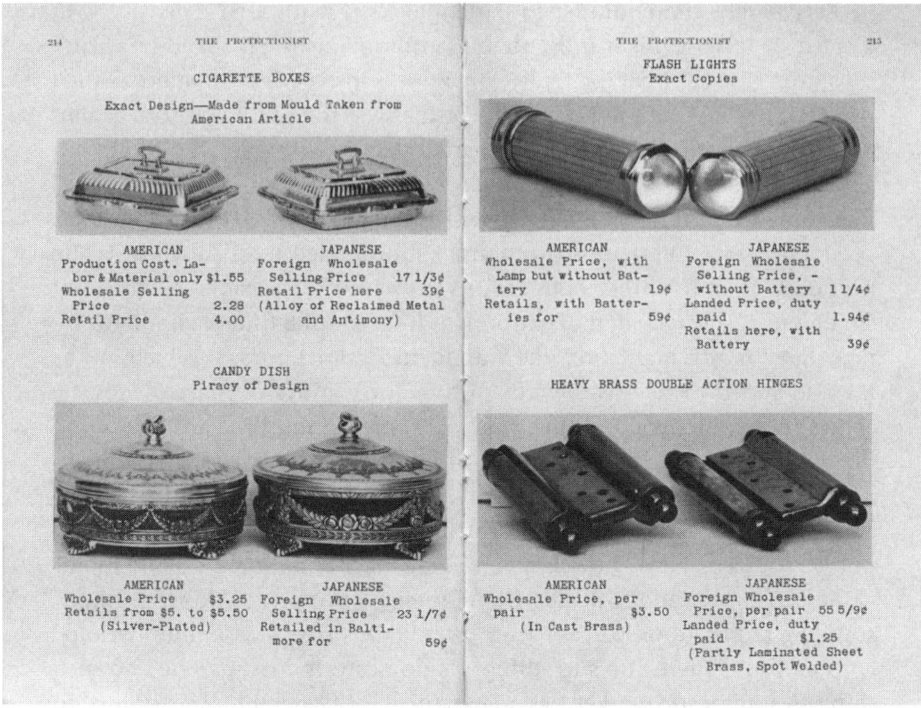

Figure 5.15. Following the passage of the Buy American Act in 1933, this photospread documented examples of "counterfeit" goods made in Japan and sold in the United States. Readers were assumed to regard the Japanese copies as inferior, but the visual evidence—especially in repetition—undermined claims of innate difference. *The Protectionist*, April 1935.

from the threat of Asiatic labor.[200] Whereas the "coolie" worker was said to be conspicuously alien, physically unassimilable, the "Jap" commodity was feared to be disconcertingly indistinct. Who could tell the difference between an American candy dish and a Japanese copy (fig. 5.15)? Who could distinguish between an American muffler and a Japanese muffler? Yes, in outer appearance, the cars were dissimilar. Japanese cars were compact, and American autoworkers needed no help spotting them—and vandalizing them—in parking lots.[201] Japanese car parts, though, were concealed, able to pass without detection: a Ford F-150 was as likely as a Nissan to run on some fraction of foreign parts. By their nature, parts triggered an anxiety about molecules rather than hordes—more akin to a fear of an infection of migrant capital than of an invasion of migrant labor.

Xenophobia intensified as Nissans filled the highways, with the zone system in the shadow of an encroaching Yellow Peril. The American auto industry was in dire straits, epitomized by Chrysler's bailout by Congress in 1979. Hundreds of thousands of autoworkers were facing cascades of layoffs. And they were finding little consolation from the UAW leadership, which was telling them to learn to live with "jointism." This accommodationist strategy was incensing many UAW locals, seemingly to the point of terrorizing Asian Americans—most infamously, the vicious murder of Vincent Chin, a Chinese American engineer, by a white Chrysler superintendent and his white stepson, in Detroit in 1982.[202] Part of the tragedy of this racist violence was its misdirection, its misapprehension of the territoriality of capital. Not only had Japan not imposed the global assembly line on the United States, but, in the auto industry, Japanese capital was not its sole beneficiary either. While Japanese automakers were early users of subzones, every single American automaker soon followed suit. By 1989, Detroit hosted an astounding eighteen subzones, and all but Subzone 70I, for Mazda, were for the Big Three. Not that the presence of these paper enclaves eluded autoworkers alone. A novel like Michael Crichton's *Rising Sun*, published in 1992, at the climax of this period, trafficked in nativism, but its high-octane caricature of Japanese executives as gangsters at war for foreign turf necessarily bypassed the terrain of the foreign-trade zone, where such neat divisions evaporated along with the tariffs attached to them. As the cultural theorist Masao Miyoshi mused, "Is Crichton so emphatic about national unity and integrity because he wants to conceal its absence?"[203]

"National unity" was undoubtedly the bugaboo for Congress in its oversight of the zone system in these years. If in the thirties, forties, and fifties the question was whether a city or county should bother to sink funds into the launch of a foreign-trade zone, by the eighties that was moot—every Podunk town now wanted one—and the issue was how it all added up. Such was the consensus among the zone commentariat. In addition to growing numbers of students in business and the social sciences, the General Accounting Office (GAO) and the International Trade Commission (ITC) both completed reports in 1984 that declared that the zone system was used overwhelmingly for importing, not for reexporting. They found that employment gains were "inconclusive," in the words of the GAO; as the ITC noted, an increase in zone-based employment might indicate only that an existing facility had been designated a zone, not that new jobs had been created. Most forcefully, they highlighted that the subzone was at the root of the system's mushrooming: between 1973 and 1983, the value of zone activities "soared" from $161 million to $4 billion, and the subzone share of this Gross Zone Domestic Product, if you will, rose from 29% to 62%.[204]

One point on which the two reports conflicted concerned the system's divisiveness. While the ITC lingered on tumult within the auto industry and on complaints from parts makers, the GAO claimed that the auto industry was quiescent—a take that read like a fairy tale by late 1988, as parts makers caused a ruckus following a new report by the Congressional Research Service. The study left little doubt that subzones were rapidly gaining on general-purpose zones in number and far outpacing them in output. Bar graphs tracked these ratios in starkly climbing slopes (fig. 5.16). Moreover, maps comparing the numbers of subzones and general-purpose zones per state made clear that the American auto industry was in the driver's seat: no amount of Japan-bashing could distort the crosshatching of Michigan, Illinois, Indiana, and Ohio on the map of "States with Subzones"—states in which the Big Three concentrated, and which nonunion "transplants" avoided (fig. 5.17).

Two subcommittees in the House of Representatives convened hearings in 1989, dealing with the same grievances. Witnesses testified to their astonishment about the spike in subzones, to their frustration about the transplants' quasi-smuggling of foreign parts through subzones, and to their dismay about the disarray of the American auto industry. Most acute in this last regard was their distress about how to reconcile parts and wholes. Everyone now agreed that the US zone system disadvantaged American parts makers and advantaged American automakers (even if the

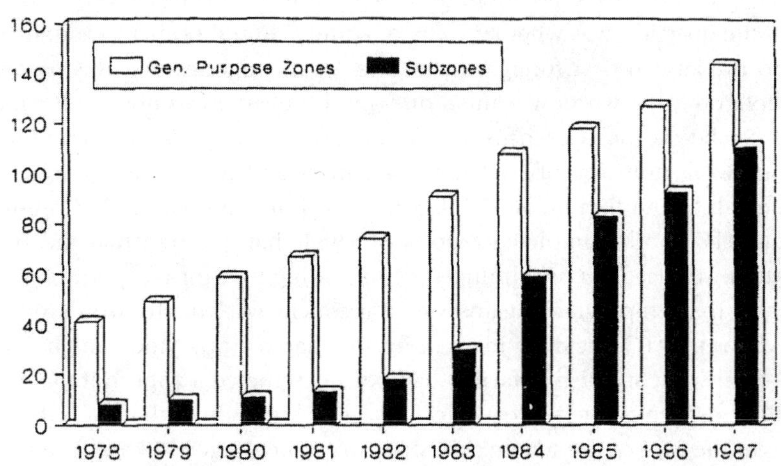

Figure 5.16. Subzones are overtaking general-purpose zones in this bar graph, from *Foreign-Trade Zones and the U.S. Automobile Industry*, October 14, 1988 (Congressional Research Service, 88-659 E).

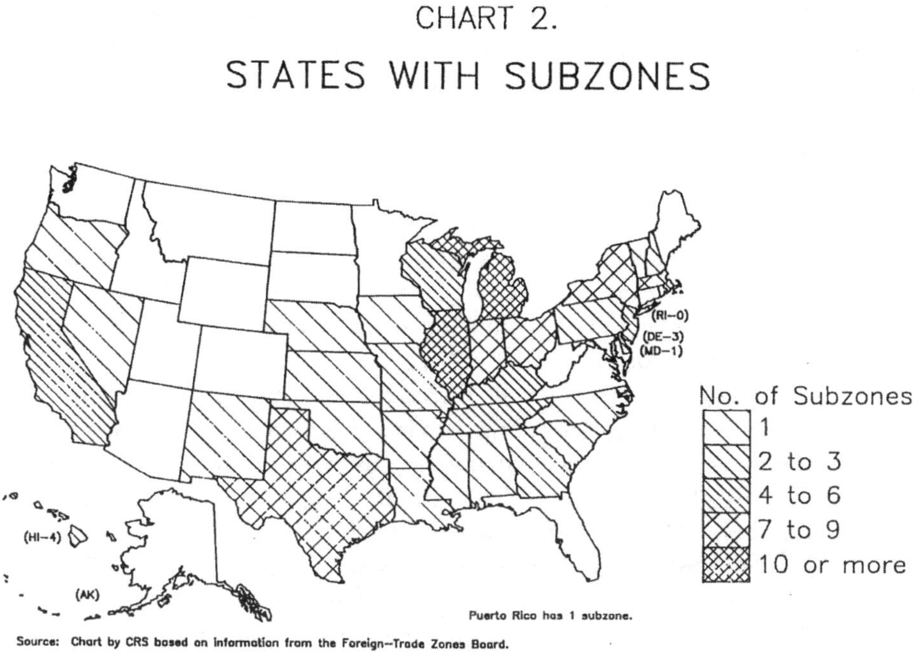

Figure 5.17. By the mid-eighties, all but four states had launched at least one general-purpose zone (not shown), but states with subzones were concentrated in the Rust Belt and the Sunbelt. From *Foreign-Trade Zones and the U.S. Automobile Industry*, October 14, 1988 (Congressional Research Service, 88-659 E).

Big Three relied on a smaller fraction of foreign parts than the transplants), and everyone worried that "national unity" was in jeopardy. The feeling was that Congress needed to find a way of righting the ship without picking sides. "We lack coherence in our trade policy," charged Congresswoman Marcy Kaptur of Toledo, Ohio, and Congressman Sander Levin of Detroit backed her up:

> Forget for a moment that it's automobiles. Sure, I come from an area and Marcy Kaptur does and others do where automobiles are no longer king or queen perhaps, but they're prince. They're important. . . . But say it were a food product or say it were some other product where the trade zones were being used to allow putting together products where the materials came from another country to get around the tariffs that are imposed on those component parts. So let's not make it regional or provincial, because there's at stake here the basic question: Should the United States have trade policy? This is a vivid example of our absolute haphazard approach to trade issues.[205]

Levin and others voiced this "basic question" as a kind of rallying cry, daring themselves to assert their collective power as legislators, elected by the people for the people. An industrial policy needed to be ironed out by Congress, they implied, not by bureaucrats with no public accountability or, for that matter, public visibility. In pressing on this demand they cribbed from the parts makers' script; as the general counsel of the Cycle Parts and Accessories Association had said to a reporter in 1984, "I challenge you to name another federal agency with so much power with such a tiny staff."[206] Not only was the FTZ Board giving a leg up to foreign corporations and sowing discord among American corporations; it was also downright antidemocratic.

Notwithstanding the fervor of these criticisms, the answer was, in a word, crickets. Nothing came of the two hearings, and in fact the zone system continued to grow exponentially. Yet was this so surprising? In 1989, there was no alternative. As a good-faith effort to ward off allegations of crypto-policymaking, the FTZ Board could have devised ways to solicit more input from the citizenry, but transparency alone would not have appeased the naysayers. The real difficulty was that no one was keen to lasso the sacred cow of free trade. "The free trade theory," as Congresswoman Kaptur called it when she too dutifully bowed down to it, was held up as an ideal, but also as no more than that—an ideal, a horizon, a categorical imperative.[207] Politicians of all persuasions seemed to believe that the ideal of free trade was irrelevant to the realpolitik of everyday transactions between nation-states. "I really think unfettered free trade is kind of like a subatomic particle," as a Republican from California confessed during one hearing. "It may exist somewhere at some time but very briefly."[208] So, no one was advocating for a flat world of free movement, not for capital and most definitely not for labor. Nor, needless to say, was anyone angling for a mandate for comprehensive federal planning on a macro or a micro level. No one was talking about nationalizing the infrastructure of capital circulation. No one was suggesting that the FTZ Board might be revamped to be able to finance ports or plants.[209] It seemed to be a given that national policy meant rules (or, in the Reagan era, the easing of rules), not dollars. It was the Soviets who ran factories, not the Americans, and everyone knew how the Soviets were faring.

What was ironic about the impasse was that the businessmen who had provoked it by clamoring for congressional attention were coming off as far more eager for state action than were the politicians they pestered. This mismatch bore out a remark by California governor Jerry Brown from the late seventies that "many businessmen are growing weary of the rigors of the free market," an alarm he sounded when describing a junket to Tokyo to sell the Golden State (subzones included!) to Toyota, Honda, and Nissan: "Sometimes businessmen almost operate as though they'd feel more comfortable in a Marxist state where they could just deal with a few commissars who would tell them what the production goals were, what quota they had as part of the overall mix," Governor Moonbeam fretted to *Barron's*. "But we live in a free economy; there's a great deal left to the market and to uncertainty."[210] Mostly, Brown felt, cities needed to be left to their own devices; while he recognized the tendency of "balkanization where each city is warring with the others to get plants," he also refused to step in to orchestrate peace treaties. Brown's pragmatic brand of market fundamentalism would suffuse the conversation a decade later. Politicians thought of the foreign-trade zone as—for better or for worse—"marginal," "surgical," as a tactic available to "the comptrollers and the CPAs."[211] They knew it ensured a "race to the bottom," a phrase coined during the Gilded Age that was reminted during the eighties. They understood that it compelled replication, that if one firm exploited it, then rival firms were pressured to as well, but because they pledged themselves to free trade, they saw no role for state action. Small wonder that an executive testified that after he pointed out to the FTZ Board that a rival firm would undercut his firm if it was allowed to use a subzone to import foreign parts, the FTZ Board responded by recommending that his firm apply for its own subzone, "as if turning the whole industry into a foreign trade zone would solve the problem."[212]

An air of futility hung over these testimonials, not only because of the laughable tautology of a zone as the remedy for the ills of a zone but also because the brass ring that everyone was grasping for—an infusion of "manufacturing jobs," or what Reagan-era wonks heralded as "reindustrialization"—was beyond reach.[213] Culturally and politically, "manufacturing" was a relic if what it signified was a Fordist compact between labor, capital, and the nation-state, guaranteeing a stable wage and a panoply of benefits for a white man to support a wife and 2.3 children. Politicians paid homage to it as a pillar of Americanism, but it was never to be resurrected. No amount of white papers on "reindustrialization" would bring back the River Rouge, or some approximation of it retooled for the global assembly line, because, as Congressman Levin admitted, industrial capital was no longer king: as two Marxist philosophers were to write in the twilight of the twentieth century, "The Detroit auto factory of the 1930s stood at the

Figure 5.18. This advertisement for Zone 44 in central New Jersey ran for a number of months in 1988, rendering "labor" as "real estate." Zone 44 was the Rockefeller Group's largest holding after Rockefeller Center in Manhattan. In the decades since, the Rockefeller Group has become a leading developer of foreign-trade zones, built on agricultural land in exurban areas. *New York Times*, April 17, 1988.

pinnacle of the global economy in the dominant position and producing the highest value; the 1990s auto factory, whether in São Paulo, Kentucky, or Vladivostok, occupies a subordinate position in the global economy—subordinated to the high-value production of services."[214] Even as "factories" opened in the South and stayed open in the North, both thanks in part to the zone concept (and to its spin-off, the enterprise zone), they were not salvaging a way of life: they were hastening its recomposition.[215]

So we come full circle to the splintered urbanism of the postmodern era. Belgian beers in Baltimore. São Paulo in place of Detroit, São Paulo inside of Los Angeles. Nothing was what it seemed, and the foreign-trade zone was both a symptom and a cause. A decade prior, John Egerton, the bard of Nissan in Tennessee, had announced "the Southernization of America," memorializing the waning of antagonisms and antinomies along the Mason-Dixon. "Southernization" signaled integration for him, and yet segregation is what he prophesied. "South Africanization," in this vein, was the term favored by those who beheld the zone world.[216] "South Africanization" captured the pluralities of the United States: the new abundance of "labor, labor, labor" (fig. 5.18), on the one hand, and the labor of abundance, on the other—the profusion of gated communities and gated industrial parks, zones of citizenship.

CONCLUSION

Free Shipping!

It's amazing how many educated minds' eyes still visualize docks in the imagery of, say, Quentin Hughes' Seaport—tall craggy warehouses, masts, cranes and funnels silhouetted against the sky, picturesque Trotskyites in silk mufflers toting that box, lifting that bale, getting a little drunk and landing in the Tower magistrates' court. But this is now an iconography of death, all the standard images of rich clutter belong to a world that has had it.

—Reyner Banham, "Flatscape with Containers," *New Society* (1967)

If there is a single object that can be said to embody the disavowal implicit in the transnational bourgeoisie's fantasy of a world of wealth without workers, a world of uninhibited flows, it is this: the container, the very coffin of remote labor-power.

—Allan Sekula, *Fish Story* (1995)

We pack and deliver like UPS trucks.

—M.I.A., "Paper Planes" (2008)

One truth of the posttruth era, judging from commentary on globalization, is that the shipping container is frictionlessness incarnate. Once it came into widespread use after the Vietnam War, the box seemed to vaporize the costs of transportation. It enabled shippers to opt out of the tedium and expense of landing freight onshore. It fused ships with trains and trucks—it transformed the high seas into highways. In consequence, the container "made the world smaller and the world economy bigger." And in its wake, emblems of class struggle on the piers drifted away, as the seaport hardened into a "flatscape." Trotskyists and Terry Malloys no longer huddled on the waterfront. As the tech tycoon Bill Gates has mused, "Today it seems crazy that a ship would dock and somebody would get off with a piece of paper to show what's in the cargo hold."[1]

But this story is oddly truncated. What it omits is the fact that the container—so often conjured as a subject rather than an object—required some help in achieving this Zeus-like feat. People had to produce enough stuff to fill it. And people still had to load and unload it. In the first instance, in other words, "cheap labor" was needed, amassed in export-processing zones in the Global South. From Taiwan to Nicaragua, these new enclosures helped ensure that containers were crammed with Air Jordans and G.I. Joes. In the second instance, an infrastructure was needed, dispersed from the water's edge to Main Street, USA. Essential to this infrastructure have been "inland ports," also known as "dry ports." Initially these outposts were called "interior ports of entry," when Congress authorized them to receive bonded goods via bonded carriers in 1870. "Airports of entry" were added to the customs territory in 1928, and now deserts and prairies are dotted by harbors. Longshoremen are not extinct. They are driving forklifts in exurbs like Joliet, Illinois.[2]

These conditions of possibility must be reckoned with in order to give a full account of "globalization." As it is, they rarely enter into the equation when the container is marveled at for minimizing the friction of space.[3] Which is not to dispute the claim of monumental change. Undoubtedly, distribution charges have plummeted. Yet they have not vanished. They have been reallocated, qualitatively as much as quantitatively. A clue that the numbers are deceptive is the ploy of "free shipping," which, like colored lattes at Starbucks, has mutated from a holiday-season stunt to a year-round norm, and which you do not need expertise in semiotics to decode as a disavowal or mystification that explains away what might otherwise be evident. As the free-marketeer himself, Milton Friedman, liked to pronounce, there's no such thing as a free lunch! Free shipping is not free—free of handling. The container does not eliminate handling but instead relocates it.[4]

This is easier to see if we see like a warehouse. Those who know all too well that shipping is not free are those who profit off of it. From the storeroom we can discern a paradox that goes to the heart of how we apprehend capitalism. How is that moving the goods is so much less expensive than making them, when warehouses are spreading faster than factories? Are warehouses merging with factories? Are moving and making progressively conjoined? Clearly something more than "simple storage" is transpiring in those warehouses, or else why build them?

Figure c.1. A concrete abstraction: a photograph is used to create a drawing to advise how best to maximize space (vertical and horizontal) in a warehouse. American Warehousemen's Association, *Proceedings of the American Warehousemen's Association* (Pittsburgh, 1922).

Why, indeed. The history of warehousing reveals that warehousemen have been responding to this provocation by trying to broaden the meaning of warehousing for nearly as long as the industry has existed. Their efforts have centered on two agendas: how to optimize the efficiency of the warehouse and how to expand the menu of services offered within it. Glimmers of both sensibilities are evident in a drawing that a warehouseman from Boston used to illustrate his speech to the American Warehousemen's Association in 1922 (fig. c.1). The first is more salient. Piles of items of assorted shapes and sizes crowd the frame. The harmoniousness of ceiling joists running in parallel lines sets off the cacophony of items teetering in jagged stacks. The lesson is plain: "IPD" or "individual package delivery" is the bane of the warehouse, wasting space (vertical as well as horizontal) and impeding access. The second attitude is indicated in the blankness of these forms. This "picture" was "reproduced from a photograph," suggesting that its geometric simplicity was intentional. The variation among the items, outlined so starkly, invites us to bear in mind that different classes of commodities yield different possibilities for fee-based enhancements. Some might merit relabeling or repackaging. Others, grading or sorting. Their incongruity is a hindrance but also an opportunity, one that the shipping container—in black-boxing that heterogeneity—discourages us from appreciating.[5]

The foreign-trade zone came about in this second sense, as a service for a subset of these items, those originating outside the United States. At its core, that is, the zone has always been a warehouse complex. Boosters of the zone system, whether public officials or private businessmen, have hustled on behalf of storage facilities and commercial property. While manufacturers like Ford and Toyota have become the names most likely to grace headlines about the zone system, they have merely patronized it. They have never led the charge in erecting it. The zone has been the totem of a kind of cargo cult, a means to lure warehouse tenants to this or that tract of land. It has been branded by its location (or location, location, location). It has been a warehouse positioned to facilitate circulation, to articulate a local economy with the global economy. Even after Congress sanctioned "manufacturing," circulation has remained the purpose of the zone; even when it has appeared as a factory, it has functioned as a warehouse.

To classify the foreign-trade zone as a warehouse is to emphasize that it is time-bound. Superficially what distinguishes the zone is its anomalous spatiality: the fence. Fundamentally, though, what crosscuts that bifurcated territory is the zone's unique temporality. In the vernacular of warehousing, the zone is a space of "dwell time." Dwell time is a period of shifting gears, the interval of disconnection in a connection. It is a pause, a conjunction—the term also refers to a bus idling at a curb, a soldier visiting family between deployments.[6] To the extent that it is conceived as empty time, it is deemed nonproductive. But it can be occupied, too, as when airports host shopping malls (descendants of duty-free boutiques).[7] Across this range of practices, the common denominator is ephemerality. Except in the context of the zone. The weirdness of the zone—and of most ways of organizing post-Fordist flexibility, such as temporary labor—lies in how it prolongs the interlude. In the zone, cargoes can sit on US soil and outside US customs territory, on the edge of the national market, indefinitely. There is no time limit. And as they sit, they are not stationary. Legally, they are "in transit," for however many days or months or years. They are transitioning from one owner to another, one customs territory to another. It is by this logic that the zone is a warehouse and not a factory: goods cannot be simultaneously in transit and in a process of manufacturing.[8] (Unless they can, and it is the content of the term *manufacturing* that cannot be pinned down.)[9]

This notion of dwell time helps elucidate media reports that contend that in the Rust Belt warehousing is the new manufacturing. And it suggests why foreign-trade zones have continued to open even as tariffs have continued to fall. By 1989, the zone system was dominated by auto-assembly plants. But many of those single-tenant subzones were doomed as the auto industry tanked.[10] Replacing them were zone operators who were angling to aggregate multiple tenants in hubs. These projects took shape as industrial parks, like the "International Trade Center" in Mt. Olive Township, New Jersey, "667 acres of hilly, wooded land" an hour's drive west from the container terminals in Newark and Elizabeth.[11] Mt. Olive, a site within the jurisdiction of Zone 44, opened in 1983 as the Rockefeller Group's first foray off US customs territory (not counting Rockefeller Center in Manhattan, which Congress designated a "free port" in 1932, to permit duty-free exhibitions).[12] It was an indication of the appetite for zones constructed on spec. These gated communities were plotted along highways and beside airports so as to install warehouses—and "light assembly" inside warehouses—within easy reach of retailers (and beyond reach of inventory taxes, in some states).[13] The overwhelming majority of goods that left these zones were "imported" into the United States, the vision of an empire of reexport by now long forgotten. Or at most they went south to Mexico or north to Canada, starting in the mid-1990s. As borne out by "AllianceTexas," or Zone 196, a master-planned development owned by the Perot Group and anchored by "the world's first 100% industrial airport," the North American Free Trade Agreement (NAFTA) broadened the orbit of the zone system. Far from rendering it moot, NAFTA meant that zones along the "NAFTA corridor" from Chicago to Laredo were guaranteed to capture more customers as traffic increased.[14] After all, a host of tariffs and customs regulations had stayed in effect.

AllianceTexas—"subsuming the name of the state within its own name," the architectural theorist Keller Easterling wryly observes—is an index of how this species of warehouses has not sprouted willy-nilly, like weeds.[15] It has been genetically modified in laboratories of public-private experimentation. The Perot Group was no lone ranger; it banked on reams of local and state subsidies. And AllianceTexas was designed as a node, not a final destination; it anticipated synergies with similar conurbations along the NAFTA corridor such as Kansas City's SmartPort, a sprawling platform wired to two foreign-trade zones, Zones 15 and 17. These "technopoles" have pioneered a regionalism characterized by "splintering" political economies.[16] Fused with each other, they have been immunized from their immediate neighborhoods (whose air they have polluted). As the geographer Juan De Lara has shown in a study of Southern California's Inland Empire (a hot spot for the Rockefeller Group and home to sites within Zones 50, 202, 236, 243, and 244), port authorities in Long Beach have helped auction off farms two hundred miles from the seacoast.[17] Although this centralization of decentralization has been easy to miss from the ground, it has been stark from the sky.[18]

The zone system is itself a microcosm of this tendency toward coordinated fragmentation. During the 1990s, the map started to resemble a pinball machine. I learned at the World Free Zone Convention in Ras Al Khaimah in 2010, for instance, over a lunch of Tex-Mex fajitas, that Zone 147 in central Pennsylvania was configured with the aid of aerial data. Customs rules mandated that sites within a zone be contiguous. But Zone 147's managers, using satellite imagery of electrical and rail lines to show contiguity, persuaded the FTZ Board to let them sponsor sites many miles apart. Stretching in this manner has been magnified since 1991, when the "circle of adjacency" stipulated by the FTZ Board—the maximum distance from the outer limit of a port of entry allowable for a site—was enlarged from thirty-five to sixty miles.[19] The upshot has been that the spatial form of the foreign-trade zone has grown fuzzier. "The island model is obsolete," the president of the National Association of Foreign-Trade Zones told me in 2007: the zone is not an enclave; it is a "trade program." Media coverage had already confirmed as much, lingering less on issues of territoriality. In 1993, the *New York Times* ran a primer on the zone system to parse what the Perot Group was up to at AllianceTexas. Even with an infographic on the ABCs of zones—noteworthy for how it featured "widgets," ignoring camels and Brazil nuts and car radios—it said nothing about the fence.[20]

This generalization or normalization of the foreign-trade zone was hardly the direct cause of the growth of the warehousing industry. Compared to trade agreements like NAFTA, the zone was trivial. And yet in that very spirit it was emblematic, for the race to the bottom was a sprint, not a marathon. The flatter the world, the narrower the margins. Amid the turbulence of just-in-time supply chains, dwell time was not to be wasted. Proselytizers like the *New York Times* columnist Thomas Friedman were effusing about globalization as if the removal of "trade barriers" was the key to universal prosperity, but of course, in capitalism, which turns on the production of difference, competition was intensifying as the shipping container was traveling. In this atmosphere, the zone was standardized as an adornment of "logistics clusters" like AllianceTexas. "It's a shingle you hang out for the world that shows you understand international trade," suggested a representative of Zone 65 (Panama City, Florida) in 1994. "It enhances the real estate, if you will."[21]

Increasingly, overseeing the movement of the shipping container between these logistics clusters has been a glorified version of the age-old warehouser: the 3PL, or third-party logistics provider. The 3PL has led the latest wave of additions to the zone ranks. An exemplar has been UPS Supply Chain Solutions, a division of UPS. At its campus in Louisville, Kentucky, UPS operates a site within Zone 29 that employs 750 people in "customs brokerage services." The advantages to these activities are found almost as much in their proximity to UPS's other offerings in Louisville as in their cost savings. UPS, in short, demonstrates how the 3PL has emerged as the handler merchant for the age of the digital border. Trade liberalization has not equaled bureaucratic relaxation. Paperwork is as abundant as ever. And the federal government's expectation for security is onerous. Smoothing over these wrinkles, a 3PL like UPS is akin to a concierge desk next to a checkpoint. Regardless of the magnitude of the tariffs at stake, the 3PL, when stationed at a high-volume crossroads, has proven to be an outstanding fit for a zone site. "Foreign-trade zones are complicated," reads the banner on the website for UPS Zone Solutions. "We make them simpler."[22] Frictionlessness. For a price.

It is unsurprising that UPS, a freight forwarder, is in the mix. What, though, of the two principal drivers of this new regime of accumulation? Walmart and Amazon seem to take divergent approaches to the foreign-trade zone. Both, needless to say, depend on warehousing. But the zone seems to factor in for one and not the other. Walmart seems to be a zone user. It applied for two subzones in the early 1990s: Subzone 75B in Buckeye, Arizona, and Subzone 104B in Savannah, Georgia, were slated as centerpieces of Walmart's "international division," created in 1993. Reexport was a special aim, with interest in "assembly/processing" of stereo systems and camera kits for Europe and Latin America. (Each enterprise seems to have flopped: Subzone 75 was terminated, and Subzone 104B is inactive.) Amazon, meanwhile, seems not to have bothered with the zone system. The shoe retailer that it acquired in 2009, Zappos, operates a site in Zone 29 (part of the Louisville logistics cluster). Otherwise, none of Amazon's fulfillment centers seem to be on the grid. The reason might have to do with the contrast in how goods are sorted in a Walmart distribution center versus in an Amazon fulfillment center—homogenized versus randomized, pallets versus bins. Amazon has dispensed with the stack, stashing items according to available slots, which shift minute to minute, such that, presumably, a zone for duty-free goods would be impossible to segregate.[23]

That said, short of conducting interviews with employees or obtaining internal documents, we will never be able to confirm precisely how or if Walmart or Amazon participates in the zone system. Public sources yield few answers. The FTZ Board's online database is comprehensive in listing the names of operators of zone sites and subzones, but the clients of those operators go unidentified. This erasure is not due to subterfuge, I must stress. It is an aspect of the epistemology of the supply chain.[24] The preponderance of 3PLs is what obscures much of the roster. And that matters since Walmart, for one, has partnered quite extensively with 3PLs. The majority of the "import distribution centers" that Walmart relies on in the United States—the facilities where duty-free handling would be most warranted—are outsourced to 3PLs. Therefore, if we trail the 3PLs we can piece together suites of custodians and zone sites, glimpsing how our lives are terraformed by offshore-onshore conveyor belts.

Or, it turns out, we can glean parallel evidence from blogs and community-based news. From an article out of Columbus, Ohio, critical of NAFTA we gather that Walmart was tied to Zone 138 (which the FTZ Board's site gives no hint of). And from articles and cellphone videos out of Chicago, we learn that Walmart connects to a site in Zone 22 (which converges on the Burlington Northern railroad featured in figure 5.9), where, in October 2012, security guards in riot gear—twenty-first century Pinkertons—confronted members and allies of Warehouse Workers for Justice (WWJ), who were supporting a strike by blocking the gates to property controlled by Schneider Logistics, a 3PL (fig. c.2). WWJ's website informs us that 150,000 people work in warehouses in the Chicago region.[25] A six-figure number, rounded off to a block of zeroes. It's assumed to be a shocking statistic. People *work* in warehouses? Assemblies like WWJ are making visible the invisible labors of circulation. Who packed and delivered your computer? How much do you—do they, do we—pay for free shipping?

One of the articles on the WWJ standoff emphasizes that security guards were present at Schneider Logistics in a regular capacity because the site was in a foreign-trade zone. Whether or not this assertion is accurate—whether or not the site was activated in 2012—is tough to verify. But it is beside the point if this site was online. Regardless of whether Zone 22 was implicated in this scene, zones across the Pacific Ocean surely were. Schneider was dealing with shipping containers—"coffins of remote labor power," in the words of photographer Allan Sekula—that were stamped by the same enclaving imperative (fig. c.3). It is all of a piece. The zone

Figure c.2. Police aligned with Walmart confront protesters aligned with Warehouse Workers for Justice in Joliet, Illinois, on October 1, 2012. Joe Stupec. Reproduced with permission.

Figure c.3. "Containers used to contain shifting sand dunes." Image 78 in Allan Sekula, *Fish Story* (Düsseldorf: Richter Verlag, 1995). Reproduced with permission from Allan Sekula Studio.

concept boasts a global history, to which the United States has contributed since the late nineteenth century. Even earlier, when we consider the bonded warehouse. In charting this genealogy, I have stayed with the spatial form, tracking its permutations. And along the way I have tried to estrange the geographies of circulation, not to take them for granted. It used to be that a book on a port offered a window on the world: Albion's *The Rise of New York Port* (1939), Sinclair's *The Port of New Orleans* (1942). Or an essay—Ernest Ingersoll's "The Lading of a Ship" (1877). Now we strain for other perspectives on that totality with the port itself unrecognizable. Chicago, by some estimates, is the third-largest container port on the planet, after Hong Kong and Singapore. It is so hard to see. But what is obvious is that these are not open fields. These are walled landscapes. They host net-works, in that old sense of that word. Not the social networks that we hear so much about but the physical net-works, the nets arrayed to catch fish who think they are swimming free.

ACKNOWLEDGMENTS

This project began at Yale University, in the program in American studies—a free zone in the ideal sense. I am forever grateful to, and in awe of, my advisors in American studies. Jean-Christophe Agnew's challenging and often bewildering seminar on the history of capitalism and culture made me realize what exactly I was up to in graduate school. I cannot overstate his influence on my thinking, or my respect for him as a scholar who is as kind and generous as he is genius. Michael Denning never failed to inspire me with his curiosity and commitment. He asks the best questions—a single observation of his could turn everything inside out. And Laura Wexler was the first to prod me to explore the visual culture of the supply chain. She showed me, not least, how to approach capital as a way of seeing. In addition I was fortunate to learn from numerous other outstanding teachers, including Nigel Alderman, Jon Butler, Charlotte Cotton, Kate Dudley, Glenda Gilmore, Paul Gilroy, Bob Gordon, David Graeber, Matt Jacobson, and Joanne Meyerowitz. Thanks also to Keller Easterling for her counsel on how to structure this project, and to Michael Denning, John McKay, and other regulars for countless memorable discussions in the Working Group on Marxism and Cultural Theory.

So many others at Yale taught me, too, in the classroom and beyond, and in particular I want to acknowledge Mike Amezcua, Francesca Ammon, Adam Arenson, Kimberly Brown, Debbie Dinner, Andrew Friedman, Melíssa Garcia, Megan Glick, Sumanth Gopinath, Sarah Haley, Tisha Hooks, Nicole Ivy, Amanda Izzo, Michael Likosky, April Merleaux, Bethany Moreton, Naomi Paik, Nick Parillo, Miriam Posner, Aaron Sachs, Andy Seal, Vicki Shepard, Kate Unterman, Suzanna Urminska, and Charlie Veric. Outside of New Haven, I am thankful for encounters in person and over email with Jonny Bunning, Charmaine Chua, Patrick Chung, Martin Danyluk, Monika

Dommann, Nelson Lichtenstein, Gautham Rao, Seth Rockman, Dan Rood, Andrew Sandoval-Strausz, Stuart Schrader, Augustine Sedgewick, Naoko Shibusawa, Sally Stein, and Susie Strasser. A special thanks to Michael Zakim for sharing his depth of knowledge and for offering his vote of confidence at a crucial juncture. For opportunities to present at workshops—not to mention for the insights I have gleaned from their own scholarship—I thank Eric Arnesen, Kevin Coleman, Deb Cowen, Jay Driskell, Matt Hockenberry, Roger Horowitz, Jeff Sklansky, and Christy Thornton. I am very appreciative of the commentators, copanelists, and audience members at these and other gatherings for their astute reponses to my work.

I started the research for this project in Staten Island, where I enjoyed hunting for materials with Carlotta DeFillo in the archives of the Staten Island Historical Society, and with Steve Zaffarano in the photo morgue of the Staten Island Advance. My thanks as well to Maxine Friedman in Staten Island and to the myriad other librarians and archivists who helped me unearth sources from New York City to Seattle. None of these trips would have been feasible, of course, without funding for travel and more. For financial support I thank the MacMillan Center, the Beinecke Rare Book and Manuscript Library, and the Howard Lamar Center for the Study of Borders and Frontiers, all at Yale; the Center for the Study of the Global South at Tulane University; the American Council of Learned Societies; and the Columbia College Facilitating Fund at George Washington University. Two residential fellowships gave me not only time to hunker down but also exposure to new ideas. I thank all of the other fellows whose brilliance I soaked in at the Center for the Humanities at Wesleyan University in 2012–13, and at the Kluge Center at the Library of Congress in 2015–16, where collegiality was fostered and modeled by Mary Lou Reker, Travis Hensley, and Jason Steinhauer, and where Theo Christov was my sabbatical comrade.

Over the duration of this project I published two journal articles, and in both cases I benefited a tremendous amount from the rigorous and constructive criticism I received from editors and anonymous readers. I thank Amy Chazkel, David Serlin, and the editorial collective of the *Radical History Review* for their valuable input on the first piece, which I wrote at an early stage. And I thank Charmaine Chua, Deb Cowen, Martin Danyluk, and Laleh Khalili for their expert guidance of the second, which was part of a special issue for *Environment and Planning D: Society and Space*; Charmaine and Martin, especially, proved to be fantastic interlocutors.

While tackling the book manuscript I was blessed with feedback from George Henderson, Jon Levy, and Andrew Zimmerman in a book workshop facilitated by Gayle Wald. I thank this brain trust for the fabulous array of ideas I was left with, more than I could manage to engage. Soon afterward I connected with Tim Mennel, editor extraordinaire, who nudged me even further with his own impressions and with reports from two readers who pinpointed dozens of important issues. I am immensely appreciative of Tim for recruiting these heroic, sagacious readers and then for coaching me as I executed revisions, before George Roupe's final round of meticulous copyediting. My thanks to Rachel Unger, Tamara Ghattas, and Tyler McGaughey for their patience in shepherding me through the editorial and production process, and to Shiraz Abdullahi Gallab for her panache with the book cover. My thanks as well to Leslie Cohen for help with proofreading and to Kurt Newman for help with indexing, and to Dean Yongwu Rong at George Washington University for two grants to offset production costs.

Speaking of that school next to Mar-a-Lago North, I feel incredibly lucky to have landed in the haven that is American studies at GW. From my very first trip to campus—when I was welcomed with such warmth by Tom Guglielmo and Jen Nash—I have continually marveled at the department's wealth of talent and good will. For an ideal mix of intellectualism and irreverence, I thank as well Libby Anker, Mona Azadi, David Bjelajac, Jamie Cohen-Cole, Chad Heap, Nicole Ivy, Melani McAlister, Amber Musser, Suleiman Osman, Elaine Peña, and Gayle Wald, with cheers for Chad, Melani, and Gayle for their mentorship. Seminars and collaborations with graduate students have been enormously fun and fruitful for me, and I am indebted specifically to Vyta Baselice and Robert Ramaswamy for dialoguing with me about this manuscript. A shout-out, too, to Kim Probolus and Megan Black and all of the other students who have been coconspirators. Elsewhere in the orbit of GW, my thanks to Leah Richardson for a fascinating partnership in the digital humanities and to Johanna Bockman and Andrew Zimmerman for their wisdom.

Two communities have loomed large in the development of this project. In New Haven, I treasured the camaraderie of Guang-Shing Cheng, Dina Pollock and Jacinto Lirola, Martina Droth and Nick Mead, and the late Irm and Morris Wessel. I was also infinitely grateful for the talents of Sandy Malmquist and the teachers at the Creating Kids Child Care Center, whose labors freed me up to start writing. In Takoma Park, MD, which is now home, I hail the many friends and neighbors who have been both so encouraging and so wonderfully distracting, especially Angie Nichols-Friedman and Brian Friedman, and Michele Bollinger and Dave Zirin.

Aaron Carico, Sophia Lee, and Rebecca McKenna have been unstintingly loyal and fierce friends since graduate school, and each of them has made a huge impact on this project in talking it through with me and reviewing drafts, and in the examples of their own books. I am so, so thankful for their advice and overall awesomeness. Irene Cheng and Jennifer Ching have been essential sounding boards for even longer, on this project and so much else. They have continually enlarged my perspective. Jenn has been my lifeline since our first week of college and is one of the most hilarious and thoughtful (and hilarious) people I know. My extended family has been equally supportive over the years. Endless thanks particularly to Ron and Joan Resetarits, Barry Orenstein, and Max Kay and Natalie Orenstein (and Lilah!). My sister Natalie has been there for me in every possible way. And as to the deep roots of my work in Modesto, CA, I thank my parents, Robert and Ginny Orenstein, my earliest instructors in the ABCs of American studies, for nurturing my imagination and enabling me to act to it.

Finally, I struggle to express my profound gratitude to the two people whose care and companionship have sustained me most throughout this project. My husband, Ron Resetarits, has been right at my side in the marathon in innumerable ways, from brainstorming with me, to pestering me for pages, to building me bookcases. And our son, Bruno Resetarits, has been just as attentive, first crab-crawling to those bookcases to gnaw at my books, and now visiting me at my desk to root me on with hugs, jokes, and my daily dose of sports trivia. Our life together is a gift. I dedicate this book to them, with love.

NOTES

INTRODUCTION

1. "Every citizen deserves the right to know where their products are made," testified Senator Barbara Mikulski of Maryland. "I also do not want us to be a society," she added, "where all we do is put on the hubcaps and then call that an American car." Committee on Commerce, Science, and Transportation, *The American Automobile Labeling Act*, 102nd Cong., 2nd sess., June 24, 1992, 5.
2. "Role of Foreign-Trade Zones in World Trade Significantly Enlarged," *Foreign Commerce Weekly*, June 26, 1950.
3. Wolters Kluwer, "Global Tax Coverage," https://www.lowtax.net/lowtax/html/offon/offonhom.html. "Landed" is an antiquated term. The current convention is to refer to goods as "entered for consumption" when they leave a zone for distribution inside the United States.
4. For two best-selling renditions of the genre of commodity history, see Donovan Hohn, *Moby-Duck: The True Story of 28,800 Bath Toys Lost at Sea and of the Beachcombers, Oceanographers, Environmentalists & Fools, Including the Author, Who Went in Search of Them* (New York: Penguin, 2012); and Pietra Rivoli, *The Travels of a T-Shirt in the Global Economy: An Economist Examines the Markets, Power, and Politics of World Trade* (Hoboken, NJ: John Wiley and Sons, 2009).
5. For cultural studies of Trumpism and deindustrialization, see Jasper Bernes on the Dodge Challenger as "white revanchism incarnate" in "Our Streets," Verso Books blog, August 24, 2017, https://www.versobooks.com/blogs/3371-our-streets; and Thuy Linh Tu and Nikhil Pal Singh on textile factories in Alabama in "Morbid Capitalism and Its Racial Symptoms," *n+1* 30 (Winter 2018), https://nplusonemag.com/issue-30/essays/morbid-capitalism/.
6. David Harvey, *Spaces of Global Capitalism: Towards a Theory of Uneven Geographical Development* (New York: Verso, 2006), 107. On the invention of the national economy as "an epistemological project of the state," see Hannah Appel, "Toward an Ethnography of the National Economy," *Cultural Anthropology* 32, no. 2 (2017): 294–322.
7. An Act for Laying a Duty on Goods, Wares, and Merchandises Imported into the United States, 1 *US Statutes at Large* 26 (July 4, 1789).
8. US Tariff Commission, *Study of Temporary Entry Provisions of Title 19 of the United States Code*, TC Publication 170 (Washington, DC, March 1966). In the history of

the spatial forms of capitalism, 1789 and 1989 are not necessarily far apart. The foreign-trade zone emerged in a cyclical spiral more than a punctuated line, to borrow from William H. Sewell Jr., "The Temporalities of Capitalism," *Socio-Economic Review* 6, no. 3 (2008): 517–37. Histories of racial capitalism are revealed less in "the *ordering* of things" than in "the *order* of things," writes Cedric J. Robinson in *Black Marxism: The Making of the Black Radical Tradition* (1983; Chapel Hill: University of North Carolina Press, 2000), 177.

9. Two weeks after the second hearing, the Berlin Wall crumbled. Joshua Clover detects reverberations of this event in the pop music of 1989, "the most geopolitically laden year since at least 1945," in *1989: Bob Dylan Didn't Have This to Sing About* (Berkeley: University of California Press, 2009).
10. Foreign-Trade Zones Board (https://enforcement.trade.gov/ftzpage/index.html). Aside from what was Zone 2 in Mobile, Alabama, which was expunged from the roster, these numbers do not parse general-purpose zones and subzones as "active" versus "inactive," another topic in its own right.
11. As I detail in chapter 5, this fearmongering was not new. Witness a headline from a magazine founded by Lyndon LaRouche: Susan Cohen, "Cushman & Wakefield Brings Hong Kong to N.J.," *Executive Intelligence Review* 6, no. 39 (1979): 10–11.
12. Susan Tiefenbrun, *Tax Free Trade Zones of the World and in the United States* (Cheltenham, UK: Edward Elgar, 2012), 1.
13. Naomi Klein, *No Logo: No Space, No Choice, No Jobs* (New York: Picador, 2002), 347. On the National Labor Committee's investigation of Gifford and Walmart, see Kitty Krupat, "From War Zone to Free Trade Zone," in *No Sweat: Fashion, Free Trade, and the Rights of Garment Workers*, ed. Andrew Ross (New York: Verso, 1997), 51–78. For a poignant denunciation of the Kingston Free Zone in Jamaica see *Life and Debt*, DVD, directed by Stephanie Black, 2001 (New York: New Yorker Video, 2003).
14. Ho Kwon Ping, "Birth of the Second Generation," *Far Eastern Economic Review*, May 18, 1979, 78. Contemporary scholarship on zones slants toward zones outside the United States. Scholars who have shaped my thinking include Jonathan Bach, "Modernity and the Urban Imagination in Economic Zones," *Theory, Culture & Society* 28, no. 5 (2011): 98–122; Xiangming Chen, "The Evolution of Free Economic Zones and the Recent Development of Cross-National Growth Zones," *International Journal of Urban and Regional Research* 19, no. 4 (1995): 593–621; Keller Easterling, *Enduring Innocence: Global Architecture and Its Political Masquerades* (Cambridge, MA: MIT Press, 2005); Michael Likosky, *The Silicon Empire: Law, Culture, and Commerce* (London: Ashgate, 2005); and Leslie Sklair, *Assembling for Development: The Maquila Industry in Mexico and the United States* (Boston: Unwin Hyman, 1989).
15. Catalogers added "free ports and zones" to the official list of LOC Subject Headings in 1948. Paul Weiss, email message to author, July 7, 2009.
16. Patrick Neveling, "Export Processing Zones, Special Economic Zones and the Long March of Capitalist Development Policies during the Cold War," in *Decolonization and the Cold War: Negotiating Independence*, ed. Leslie James and Elisabeth Leake (London: Bloomsbury, 2015), 63–84.
17. This summary does not count my own article, "Foreign-Trade Zones and the Cultural Logic of Frictionless Production," *Radical History Review* 109 (Winter 2011): 36–61, or the hundreds of articles in the realms of business and law (none of which derive from archival research). The only two books on the subject, one by a geography professor and the other by a management professor, are artifacts themselves: William A. Dymsza, *Foreign-Trade Zones and International Business* (Trenton: New

Jersey Department of Conservation and Economic Development, 1964); and Richard S. Thoman, *Free Ports and Foreign-Trade Zones* (Ithaca, NY: Cornell Maritime, 1956). One of the few acknowledgments of foreign-trade zones in a work of history is in the "neo-Hamiltonian" Michael Lind's *Land of Promise: An Economic History of the United States* (New York: Harper, 2013), 452–53.

18. Mason B. Williams, *City of Ambition: FDR, La Guardia, and the Making of Modern New York* (New York: W. W. Norton, 2013), 200.
19. Kenneth T. Jackson, ed., *The Encyclopedia of New York City*, 2nd ed. (New Haven, CT: Yale University Press, 2010), 1230, 1234.
20. Emanuel Celler, *You Never Leave Brooklyn: The Autobiography of Emanuel Celler* (New York: John Day, 1953).
21. Emanuel Celler, "Transcript of Proceedings of the Examiners Committee, Foreign-Trade Zones Board," November 12, 1935, 15, folder 4, box 12, Free Port Records, Staten Island Historical Society (Staten Island, NY) (hereafter Free Port Records).
22. Emanuel Celler, "Comments before the National Association of Foreign-Trade Zones 1976 National Conference," September 13, 1976, 9. My thanks to Greg Jones of the National Association of Foreign-Trade Zones for sharing this transcript.
23. Thomas E. Lyons, "Why Not a Foreign-Trade Zone at New Orleans?," speech, May 18, 1942, 1, folder 6, box 8, Free Port Records.
24. Carter R. Bryan, "Like the Pea in the Shell Game," *Foreign Commerce Weekly*, February 21, 1942.
25. This quote is from me, from the article in *Radical History Review* cited above, and now I want to qualify it. While I continue to be informed by scholarship on "mutations in sovereignty and citizenship," to reference Aihwa Ong, I dislike how—in relation to the US zone system—the term *denationalization* connotes a weakened nation-state. On what Ong calls "graduated sovereignty," see Ong, *Neoliberalism as Exception: Mutations in Citizenship and Sovereignty* (Durham, NC: Duke University Press, 2006); John Ruggie, "Territoriality and Beyond: Problematizing Modernity in International Relations," *International Organization* 47, no. 1 (Winter 1993): 139–74; and Saskia Sassen, *Territory, Authority, Rights: From Medieval to Global Assemblages* (2006). On sovereignty and customs regimes, specifically, see Brenda Chalfin, *Neoliberal Frontiers: An Ethnography of Sovereignty in West Africa* (Chicago: University of Chicago Press, 2010); and Josiah Heyman, "Ports of Entry as Nodes in the World System," *Identities: Global Studies in Culture and Power* 11, no. 3 (2004): 303–27.
26. "Somber and Sound," *Detroit Free Press*, June 15, 1965. Here I might add that US foreign-trade zones are a far cry from the postnational islands that libertarians evangelize for, whether charter cities or seasteads. Exhibit A of this gospel: Mark Frazier, "Emergence of a New Hanseatic League: How Special Economic Zones Will Reshape Global Governance," *Chapman Law Review* 21, no. 2 (2018): 333–406. For historical context, see Raymond B. Craib, "Egotopia," *Counterpunch*, August 24, 2018, https://www.counterpunch.org/2018/08/24/egotopia/.
27. James Ferguson, *The Anti-Politics Machine: Development, Depoliticization, and Bureaucratic Power in Lesotho* (Minneapolis: University of Minnesota Press, 1994).
28. Julius Henry Cohen, Senate Committee on Commerce, *Free Zones in Ports*, 66th Cong., 1st sess., October 10, 1919, 15; Senator Joseph E. Ransdell, 67th Cong., 2nd sess., *Congressional Record* 62, August 16, 1922, 11411; Emanuel Celler, House Committee on Ways and Means, *Foreign-Trade Zones*, 80th Cong., 2nd sess., May 10, 1948, 12.

29. See, for instance, Dan McGraw, "Free Trade Zone Is Perot's Own Nafta," *Chicago Tribune*, September 18, 1993.
30. Charles Peters, "A Neoliberal's Manifesto," *Washington Monthly*, May 1983, 11.
31. Bob Wiedrich, "Foreign Trade Zones Languish," *Chicago Tribune*, September 15, 1981.
32. Robert Murray Haig, "Toward an Understanding of the Metropolis," *Quarterly Journal of Economics* 40, no. 2 (1926), 184. Haig anticipates Lewis Mumford's gloss on the metropolis as a "processing center," in *The City in History: Its Origins, Its Transformations, and Its Prospects* (New York: Harcourt, 1961). On Mumford, see Alberto Toscano, "Logistics and Opposition," *Mute* 3, no. 2 (August 9, 2012), http://www.metamute.org/editorial/articles/logistics-and-opposition. On "work," see Augustine Sedgewick, "Against Flows," *History of the Present* 4, no. 2 (Fall 2014): 143–70. On "friction-free capitalism," see chapter 8 in Bill Gates with Nathan Myhrvold and Peter Rinearson, *The Road Ahead*, rev. ed. (New York: Penguin, 1996). On frictionlessness as both a design aesthetic and an economic idiom during the Fordist era, see Jeffrey L. Meikle, *Twentieth Century Limited: Industrial Design in America, 1925–1938* (Philadelphia: Temple University Press, 1979).
33. On the infrastructure of cyberspace, see, for example, Donald MacKenzie, "Be Grateful for Drizzle," *London Review of Books* 36, no. 17 (2014): 27–30; and Nicole Starosielski, *The Undersea Network* (Durham, NC: Duke University Press, 2015).
34. These insights on the labors of leisure in the digital sphere are indebted to feminist scholarship, such as Astra Taylor, "The Automation Charade," *Logic* no. 5 (2018), https://logicmag.io/05-the-automation-charade/. On the Roomba see Neta Alexander, "From Dust to Drone: Roomba Aesthetics and Non-Human Cinema," *Flow*, March 27, 2017, https://www.flowjournal.org/2017/03/from-dust-till-drone/. For a related intervention about the built environment, see Hilary Sample, *Maintenance Architecture* (Cambridge, MA: MIT Press, 2016).
35. My thanks to Andrew Zimmerman for this phrase and for conversations about "the hidden abode of production."
36. Such scholars homogenize the qualitative forms of capital into quantitative flows of finance capital. This tendency is most explicit in Vanessa Ogle, "Archipelago Capitalism: Tax Havens, Offshore Money, and the State, 1940s–1970s," *American Historical Review* 122, no. 5 (2017): 1431–58; and Ronen Palan, *The Offshore World: Sovereign Markets, Virtual Places, and Nomad Millionaires* (Ithaca, NY: Cornell University Press, 2003). I concur with Jonathan Bach: "A Zone may contain a tax haven but is not historically co-extensive with it; the focus is production not evasion." Bach, "Modernity and the Urban Imagination in Economic Zones," 100.
37. And it is out of stock in the historiography of capitalism. "The role of the warehouse in the twentieth-century economy is something of a 'black box,' hidden from view and largely taken for granted," writes Shane Hamilton, *Trucking Country: The Road to America's Wal-Mart Economy* (Princeton, NJ: Princeton University Press, 2008), 272n29. David Mitch provides a historical taxonomy of warehousing in "Public Warehousing," in *Extractives, Manufacturing and Services: A Historiographical and Bibliographical Guide*, ed. David O. Whitten (Westport, CT: Greenwood, 1997), 377–406. Monika Dommann is writing a global history of the warehouse since 1800 (in German), of which outtakes include "'Be Wise—Palletize,' Die Transformationen eines Transportbretts zwischen den USA und Europa im Zeitalter der Logistik," *Traverse* 16, no. 3 (2009): 21–35; "Verbandelt im Welthandel: Spediteure und ihre Papiere seit dem 18. Jahrhundert," *WerkstattGeschichte* 58 (2012): 29–48; "Handling,

Flowcharts, Logistik: Zur Wissensgeschichte und Materialkultur von Warenflüssen," *Zürcher Jahrbuch für Wissensgeschichte* 7 (2011): 75–103; and "Warenräume und Raumökonomien: Kulturtechniken des Lagerns," *Tumult: Schriften zur Verkehrswissenschaft* 38 (2012): 50–62. To expand on Hamilton's footnote, while warehousing is implicated by business historians in studies of wholesaling, marketing, and so forth, it is not taken up as a business unto itself. Similarly neglected is the warehouse as a spatial form adjacent to but autonomous from the chain store and the department store. On these frontstage assemblages, see Andrew K. Sandoval-Strausz, "Spaces of Commerce: A Historiographic Introduction to Certain Architectures of Capitalism," *Winterthur Portfolio* 44, no. 2/3 (2010): 143–58.

38. Elizabeth Hinton, *From the War on Poverty to the War on Crime: The Making of Mass Incarceration in America* (Cambridge, MA: Harvard University Press, 2016), 210–11.

39. More showcases of the abandoned or deserted warehouse were films like *This Gun for Hire* (1942) and *Asphalt Jungle* (1950), and parodying it are films like *Reservoir Dogs* (1992) and *Synecdoche, New York* (2008), in which the past is, literally, per Arjun Appadurai, "a synchronic warehouse of cultural scenarios." Appadurai, *Modernity at Large: Cultural Dimensions of Globalization* (Minneapolis: University of Minnesota Press, 1996), 30. Another pastiche is the music video for Michael Jackson's "Beat It" (1982).

40. Robert Levy, "Wizard of the Warehouse," *Dun's Review and Modern Industry*, May 1966, 49.

41. Alice Griffin, *Understanding Arthur Miller* (Columbia: University of South Carolina Press, 1996), 96.

42. In 1946, Alfred Kazin extolled these warehouses as emblems of "old New York": "There are warehouses cut into the belly of the anchorages of the bridge, and the clerks who sit in stools in them have migrated from prints of old London." Kazin, "Brooklyn Bridge," *Harper's Bazaar*, September 1946, 397. See also Ada Louise Huxtable, "Farewell, Old New York," *New York Times*, November 18, 1973. For a jab at mid-twentieth-century warehouses as antiques, see "The Push-Button Warehouse," *Fortune*, December 1956, 140.

43. Similar associations are triggered on the prairies. The photographer Frank Gohlke muses about "lost worlds," "vanished empires," and "abandoned cities" in *Measure of Emptiness: Grain Elevators in the American Landscape* (Baltimore: Johns Hopkins University Press, 1992), 14.

44. Barbara Swift, "Queer Cargoes," *New Orleans Port Record*, March 1947, 13. Miles Ogborn stakes out seaports as "points of articulation" in the "local history of capitalism" in "Making Connections: Port Geography and Global History," in *Organización del Espacio en el México Colonial: Puertos, Ciudades y Caminos*, ed. Lourdes de Ita Rubio (Instituto de Investigaciones Históricas, UMSNH, 2012), 97–120. Virginia Woolf testifies to the seaport as a tableau of global capitalism in "The London Docks," *Good Housekeeping*, December 1931; see also the chapter on Alice Austen in Laura Wexler, *Tender Violence: Domestic Visions in an Age of U.S. Imperialism* (Chapel Hill: University of North Carolina Press, 2000). On the visuality of the transition from "queer cargoes" (bulk cargoes) to shipping containers, see Allan Sekula, *Fish Story* (Düsseldorf: Richter Verlag, 1995); and Güven Incirlioglu and Hakan Topal, eds., *The Sea-Image: Visual Manifestations of Port Cities and Global Waters* (New York: Newgray, 2011).

45. David E. Nye, *America's Assembly Line* (Cambridge, MA: MIT Press, 2013), 45.

46. "Circulation" can refer to the physical distribution of commodity capital, as well

as to the circulation of value through different forms of appearance like commodity capital, finance capital, and rentier capital. These two circulations are "almost always intertwined," writes Jasper Bernes. (For example, the warehouse facilitates both the transfer of commodities and the release of credit via the warehouse receipt and the customs bond.) See Bernes, "Logistics, Counterlogistics and the Communist Prospect," *End Notes* 3 (2014), https://endnotes.org.uk/issues/3/en/jasper-bernes-logistics-counterlogistics-and-the-communist-prospect; Joshua Clover, *Riot. Strike. Riot: The New Era of Uprisings* (New York: Verso, 2016); and Deborah Cowen, *The Deadly Life of Logistics: Mapping Violence in Global Trade* (Minneapolis: University of Minnesota Press, 2014).

47. Because the zone is a state space (a public utility, for that matter), what happens in it is scrutinized by lawyers, and keywords like "manufacturing" are scrupulously vetted. Vagueness is not viable. The archive of the zone therefore helps to demystify the intellectual history of capitalism, similar to how copyright law sheds light on the commodification of images. As Jane M. Gaines observes, "In entertainment law, the economic motive is written all over the face of things, as opposed to the way it appears in narrative fictions—in disguised and inverted forms." Gaines, "The Absurdity of Property in the Person," *Yale Journal of Law and Humanities* 10, no. 2 (1998): 539.

48. White House, Office of the Press Secretary, "Remarks by the President on the American Auto Industry and American Economy at Chrysler Auto Plant," July 30, 2010, https://obamawhitehouse.archives.gov/the-press-office/remarks-president-american-auto-industry-and-american-economy-chrysler-auto-plant.

49. I refer here less to lines in the sand than to the "boundary struggles" that Nancy Fraser posits as integral to capital accumulation. Fraser, "Behind Marx's Hidden Abode," *New Left Review* 86 (2014): 55–72. On lines in the sand and "state ordering," see Brenda Chalfin, "Global Customs Regimes and the Traffic in Sovereignty," *Current Anthropology* 47, no. 2 (2006): 246. On boundaries as "differentials"—gender, race, nature—"that allow value to flow, to valorize and realize itself" (and on the seaport as "the management of the differential"), see Joshua Clover and Juliana Spahr, "Gender Abolition and Ecotone War," *South Atlantic Quarterly* 115, no. 2 (2016): 304, 308.

50. The "hallmark" of the zone is "its legal re-designation of activities within a delimited space." Bach, "Modernity and the Urban Imagination in Economic Zones," 100. Studies of marketplaces that have influenced me include Jean-Christophe Agnew, *Worlds Apart: The Market and the Theater in Anglo-American Thought, 1550–1750* (Cambridge: Cambridge University Press, 1986); Aaron Carico, *Black Market: Slavery, Capitalism, and American Culture after 1865* (Chapel Hill: University of North Carolina Press, forthcoming); and Rebecca Tinio McKenna, *American Imperial Pastoral: The Architecture of US Colonialism in the Philippines* (Chicago: University of Chicago Press, 2017).

51. Siegfried Giedion, *Mechanization Takes Command: A Contribution to Anonymous History* (New York: Oxford University Press, 1948), 3. See also Jean-Christophe Agnew, "Anonymous History," in *Capitalism Takes Command: The Social Transformation of Nineteenth-Century America*, ed. Michael Zakim and Gary J. Kornblith (Chicago: University of Chicago Press, 2012), 277–84.

52. The indictment of "capital-C Capital" is from Seth Rockman, "What Makes the History of Capitalism Newsworthy?" *Journal of the Early Republic* 34, no. 3 (2014): 448. For critiques of "neoempiricism," see Brian Connolly, "Against Accumulation," *J19: The Journal of Nineteenth-Century Americanists* 2, no. 1 (2014): 172–79; Kieran Healy,

"Fuck Nuance," *Sociological Theory* 35, no. 2 (2017): 118–27; Joan W. Scott, "Against Eclecticism," *Differences* 16, no. 3 (2005): 114–37. In a visual register, see Alexander Galloway, "Are Some Things Unrepresentable?" *Theory, Culture & Society* 28, no. 7–8 (2011): 85–102.

53. "We know well the dangers of taking the part for the whole, but it is difficult to imagine the whole without those metonymic devices," Michael Denning writes in "Representing Global Labor," *Social Text* 25, no. 3 (2007): 142. See also Leigh Claire La Berge, *Scandals and Abstraction: Financial Fiction in the Long 1980s* (Oxford: Oxford University Press, 2014); Sianne Ngai, "Visceral Abstractions," *GLQ: A Journal of Lesbian and Gay Studies* 21, no. 1 (2015): 33–63; and Alberto Toscano, "The Open Secret of Real Abstraction," *Rethinking Marxism* 20, no. 2 (2008): 273–87. The turn from the real abstractions of "capital" and "labor" to the metaphysics of "power" can amount to a turn away from exploitation, as Fredric Jameson observes:

> For Marxism, indeed, the categories of power are not the ultimate ones, and the trajectory of contemporary social theory (from Weber to Foucault) suggests that the appeal to it is often strategic, and involves a systematic displacement of the Marxian problematic. No, the ultimate form of the "nightmare of history" is rather the fact of labor itself, and the intolerable spectacle of the backbreaking millennial toil of millions of people from the earliest moments of human history. The more existential versions of this dizzying and properly unthinkable, unimaginable spectacle—as in horror at the endless succession of "dying generations," at the ceaseless wheel of life, or at the irrevocable passage of Time itself—are themselves only disguises for this ultimately scandalous fact of mindless alienated work and of the irremediable loss and waste of human energies, a scandal to which no metaphysical categories can give a meaning. (Jameson, "Marxism and Historicism," in *The Ideologies of Theory: The Syntax of History* [Minneapolis: University of Minnesota Press, 1988], 162)

For a similar critique, written with an eye to the global assembly line, see Gayatri Chakravorty Spivak, "Scattered Speculations on the Question of Value," *Diacritics* 15, no. 4 (1985): 73–93.

54. Alberto Toscano and Jeff Kinkle, *Cartographies of the Absolute* (Hants, UK: Zero Books, 2015), 44.
55. I love how Siegfried Giedion deploys visual material as a hypertext: "To facilitate the reading, special care was taken in the choice and the layout of illustrations. Captions are provided in such a way as to convey the broad outline independently of and simultaneously with the text." Giedion, *Mechanization Takes Command*, vii.
56. Which, again, is not to say *not* abstract but rather abstract *and* concrete.
57. Roland Barthes, "The Rhetoric of the Image," in *Image, Music, Text*, trans. Stephen Heath (New York: Hill and Wang, 1977), 44. On photographs as historical evidence, see Kevin Coleman, Daniel James, and Jayeeta Sharma, "Photography and Work," *Radical History Review* 132 (2018): 1–22; and Jennifer Tucker, "Entwined Practices: Engagements with Photography in Historical Inquiry," *History and Theory* 48, no. 4 (2009): 1–8. On photographs in the archive of American capitalism, see Elspeth Brown, *The Corporate Eye: Photography and the Rationalization of American Commercial Culture, 1884–1929* (Baltimore: Johns Hopkins University Press, 2005); David E. Nye, *Image Worlds: Corporate Identities at General Electric, 1890–1930* (Cambridge, MA: MIT Press, 1985); Allan Sekula, "Photography between Labour and Capital," in *Mining Photographs and Other Pictures, 1948–1968*, ed. Benjamin H. D. Buchloh and Robert Wilkie (Halifax: Press of the Nova Scotia College of Art and Design, 1983),

193–268; and Alan Trachtenberg, *Reading American Photographs: Images as History, Mathew Brady to Walker Evans* (New York: Hill and Wang, 1989).

58. Walter Johnson, "The Pedestal and the Veil: Rethinking the Capitalism/Slavery Question," *Journal of the Early Republic* 24, no. 2 (2004): 299–308. On the aesthetic of instrumentalism, see Allan Sekula, "The Instrumental Image: Steichen at War," *Artforum* 14, no. 4 (1975): 26–35; and Alberto Toscano, "The Mirror of Circulation: Allan Sekula and the Logistical Image," *EPD: Society and Space* 36, no. 4 (2018), https://societyandspace.org/2018/07/30/the-mirror-of-circulation-allan-sekula-and-the-logistical-image/.

59. As George Steinmetz writes, "Repeated patterns or regularities that persist over time and generalize across space are the truly puzzling anomalies." Steinmetz, "On the Articulation of Marxist and Non-Marxist Theory in Colonial Historiography," *Journal of World-Systems Research* 20, no. 2 (2014): 285.

60. "4 Trade Groups Act to Speed Free Port," *New York Times*, December 10, 1932.

61. Ralph Scanlan, "The Potentialities of a Foreign Trade Zone in the Trade of the Port of San Francisco" (PhD diss., University of California, Berkeley, 1929), 80.

CHAPTER ONE

1. Ernest Ingersoll, "The Lading of a Ship," *Harper's New Monthly Magazine*, September 1877, 481–93.

2. Clyde L. MacKenzie Jr., "Biographic Memoir of Ernest Ingersoll: Naturalist, Shellfish Scientist, and Author," *Marine Fisheries Review* 53, no. 3 (1991): 23–29. Ingersoll's way of seeing a warehouse as a palimpsest of stages of human development exemplifies Anne McClintock's concept of "panoptical time," which she links to the advent of the imperial emporium (the department store) and defines as "the image of a global history consumed—at a glance—in a single spectacle from a point of privileged invisibility." McClintock, *Imperial Leather: Race, Gender and Sexuality in the Colonial Contest* (New York: Routledge, 1995), 37. See also Kristin Hoganson, *Consumers' Imperium: The Global Production of American Domesticity, 1865–1920* (Chapel Hill: University of North Carolina Press, 2007). This engraving and its companion photograph (the chapter's visual epigraph) typify a mode of representation that came to the fore in the age of empire. Quinn Slobodian argues that "two competing ways of seeing the world economy crystallized around 1900," the panoramic map and the pointilist chronophotograph, and I propose the metonymic landscape as a third. Slobodian, "How to See the World Economy: Statistics, Maps, and Schupeter's Camera in the First Age of Globalization," *Journal of Global History* 10, no. 2 (2015): 331.

3. On the body as a symbol of circulation, see Timothy L. Alborn, "Economic Man, Economic Machine: Images of Circulation in the Victorian Money Market," in *Natural Images in Economic Thought: "Markets Read in Tooth and Claw,"* ed. Philip Mirowski (New York: Cambridge University Press, 1994), 173–96; Sara Altschuler, "From Blood Vessels to Global Networks of Exchange: The Physiology of Benjamin Rush's Early Republic," *Journal of the Early Republic* 32, no. 2 (Summer 2012): 207–32. See also Susan Buck-Morss, "Envisioning Capital: Political Economy on Display," *Critical Inquiry* 21 (Winter 1995): 434–67.

4. In terms of the social metabolism of nature, we might also equate the reservoir and the warehouse in that they were inorganic structures for extracting value from organic processes. See Jason W. Moore, *Capitalism in the Web of Life: Ecology and the Accumulation of Capital* (New York: Verso, 2015); and E. A. Wrigley, *Continuity, Chance*

and Change: The Character of the Industrial Revolution in England (Cambridge: Cambridge University Press, 1988).

5. "The United States Bonded Warehouse—the Security against Fire," *New York Herald*, July 20, 1847.
6. US Department of Commerce and Labor, *Warehousing Industry in the United States* (Washington, DC: Government Printing Office, 1903), 1036.
7. Karl Marx, *Capital* (London: Penguin, 1978), 2:225. It is in this spirit that Marxists can reclaim the heuristic of "flows" from the flat-worlders, with wealth measured by the circulation—flows—of value rather than by the accumulation of goods. On flows of value in the historiography of capitalism, see A. G. Jakes and Ahmad Shokr, "Finding Value in *Empire of Cotton*," *Critical Historical Studies* 4, no. 1 (2017): 107–36; and Gabriel Winant, "Slave Capitalism," *n+1* 17 (Fall 2013), https://www.nplusonemag.com/issue-17/reviews/slave-capitalism/.
8. Karl Marx, *Theories of Surplus Value* (Moscow: Progress Publishers, 1968), 870–75. In German, Marx wrote of warehouses as *Zirkulationreservoirs*, adopting the French-English term for "reservoir."
9. Clarence Aspinwall, *Household Goods Warehousing in the United States* (Washington, DC: American Warehousemen's Association, 1925), v.
10. "Storage Is Civilization," *Distribution & Warehousing*, April 1922, 48. Lewis Mumford would enshrine this thesis by designating the container as the paradigmatic tool of the Neolithic Age in his celebrated *The City in History: Its Origins, Its Transformations, and Its Prospects* (New York: Harcourt, 1961).
11. H. A. Haring, *Warehousing: Trade Customs and Practices, Financial and Legal Aspects* (New York: Ronald, 1925), 17.
12. American Warehousemen's Association, *Bulletins 1–8* (New York: AWA, 1900), 11.
13. On "historical copy" see "The Business Quiz," *Confectioner's Journal*, September 1922, 95. A rare example of a comparable précis on this history (in English) is in Fernand Braudel's *The Wheels of Commerce*, vol. 2 of *Civilization and Capitalism, 15th–18th Century*, trans. Siân Reynolds (New York: Harper and Row, 1982), 94–97.
14. H. H. Manchester, "A Pictorial History of the Garden," *Garden Magazine*, January 1922, 113; Manchester, "Evolution of the Bookstore," *Bookman*, May 1918, 240–51. Manchester calls attention to the relationship between the space as a noun and the space as a verb. The garden is the basis of gardening. The bank is the basis of banking. The warehouse is the basis of warehousing. Correspondingly, he throws into relief the nouns for which this equation does *not* hold—for instance, the factory.
15. H. H. Manchester, "A History of the Warehouse, IV: Other Factors in Its Development," *Distribution & Warehousing*, December 1922, 14.
16. H. H. Manchester, "A History of the Warehouse since 2200 B.C.," *Distribution & Warehousing*, May 1922, 20.
17. H. H. Manchester, "A History of the Warehouse, III: In the Middle Ages," *Distribution & Warehousing*, October 1922, 20.
18. The Dutch West India Company backed one of the New World's earliest warehouses in the "factory" of New Amsterdam in 1623. The first Congress of the United States followed suit with a "factory system" in an "Act to Regulate Trade and Intercourse with the Indian Tribes" in 1791. See David A. Nichols, *Engines of Diplomacy: Indian Factories and the Negotiation of American Empire* (Chapel Hill: University of North Carolina Press, 2016); and Ora Brooks Peake, *A History of the United States Factory System, 1795–1822* (Denver: Sage Books, 1954). The apostle of American Empire

Frederick Jackson Turner detailed how such factories triggered "all the transforming forces that accompany the intercourse of a higher with a lower civilization." Turner, *The Character and Influence of the Indian Trade in Wisconsin* (Baltimore: Johns Hopkins University Press, 1891), 3.

19. On the etymology of "factory," see R. Whatley Cooke-Taylor, *Introduction to a History of the Factory System* (London: Richard Bentley and Son, 1886) 1–6. See also Susan Buck-Morss, *Hegel, Haiti, and Universal History* (Pittsburgh: University of Pittsburgh Press, 2009), 101–4; and Marcus Rediker, *The Slave Ship: A Human History* (New York: Penguin, 2007), 44.
20. Saidiya Hartman, *Lose Your Mother: A Journey along the Atlantic Slave Route* (New York: Farrar, Straus and Giroux, 2007), 111.
21. Scholars in critical carceral studies have rejected this binary by embedding prisons in capitalism, such as Ruth Wilson Gilmore, *Golden Gulag: Prisons, Surplus, Crisis, and Opposition in Globalizing California* (Berkeley: University of California Press, 2007).
22. Haring, *Warehousing*, 22.
23. Marx, *Capital*, 2:218. "Because it did not assume the form of a commodity stock, Adam Smith thus confused the form of the stock with the stock itself, and believed that society previously lived from hand to mouth, abandoning itself to the hazards of the next day. This is a childish misunderstanding."
24. Haring, *Warehousing*, 4.
25. See Leonard J. Arrington, *Great Basin Kingdom: An Economic History of the Latter-Day Saints, 1830–1900* (Cambridge, MA: Harvard University Press, 1958).
26. On the plan in Philadelphia, see Andrew Shankman, *Crucible of American Democracy: The Struggle to Fuse Egalitarianism and Capitalism in Jeffersonian Pennsylvania* (Lawrence: University Press of Kansas, 2004), 165.
27. Charles Postel, *The Populist Vision* (New York: Oxford University Press, 2007), 17, 116, 233–37.
28. See Bronislaw Malinowski, *Argonauts of the Western Pacific* (London: Routledge and Sons, 1922). Karl Polanyi leaned on Malinowski in stressing the centrality of storage to the economy of redistribution in *The Great Transformation: The Political and Economic Origins of Our Times* (Boston: Beacon, 1971), 50–55.
29. H. H. Manchester, "A History of the Warehouse, V: The Earliest American Warehouses," *Distribution & Warehousing*, April 1923, 20.
30. See, for instance, Elva Tooker, *Nathan Trotter: Philadelphia Merchant, 1787–1853* (Cambridge, MA: Harvard University Press, 1955).
31. H. H. Manchester, "A History of the Warehouse, VII, Early America, 2: The Development Inland, 1800–1850," *Distribution & Warehousing*, September 1924, 21.
32. Walt Whitman in "Crossing Brooklyn Ferry," as quoted in Malka Simon, "The Space of Production: Brooklyn and the Creation of an Urban Industrial Landscape" (PhD diss., New York University, 2009), 1. Simon notes that these warehouses—"a mass of repetitiveness"—were best comprehended from the water (56–57). For a window on the shift from storehouse to warehouse, see the Pierrepont Papers at the Brooklyn Historical Society.
33. George H. Ireland, 1877, Improvement in Toys, US Patent 195,011, filed December 18, 1876, and issued September 11, 1877.
34. Robert A. M. Stern, Thomas Mellins, and David Fishman, *New York 1880* (New York: Monacelli, 1999), 468. The authors devote an entire section to warehouses in this volume, but they make no explicit mention of them in the 1900, 1930, and 1960

volumes. This pattern accords with most architectural surveys. On the pivot of 1880, see Leonard K. Eaton, "Warehouses and Warehouse Districts in Mid-American Cities," *Urban History Review* 11, no. 1 (1982): 17–26.

35. *Prospectus of the Atlantic Dock Company* (New York: George F. Nesbitt, 1840); Simon, "The Space of Production," 59–66; Edwin G. Burrows and Mike Wallace, *Gotham: A History of New York City to 1898* (New York: Oxford University Press, 1999), 653–54.
36. See Henry R. Stiles, *A History of the City of Brooklyn* (Brooklyn: Published by Subscription, 1867), 1:59. Similarly, the *Brooklyn Eagle* published numerous features on the new docks, e.g., "Thirty-Eight Years of Progress," *Brooklyn Eagle*, May 16, 1874.
37. Glenn Porter and Harold C. Livesay, *Merchants and Manufacturers: Studies in the Changing Structure of Nineteenth-Century Marketing* (Baltimore: Johns Hopkins University Press, 1971).
38. Walter C. Reid, "The Development of the Household Goods Storage Business," in *The Transfer and Storage Directory* (New York: Transfer and Storage Publishing Corporation, 1916), 16.
39. "In a Storage Warehouse: Curious Features of a Comparatively New Business," *New York Tribune*, January 17, 1897.
40. US Department of Commerce and Labor, *Warehousing Industry in the United States*, 1049.
41. "Moving Romances to the Storage House," *Distribution & Warehousing*, June 1922, 37.
42. "In a Storage Warehouse: Curious Features of a Comparatively New Business," *New York Tribune*, January 17, 1897; Margery Rae, "There's More to Moving than Motion," *Nation's Business*, April 1939, 36. See also Clarence A. Aspinwall, "The Evolution of the Storage Warehouse," *Financial Review*, February 5, 1897, 6; and Aspinwall, *Household Goods Warehousing in the United States*. On singularization, see Jean-Christophe Agnew, "The Give-and-Take of Consumer Culture," in *Commodifying Everything: Relationships of the Market*, ed. Susan Strasser (London: Routledge, 2003), 11–39. On the contemporary landscape of self-storage, see the thematic issue "Shelf Life," *Harvard Design Magazine* no. 43 (Fall/Winter 2016).
43. Haring, *Warehousing*, 385.
44. Recent work on cold-storage warehouses includes Susanne Freidberg, *Fresh: A Perishable History* (Cambridge, MA: Harvard University Press, 2009); Michael Osman, *Modernism's Visible Hand: Architecture and Regulation in America* (Minneapolis: University of Minnesota Press, 2018); Jonathan Rees, *Refrigeration Nation: A History of Ice, Appliances, and Enterprise in America* (Baltimore: John Hopkins University Press, 2013); and "Perishable: An Exploration of the Refrigerated Landscape of America," a multimedia study by Nicola Twilley and the Center for Land Use Interpretation, www.clui.org/section/perishable-exploration-refrigerated-landscape-america. On frozen cadavers as well as frozen chickens, see Joanna Radin and Emma Kowal, eds., *Cryopolitics: Frozen Life in a Melting World* (Cambridge, MA: MIT Press, 2017).
45. "Artificial Cold on Tap," *Chicago Daily Tribune*, November 1, 1888.
46. James F. O'Gorman, "A Bogardus Original," *Architectural Review*, February 1970, 155–56. Moreover, "Between 1850 and 1880 the use of iron columns for the means of support for the floors of a building defined the construction of office buildings, warehouses, and department stores." Siegfried Giedion, *Space, Time, and Architecture*, 5th ed. (Cambridge, MA: Harvard University Press, 1967), 195.
47. "New Engineering and Architectural Firm Organized," *Construction News*, May 3, 1913.

48. American Warehousemen's Association, *Traveling the Road of Logistics: The Evolution of Warehousing and Distribution* (Chicago: American Warehousemen's Association, 1991). The AWA replaced the Associated Transfer and Storage Companies, which had been formed in 1884 by firms that stored farm equipment. The "American Warehousemen's Association" was not rechristened as the "American Warehousers' Association" until the 1990s.
49. American Warehousemen's Association, *Warehousing, Storage, and Forwarding Reference* (Kansas City: Tew-Lyle, 1892).
50. Ruth Dutilh Jenkins, "Mr. Storage Executive: Meet Mrs. Warehouseman," *Distribution & Warehousing*, February 1922, 34–35, 50.
51. Revolutionaries targeted warehouses for expropriation. "The integrity of the Russian warehouse has been shattered. Warehousemen have been powerless to prevent the looting of warehouses and granaries, and the warehousing industry of that country has made a failure as disastrous as that of the banking system." Haring, *Warehousing*, 28. At the same time, warehousing thwarted revolution. A textbook recommends "strike protection" as one pragmatic reason to patronize public warehouses—to ensure back inventories should a supply chain snap. Albert G. Sweetser, *Financing Goods* (Newton, MA: Albert G. Sweetser, 1957), 199.
52. Haring, *Warehousing*, 99.
53. The columns were collected in H. A. Haring, *New Business for Warehouses* (New York: Distribution and Warehousing Publications, 1931), 28.
54. Haring, *New Business for Warehouses*, 181.
55. Albert Haring, "The Public Warehouse an Essential Tool in Wholesale Distribution," *Journal of Marketing* 1, no. 2 (October 1936): 106–14. Albert Haring was the son of H. A. Haring.
56. Porter and Livesay, *Merchants and Manufacturers*, 218.
57. H. H. Manchester dates the first warehouse receipts to 1318, qualifying that it was not until the early eighteenth century that they were exchanged as "checks." He contends that "the first banks were developed out of this custom of receiving valuables on deposit." Manchester, "A History of the Warehouse, IV," 16.
58. At tobacco-inspection warehouses, farmers exchanged tobacco for "tobacco notes," which they used to pay taxes and to buy other commodities. For a Habermasian meditation on tobacco auction warehouses, see Pete Daniels, "Reasons to Talk about Tobacco," *Journal of American History* 96, no. 3 (December 2009): 663–77.
59. American Warehousemen's Association, *Traveling the Road of Logistics*, 29; Haring, *Warehousing*, 28. A company in Milwaukee came to be known as "the bank" because of the success of the faux folklore in its ad copy. "This Warehouse Is a Bank," *Distribution & Warehousing*, February 1922. The company is going strong: www.hansenstorage.com.
60. As he wrote of receipts for cotton and iron, "A house that is sold by A to B circulates as a commodity, but it does not get up and walk. . . . What actually moves here is the property title to the thing and not the thing itself." Marx, *Capital*, 2:226. On paperwork and finance, see Seth Rockman, introduction to "Forum: The Paper Technologies of Capitalism," *Technology and Culture* 58, no. 2 (2017): 487–505.
61. On the alteration of the sack into the carload, see William Cronon, *Nature's Metropolis: Chicago and the Great West* (New York: W. W. Norton, 1991), 104–9.
62. The dean of business historians dates the origins of mass distribution to the marketing of grain and cotton in the 1840s. Alfred D. Chandler Jr., *The Visible Hand:*

The Managerial Revolution in American Business (Cambridge, MA: Harvard University Press, 1977), 209.

63. "Farmers or shippers took their wheat or corn to an elevator operator as if they were taking gold or silver to a banker." Cronon, *Nature's Metropolis*, 120.
64. "One scholar [in 1896] called the introduction of these general receipts 'the most important step in the history of the grain trade.'" Morton Rothstein, "Antebellum Wheat and Cotton Exports: A Contrast in Marketing Organization and Development," *Agricultural History* 40, no. 2 (1966): 97.
65. William J. Brown, *American Colossus: The Grain Elevator, 1843 to 1943* (Cincinnati: Colossal Books, 2009), 12.
66. The United States led the world in the invention of grain elevators. George Frederick Zimmer, *The Mechanical Handling of Material* (London: Crosby Lockwood and Son, 1905), 436.
67. Cronon, *Nature's Metropolis*, 120–47; Ann Fabian, *Card Sharps and Bucket Shops: Gambling in Nineteenth-Century America* (Ithaca, NY: Cornell University Press, 1990); George L. Henderson, *California and the Fictions of Capital* (Philadelphia: Temple University Press, 2003); Jonathan Ira Levy, "Contemplating Delivery: Futures Trading and the Problem of Commodity Exchange in the United States, 1875–1905," *American Historical Review* 111, no. 2 (April 2006): 307–35; Scott Reynolds Nelson, *A Nation of Deadbeats: An Uncommon History of America's Financial Disasters* (New York: Random House, 2012); Jeffrey C. Williams, "The Origin of Futures Markets," *Agricultural History* 56, no. 1 (1982): 306–16.
68. Haring, *Warehousing*, 67.
69. Fred'k H. Cooke, "The Application of the Commerce Clause to the Intangible," *University of Pennsylvania Law Review* 58 (April 1910): 411–25.
70. Oliver Wendell Holmes Sr., "The Stereoscope and the Stereograph," in *Classic Essays on Photography*, ed. Alan Trachtenberg (New Haven, CT: Leete's Island Books, 1980), 80–81. See also Allan Sekula, "The Traffic in Photographs," *Art Journal* 41, no. 1 (Spring 1981): 15–25. Peter Knight writes in an absorbing essay on images of the stock market that "American capitalism became increasingly difficult to 'see' in this period," and while I agree, I find Knight's inattention to photography to short shrift his analysis of abstraction, which he treats as an aesthetic style and not also as an aesthetic logic and therefore as a trait of modernism and not also of realism. Knight, "Representations of Capitalism in the Gilded Age and Progressive Era," in *American Capitalism: New Histories*, ed. Sven Beckert and Christine Desan (New York: Columbia University Press, 2018), 236–56.
71. The warehouse assured tangibility, even when tangibility no longer entered into the equation. So testified a merchant at a hearing on futures markets: "If I wish to buy grain, believing it is selling too cheaply, I can do it without expense merely by finding a responsible man who holds views opposite to mine. His contract is as good and as safe *as if I had the stuff locked up in warehouses*" (emphasis added). House Committee on Agriculture, *Fictitious Dealings in Agricultural Products*, 52nd Cong., 3rd sess., February 4, 1892, 303.
72. Marx, *Theories of Surplus Value*, 871.
73. As Henderson observes, "The very processes that interrupt the circulation of one capital are processes which may be the condition for the circulation of another." Henderson, *California and the Fictions of Capital*, 42. See also David Harvey, *The Limits to Capital* (London: Verso, 2006), 239–82.

74. At the AWA's 1893 convention, a warehouseman vented: "I would like to say that as far as my observation has gone, no banker cares for these warehouse receipts as collateral, unless they had it drummed into their heads by the warehouseman that the security is of the best, and that their money is better secured than in almost any other way. . . . After they have had it forced into them they liked it." American Warehousemen's Association, *Proceedings of the Third Annual Meeting of the American Warehousemen's Association* (Kansas City: George W. Tew, 1893), 63.
75. Elizabeth Sanders, *The Roots of Reform: Farmers, Workers, and the American State, 1877–1917* (Chicago: University of Chicago Press, 1999), 298–303; Haring, *Warehousing*, 329–45.
76. "A warehouse is more than is implied in the common application of the word, i.e., a place to store goods. As a rule it is the safekeeping premises for bank collateral." Robert H. Bean, *Subsidiary Warehousing: Not an Approved Substitute for the Bona Fide Warehouseman* (New York: American Acceptance Council, [undated pamphlet, ca. 1920s]), 12, 4.
77. An act to extend the warehousing system by establishing private bonded warehouses, 10 *US Statutes at Large* 270 (March 28, 1854).
78. For a few intriguing analyses by legal scholars—published well before the practice became a regular facet of "inventory financing"—see Harold F. Birnbaum, "Form and Substance in Field Warehousing," *Law and Contemporary Problems* 13, no. 4 (Autumn 1948): 579–92; Daniel M. Friedman, "Field Warehousing," *Columbia Law Review* 42, no. 6 (June 1942): 991–1013; and Neil H. Jacoby and Raymond J. Saulnier, "Nature and Development of Field Warehousing," in *Financing Inventory on Field Warehouse Receipts*, ed. Neil H. Jacoby (Washington, DC: National Bureau of Economic Research, 1944), 9–18.
79. Haring, *Warehousing*, 176.
80. Herbert Bratter, "Teaching Credit New Tricks," *Nation's Business*, April 1944, 32, 34, 60; William Hurd Hillyer, "Wartime Guides for Your Business," *Barron's*, December 7, 1942.
81. Norman C. Miller, *The Great Salad Oil Swindle* (New York: Penguin, 1965), 71. On the financialization of storage via a case study of oil tanks, see Michael Simpson, "The Annihilation of Time by Space: Pluri-Temporal Strategies of Capital Circulation," *Environment and Planning E: Nature and Space* 2, no. 1 (2019): 110–28.
82. For a summary, see "The Man Who Fooled Everybody," *Time*, June 4, 1965. A young Warren Buffett made one of his first killings on the depreciated AmEx stock.
83. American Warehousemen's Association, *Warehousing General Merchandise* (Chicago: American Warehousemen's Association, 1923), 379–80.
84. "The Warehouse Trust," *Brooklyn Eagle*, March 28, 1888.
85. "Hammering the Trusts," *Brooklyn Eagle*, October 19, 1888.
86. "A Man Who Defied the Trust Now Laughs at It," *Brooklyn Eagle*, December 19, 1888. The trust was reinstituted in 1895, covering all of the Brooklyn warehouses. Within five years, it was in receivership. See "Warehouse Combine a Fact," *Brooklyn Eagle*, January 6, 1895; and "Workers of the Trusts," *Brooklyn Eagle*, April 18, 1900.
87. Niven Busch Jr., "Over Babel," *New Yorker*, April 2, 1927, 26.
88. F. B. Copley, "Irving T. Bush," *American Magazine* 76, no. 4 (October 1913): 57.
89. Irving T. Bush, *Working with the World* (Garden City, NY: Doubleday, Doran, 1928), 12. On Bush Terminal, see Simon, "The Space of Production," 160–87.
90. Haring, *Warehousing*, 13.

91. For example, see House Committee on Agriculture, "Fictitious Dealings in Agricultural Products," 30, 53, 63.
92. "Now, Schmidt, you are a first-class pig-iron handler and know your business well. You have been handling at the rate of 12 tons per day. I have given considerable study to handling pig iron, and feel sure that you could do a much larger day's work than you have been doing. Now don't you think that if you really tried you could handle 47 tons of pig iron per day, instead of 12 tons?" Frederick Winslow Taylor, *The Principles of Scientific Management* (New York: Harper and Brothers, 1911), 46.
93. Lindy Biggs, *The Rational Factory: Architecture, Technology, and Work in America's Age of Mass Production* (Baltimore: Johns Hopkins University Press, 1996), 111.
94. Horace Lucien Arnold and Fay Leone Faurote, *Ford Methods and the Ford Shops* (New York: Engineering Magazine Company, 1915), 37.
95. Henry Ford, as quoted in James M. Wilson, "Henry Ford's Just-in-Time System," in *Henry Ford: Critical Evaluations in Business and Management*, ed. John C. Wood and Michael C. Wood (London: Routledge, 2003), 1:307. See also David E. Nye, *America's Assembly Line* (Cambridge, MA: MIT Press, 2013), 27, 48. On procurement as a facet of supply-chain management at Ford, see Damon Yarnell, "Ford Motor Company's Lost Chapter: Purchasing Routine and the Advent of Mass Production," in *The Emergence of Routines: Entrepreneurship, Organization, and Business History*, ed. Daniel M. G. Raff and Philip Scranton (New York: Oxford University Press, 2017), 139–70.
96. Albert Kahn, *The Design and Construction of Industrial Buildings* (London: Technical Journals, 1917), 5–6. See also Reyner Banham, *A Concrete Atlantis: U.S. Industrial Building and European Modern Architecture, 1900–1925* (Cambridge, MA: MIT Press, 1986); Betsy Hunter Bradley, *The Works: The Industrial Architecture of the United States* (New York: Oxford University Press, 1999); Federico Bucci, *Albert Kahn: Architect of Ford* (New York: Princeton Architectural, 2002); and Amy E. Slaton, *Reinforced Concrete and the Modernization of American Building, 1900–1930* (Baltimore: Johns Hopkins University Press, 2001).
97. "The Use of Warehouses as Distribution Centers," *Bulletins 21–34* (New York: American Warehousemen's Association, 1902), 242.
98. American Warehousemen's Association, *Warehousing General Merchandise*, 334, 337.
99. "Warehousing Reforms," *The Nation's Business*, July 1923, 52.
100. On the centrality of paperwork to the circulation of capital see James R. Beniger, *The Control Revolution: Technological and Economic Origins of the Information Society* (Cambridge, MA: Harvard University Press, 1986); and Yves de la Haye, *Marx & Engels on the Means of Communication (the Movement of Commodities, People, Information & Capital)* (New York: International General, 1979).
101. American Warehousemen's Association, *Warehousing General Merchandise*, 340–41.
102. "To the uninitiated," H. A. Haring noted, "warehouse merchandise schedules are not unlike a railroad tariff in intricacy." Haring, *Warehousing*, 33. As Karl Marx commented on the infamous railroad tariffs, "The railway magnates have shown greater genius in inventing fantastic species than have botanists or zoologists." Marx, *Capital*, 2:228.
103. Mr. Spear, "Standardization of Basis for Rates," in *Proceedings of the Twenty-Eighth Annual Meeting of the American Warehousemen's Association* (New York, 1918), 148. The man-hour marks warehousing's leap from mercantile to industrial cost accounting, from buying low and selling high, as Jonathan Levy sketches, to calculat-

ing production costs. See Levy, "Accounting for Profit and the History of Capital," *Critical Historical Studies* 1, no. 2 (Fall 2014): 183.

104. American Warehousemen's Association, *Warehousing General Merchandise*, 342.
105. On the marginalists, see Rosanne Currarino, "The Politics of 'More': The Labor Question and the Idea of Economic Liberty in Industrial America," *Journal of American History* 93, no. 1 (June 2006): 32.
106. Marx, *Capital*, 2:214.
107. American Warehousemen's Association, *Warehousing General Merchandise*, 349.
108. American Warehousemen's Association, *Warehousing General Merchandise*, 348. On protests of watches, see Hugh G. J. Aitken, *Taylorism at Watertown Arsenal: Scientific Management in Action, 1908–1915* (Cambridge, MA: Harvard University Press, 1960).
109. American Warehousemen's Association, *Warehousing General Merchandise*, 342.
110. American Warehousemen's Association, *Warehousing General Merchandise*, 342.
111. Marx discusses the productivity of service workers, which he dismisses as "of microscopic significance within the mass of capitalist production." Marx, *Capital* 1:1044–49; see also Harry Braverman, *Labor and Monopoly Capital: The Degradation of Work in the Twentieth Century*, 25th anniv. ed. (New York: Monthly Review Press, 1998), 284–93; Ian Gough, "Marx's Theory of Productive and Unproductive Labor," *New Left Review* 76 (November–December 1972): 47–72; and for definitions from contemporary Marxists, see Anwar M. Shaikh and E. Ahmet Tonak, *Measuring the Wealth of Nations: The Political Economy of National Accounts* (New York: Cambridge University Press, 1994), 20–37; and Richard Walker, "Is There a Service Economy? The Changing Capitalist Division of Labor," *Science & Society* 49, no. 1 (1985): 42–83. Jason E. Smith clarifies that "productivity" (like that of warehouse work) is situational: "The same activity—say, emptying bedpans—can be unwaged when performed by family members, 'unproductive' when a health-care aide is paid out of that same family's personal income, and 'productive' when the health-worker's wages are paid by an employer who sells the employee's services to a consumer. . . . [T]he difference is not in the concrete activity itself, but in the social form within which the activity is embedded." Smith, "Jobs, Bullshit, and the Bureaucratization of the World," *Brooklyn Rail*, July 11, 2018, https://brooklynrail.org/2018/07/field-notes/Jobs-Bullshit-and-the-Bureaucratization-of-the-World.
112. American Warehousemen's Association, *Proceedings of the Thirty-Second Annual Meeting of the American Warehousemen's Association* (Pittsburgh, 1923), 73. See also, for instance, "Wanted: A Definition of 'Distribution' as Applied to Warehousing," *Distribution & Warehousing*, November 1924, 7–8.
113. Marx, *Capital*, 2:229, 209. As Neil Smith writes, "Hitherto no one has discovered the art of transporting commodities and objects from one place to another without changing their location." Smith, *Uneven Development: Nature, Capital, and the Production of Space* (1984; Athens: University of Georgia Press, 1990), 117. See also Henderson, *California and the Fictions of Capital*, 30–44.
114. Rebecca Solnit quotes Ulysses S. Grant and Ralph Waldo Emerson using this phrase in 1839 and 1844, respectively, in *River of Shadows: Eadweard Muybridge and the Technological Wild West* (New York: Viking Penguin, 2003), 9–11. Wolfgang Schivelbusch also notes its popularity in Europe during the 1830s in *The Railway Journey: The Industrialization of Time and Space in the Nineteenth Century* (Berkeley: University of California Press, 1977), 33–44, 194. Putting capital in the driver's seat, Marx famously reworked the phrase into "the annihilation of space *by* time" (emphasis added).
115. Henry George, *Protection or Free Trade: An Examination of the Tariff Question* (London:

Kegan Paul, Trench, 1886), 71; Michael Denning, *The Cultural Front: The Laboring of America Culture in the Twentieth Century* (New York: Verso, 1996), 125. George, too, invoked the metaphor of the reservoir when discussing distribution.

116. Alvin E. Dodd, "The Domestic Distribution Department of the Chamber of Commerce of the United States and the Future of Warehousing," in American Warehousemen's Association, *Proceedings of the Thirty-Second Annual Meeting*, 114.
117. In an essay about Walmart, Fredric Jameson gives reason to think that the modern warehouse might illuminate a path through the "binary tension between production and distribution, which we do not seem to be able to think our way out of." Jameson, *Valences of the Dialectic* (New York: Verso, 2009), 423, 424.
118. "Encasement" is Quinn Slobodian's helpful term for the desideratum of neoliberals like Friedrich Hayek and Ludwig von Mises, who called for supranational institutions to shield markets from politics. Slobodian, *Globalists: The End of Empire and the Birth of Neoliberalism* (Cambridge, MA: Harvard University Press, 2018). The *Freihafen*, or free zone, as I present it in chapter 3, is an encasement in miniature.
119. American Warehousemen's Association, *Proceedings of the Sixth Annual Meeting of the American Warehousemen's Association* (Boston, 1896), 53.
120. Arthur L. Dahl, "Using Gravity to Solve Transportation Problems," *Industrial Management* 66, no. 2 (1923): 104.
121. American Warehousemen's Association, *Traveling the Road of Logistics*, 66.
122. Articles on the conveyor belt and its cousins are legion in magazines and trade journals of the Fordist era. Many are lavishly illustrated with photographs of "the handling picture," so described in "Mechanical Handling: A New Production Manager," a special issue of *Factory and Industrial Management* 80, no. 2 (1930): 271.
123. Matthew William Potts, "Introducing Equipment to Warehouse Labor," *Distribution & Warehousing*, August 1922, 29.
124. George E. Squier, "Economic Utilization of Storage Space," *Distribution Economy*, November 1928, 58.
125. "Serving American Workmen," *Materials Handling and Distribution*, June 1931, 17.
126. While unions of notable size, like the warehouse divisions of the International Longshore and Warehouse Union and the Teamsters, did not form until the 1930s, local shops surfaced in the late 1890s. On the ILWU, see Harvey Schwartz, *The March Inland: Origins of the ILWU Warehouse Division, 1934–1938* (Los Angeles: Institute of Industrial Relations, 1978).
127. Potts, "Introducing Equipment to Warehouse Labor," 29; "Serving American Workmen," *Materials Handling and Distribution*, June 1931, 17.
128. "Materials Handling: The New Word in Industry," *Fortune*, June 1948, 96.
129. US Department of Commerce and Labor, *Warehousing Industry in the United States*, 1065. The galaxy beneath the ceiling was the final frontier in warehouses and factories alike; see, for instance, Frank E. Gooding, "The Sky's the Limit," *Mill & Factory*, January and February 1939.
130. "Break-bulk" refers to cargo that is too individualized to be shipped in bulk containers. On the ILWU's fight against the pallet, see Augustine Sedgewick, "The American System in the World Depression, 1932–1941: The Case of the Coffee Trade" (PhD diss., Harvard University, 2011), 160–65. For a short history of the pallet see Jacob Hodes, "Whitewood under Siege," *Cabinet* 52 (Winter 2013–14): 21–28.
131. The term *palletization* first appeared in newspapers at the end of World War II, such as in "Terminal Sets Record in Handling Freight," *Wilmington Morning News*, June 21, 1945.

132. See Samuel G. Spear, *Warehousing in World War II* (Chicago: Traffic Service Corporation, 1947); and "The Army Supply Program," *Fortune*, February 1943.
133. Harvard Business School was ahead of the pack in reinterpreting marketing as the study of "the problem of distribution." William Leach, *Land of Desire: Merchants, Power, and the Rise of a New American Culture* (New York: Random House, 1993), 161.
134. Chester Whitney Wright, *Economic History of the United States*, 2nd. ed. (New York: McGraw-Hill, 1949), 633.
135. Henry A. Wallace, "Food, Farmers, and Fundamentals," *Survey Graphic* 30, no. 7 (1941): 390.
136. Benjamin Graham, *Storage and Stability: A Modern Ever-Normal Granary* (New York: McGraw-Hill, 1937), v. Graham's pitch was also echoed by Friedrich Hayek and his disciples. See Milton Friedman, "Commodity-Reserve Currency," *Journal of Political Economy* 59, no. 3 (1951): 203–32.
137. John Maynard Keynes, "The Policy of Government Storage of Food-Stuffs and Raw Materials," *Economic Journal* 48, no. 191 (1938): 459.

CHAPTER TWO

1. Untitled Circular, October 11, 1852, 5, folder 3, box 1, Crystal Palace Papers, New York Historical Society (hereafter CP Papers). For background, see Edwin G. Burrows, *The Finest Building in America: The New York Crystal Palace, 1853–1858* (New York: Oxford University Press, 2018); Rem Koolhaas, *Delirious New York: A Retroactive Manifesto for Manhattan* (New York: Monacelli, 1994), 23–27; Robert C. Post, "Reflections of American Science and Technology at the New York Crystal Palace Exhibition of 1853," *Journal of American Studies* 17, no. 3 (1983): 337–56; and Michael Zakim, "Importing the Crystal Palace," in *American Capitalism: New Histories*, ed. Sven Beckert and Christine Desan (New York: Columbia University Press, 2018), 337–60.
2. "The New York Crystal Palace," newspaper clipping, undated, folder 4, box 1, CP Papers.
3. Untitled circular, October 11, 1852, 12, folder 3, box 1, CP Papers.
4. Walt Whitman, "Song of the Exposition," *Leaves of Grass* (Boston: Small, Maynard, 1904), 160.
5. Samuel Clemens, as quoted in Edwin G. Burrows and Mike Wallace, *Gotham: A History of New York City to 1898* (New York: Oxford University Press, 1999), 670.
6. Untitled circular, October 11, 1852, 10, folder 3, box 1, CP Papers.
7. "The New York Crystal Palace Exhibition," *Sun*, July 11, 1853.
8. Walter Benjamin, "Paris, Capital of the Nineteenth Century," in *Reflections: Essays, Aphorisms, Autobiographical Writings*, ed. Peter Demetz (1935; New York: Schocken Books, 1986), 147. See also Sigfried Giedion, *Space, Time, and Architecture*, 5th ed. (Cambridge, MA: Harvard University Press, 1967), 195, 234. Susan Buck-Morss observes: "Benjamin noted that these buildings were connected with transitoriness in both the spatial sense (as railroad stations, places of transit) and the temporal one (as galleries for world exhibitions, typically torn down after they closed)." Buck-Morss, *The Dialectics of Seeing: Walter Benjamin and the Arcades Project* (Cambridge, MA: MIT Press, 1989), 130.
9. "Crystal Palace—The Probable Disappointment of the People," *Sunday Atlas*, March 27, 1853; untitled circular, October 11, 1852, 3, folder 3, box 1, CP Papers; Daniel Webster to Theodore Sedgwick, ca. October 1852, folder 13, box 2, CP Papers.
10. Charles Bright and Michael Geyer, "Benchmarks of Globalization: The Global Condition, 1850–2010," in *A Companion to World History*, ed. Douglas Northrop (Mal-

den, MA: Blackwell, 2012), 285–300; Bright and Geyer, "Where in the World Is America? The History of the United States in a Global Age," in *Rethinking America in a Global Age*, ed. Thomas Bender (Berkeley: University of California Press, 2002), 63–100.

11. Philip S. Foner, *Business and Slavery: The New York Merchants and the Irrepressible Conflict* (Chapel Hill: University of North Carolina Press, 1941), 1.
12. "Memoirs of Robert J. Walker by Mrs. M. W. Cook" (unpublished, 1873), 38, vol. 6, Papers of Robert J. Walker, Library of Congress.
13. Alfred E. Eckes Jr., *Opening America's Market: U.S. Foreign Trade Policy Since 1776* (Chapel Hill: University North Carolina Press, 1995), 49.
14. Theodore Sedgwick to James Guthrie, October 8, 1853, 1, folder 6, box 2, CP Papers.
15. The lock's free-floating presentation was consistent with official patent drawings, which were mandated to focus solely on the object under consideration and to be readable "at a glance." See William J. Rankin, "'Person Skilled in the Art' Is Really Quite Conventional: Patent Drawings and the Persona of the Inventor, 1870–2005," in *Making and Unmaking Intellectual Property: Creative Production in Legal and Cultural Perspective*, ed. Mario Biagioli, Peter Jaszi, and Martha Woodmansee (Chicago: University of Chicago Press, 2011), 55–75.
16. On twenty-first-century securitization of art in free zones, see "Swiss Freeports Are Home for a Growing Treasure of Art," *New York Times*, July 21, 2012; "Über-Warehouses for the Ultra-Rich," *Economist*, November 23, 2013; "One of the World's Greatest Art Collections Hides Behind This Fence," *New York Times*, May 28, 2016; and Atossa Araxia Abrahamian, "Inside the New 'Fortress' in New York City That's Housing Millions of Dollars of Art," *Artsy*, May 29, 2018, https://www.artsy.net/article/artsy-editorial-harlem-warehouse-millions-dollars-worth-art. See also Mirjam Brusius and Kavita Singh, eds., *Museum Storage and Meaning: Tales from the Crypt* (New York: Routledge, 2018); Stefan Heidenreich, "Freeportism as Style and Ideology: Post-Internet and Speculative Realism, Part I," *e-flux journal* 71 (2016); and Hito Steyerl, *Duty Free Art: Art in the Age of Planetary Civil War* (New York: Verso, 2017), chapter 7.
17. An Act to Establish a Warehousing System, 9 *US Statutes at Large* 53 (August 6, 1846). See also Daniel S. Margolies, "'Factors of Universal Commerce': Bonded Warehousing and the Spatialities of Mid-Nineteenth Century American Foreign Trade Policy," *World History Bulletin* 29, no. 1 (2013): 19–25; and Gautham Rao, "Cities of Ports: The Warehousing Act of 1846 and the Centralization of American Commerce," *Thresholds* no. 34 (2007): 34–37.
18. An Act for the Erection of United States Prisons and for the Imprisonment of United States Prisoners, 26 *US Statutes at Large* 839 (March 3, 1891). The banking system is an example that warehousemen have envied.
19. Robert J. Walker, *Report from the Secretary of the Treasury on the Warehousing System*, 30th Cong., 2nd sess., Ex. Doc. 57 (1849), 15.
20. Albert G. Sweetser, "The Public-Utility Status of Commercial Warehousing in the United States" (PhD diss., American University, 1961), 30–121.
21. A. K. Sandoval-Strausz, "Travelers, Strangers, and Jim Crow: Law, Public Accommodations, and Civil Rights in America," *Law and History Review* 23, no. 1 (Spring 2005): 53–94.
22. Gautham Rao, *National Duties: Custom Houses and the Making of the American State* (Chicago: University of Chicago Press, 2016); Edward Stanwood, *American Tariff Controversies in the Nineteenth Century* (Boston: Houghton, Mifflin, 1903), 1:170.

23. An Act to Regulate the Collection of Duties on Imports and Tonnage, 1 *US Statutes at Large* 675 (March 2, 1799).
24. On the evolution of the credit system, see Senator John Adams Dix, "The Warehousing System," 29th Cong., 1st sess., *Congressional Globe* 15, June 19, 1846, 996–99. On the auction houses, see Norman Sidney Buck, *The Development of the Organisation of the Anglo-American Trade, 1800–1850* (New Haven, CT: Yale University Press, 1925), 121–50; and Ira Cohen, "The Auction System in the Port of New York, 1817–1837," *Business History Review* 45, no. 4 (1971): 488–510.
25. Rao, *National Duties*, 89.
26. Robert Ralston et al., *Essay on the Warehousing System and Government Credits of the United States* (Philadelphia: Philadelphia Chamber of Commerce, 1828), 13, 25.
27. An Act to Modify the Act of the Fourteenth of July, One Thousand Eight Hundred and Thirty-Two, and All Other Acts Imposing Duties on Imports, 4 *US Statutes at Large* 630 (March 2, 1833).
28. Dix, *The Warehousing System*, 999. On the Black Tariff, see Stanwood, *American Tariff Controversies in the Nineteenth Century*, 1:1–37.
29. William Edward Dodd, *Robert J. Walker, Imperialist* (Chicago: Chicago Literary Club, 1914), 11.
30. James P. Shenton, *Robert John Walker: A Politician from Jackson to Lincoln* (New York: Columbia University Press, 1961), 12. Walker, a historiographic Zelig, grappled with many of the banner issues of the long nineteenth century—the tariff, the banks, Texas, Mexico, and Bleeding Kansas—not to mention that he argued before the Supreme Court for states' rights to control the domestic slave trade. Yet as Shenton observed, "he seems destined to remain a footnote to history" (xv).
31. On the rhetoric of Walker's push for annexation of Texas, see Stephen John Hartnett, *Democratic Dissent and the Cultural Fictions of Antebellum America* (Urbana: University of Illinois Press, 2001), 93–131. On Natchez and its environs during the 1830s, see Edward E. Baptist, "Toxic Debt, Liar Loans, Collateralized and Securitized Human Beings, and the Panic of 1837," in *Capitalism Takes Command: The Social Transformation of Nineteenth-Century America*, ed. Michael Zakim and Gary J. Kornblith (Chicago: University of Chicago Press, 2012), 69–92. See also David Kazanjian, *National Culture and the Colonizing Trick: Imperial Citizenship in Early America* (Minneapolis: University of Minnesota Press, 2003).
32. Shenton, *Robert John Walker*, 76. At a moment when Britain was about to abolish the protectionist Corn Laws, Walker's report bolstered the Cobdenites, who argued that Britain should import grain to develop markets for British manufactured goods among grain farmers in the United States. See Scott C. James and David A. Lake, "The Second Face of Hegemony: Britain's Repeal of the Corn Laws and the American Walker Tariff of 1846," *International Organization* 43, no. 1 (Winter 1989): 1–29.
33. Robert J. Walker, *1845 Treasury Report* (Washington, DC, 1846), 14.
34. Walter Johnson, *River of Dark Dreams: Slavery and Empire in the Cotton Kingdom* (Cambridge, MA: Harvard University Press, 2013); on Calhoun, see Manisha Sinha, *The Counterrevolution of Slavery: Politics and Ideology in Antebellum South Carolina* (Chapel Hill: University of North Carolina Press, 2000).
35. Johnson, *River of Dark Dreams*, chapter 10; on Maury, and on Confederate globalism, see Matthew J. Karp, "Slavery and American Sea Power: The Navalist Impulse in the Antebellum South," *Journal of Southern History* 77, no. 2 (2011): 284–324, and Matthew J. Karp, *This Vast Southern Empire: Slaveholders at the Helm of American Foreign Policy* (Cambridge, MA: Harvard University Press, 2016).

36. Harry Bluff, "To the Memphis Convention," *Southern Literary Messenger*, October 1845, 585. In the futuristic novel written by Virginia slaveholder Edmund Ruffin, Norfolk replaces New York City as "the chief seaport and commercial mart on the Atlantic Coast," notes John Majewski. Secessionists like Ruffin "criticized the US tariff exclusively on distributional grounds: it benefitted one region at the expense of another." Majewski, *Modernizing a Slave Economy: The Economic Vision of the Confederate Nation* (Chapel Hill: University of North Carolina Press, 2009), 116, 128.
37. Jay Gitlin, Barbara Berglund, and Adam Arenson, eds., *Frontier Cities: Encounters at the Crossroads of Empire* (Philadelphia: University of Pennsylvania Press, 2012).
38. The federal government should regulate trade among the states, Walker conceded, except for "this local and peculiar question of slaves, and their sale and transportation from state to state." Walker pressed for a definition of slaves as property, but not as "articles of commerce." Slaves were not "merchandise"; they were not equivalent to "universal articles of commerce." Slaves were persons, "stamped [with] the character of property." ("It as *persons* they are enumerated under the census," he wrote, "and as such taxation and representation apportioned according to the three-fifths of their *numbers*, not their *value*.") And as persons they were property only where a state declared them to be, which was why slavery was a local matter. Mississippi sanctioned the treatment of people as property, while Massachusetts did not, and neither state could impose its standards of property on the other. Walker pulled off a neat reversal, portraying northerners as guilty of rendering people as commodities: "How strangely inconsistent are the arguments of the abolitionists," he observed, in his *Groves v. Slaughter* brief. "They say men are not property, and cannot be property by virtue of any laws of congress or of the states; and yet that as such, *commerce* in them among the states may be regulated by congress, and by congress alone." Robert J. Walker, "Argument of Robert J. Walker, Esq., Before the Supreme Court of the United States, on the Mississippi Slave Question, at January Term, 1841," reprinted in *Southern Slaves in Free State Courts: The Pamphlet Literature*, ed. Paul Finkelman (New York: Garland Publishing, 1988), 2:124, 126, 123, 131, 125. On im/migration and *Groves v. Slaughter*, see Mary Sarah Bilder, "The Struggle over Immigration: Indentured Servants, Slaves, and Articles of Commerce," *Missouri Law Review* 61, no. 4 (Fall 1996): 807–12; and Adam M. McKeown, *Melancholy Order: Asian Migration and the Globalization of Borders* (New York: Columbia University Press, 2008), 98–99.
39. "Nothing moved in this economy without money." Johnson, *River of Dark Dreams*, 43. See also Jeffrey Sklansky, "Labor, Money, and the Financial Turn in the History of Capitalism," *Labor* 11, no. 1 (2014): 23–46.
40. "The instruments of exchange" is Fernand Braudel's category of analysis in *The Wheels of Commerce*, vol. 2 of *Civilization and Capitalism, 15th–18th Century*, trans. Siân Reynolds (New York: Harper and Row, 1982), chapter 1.
41. On Americans' impressions of British docks, see Tamara Plakins Thornton, "Capitalist Aesthetics: Americans Look at the London and Liverpool Docks," in *Capitalism Takes Command*, ed. Zakim and Kornblith, 169–98. Thornton hypothesizes that these encounters influenced American textile factories, but she neglects how the British docks led to the American docks. For a brief history of the British system, see Colum Giles and Bob Hawkins, *Storehouses of Empire: Liverpool's Historic Warehouses* (London: English Heritage, 2004).
42. H. van Driel, *Four Centuries of Warehousing: Pakhoed, The Origins and History, 1616–1967*, trans. J. W. Watson (Rotterdam: Royal Pakhoed N.V., 1992).
43. Phillip Magness traces this intellectual history in "Walker and the Warehousing Act

of 1846: A Study in Policy Entrepreneurship" (paper presented at the Policy History Conference, St. Louis, Missouri, May 29–June 1, 2008), in author's possession.

44. John Hedley Higginson, *Tariffs at Work* (London: P. S. King and Son, 1913), 130, 78.
45. John Quincy Adams, "The Public Deposits," 23rd Cong., 1st sess., *Congressional Globe* 10, March 12, 1834, 2976.
46. Johnson, *River of Dark Dreams*, 291.
47. Robert J. Walker, *1846 Treasury Report* (Washington, DC, 1847), 16.
48. James and Lake, "The Second Face of Hegemony," 11.
49. The Treasury Department did not attempt the burdensome task of monitoring these statistics during the telegraph era. At most, customs clerks gave reexport statistics in aggregate: X number of goods were warehoused in Y year, and Z number were withdrawn for export.
50. Walker, *1846 Treasury Report*, 98–111.
51. Legal scholars use ports of entry as a metaphor if they mention them at all. See, e.g., Judith Resnik, "Law's Migration: American Exceptionalism, Silent Dialogues, and Federalism's Multiple Ports of Entry," *Yale Law Journal* 115, no. 7 (May 2006): 1564–1670.
52. For a step-by-step tutorial in the landing of imports, see Richard Wheatley, "The New York Custom House," *Harper's New Monthly Magazine*, June 1884, 38–61.
53. Someone needs to write an indigenous history of customs territory, guided by Manu Karuka, *Empire Tracks: Indigenous Nations, Chinese Workers, and the Transcontinental Railroad* (Berkeley: University of California Press, 2019).
54. Rao, *National Duties*, 67.
55. An act to regulate the collection of the duties imposed by law on the tonnage of ships or vessels, and on goods, wares, and merchandise, 1 *US Statutes at Large* 29 (July 31, 1789).
56. Johnson, *River of Dark Dreams*, 294. See also William Cronon, *Nature's Metropolis: Chicago and the Great West* (New York: W. W. Norton, 1991); D. W. Meinig, *The Shaping of America: A Geographical Perspective on 500 Years of History*, vol. 3, *Transcontinental America* (New Haven, CT: Yale University Press, 1995); and Richard White, *Railroaded: The Transcontinentals and the Making of Modern America* (New York: W. W. Norton, 2011).
57. Senate, "Memorial of a Number of Citizens of Chicago, Illinois, Praying to Have that Place Constituted a Port of Entry," 26th Cong., 1st sess., April 6, 1840. See also House, "Port of Entry at Cincinnati, Ohio," 4th Cong., 2nd sess., February 13, 1817; Senate, "Memorial of Sundry Merchants of St. Louis, in the State of Missouri, Praying That St. Louis May Be Made a Port of Entry," 19th Cong., 1st sess., December 30, 1825; House, "Port of Entry, Zanesville," 23rd Cong., 2nd sess., February 6, 1835; and An Act to Establish the Collection District of Chicago, 9 *US Statutes at Large* 38 (July 16, 1846).
58. Hugh McCulloch to William B. Peters, March 13, 1868, in *Letters Sent Relating to Customs and Internal Revenue Warehouses, General Records of the Department of the Treasury*, RG 56, National Archives and Records Administration, College Park, MD (hereafter Treasury Records), 1:36.
59. John E. Hartley to James A. Magruder, February 18, 1868, *Letters Sent Relating to Customs and Internal Revenue Warehouses*, Treasury Records, 1:25, 15.
60. An Act to Extend the Warehousing System by Establishing Private Bonded Warehouses, 10 *US Statutes at Large* 270 (March 28, 1854). The Customs Service contin-

ued to operate public warehouses as adjuncts of customhouses, to store imports during appraisal.

61. Confederate States of America, *Compilation of the Tariff Act, of the Confederate States of America, Approved May 21st, 1861* (New Orleans: Corson and Armstrong, 1861). See also "The Interior Ports of Entry in the Confederate States," *Chicago Tribune*, April 1, 1861.
62. "The Warehousing System," *North American*, January 31, 1867. For an earlier example, see "The Warehousing System," *Boston Daily Advertiser*, May 26, 1860.
63. "The Warehousing System: Its Hostility to American Interests and Industry," *New York Daily Tribune*, June 20, 1868.
64. House Committee on Manufactures, *The Protective Policy and the Warehousing System*, 40th Cong., 2nd sess., June 22, 1868, 29.
65. "Decline of Business at the Bonded Warehouse," *New York Herald*, October 15, 1857.
66. David Mitch, "Public Warehousing," in *Extractives, Manufacturing and Services: A Historiographical and Bibliographical Guide*, ed. David O. Whitten (Westport, CT: Greenwood, 1997), 377–406. Mitch shared a longer version of his helpful essay, from which I gleaned these figures.
67. An Act to Provide Internal Revenue to Support the Government, to Pay Interest on the Public Debt, and for Other Purposes, 14 *US Statutes at Large* 155 (July 13, 1866).
68. Consider this vignette from the *Lowell Daily Citizen and News*, May 6, 1869: "A traveler in Kentucky thinks he is in the midst of Arcadian simplicity, but at every station . . . a 'bonded warehouse' flashes upon the sight, and every stream is dammed at all favorable places to give water power for huge establishments, which seem, at first to be factories, but turn out . . . to be distilleries. The whole agricultural industry of central Kentucky is given to raising grain to feed mules and distilleries, and the entire mercantile enterprise of the people is centered on horse-jockeying and spirit-selling."
69. Senate Committee on Finance, Report No. 102, 50th Cong., 1st sess., January 31, 1888, 1.
70. "The difference between the Sub-Treasury bill desired by the farmers and the bonded warehouse privileges already extended to whiskey-dealers by the Federal Government is not a very great one. The farmers want warehouses for their corn while it is still fit to support life. The whiskey dealers get warehouses where they can store the corn for three years, after it has been converted in murderous whiskey. The farmers want Treasury notes issued on their products; the whiskey dealers get warehouse certificates from Uncle Sam which answer about the same purpose. If the Sub-Treasury scheme is ridiculous, what is the bonded warehouse scheme?" Reprinted from the *Voice* (New York), in *The Progressive Farmer*, June 23, 1891.
71. Rebecca Latimer Felton, *My Memoirs of Georgia Politics* (Atlanta: Index Printing, 1911), 642. Charles Macune and other authors of the subtreasury plan repeatedly invoked the whiskey warehouse as a prototype. John Hicks, *The Populist Revolt: A History of the Farmer's Alliance and the People's Party* (Minneapolis: University of Minnesota Press, 1931), 191–92.
72. "Jake, the Barber Played Tag with Law More than 20 Years," *Sunday Morning Star*, February 21, 1943.
73. Walker's biographer calls the report "the definitive work" on the British docks. Shenton, *Robert John Walker*, 243.

74. Walker, *Report from the Secretary of the Treasury on the Warehousing System*, 8. Walker never discusses theft, probably because he regarded it as a given. See also Peter Linebaugh, *The London Hanged: Crime and Civil Society in the Eighteenth Century*, 2nd ed. (New York: Verso, 2003), 371–401.
75. Thornton, "Capitalist Aesthetics," 196.
76. Walker, *Report from the Secretary of the Treasury on the Warehousing System*, 5.
77. Malka Simon, "The Space of Production: Brooklyn and the Creation of an Urban Industrial Landscape" (PhD diss., New York University, 2009), 58.
78. Samuel B. Collins, *The Great Fire: Sworn Testimony of the Witnesses Examined by Fire Marshall Blackburn, in Reference to the Causes of the Fire at Patterson's Bonded Warehouse* (Philadelphia: E. C. Markley and Son, 1869), 58, 9, 19, 117–18.
79. Walker, *Report from the Secretary of the Treasury on the Warehousing System*, 16–31.
80. American Warehousemen's Association, *Warehouse, Storage, and Forwarding Reference* (Kansas City: Tew-Lyle, 1892), 40–41.
81. See J. H. Morrell, Floodway for Warehouses, US Patent 165,247, filed May 28, 1875, and issued July 6, 1875 (Morrell's is often ranked as the first household storage warehouse in the nation); and P. G. Hubert, Storage Warehouse and Method of Storing Materials, US Patent 372,850, filed August 27, 1887, and issued November 8, 1887.
82. Talbot Faulkner Hamlin, *The Pageant of America: A Pictorial History of the United States*, vol. 13, *The American Spirit in Architecture* (New Haven, CT: Yale University Press, 1926), 257. See also Russell Sturgis, "The Warehouse and the Factory in Architecture," *Architectural Record* 15, no. 1 (1904): 1–17; and Sturgis, "The Warehouse and the Factory in Architecture—II," *Architectural Record* 15, no. 2 (1904): 123–33. Sturgis set apart the warehouse and the factory from the office.
83. Joseph Nimmo Jr., *First Annual Report on the Internal Commerce of the United States*, 44th Cong., 2nd sess., House Exec. Doc. 46, pt. 2 (1877), 133. Albro Martin offhandedly claimed that this provision helped to remap the nation's economic geography, referring to it as "an obscure section" of "a little noted U.S. statute," in *Railroads Triumphant: The Growth, Rejection, and Rebirth of a Vital American Force* (New York: Oxford University Press, 1992), 192. Daniel S. Margolies touches on the history of bonded transport in the Mexican borderlands in *Spaces of Law in American Foreign Relations: Extradition and Extraterritoriality in the Borderlands and Beyond, 1877–1898* (Athens: University of Georgia Press, 2011).
84. Senator Thomas F. Bayard, "Tax Bill," 41st Cong., 2nd sess., *Congressional Globe* 42, July 5, 1870, 5206.
85. The legal apparatus for in-bond transport helped pave the way for the railroad. In 1831, for example, Congress elevated the Mississippi River to international stature by authorizing in-bond transport to seven interior cities. An Act Allowing the Duties on Foreign Merchandise Imported into Pittsburg, Wheeling, Cincinnati, Louisville, St. Louis, Nashville, and Natchez, to Be Secured and Paid at Those Places, 4 *US Statutes at Large* 480 (March 2, 1831).
86. "Chicago Imports," *Chicago Tribune*, July 1, 1868.
87. Senator George Frisbie Hoar, "Homesteads and Right of Way in Alaska," 55th Cong., 2nd sess., *Congressional Record* 31, March 2, 1898, 2370.
88. Simon J. McLean, "Canadian Railways and the Bonding Question," *Journal of Political Economy* 7, no. 4 (September 1899): 500–42.
89. Joseph Nimmo Jr., Senate Committee on Relations with Canada, *Relations with Canada*, 51st Cong., 1st sess., April 26, 1890, 898.

90. An Act to Protect the Revenue, 14 *US Statutes at Large* 329 (July 28, 1866).
91. "The Port of Entry Bill," *Evansville Daily Journal*, March 18, 1870.
92. Senator Lyman Trumbull, "Tax Bill," 41st Cong., 2nd sess., *Congressional Globe* 42, July 5, 1870, 5216. Bitterness toward the Empire City dominated these debates, as in a speech by an Ohio congressman:

> The tribute we pay her is double and treble; for not only do we import, but we also export over her counters. Constrained to buy of her, we must sell to her in order to pay for what we buy; and being obliged to buy of and sell to her, we are compelled to make her our banker; to constitute her, without bond or security, our agent, factor, and broker; give into her hands the key and the purse, and submit ourselves her commercial tributaries and subjects. This city by the sea contains, perhaps, one fortieth of the population of the Republic, yet nearly three fourths, thirty-fortieths, of our national imports and exports pass through her hands. (Congressman Job E. Stevenson, "Internal Commerce," 41st Cong., 2nd sess., *Appendix to the Congressional Globe* 42, June 28, 1870, 604)

See also David M. Scobey, *Empire City: The Making and Meaning of the New York City Landscape* (Philadelphia: Temple University Press, 2002).
93. Senator George F. Edmunds, "Tax Bill," 41st Cong., 2nd sess., *Congressional Globe* 42, June 30, 1870, 5042.
94. Senator Justin Smith Morrill, "Tax Bill," 41st Cong., 2nd sess., *Congressional Globe* 42, July 5, 1870, 5208.
95. Senator Zachariah Chandler, "Tax Bill," 41st Cong., 2nd sess., *Congressional Globe* 42, July 5, 1870, 5210.
96. Leo Marx, *The Machine in the Garden: Technology and the Pastoral Ideal in America*, 35th anniv. ed. (New York: Oxford University Press, 1964), 194.
97. Morrill, "Tax Bill," 41st Cong., 2nd sess., *Congressional Globe* 42, 5207.
98. Andrew Wender Cohen argues that the need to police the customs border was a catalyst for state formation in the nineteenth century in *Contraband: Smuggling and the Birth of the American Century* (New York: W. W. Norton, 2015).
99. George S. Boutwell, letter, "Tax Bill," 41st Cong., 2nd sess., *Congressional Globe* 42, July 5, 1870, 5209.
100. For a short overview of the Lefebvrean theory of absolute space, see David Harvey, "Space as a Keyword," in *Spaces of Global Capitalism: Towards a Theory of Uneven Geographical Development* (London: Verso, 2006), 117–48.
101. "Chicago Imports," *Chicago Tribune*, July 1, 1868.
102. Senator John Sherman, "Tax Bill," 41st Cong., 2nd sess., *Congressional Globe* 42, June 30, 1870, 5042.
103. "Would it not probably be wiser not to extend it too far; but let us see how it would work in the larger places, and then, at any future time, when it may be judiciously extended to cities of less population, that can be done?" Senator Charles D. Drake, "Tax Bill," 41st Cong., 2nd sess., *Congressional Globe* 42, June 30, 1870, 5042. Much the same was said of the foreign-trade zone.
104. On Cairo, see Nick Yablon, *Untimely Ruins: An Archaeology of American Urban Modernity, 1819–1919* (Chicago: University of Chicago Press, 2010).
105. For an overview of these regulations, see "Transportation of Goods in Bond," *Chicago Tribune*, May 15, 1871. For an example of the official language about routes—in effect as of the 1866 statute—see Hugh McCulloch to George J. Stannard, May 5,

1868, *Letters Sent Relating to Customs and Internal Revenue Warehouses*, Treasury Records, 1:36.

106. Peter Z. Grossman, *American Express: The Unofficial History of the People Who Built the Great Financial Empire* (New York: Crown, 1987), 100.
107. On railroads and empire, see Karuka, *Empire's Tracks*; and Rosa Luxemburg, *The Accumulation of Capital*, trans. Agnes Schwarzschild (1913; London: Routledge, 2003), chapter 30.
108. Edward King, *The Great South: A Record of Journeys in Louisiana, Texas, the Indian Territory, Missouri, Arkansas, Mississippi, Alabama, Georgia, Florida, South Carolina, North Carolina, Kentucky, Tennessee, Virginia, West Virginia, and Maryland* (Hartford, CT: American Publishing, 1875), 58. See also Scott P. Marler, *The Merchant's Capital: New Orleans and the Political Economy of the Nineteenth-Century South* (Cambridge: Cambridge University Press, 2013).
109. Joseph Nimmo, *Report on the Internal Commerce of the United States for the Fiscal Year 1881–1882* (Washington, DC: Government Printing Office, 1884), 72.
110. Nimmo, *Report on the Internal Commerce of the United States*, 78.
111. Deborah Cowen and Neil Smith, "After Geopolitics? From the Geopolitical Social to Geoeconomics," *Antipode* 41, no. 1 (2009): 22–48.
112. See House, *Letters, Reports, and Other Papers Relative to Locks and Seals Used in Internal Revenue and Customs Service of the Government*, 44th Cong, 1st sess., Mis. Doc. 191 (1876), 1–144.
113. "The American Seal Lock," *Scientific American*, December 21, 1872, 392.
114. "Bonded Goods," *New York Times*, January 6, 1871.
115. "Amended Regulations for the Transportation of Merchandise in-Bond," *Chicago Tribune*, April 22, 1871.
116. "Practical Workings of the Bonded Car System," *Railroad Gazette*, September 9, 1871, 261.
117. Ben Kafka, *The Demon of Writing: Powers and Failures of Paperwork* (Cambridge, MA: MIT Press, 2012).
118. "A North Carolinian" [pseud.], *Slavery Considered as General Principles; or, a Grapple with Abstractionists* (New York: Rudd and Carleton, 1861).
119. Congressman Job E. Stevenson, "Internal Commerce," 41st Cong., 2nd sess., *Appendix to the Congressional Globe* 42, June 28, 1870, 605.
120. Walter Johnson, *Soul by Soul: Life inside the Antebellum Slave Market* (Cambridge, MA: Harvard University Press, 1999).
121. Slavery, Johnson observes, highlighted "the uneasy frontier between value and its physical form." The slave commodity had to traverse "a territory in which things could be measured and compared by a price, but in which that price always had to be paid in physical—movable, fakeable, and boostable—form." Johnson, *River of Dark Dreams*, 66–67.
122. One last twist on the deterritorialization of the commodity vis-à-vis the bond is in the realm of "situs," the legal concept for the whereabouts of property. Situs usually comes up around questions of taxation—whether that bale of cotton or that hogshead of sugar is subject to New York State tax depends on whether its situs is in New York State. Yet thanks to these various legal and technical mechanisms of movement, location was becoming more and more complex. A bale of cotton might be physically in Manhattan, but its situs might be in New Orleans, where the bill of lading for it was held. There was a rift emerging between what we might call (physi-

cal) possession and (legal) ownership, and the bonded warehouse figured large in that transition.

123. John Ruskin had derided the iron horse for reducing passengers to "human parcels." Wolfgang Schivelbusch, *The Railway Journey: The Industrialization of Time and Space in the Nineteenth Century* (Berkeley: University of California Press, 1977), 38.
124. US secretary of commerce and labor, *Facts Concerning the Enforcement of the Chinese-Exclusion Laws*, May 25, 1906, 59th Cong., 1st sess., H. Doc. 847, 15.
125. "Clink of Gold Draws Chinese," *Clarence Courier*, October 31, 1906.
126. "Keeping Track of the Chinese," *Washington Post*, October 1, 1889.
127. Robert Chao Romero, *The Chinese in Mexico, 1882–1940* (Tucson: University of Arizona Press, 2010), 35–39.
128. "Shipped in Bond," *Morning Call*, May 21, 1893.
129. "A Chinese Party," *Montreal Daily Witness*, November 7, 1890.
130. US secretary of commerce and labor, *Facts Concerning the Enforcement of the Chinese-Exclusion Laws*, 39.
131. An Act to Prohibit the Coming into and to Regulate the Residence within the United States, Its Territories, and All Territory under Its Jurisdiction, and the District of Columbia, of Chinese and Persons of Chinese Descent, 32 *US Statutes at Large* 176 (April 26, 1902).
132. Mae Ngai, *The Lucky Ones: One Family and the Extraordinary Invention of Chinese America* (Boston: Houghton Mifflin Harcourt, 2010), 107.
133. "The Great Exhibition," *New York Times*, September 11, 1875.
134. As the head collector for the 1893 Columbian Exposition in Chicago told a reporter,

> When foreign goods arrive at New York and other original entry ports, destined for the World's Fair, they will be loaded on cars under the eyes of customs inspectors, and the car doors sealed by the inspectors. Arriving here the cars will be switched into the park, where the seals will be broken by the inspectors, who will remain in charge until the exhibits have been appraised and put into place. The lists will be carefully checked over after the exhibits have been arranged to make certain that none have been removed. Lists will be furnished the Columbia Guards on duty around the exhibits, and they are to assist the Customs Inspectors against any attempt to circumvent the customs regulations. The inspectors will make occasional rounds of the exhibits in their charge, keeping a watchful eye on the goods, although anything like an offensive surveillance will be avoided. ("Customs Service at the Fair," *Chicago Daily Tribune*, December 24, 1892)

Another collector gave a similar accounting on the eve of the Atlanta Cotton Exposition, which coincided with Atlanta's designation as a port of entry: "With Madison Davis, Surveyor of the Port of Atlanta," *Daily Constitution*, July 12, 1881. For a full report, see Senate, *Cotton States and International Exposition, Atlanta, Georgia, Customs Service Report*, 54th Cong., 1st sess., May 9, 1896, S. Doc. 255. For pamphlets and sample documents, see the records of the Centennial Exhibition, Collection 1544, box 1, Historical Society of Pennsylvania (Philadelphia).

135. "List of Ports at Which Bonded Warehouses Are Established," *Bulletins 59–70* (New York: AWA, 1905), 152. China granted US citizens the right to establish bonded warehouses in Chinese open ports in the Treaty between the United States and China for the Extension of Commercial Relations between Them, U.S.-China, art. VI, Oct. 8, 1903, 33 Stat. 2208.

CHAPTER THREE

1. This column plays on an article reprinted the previous day from the *Omaha World-Herald*: "Matrimony Admits One to Bliss and United States Also," *Baltimore Sun*, January 27, 1927.
2. A member of California's Board of State Harbor Commissioners drew this comparison during a US Senate hearing on free zones. See note 141 to this chapter.
3. "Mr. Corbin's Free Port," *Chicago Daily Tribune*, February 25, 1896. The Tariff Commission found that Congress's practice of designating world's fairs as bonded warehouses was a precedent for authorizing free zones. US Tariff Commission, *Information Concerning Free Zones in Ports of the United States* (Washington, DC, 1919), 91.
4. Edwin J. Clapp, "Foreign Trading Zones in Our Seaports," *American Economic Review* 12 (June 1922): 263. For an example of an article that equates Hamburg's legal and physical infrastructure, see "The Coming of the Mechanically Perfect 'Free Port,'" *Americas* 14 (May 1918): 4–10.
5. National borders are as prone to induce flows of capital and labor as to impede them. This is a "central thesis" of Sandro Mezzadra and Brett Neilson, *Border as Method, or, The Multiplication of Labor* (Durham, NC: Duke University Press, 2013), ix; see also Paul Kramer, "Power and Connection: Imperial Histories of the United States in the World," *American Historical Review* 116, no. 5 (December 2011): 1353.
6. "Claim It Is Cheaper to Store Whiskey at Hamburg," *Bulletins 35–46* (New York: American Warehousemen's Association, 1903), 262.
7. William Kent, untitled speech, ca. 1919, 2, folder 224, box 79, William Kent Family Papers, Yale University Manuscripts and Archives (hereafter Kent Papers).
8. The notion of a "tariff wall" spread in 1926 via a table-size map of Europe on which each nation was hemmed in by miniature bricks, a model built by a British politician to help his compatriots "visualize" the perils of economic nationalism. See Mike Heffernan and Benjamin J. Thorpe, "'The Map That Would Save Europe': Clive Morrison-Bell, the Tariff Walls Map, and the Politics of Cartographic Display," *Journal of Historical Geography* 60 (April 2018): 24–40; and Quinn Slobodian, *Globalists: The End of Empire and the Birth of Neoliberalism* (Cambridge, MA: Harvard University Press, 2018), 37–42.
9. John Gallagher and Ronald Robinson, "The Imperialism of Free Trade," *Economic History Review* 6, no. 1 (August 1953): 3.
10. Roy MacElwee, *Ports and Terminal Facilities* (New York: McGraw-Hill, 1918), 291.
11. Teemu Ruskola, *Legal Orientalism: China, the United States, and Modern Law* (Cambridge, MA: Harvard University Press, 2013), 110. See also Lisa Lowe, *The Intimacies of Four Continents* (Durham, NC: Duke University Press, 2015). On extraterritoriality in the encounter between the United States and Mexico, see Daniel S. Margolies, *Spaces of Law in American Foreign Relations: Extradition and Extraterritoriality in the Borderlands and Beyond, 1877–1898* (Athens: University of Georgia Press, 2011). Generally, see Lauren Benton, *Law and Colonial Cultures: Legal Regimes in World History, 1400–1900* (New York: Cambridge University Press, 2001); Kal Raustiala, *Does the Constitution Follow the Flag? The Evolution of Territoriality in American Law* (New York: Oxford University Press, 2011).
12. For example, Vanessa Ogle juxtaposes "archipelago capitalism" with "territorial capitalism" in "Archipelago Capitalism: Tax Havens, Offshore Money, and the State, 1950s–1970s," *American Historical Review* 122, no. 5 (2017): 1431–58. Yet the term *territorial capitalism* is redundant. Capitalism has been deterritorialized and reterritorialized at new scales and in new state spaces, but it has never been nonterritorial

or permanently deterritorialized (as any dockworker, truck driver, server-farm technician, or bank teller can attest). For refutations of the conceit of nonterritoriality or postterritoriality, see Stuart Elden, "Missing the Point: Globalization, Deterritorialization and the Space of the World," *Transactions of the Institute of British Geographers* 30, no. 1 (2005): 8–19; Manu Goswami, "AHR Conversation: History after the End of History: Reconceptualizing the Twentieth Century," *American Historical Review* 121, no. 5 (December 2016): 1571–72; and Saskia Sassen, "Territory and Territoriality in the Global Economy," *International Sociology* 15, no. 2 (2000): 372–93.

13. On the imperial history of the camp, see Enzo Traverso, *The Origins of Nazi Violence*, trans. Janet Lloyd (New York: New Press, 2003).
14. "Summer Madness," *Honolulu Advertiser*, July 11, 1916.
15. Philip B. Kennedy, *Digest of a Report to the Foreign Trade Committee of the Merchants' Association of New York on a Comparative Study of the Economic, Industrial and Comparative Conditions in the Free Ports of Europe and the Port of New York* (New York: Merchants' Association of New York, 1914), 8; San Francisco Chamber of Commerce quoted in US Tariff Commission, *Information Concerning Free Zones in Ports of the United States*, 42.
16. As a result, people almost always spoke of the "free port" and not the "free zone" or "foreign-trade zone" up through the turn of the twentieth century, and then used the terms interchangeably until the 1960s.
17. As a banker elaborated in December of 1860, "I would have New York a free city—not a free city with respect to the liberty of the negro, but a free city in commerce and trade." Philip S. Foner, *Business and Slavery: The New York Merchants and the Irrepressible Conflict* (Chapel Hill: University of North Carolina Press, 1941), 286. See also Michael Zakim, "The Dialectics of Merchant Capital: New York City Businessmen and the Secession Crisis of 1860–61," *New York History* 87, no. 1 (2006): 67–87.
18. Christian Schulze, *International Tax-Free Trade Zones and Free Ports* (Durban, South Africa: Butterworths, 1997), 1.
19. Geographers started using this term around World War I. E.g., Kennedy, *Digest of a Report to the Foreign Trade Committee*, 12; MacElwee, *Ports and Terminal Facilities*, 381; Karl D. Reyer, "Free Ports: The Importance of Geographic Factors in Determining Their Successful Operations" (M.A. thesis, Ohio State University, 1925), 5.
20. Frances Armytage, *The Free Port System in the British West Indies: A Study in Commercial Policy, 1766–1822* (London: Longmans, Green, 1953), 2. Seymour Drescher calls the free port system "a carefully controlled breach in the mercantilist network." Drescher, *Econocide: British Slavery in the Era of Abolition*, 2nd ed. (1977; Chapel Hill: University of North Carolina Press, 2010), 56. See also Gerald S. Graham, "The Origin of Free Ports in British North America," *Canadian Historical Review* 22, no. 1 (1941): 25–34.
21. The Free Port Acts cemented London's stature as an entrepôt, within three decades catalyzing the West India Docks and the British bonded warehousing system to facilitate reexport of commodities from non-British colonies (hence subject to British tariffs).
22. On France, see Armytage, *The Free Port System in the British West Indies*, 55. On Saint Eustatius, see Mordechai Arbell, *The Jewish Nation of the Caribbean: The Spanish-Portuguese Jewish Settlements in the Caribbean and the Guianas* (Jerusalem: Geffen, 2002), 179–82. On Spain, see John Fisher, "Imperial 'Free Trade' and the Spanish Economy, 1778–1796," *Journal of Latin American Studies* 13, no. 1 (1981): 21–56.

See also Adam Smith, *The Wealth of Nations*, part 2 (P. F. Collier and Son, 1902), 318.

23. Michael Jarvis, *In the Eye of All Trade: Bermuda, Bermudians, and the Maritime Atlantic World, 1680–1783* (Chapel Hill: University of North Carolina Press, 2010), 180.
24. Seymour Drescher underlines that the free ports "enhanced the re-export of British-carried slaves to the foreign colonies"—"on the very eve of the first abolitionist campaign, one of the two significant moves toward liberalized trade was intimately bound up with the extension, not diminution, of the commerce in human beings." Drescher, *From Slavery to Freedom: Comparative Studies in the Rise and Fall of Atlantic Slavery* (New York: Macmillan, 1999), 12–13. Scholars have begun to mine the history of early modern European free ports. See Corey Tazzara, *The Free Port of Livorno and the Transformation of the Mediterranean World* (New York: Oxford University Press, 2017); and University of Helsinki, "A Global History of Free Ports: Capitalism, Commerce and Geopolitics (1600–1900)," https://www.helsinki.fi/en/researchgroups/a-global-history-of-free-ports.
25. "St. Thomas," *Gleason's Pictorial Drawing-Room Companion*, April 10, 1852, 240.
26. For an overview of this vocabulary, see David Harvey, "Space as a Keyword," in *Spaces of Global Capitalism: Towards a Theory of Uneven Geographical Development* (New York: Verso, 2006), 119–48.
27. In the typology of spaces of colonialism, it was akin to a "maritime enclave," "those islands, harbors, and other strategic points that were occupied as bases for the purpose of global military and naval operations, sometimes with the added purpose of trading and commercial interaction with a mainland"—although its sole purpose was commercial. Robert J. C. Young, *Postcolonialism: An Historical Introduction* (Malden, MA: Blackwell, 2001), 17.
28. Graham, "The Origin of Free Ports in British North America," 31–34.
29. Senator Samuel Smith, "Discriminating Duties," 19th Cong., 1st sess., *Register of Debates* 21, pt. 144, April 18, 1826, 578.
30. William A. Whitehead, *Contributions to the Early History of Perth Amboy and Adjoining Country* (New York: D. Appleton, 1856), 1.
31. Henry Scofield Cooley, *A Study of Slavery in New Jersey* (Baltimore: John Hopkins Press, 1896), 15.
32. *Letter Book of John Watts: Merchant and Councillor of New York, January 1, 1762–December 22, 1765* (New York: New York Historical Society, 1928), 31.
33. Graham Russell Hodges, *Slavery and Freedom in the Rural North: African Americans in Monmouth County* (Lanham, MD: Rowman and Littlefield, 1997), 49. On slavery in Perth Amboy and New Jersey, see also James J. Gigantino II, "Trading in Jersey Souls: New Jersey and the Interstate Slave Trade," *Pennsylvania History* 77, no. 3 (Summer 2010): 281–302; Edgar J. McManus, *Black Bondage in the North* (Syracuse, NY: Syracuse University Press, 1973), 13, 22–23; and Whitehead, *Contributions to the Early History of Perth Amboy and Adjoining Country*, 317–19.
34. "Free Ports," *Providence Patriot*, March 13, 1822; "Free Port in Hayti," *Norwich Courier*, July 3, 1822; "Free Port in the Pacific," *Baltimore Gazette and Daily Advertiser*, October 29, 1827; "Tampico a Free Port," *Boston Weekly Messenger*, September 24, 1829; "Pampatar, a Free Port," *Baltimore Patriot*, November 16, 1829; "Maracaibo a Free Port," *New York Mercury*, October 3, 1832. And these were the free ports that made the news, thanks to letters from US consuls; still more may have escaped mention.

35. Albert Anthony Giesecke, *American Commercial Legislation before 1789* (New York: D. Appleton, 1910), 103.
36. Charles A. Beard, *An Economic Interpretation of the Constitution of the United States* (New York: Free Press, 1913), 175. Citing Beard, Richard Posner terms the Commerce Clause "a charter of free trade." Posner, "The Constitution as an Economic Document," *George Washington Law Review* 56, no. 1 (1987): 17. For historical analyses of the United States as a "free trade area," see Richard Franklin Bensel, *The Political Economy of American Industrialization, 1877–1900* (New York: Cambridge University Press, 2000); Herbert Hovenkamp, *Enterprise and American Law, 1836–1937* (Cambridge, MA: Harvard University Press, 1991); and Allan Kulikoff, *The Agrarian Origins of American Capitalism* (Charlottesville: University Press of Virginia, 1992).
37. Senator George M. Dallas, Revenue Collection Bill, 22nd Cong., 2nd sess., *Register of Debates*, February 8, 1833, 416.
38. The Supreme Court had to bring states to heel by striking down obstructions to trade, as in 1878 when it annulled a Pennsylvania law that taxed out-of-state goods sold at auction. Bensel, *The Political Economy of American Industrialization*, 325.
39. On List, I have benefitted from Marc-William Palen, *The "Conspiracy" of Free Trade: The Anglo-American Struggle over Empire and Economic Globalisation, 1846–1896* (Cambridge: Cambridge University Press, 2016); Roman Szporluk, *Communism and Nationalism: Karl Marx versus Friedrich List* (New York: Oxford University Press, 1988); and Keith Tribe, *Strategies of Economic Order: German Economic Discourse, 1750–1950* (Cambridge: Cambridge University Press, 1995). List has been resurrected by contemporary critics of global capitalism of all political persuasions. See Patrick J. Buchanan, "Say Goodbye to the Mother Continent," January 1, 2002, https://buchanan.org/blog/pjb-say-goodbye-to-the-mother-continent-409; and Ha-Joon Chang, *Kicking Away the Ladder: Development Strategy in Historical Perspective* (New York: Anthem, 2002).
40. On the Pennsylvania scene, see Andrew Shankman, "'A New Thing on Earth': Alexander Hamilton, Pro-Manufacturing Republicans, and the Democratization of American Political Economy," *Journal of the Early Republic* 23, no. 3 (Fall 2003): 323–52.
41. Friedrich List, "Letter I," *Outlines of American Political Economy* (Philadelphia: Samuel Parker, 1827), 7.
42. Friedrich List, "Letter II," *Outlines of American Political Economy* (Philadelphia: Samuel Parker, 1827), 10.
43. Karl Marx, in turn, rejected Listian nationalism as bourgeois mystification: "The nationality of the worker is neither French, nor English, nor German, it is *labour, free slavery, self-huckstering*. His government is neither French, nor English, nor German, it is capital. His native air is neither French, nor English, nor German, it is *factory air*. The land belonging to him is neither French, nor English, nor German, it lies a few feet *below the ground*." Quoted in Szporluk, *Communism and Nationalism*, 35.
44. Stuart Elden, *The Birth of Territory* (Chicago: University of Chicago Press, 2013), 7.
45. In 1889, Togo and other German possessions on the "slave coast" of Africa were joined with those of France in "one common customs territory." See "Progress in Africa," *African Repository* 65, no. 1 (1889): 4. In 1901, the US Supreme Court ruled that a temporary tariff on commerce between Puerto Rico and the mainland United States was not in conflict with the island's status as a part of the US customs territory because the US customs territory was distinct from the US domestic territory.

Puerto Rico was in the former but not in the latter—it was "foreign in a domestic sense." Merchants in San Juan could not export oranges duty-free to New York City since Puerto Rico was not in the US domestic territory, but also they could not import, say, coal duty-free from Liverpool since Puerto Rico was in the US customs territory. "Primarily Porto Rican products were taxed not for the benefit of Porto Rico," the British journalist Sydney Brooks elaborated at the time, "but to establish the principle, now ratified by the Supreme Court, that Imperialism did not imply free trade even with the Empire." "And as regards the outer world," he added, "the American navigation laws will be extended to fence the colonies in and preserve them to American trade." Brooks, "Protectionist Empire," *Fortnightly* 70, no. 416 (1901), 238; see also Benjamin O. Fordham, "Protectionist Empire: Trade, Tariffs, and United States Foreign Policy, 1890–1914," *Studies in American Political Development* 31, no. 2 (2017): 170–92. The Supreme Court decision is *Downes v. Bidwell*, 182 US 244 (1901). On *Downs v. Bidwell* and the other "Insular Cases," see Christina Duffy Burnett and Burke Marshall, eds., *Foreign in a Domestic Sense: Puerto Rico, American Expansion, and the Constitution* (Durham, NC: Duke University Press, 2001); and Sarah Cleveland, "Powers Inherent in Sovereignty: Indians, Aliens, Territories, and the Nineteenth Century Origins of Plenary Power over Foreign Affairs," *Texas Law Review* 81, no. 1 (2002): 226.

46. Quoted in Robert Walter Johannsen, *Stephen A. Douglas* (Urbana: University of Illinois Press, 1997), 832.
47. Congressman Richard W. Townshend, speech, 48th Cong., 2nd sess., *Appendix to the Congressional Record* 16, January 10, 1885, 33, 29. Townshend was not the first to broach this scenario in Douglas's wake. See, for example, "An American Zollverein," *Chicago Daily Tribune*, September 6, 1878.
48. Congressman William McAdoo, Post-Office Appropriation Bill, 49th Cong., 1st sess., *Congressional Record* 17, May 19, 1886, 4702.
49. "An American Zollverein: How It Strikes the European Mind," *New York Tribune*, August 19, 1889.
50. José Martí, "The Washington Pan-American Congress," in *Inside the Monster: Writings on the United States and American Imperialism*, trans. Elinor Randall, ed. Philip S. Foner (New York: Monthly Review Press, 1975), 357. Some recognized that the United States itself was structured as a customs union: "Just as the 45 States of the American Union, covering many degrees of latitude, and many varieties of soil and climate, prosper under *internal free trade* so it might reasonably be expected that Mexico would gain by unrestricted commercial intercourse with its mighty neighbor." *Mexican Herald*, "North American Customs Union," August 23, 1898.
51. "Personal and Political," *Hartford Daily Courant*, June 18, 1866.
52. Mary Louise Pratt, *Imperial Eyes: Travel Writing and Transculturation* (New York: Routledge, 1992), chapter 4.
53. Wharton Barker, "American Commercial Union," *North American Review* 178, no. 569 (March 1904): 345–46.
54. Although *Freihafen* means "free port," this new district was recognized as a repudiation of Hamburg's prior status as a *Freihafen*.
55. I borrow the phrase from Nezzar Alsayyad and Ananya Roy, "Medieval Modernity: On Citizenship and Urbanism in a Global Era," *Space and Polity* 10, no. 1 (2006): 1–20.
56. Richard J. Evans, *Death in Hamburg: Society and Politics in the Cholera Years* (London: Penguin Books, 2005), 4.

57. "N.Y. Foreign Trade Zone Seeks Bigger Role in Post-War Commerce," *Wall Street Journal*, October 26, 1945.
58. "There was no truly international economy before the Hanseatic League," notes Fernand Braudel in *The Perspective of the World*, vol. 3 of *Civilization and Capitalism, 15th–18th Century*, trans. Siân Reynolds (Berkeley: University of California Press, 1992), 102.
59. "Of the Maritime Legislation of the Middle Ages," *Eastern Argus*, April 15, 1828. See also "The Hanse Towns," *New Orleans Times-Picayune*, August 14, 1870.
60. See, for instance, Walter Zinn, "The Hanseatic League and the Nature of Multinational Business," *Proceedings of the Second Workshop in Marketing History*, ed. Stanley D. Hollander and Terence Nevitt (1985): 86–97.
61. "Lübeck and the Hanseatic League," *National Magazine* 8, no. 47 (September 1860): 251.
62. "That German commerce does not need the Jews is proven by the Fuggers, the Welsers, and the Hanseatic League, none of which succumbed to Jewish influence," wrote Konstantin von Gebsattel, a retired general and supporter of the Pan-German League, in 1913, quoted in J. C. G. Rohl, *From Bismarck to Hitler: The Problem of Continuity in German History* (New York: Barnes and Noble, 1970), 50. See also Oliver Cox, *The Foundations of Capitalism* (New York: Philosophical Library, 1959), 196.
63. The free zone was the epitome of Alfred Thayer Mahan's notion of "sea power." On Mahan with a German accent, see Christopher L. Connery, "Ideologies of Land and Sea: Alfred Thayer Mahan, Carl Schmitt, and the Shaping of Global Myth Elements," *Boundary 2* 28, no. 2 (2001): 173–201.
64. Cox, *Foundations of Capitalism*, 188. "We can be sure," writes Christopher A. McAuley, Cox's biographer, "that Cox took note of the parallels between Trinidad's economic relationship with an imperial England and a younger England's economic relationship with the Hansards." McAuley, "Oliver C. Cox and World Systems Theory," in *American Capitalism: Social Thought and Political Economy in the Twentieth Century*, ed. Nelson Lichtenstein (Philadelphia: University of Pennsylvania Press, 2006), 186.
65. Scholars have long ranked the Hansards as early practitioners of extraterritoriality. See, for instance, Shih Shun Liu, *Extraterritoriality: Its Rise and Decline* (New York: Columbia University Press, 1925).
66. Brooks Adams, *The New Empire* (New York: Macmillan, 1902), 62.
67. Friedrich List, *The National System of Political Economy*, trans. Sampson S. Lloyd (1841; London: Longmans, Green, 1928), 10–21.
68. MacElwee, *Ports and Terminal Facilities*, 381.
69. Clapp, "Foreign Trading Zones in Our Seaports," 262.
70. On the *zona libre*, see Samuel E. Bell and James M. Smallwood, *The Zone Libre, 1858–1905: A Problem in American Diplomacy* (El Paso: Texas Western, 1982); Margolies, *Spaces of Law*; and David M. Pletcher, *The Diplomacy of Trade and Investment: American Economic Expansion in the Hemisphere, 1865–1900* (Columbia: University of Missouri Press, 1997), 84–91. On the *zones franches*, see Charles Biermann, "The Franco-Swiss Free Zones," *Geographical Review* 13, no. 3 (1923): 368–76; and Louis Schulthess, "The Franco-Swiss Free Zones," *Foreign Affairs*, December 15, 1924. When France abolished the zones in 1923, *Commerce Reports* noted that "the French customs line was transferred to the political frontier." "France," *Commerce Reports*, December 31, 1923, 904.
71. Sutton E. Griggs, *Imperium in Imperio* (Cincinnati: Editor Publishing, 1899).

72. Clapp, "The Free Port as an Instrument of World Trade," in *American Problems of Reconstruction*, ed. Elisha M. Friedman (New York: E. P. Dutton, 1918), 249.
73. Reyer, "Free Ports," 24–25.
74. Germany razed the old village of Qingdao in 1898–99 to construct the free port's commercial district, relocating Chinese to segregated residential zones. See US Tariff Commission, *Colonial Tariff Policies* (Washington, DC: Government Printing Office, 1922), 262; and George Steinmetz, *The Devil's Handwriting: Precoloniality and the German Colonial State in Qingdao, Samoa, and Southwest Africa* (Chicago: University of Chicago Press, 2007), chapter 7.
75. Clapp, "The Free Port as an Instrument of World Trade," 248.
76. Reyer, "Free Ports," 26.
77. Charles Gide, *Political Economy*, 3rd ed., trans. C. William A. Veditz (Boston: D. C. Heath, 1913), 266.
78. *The Copenhagen Free Port Co.* (Copenhagen: Hertz's Bogtrykkeri, 1923), 23.
79. MacElwee, *Ports and Terminal Facilities*, 414–18.
80. *The Key to the Baltic* (Copenhagen: Hertz's Bogtrykkeri, 1920); on Norway and Finland, see MacElwee, *Ports and Terminal Facilities*, 414; on Sweden, a sampling of coverage includes "Malmö Free Port Nears Completion," *Swedish-American Trade Journal* 15 (October 1921): 352–55; "Göteborg, Principal Port in the North, Establishes Free Port," *Swedish-American Trade Journal* 15 (November 1921): 384–87; "The Free Port at Stockholm," *Swedish-American Trade Journal* 16 (April 1922): 116–19; "The Free Port at Stockholm," *American Review of Reviews* 65 (June 1922): 659–60; "The Free Ports of Sweden," *World Markets*, March 28, 1923, 47–49. For a resource with photographs, maps, and charts, see US Army Corps of Engineers and US Shipping Board, *Foreign Trade Zones (or Free Ports)* (Washington, DC: Government Printing Office, 1929).
81. MacElwee, *Ports and Terminal Facilities*, 414–18; "New Free Harbor at Cadiz, Spain," *American Industries* 26, no. 9 (April 1916); "Vladivostok: Free Port Regulations," *Japan Weekly Chronicle*, January 15, 1925; "Saloniki's Free Zones," *New York Times*, May 31, 1925; "Free Zone Declared in Old Piraeus," *Hartford Courant*, April 24, 1927.
82. Under the auspices of the League of Nations, colonial free ports persisted too, such as at Haifa, whose management was entrusted to a British company. "Haifa to Be Free Port," *New York Times*, October 7, 1921.
83. J. F. Keeley to C. W. Bahr, July 19, 1924, Free Ports (Italy), Records of the Bureau of Foreign and Domestic Commerce, Record Group 151, National Archives and Records Administration (NARA) (hereafter BFDC Records); "Italy Puts Lid on Ford Dream of 'Fordonia,'" *Chicago Daily Tribune*, November 30, 1922; and "Ford Starts to Make Cars for Balkan States," *Dayton Daily News*, August 30, 1925. Ford was also in talks with Mexico and Romania. "Ford to Visit Mexico?," *New York Times*, July 9, 1924; "Mr. Ford's Offer to Rumania," *Manchester Guardian*, July 25, 1929. The company had branched out from Detroit early on, opening its first foreign assembly plant in London in 1914—three years before breaking ground on the River Rouge—and thirty-three more around the globe by the early 1930s. Gerald T. Bloomfield, "Coils of the Commercial Serpent: A Geography of the Ford Branch Distribution System, 1904–1933," in *Roadside America: The Automobile in Design and Culture*, ed. Jan Jennings (Ames: Iowa State University Press, 1990), 41. On Ford's empire see Elizabeth D. Esch, "Fordtown: Managing Race and Nation in the American Empire, 1925–1945" (PhD diss., New York University, 2003); Elizabeth D. Esch, *The Color*

Line and the Assembly Line: Managing Race in the Ford Empire (Berkeley: University of California Press, 2018); and Greg Grandin, *Fordlandia: The Rise and Fall of Henry Ford's Forgotten Jungle City* (New York: Henry Holt, 2009).

84. See the folder "Barcelona: Particulars of New Plant," box 1, accession #760, Branch Assembly Department Records Subseries, Benson Ford Research Center, Dearborn, Michigan (hereafter FMC Records).
85. "Ford Distributing System Creates a Little Empire," *Los Angeles Times*, February 6, 1927.
86. Antonio Gramsci, "Americanism and Fordism," in *Selections from the Prison Notebooks*, ed. and trans. Quintin Hoare and Geoffrey Nowell Smith (New York: International, 1971), 285.
87. See documents in the Branch Assembly Department Records Subseries, such as about Sao Paolo, Brazil, in box 2, accession #760, FMC Records.
88. "Potash and Klein," *Time*, July 19, 1926.
89. Leach, *Land of Desire*, 362. Also see William H. Becker, *The Dynamics of Business-Government Relations: Industry and Exports, 1893–1921* (Chicago: University of Chicago Press, 1982).
90. Harvey A. Sweetser to A. Raymond, June 28, 1928, Free Ports (Norway), BFDC Records.
91. New Orleans Office to Tariff Division, December 9, 1925, and Tariff Division to New Orleans Office, December 14, 1925, Free Ports (General), BFDC Records.
92. New York District Office to Division of Foreign Tariffs, "Free Ports in Spain," April 18, 1925, Free Ports (Spain), BFDC Records; M. E. Woods to Henry Chalmers, September 13, 1927, Free Ports (Sweden), BFDC Records; V. Gebelt to Henry Chalmers, September 20, 1928, Free Ports (Turkey), BFDC Records.
93. Jordan Motor Car Company Export Manager to Henry Chalmers, December 8, 1927, Free Ports (General), BFDC Records.
94. Julius Klein to L. M. Rumely, March 22, 1926, Free Ports (Spain), BFDC Records.
95. Clapp, "The Free Port as an Instrument of World Trade," 250.
96. Kennedy, *Digest of a Report to the Foreign Trade Committee*, 23.
97. Kennedy, *Digest of a Report to the Foreign Trade Committee*, 28.
98. International Chamber of Commerce, "Memorandum on the Development and Regularization of Free Zones in Ports," *Transportation*, Brochure No. 2 (Paris, 1921): 10–12. On the ICC, see Victoria de Grazia, *Irresistible Empire: America's Advance through 20th-Century Europe* (Cambridge, MA: Harvard University Press, 2005), chapter 3, and Slobodian, *Globalists*, 34–37.
99. "Germans Chief Rum-Runners," *Boston Daily Globe*, December 15, 1925.
100. De Grazia, *Irresistible Empire*, 131.
101. "Malmö Free Port Nears Completion," 352.
102. Rosewater had immigrated from Bohemia in 1853. As a young telegraph operator he had tapped out the Emancipation Proclamation to the world. Kathryn Hellerstein, "A Letter from Lincoln's Jewish Telegrapher," *Jewish Quarterly Review* 94, no. 4 (2004): 625–36. Erastus Wiman, a real estate developer in Staten Island (and likely the earliest proponent of a foreign-trade zone on Staten Island), claimed that Rosewater had sold President Benjamin Harrison on the zone concept. See Wiman, *Chances of Success* (New York: Stanley Bradley, 1893), 184.
103. Victor Rosewater, "Free Port Proposed in 1891," *New York Times*, December 14, 1932.
104. Corbin's plan was three pronged: a steamship line between Montauk and Milford

Haven in Wales, a free zone at Montauk, and a tunnel carrying tracks from Montauk under the East River to Manhattan. His partners were Watson B. Dickerman (president of the New York Stock Exchange), Charles M. Pratt (later a vice president at Standard Oil), and Corbin's son-in-law George S. Edgell. Austin Corbin to William E. Chandler, April 9, 1895, box 97, Papers of William E. Chandler, Library of Congress (hereafter Chandler Papers). See also Austin Corbin, "Quick Transit between New York and London," *North American Review* 161, no. 468 (November 1895): 513–27; "The Brooklyn-Jersey City Tunnel," *Washington Post,* October 17, 1894.

105. "Austin Corbin's Wild Boars," *New York Tribune,* September 28, 1890.
106. Edward A. Bowers to William E. Chandler, April 30, 1894, box 93, Chandler Papers.
107. Mildred H. Smith, *Early History of the Long Island Railroad, 1834–1900* (Uniondale, NY: Salisbury, 1958), 39–52; *Coney Island and the Jews* (New York: G. W. Carleston, 1879).
108. "Austin Corbin Acquires 5,500 Acres of Land at Montauk Point," *New York Times,* June 1, 1895; John A. Strong, *The Montaukett Indians of Eastern Long Island* (Syracuse, NY: Syracuse University Press, 2001); Austin Corbin to William E. Chandler, February 15, 1895, box 97, Chandler Papers.
109. "Mr. Corbin's Free Port," *Chicago Daily Tribune,* February 25, 1896. "The free port will be exactly like a manufacturer's bonded warehouse as now located at the water's edge in one of our harbors. Instead of being a single building, however, a line will be drawn from the water around a tract of land of sufficient size and back to the shore, and a wall will be constructed enclosing the land, and within the enclosure there will be warehouses of various kinds, including the manufacturers' warehouses." "Mr. Corbin's Free Port Plan," *New York Tribune,* February 6, 1896.
110. Austin Corbin to William E. Chandler, May 4, 1894, box 93, Chandler Papers.
111. "An American Free Port," *Washington Post,* May 14, 1894.
112. Austin Corbin, "The Fort Pond Bay Free Port," 54th Cong., 1st sess., 1896, S. Doc. 106, 2.
113. Austin Corbin to William E. Chandler, November 15, 1895, box 99, Chandler Papers.
114. S1980, 53 Cong., 2nd sess. (April 30, 1894).
115. S561, 54th Cong., 1st sess. (December 5, 1895).
116. "Shaw Declares for Free Ports," *Boston Daily Globe,* January 31, 1907.
117. "Shaw on Free Ports," *Washington Post,* February 15, 1907. Shaw's entrance into politics is told as a crusade of antipopulism in William R. Boyd, "Leslie Mortimer Shaw," *Annals of Iowa* 34, no. 5 (1958): 321–30.
118. "Bonded Zones," *Manchester Guardian,* March 12, 1907.
119. "Statement Issued by Mr. Fitzgerald Defines His Policy," *Christian Science Monitor,* January 12, 1910.
120. "Mayor Fitzgerald Urges a Free Port for City of Boston," *Christian Science Monitor,* February 17, 1910. See also "Boston as Free Port Is Favored," *Christian Science Monitor,* March 21, 1910; "New Business Era Promised in 'Free Port' for Boston," *Boston Daily,* April 3, 1910; "Offers Hub's Free Port Bill in House," *Boston Journal,* April 9, 1910; "Fitz Back, Strong for a Free Port," *Boston Journal,* April 18, 1910; "McNary for Free Port," *Boston Daily Globe,* September 15, 1910; and "Expert Is Here from Hamburg," *Boston Globe,* February 19, 1912.
121. Philip B. Kennedy, *Digest of a Report to the Foreign Trade Committee of the Merchants' Association of New York on a Comparative Study of the Economic, Industrial and Com-*

parative Conditions in the Free Ports of Europe and the Port of New York (New York: Merchants' Association of New York, 1914).

122. "Suggest Cannon Ball Farm for Free Port Site," *Philadelphia Inquirer*, June 10, 1913.
123. As Andrew Zimmerman writes about the utility of sociological justifications of racism during this period, "Capital and colonial states move only against a background of fixed differences, and their mobility thus depends on the immobility of populations, races, cultures, and identities." Zimmerman, *Alabama in Africa: Booker T. Washington, the German Empire, and the Globalization of the New South* (Princeton, NJ: Princeton University Press, 2010), 206. On the symmetry of tariff policy and immigration policy, see Matthew Frye Jacobson, *Barbarian Virtues: The United States Encounters Foreign Peoples at Home and Abroad, 1876–1917* (New York: Hill and Wang, 2001); and April Merleaux, *Sugar and Civilization: American Empire and the Cultural Politics of Sweetness* (Chapel Hill: University of North Carolina Press, 2015).
124. Arthur McGuirk to William Kent, April 28, 1920, folder 628, box 31, Kent Papers.
125. Kent was a trust-fund friend of socialism. "Like a repentant sinner, William Kent opened his congressional campaign in 1910 with an apology for his wealth accumulated by land speculation and with a promise to use his fortune to wipe out the system by which he had accumulated it." George E. Mowry, *The California Progressives* (Berkeley: University of California Press, 1951), 95.
126. As Kent vouched in a letter to V. S. McClatchy, a eugenicist whom he supported, "I received your pamphlets on Japan and greatly appreciated them. You are exactly and entirely right." William Kent to V. S. McClatchy, August 7, 1919, folder 593, box 30, Kent Papers. Kent later wrote to fellow progressive Senator Irvine L. Lenroot:

    > When the immigration laws are reformed, it will be absolutely necessary to cut off a lot of undesirable immigration now permitted. For instance, there is no possible sense in permitting the entry of negroes, and I for my part am strongly opposed to making this country the dumping ground for the remainder of the Russian, Polish, and German Jews. We have got to a point where we must talk frankly and act strongly if we are going to preserve a race of people fit for self-government, and in the problem of self-government, assimilability, mutual understanding and good will, which cannot exist between divergent races, is of as much importance, and to my mind of greater importance, than economic value. (William Kent to Irvine L. Lenroot, February 9, 1921, 2, folder 654, box 32, Kent Papers)

127. William Kent to John P. Young, April 19, 1920, 2, folder 627, box 31, Kent Papers.
128. William Kent to J. G. Ropes, June 16, 1920, 1, folder 633, box 31, Kent Papers.
129. F. W. Taussig, "The United States Tariff Commission and the Tariff," *American Economic Review* 16, no. 1 (March 1926): 1.
130. US Tariff Commission, *Information Concerning Free Zones in Ports of the United States*.
131. All seventeen were introduced during the first session of the 66th Congress: HR414 (May 19, 1919); S556 (May 23, 1919); S1652 (June 11, 1919); HJR141 (June 26, 1919); S2288 (June 27, 1919); HJR142 (June 28, 1919); HJR223 (October 3, 1919); HR9724 (October 4, 1919); HJR224 (October 4, 1919); S3170 (October 6, 1919); HR9778 (October 7, 1919); HJR225 (October 8, 1919); HJR226 (October 9, 1919); HJR228 (October 11, 1919); HJR234 (October 17, 1919); HJR237 (October 22, 1919); HR10156 (October 24, 1919).
132. As Kent vented to Commerce Secretary Herbert Hoover, Fordney "knows nothing about commerce and little of anything else, except folklore." William Kent to Herbert Hoover, September 7, 1921, 1, folder 692, box 34, Kent Papers.

133. Roy S. MacElwee, House Committee on Ways and Means, *Foreign Trade Zones*, 66th Cong., 1st sess., October 11, 1919, 137.
134. Philip B. Kennedy, House Committee on Ways and Means, *Foreign Trade Zones*, 66th Cong., 1st sess., October 10, 1919, 41.
135. Congressman Joseph W. Fordney, House Committee on Ways and Means, *Foreign Trade Zones*, 66th Cong., 1st sess., October 10, 1919, 47. Protectionists outside of Congress latched onto this critique, such as in "No Manufacturing in Free Ports," *American Economist* 75, no. 4 (January 23, 1925): 26.
136. Congressman Nicholas Longworth and Philip B. Kennedy, House Committee on Ways and Means, *Foreign Trade Zones*, 66th Cong., 1st sess., October 10, 1919, 48.
137. J. J. Dwyer, House Committee on Ways and Means, *Foreign Trade Zones*, 66th Cong., 1st sess., October 11, 1919, 122.
138. Elihu C. Church, House Committee on Ways and Means, *Foreign Trade Zones*, 66th Cong., 1st sess., October 11, 1919, 130.
139. Wilbur F. Wakeman, House Committee on Ways and Means, *Foreign Trade Zones*, 66th Cong., 1st sess., October 10, 1919, 71.
140. W. P. Bowman, House Committee on Ways and Means, *Foreign Trade Zones*, 66th Cong., 1st sess., October 10, 1919, 84.
141. J. J. Dwyer, Senate Committee on Commerce, *Free Zones in Ports*, 66th Cong., 1st sess., October 10, 1919, 10. Dwyer made a similar case in the House the next day:

> I know very well that we have in the last 140 years become the greatest and richest nation in the world without the assistance of the proposed foreign-trade zone. But we must keep abreast of the times. Because the old-time printing press printed a paper pretty well is no reason why we should adopt the latest model. Because the old-time automobile got us around is no reason why we should not insist on getting next year's. Because wagons were useful things was no reason why we should not have adopted automobiles when they came along, if they could accelerate our progress and make it cheaper and easier. And if by this new method and device we can have less friction and less expense, less needless loss and anxiety, by improving the processes of foreign trade, why in the name of common sense should we not employ it? In addition to that, we will afford a means of livelihood for labor that does not exist now to any considerable extent. (Dwyer, House Committee on Ways and Means, *Foreign Trade Zones*, 66th Cong., 1st sess., October 11, 1919, 128)

142. Irving T. Bush to Joseph W. Fordney, reprinted in House Committee on Ways and Means, *Foreign Trade Zones*, 66th Cong., 1st sess., October 10, 1919, 75. "It seems to me like a half-digested idea, a glittering generality," Bush had observed in a lengthy interview the year before. "It is buying population that makes markets, not an ingenious scheme of duty evasion. Besides, there is a simpler way to avoid the duty than by the expensive process of establishing a free city, building the factories there, walling them in, placing a guard over them, letting the workmen in and out night and morning as if they were employed in munitions factories, and, in general, erecting this expensive artificial wall against the impalpable tariff evil which can be so much more easily conquered [by simplifying the drawback procedure]." Richard Barry, "How New York Would Fare as a Free Port," *New York Times*, January 6, 1918. Kent viewed Bush as "untruthful" and self-interested, a characterization he made in private correspondence. William Kent, "Notes on Free Zones: Concerning Personnel of Free Zone Legislation," August 5, 1919, 7, folder 53, box 56, Kent Papers.

143. Arthur McGuirk, Senate Committee on Commerce, *Free Zones in Ports*, 66th Cong., 1st sess., October 11, 1919, 64.
144. John H. Rosseter, Senate Committee on Commerce, *Free Zones in Ports*, 66th Cong., 1st sess., October 21, 1919, 112.
145. Thomas Walker Page to William Kent, February 5, 1920, 1, folder 614, box 31, Kent Papers.
146. William Kent to Lucius R. Eastman, February 11, 1920, folder 614, box 31, Kent Papers.
147. HR2228, 67th Cong., 1st sess. (April 11, 1921); S597, 67th Cong., 1st sess. (April 13, 1921); S2391, 67th Cong., 1st sess. (August 11, 1921).
148. As Thomas Walker Page put it, "[Foreign-trade zones] is a better term for this device than 'free zones,' inasmuch as the word 'free' carries the implication that fiscal policy is involved, the implication being due, in the main, to the fact that we use the expression 'free trade' as a synonym for a low tariff." Page, House Committee on Ways and Means, *Foreign Trade Zones*, 66th Cong., 1st sess., October 10, 1919, 29.
149. "Free Zones for the Port," *New York Tribune*, August 18, 1922.
150. 42 *US Statutes at Large* 978 (September 21, 1922).
151. Herbert Hoover to Wesley L. Jones, March 29, 1924, reprinted in "Foreign Trade Zones in Ports of the United States," 68th Cong., 1st sess., 1924, S. Rep. 477, 33. The first manipulating bonded warehouse opened in San Francisco, and warehousemen had tepid praise for it. "The space has been very little used," one noted. "Our manipulating warehouse is a chicken wire enclosure about ten feet square, in the corner of the top floor of one our bonded warehouses. During the past five years it has been used twice." Ralph J. Scanlan, "The Potentialities of a Foreign Trade Zone in the Trade of the Port of San Francisco" (PhD diss., University of California at Berkeley, 1929), 95.
152. As part of an incorporated territory of the United States, Honolulu was in the same customs territory as San Francisco or New York City. Henry Chalmers to C. W. Reynolds, December 9, 1926, Free Ports (Hawaii), BFDC Records.
153. In addition to the three bills from 1921, politicians introduced HRJ2, 68th Cong., 1st sess. (December 5, 1923); S2570, 68th Cong., 1st sess. (February 20, 1924); HR 9293, 68th Cong., 1st sess. (May 17, 1924); S3565, 68th Cong., 2nd sess. (December 5, 1924); HJR4, 69th Cong., 1st sess. (December 7, 1925); HR37, 69th Cong., 1st sess. (December 7, 1925); S66, 69th Cong., 1st sess. (December 8, 1925); HR 5479, 70th Cong., 1st sess. (December 5, 1927); S742, 70th Cong., 1st sess. (December 9, 1927); HR8557, 70th Cong., 1st sess. (January 5, 1928); S2356, 71st Cong., 2nd sess. (December 4, 1929); HR6592, 71st Cong., 2nd sess. (December 5, 1929). Published in support of these last two bills was yet another dense report: US Shipping Board, *Foreign Trade Zones (or Free Ports)*.
154. Hugh Lynch to Wesley L. Jones, July 10, 1929, 2, folder 3, box 45, Wesley L. Jones Papers, Special Collections, University of Washington Libraries.
155. Alfred E. Eckes Jr. comments on how frequently "infamous" and "notorious" modify "Smoot-Hawley" in *Opening America's Market: U.S. Foreign Trade Policy since 1776* (Chapel Hill: University of North Carolina Press, 1995), 100.
156. "Hoover Support Gives Impetus to Move for Less Red Tape," *Christian Science Monitor*, January 25, 1929.
157. Dick Steward, *Trade and Hemisphere: The Good Neighbor Policy and Reciprocal Trade* (Columbia: University of Missouri Press, 1975), 13.

158. Roosevelt quoted in Edward S. Kaplan, *American Trade Policy, 1923–1995* (Westport, CT: Greenwood, 1996), 46. Nitsan Chorev focuses on this "depoliticization" of trade policy: "The institutional project of globalization entails a process of *depoliticization*, where bureaucratic orientation and structural constraints dominate the process of decision making, at the expense of public debates and political deliberations." Chorev, *Remaking U.S. Trade Policy: From Protectionism to Globalization* (Ithaca, NY: Cornell University Press, 2007), 12.
159. Kaplan, *American Trade Policy, 1923–1995*, 45.
160. In addition, Congressman Wesley L. Jones of Washington, patron of the US merchant marine and sponsor of a total of seven zone bills, died in 1932.
161. Emanuel Celler, *You Never Leave Brooklyn: The Autobiography of Emanuel Celler* (New York: John Day, 1953), 5, 22.
162. Congressman Emanuel Celler, Celler Free Port Bill, 73rd Cong., 2nd sess., *Congressional Record* 78, May 29, 1934, 9855.
163. The first free-zone bill that Celler proposed—HR14454, 71st Cong., 3rd sess. (January 22, 1931)—called for Congress to charter a privately held "World Commerce Corporation," which would aid American industries by attempting to control the distribution of raw materials from abroad, partly by operating foreign-trade zones in the United States. See House Committee on the Judiciary, *To Create a World Commerce Corporation*, 71st Cong., 3rd sess., January 22, 1931. This scheme revived a bill from 1924—S3565, 68th Cong., 2nd sess. (December 5, 1924)—that had provided for a World Commerce Corporation to produce commodities such as asphalt, petroleum, and crude rubber abroad and then supply them to US industries via US free zones. Another, subsequent World Commerce Corporation became a front for the CIA. Writes Douglas Valentine, "WCC has been described as a cross between 'an import-export combine and a commercially oriented espionage network.'" Valentine, *The Strength of the Wolf: The Secret History of America's War on Drugs* (New York: Verso, 2004), 76.
164. Emanuel Celler, House Subcommittee of the Committee on Ways and Means, *Foreign Trade Zones*, 73rd Cong., 2nd sess., March 6, 1934, 6, 7. Celler's earlier bill resulted in two days of hearings as well, but it failed to proceed further.
165. Walter P. Hedden, House Subcommittee of the Committee on Ways and Means, *Foreign Trade Zones*, 73rd Cong., 2nd sess., March 6, 1934, 55.
166. In addition to smuggling, customs officials worried about how to categorize goods coming out of a zone. For a commodity subject to ad valorem duties, at what market price would its tariff rate be calculated—the price when it arrived in the zone or the price when it left? Most zones around the world used the latter price, although there were ways to use the former price if an owner so preferred (which, in turn, required paperwork to be completed within the zone, thereby undermining the goal of frictionlessness).
167. Hedden, House Subcommittee of the Committee on Ways and Means, *Foreign Trade Zones*, 73rd Cong., 2nd sess., March 6, 1934, 55.
168. John McKenzie, House Subcommittee of the Committee on Ways and Means, *Foreign Trade Zones*, 73rd Cong., 2nd sess., March 6, 1934, 44.
169. Wilbur LaRoe Jr., Senate Subcommittee on Commerce, *Foreign Trade Zones*, 73rd Cong., 2nd sess., April 11, 1934, 20.
170. Congressman Emanuel Celler, "Celler Free Port Bill," 73rd Cong., 2nd sess., *Congressional Record* 78, May 29, 1934, 9855–58.

171. William E. Evans, House Subcommittee of the Committee on Ways and Means, *Foreign Trade Zones*, 73rd Cong., 2nd sess., March 6, 1934, 52.
172. Schuyler Otis Bland, House Subcommittee of the Committee on Ways and Means, *Foreign Trade Zones*, 73rd Cong., 2nd sess., March 6, 1934, 77.
173. Celler had adopted the same tactic the year before, when he testified, "I would prefer to exclude manufacturing in the beginning. Let us try the idea of a free port first, under the conditions laid down in my bill, and then later we can if practical and reasonable expand the facilities and functions of the free port. Manufacturing at this juncture might give rise to much controversy. Let us leave it out—temporarily at least." Emanuel Celler, House Subcommittee of the Committee on Ways and Means, *Foreign Trade Zones*, 72nd Cong., 2nd sess., February 15, 1933, 6.
174. Halford Mackinder, "The Great Trade Routes," *Journal of the Institute of Bankers* 21, part I (1900): 155.
175. Congressman Emanuel Celler, "Celler Free Port Bill," 73rd Cong., 2nd sess., *Congressional Record* 78, May 29, 1934, 9855.
176. House, "Foreign Trade Zones," 73rd Cong., 2nd sess., *Congressional Record* 78, May 29, 1934, 9859.
177. Senate, "Foreign-Trade Zones in Ports of Entry," 73rd Cong., 2nd sess., *Congressional Record* 78, May 10, 1934, 8476.
178. "Roosevelt Signs Road Funds Bill," *New York Times*, June 19, 1934.
179. Daniel Immerwahr, "The Greater United States: Territory and Empire in U.S. History," *Diplomatic History* 40, no. 3 (2016): 389. See also Brooke L. Blower, "A Nation of Outposts: Forts, Factories, Bases, and the Making of American Power," *Diplomatic History* 41, no. 3 (2017): 439–59.
180. James Ferguson, "Seeing Like an Oil Company: Space, Security, and Global Capital in Neoliberal Africa," *American Anthropologist* 107, no. 3 (2005): 377–82. See also Alberto Toscano, "Lineaments of the Logistical State," *Viewpoint Magazine*, September 28, 2014, https://www.viewpointmag.com/2014/09/28/lineaments-of-the-logistical-state. On military logistics and American empire, see Pierre Bélanger and Alexander Arroyo, *Ecologies of Power: Countermapping the Logistical Landscapes and Military Geographies of the U.S. Department of Defense* (Cambridge, MA: MIT Press, 2016); Patrick Chung, "From Korea to Vietnam: Local Labor, Multinational Capital, and the Evolution of US Military Logistics, 1950–97," *Radical History Review* 133 (2019): 31–55; Deborah Cowen, "*Containing* Insecurity: Logistics Space, U.S. Port Cities, and the 'War on Terror,'" in *Disrupted Cities: When Infrastructure Fails*, ed. Stephen Graham (New York: Routledge, 2010), 69–84; and Laleh Khalili, "The Infrastructural Power of the Military: The Geoeconomic Role of the US Army Corps of Engineers in the Arabian Peninsula," *European Journal of International Relations* 24, no. 4 (2017): 911–33.
181. Andrew Friedman, *Covert Capital: Landscapes of Denial and the Making of U.S. Empire in the Suburbs of Northern Virginia* (Berkeley: University of California Press, 2013), 123; Ann Laura Stoler, "On Degrees of Imperial Sovereignty," *Public Culture* 18, no. 1 (2006): 125–46; Lowe, *The Intimacies of Four Continents*, 8.
182. Foreign-Trade Zones Board, "Description of the Device of the Seal of the Foreign-Trade Zones Board," January 29, 1936, available at https://enforcement.trade.gov/ftzpage/history/earlyyears.html.
183. Giovanni Arrighi, *The Long Twentieth Century: Money, Power, and the Origins of Our Times* (New York: Verso, 1994), 174–75.

184. Jean Gottmann, *The Coming of the Transactional City* (College Park: University of Maryland Institute for Urban Studies, 1983); Saskia Sassen, *The Global City: New York, London, Tokyo* (Princeton, NJ: Princeton University Press, 1991).

CHAPTER FOUR

1. Newbold Morris, speech, October 23, 1939, 4, folder 2, box 5, Free Port Records.
2. George Orwell, "Politics and the English Language," in *Why I Write* (1946; New York: Penguin, 2005), 115.
3. John McKenzie, "Transcript of Proceedings of the Examiners Committee, Foreign-Trade Zones Board," November 12, 1935, 8, folder 4, box 12, Free Port Records.
4. Brooklyn Chamber of Commerce, "Transcript of Proceedings of the Examiners Committee, Foreign-Trade Zones Board," November 12, 1935, 8, folder 4, box 12, Free Port Records.
5. "The day of the world entrepôt has passed," concludes J. Russell Smith in *Industrial and Commercial Geography* (New York: Holt, 1913), 865.
6. Alfred Lewis Lomax, *The Foreign-Trade Zone* (Eugene: Bureau of Business Research, University of Oregon, 1947), 10.
7. Committee for the Steuben Society of America, "In the Matter of: Application by the Board of State Harbor Commissioners for a Grant to Establish a Foreign-Trade Zone at San Francisco, California," transcript, April 28, 1937, 33, folder 3413-1595, box 4, Board of State Harbor Commissioners for San Francisco Harbor Records, California State Archive (hereafter SF Harbor Records).
8. John Dick, "Transcript of Proceedings of the Examiners Committee, Foreign-Trade Zones Board," November 12, 1935, 33, folder 4, box 12, Free Port Records.
9. "The Sheds Down at Pier 45," *San Francisco Chronicle*, June 20, 1948.
10. For an oft-cited example, see Jefferson Cowie, *Capital Moves: RCA's Seventy-Year Quest for Cheap Labor* (Ithaca, NY: Cornell University, 1999).
11. David F. Noble, *Progress without People: In Defense of Luddism* (Chicago: Charles H. Kerr, 1993); "Trade Zones Seek Wider Activities," *New York Times*, October 24, 1949. On carrier pigeons and sundry other forms of "guerrilla logistics," see Jacob Shell, *Transportation and Revolt: Pigeons, Mules, Canals, and the Vanishing Geographies of Subversive Mobility* (Cambridge, MA: MIT Press, 2015). On the iconography of manual labor in the 1930s, see Max Fraser, "Hands Off the Machine: Workers' Hands and Revolutionary Symbolism in the Visual Culture of 1930s America," *American Art* 27, no. 2 (2013): 94–117.
12. US Department of Commerce, *Regulations Governing the Establishment, Operation, Maintenance, and Administration in the United States of Foreign-Trade Zones* (Washington, DC: Government Printing Office, 1935), 1.
13. "Unwitting Pigeons Aid in Production of U.S. Medicine," *Daily Times* (Rochester, NY), October 24, 1941.
14. "Let the Pigeons Do the Work," *Daily Hawk-Eye Gazette* (Burlington, IA), October 20, 1941. The Associated Press also covered the ergot processors—e.g., "Mendicant Pigeons Are Put to Work," *Reading Eagle* (Reading, PA), October 20, 1941.
15. "Foreign Trade Zone 4: 'A Five-Acre Free City,'" *Los Angeles Times*, June 25, 1950.
16. Henri Lefebvre, *The Production of Space*, trans. Donald Nicholson-Smith (Oxford: Blackwell, 1991).
17. US Department of Commerce, *Regulations Governing the Establishment, Operation, Maintenance, and Administration in the United States of Foreign-Trade Zones*, 3–5.
18. Emanuel Celler to Rueben Goodman, April 2, 1946, and Emanuel Celler to Paul

Porter, April 16, 1946, box 9, Papers of Emanuel Celler, Manuscript Division, Library of Congress (hereafter Celler Papers).

19. Emanuel Celler to W. R. Johnson, February 8, 1946, box 9, Celler Papers.
20. "Speech of Thomas E. Lyons, Executive Secretary, FTZ Board, at the Exercises Dedicating the New Orleans FTZ," press release, November 16, 1946, 2, folder 6, box 8, Free Port Records.
21. Michel Foucault, "Of Other Spaces," trans. Jay Miskowiec, *Diacritics* 16, no. 1 (Spring 1986): 22–27.
22. "'Free Port' Plans: New York's No-Tariff Trade Zone a Big Hit; Other Cities to Try It," *Wall Street Journal*, November 14, 1944; "Foreign Trade Zone Plan to Be Outlined," *Los Angeles Times*, August 5, 1949; "Staten Island Zone Becomes a Haven for Canny and Thrifty Traders," *New York Times*, July 6, 1958; "Role of Foreign-Trade Zones in World Trade Significantly Enlarged," *Foreign Commerce Weekly*, June 26, 1950; "Where War Goods Wait," *Washington Post*, January 28, 1940; "$50,000,000 Expenditure for Jersey City," *Shipping Register and World Ports*, July 11, 1936; "Foreign Trade Zone 4: 'A Five-Acre Free City,'" *Los Angeles Times*, June 25, 1950; "A Halfway House of Trade," *Christian Science Monitor*, March 9, 1938; "Foreign-Trade Zones' Post-Victory Challenge," *Foreign Commerce Weekly*, June 16, 1945; "The Free-Port Plan New York Envisions," *New York Times*, December 18, 1932; Sterling St. John, *How to Use a Foreign Trade Zone* (Los Angeles: Los Angeles Chamber of Commerce, 1949), 4; "Free Ports," *New Yorker*, February 12, 1944, 18.
23. Timothy Mitchell, *Rule of Experts: Egypt, Techno-Politics, Modernity* (Berkeley: University of California Press, 2002).
24. "Free Trade Zone Opened at New Orleans," *Pittsfield Berkshire Evening Eagle*, May 6, 1947.
25. "Where War Goods Wait," *Washington Post*, January 28, 1940.
26. Richmond Industrial Survey, "Planning and Engineering Design: New York City Free Port," January 10, 1935, 31, folder 18, box 2, Free Port Records.
27. Edwin White Medley, "The Development of Foreign Trade Zones in the United States" (MPA thesis, American University, 1948), 82.
28. The principle that federal laws trumped state laws in foreign-trade zones was first asserted in *During v. Valente* 267 App. Div. 383, 46 NYS 2d 385 (1944). Nonetheless, this issue has continued to spark commentary in law reviews. See, for instance, Mark B. Bader, "Jurisdictional Uncertainty: The American Foreign Trade Zone," *North Carolina Journal of International Law and Commercial Regulation* 8, no. 3 (1982): 239–58.
29. "Manhattan Exporters Like Idea of Free Port Here," *Staten Island Advance*, September 4, 1935.
30. Ralph J. Scanlan to FTZ Board, "In the Matter of Application by the Board of State Harbor Commissioners for a Grant to Establish a Foreign-Trade Zone at San Francisco, California," transcript, April 24, 1937, 72, folder 3413-1595, box 4, SF Harbor Records. See also Archie Campbell Edwards, "The Bonded Warehouse vs. the Free Port" (MBA thesis, University of Washington, 1927). A typical vignette: "A shipper with a bulk load of Mexican chick peas, for example, swings his vessel alongside one of the Zone's piers. Busy dockworkers unload the peas and store them in a huge warehouse—just as if it were any other warehouse in New York harbor. But there's a big difference. The shipper can leave those peas in that warehouse as long as he wishes—*without observing customs requirements or paying customs duties required by our tariff laws*. They're as free as if they were still on the ocean." Woodrow Wirsig, "The Port within a Port," *New York Herald Tribune*, January 13, 1946.

31. Works Progress Administration, "Foreign Trade Zone No. One," April 14, 1936, 3, folder 8, box 11, Free Port Records.
32. "The Sheds Down at Pier 45," *San Francisco Chronicle*, June 20, 1948; David Graeber dubs this bind "the iron law of liberalism" in *The Utopia of Rules: On Technology, Stupidity, and the Secret Joys of Bureaucracy* (Brooklyn, NY: Melville House, 2015).
33. On "Herbert Hoover's Emerald City," completed in 1932, see Leach, *Land of Desire: Merchants, Power, and the Rise of a New American Culture* (New York: Vintage Books, 1993), 349–51.
34. On Lyons, see "Contributors' Column," *Foreign Commerce Weekly*, February 22, 1947, 3. For an early description of the FTZ Board, see Thomas E. Lyons, "Foreign Trade Zones," *Shipping Register and World Ports*, January 11, 1935.
35. Thomas E. Lyons, "VITAL Stepping Stone to U.S. World-Trade Advance," *Foreign Commerce Weekly*, January 23, 1943, 3. Others include the economist Claudius T. Murchison, author of *King Cotton Is Sick* and later the president of the Cotton-Textile Institute (see "Spinners' Treaty," *Time*, March 8, 1937); and C. C. Kirkpatrick, another alumnus of the Transportation Division of the BFDC (see C. C. Kirkpatrick to W. A. Cox, July 20, 1936, and C. C. Kirkpatrick to Lindsay Crawford, August 6, 1936, folder 3413-1587, box 4, SF Harbor Records). Even Zone 1 was led by a former cotton broker from Memphis (see "War Spurs Trade at Free Port Here," *New York Times*, November 14, 1939).
36. The FTZ Board moved to a division of the Office of International Trade in the late 1940s. For a sample of his research on warehousing, see Thomas E. Lyons, "Packing Airplanes for Export," *Distribution Economy*, November 1928: 19–21, 44, 63.
37. "Secretary of Commerce," note for files, April 16, 1934, official file 614, Franklin D. Roosevelt Presidential Library (hereafter FDRPL).
38. On Egypt, see Thomas E. Lyons, "Foreign Trade Zones and Air Commerce," May 20, 1948, 4, Free Port Records; on Latin America, see Thomas E. Lyons, *Report on Proposal to Create a Foreign-Trade Zone (or Free Port) in the Republic of Panama* (Washington, DC: Government Printing Office, 1946).
39. Emanuel Celler, House Committee on Ways and Means, *Foreign Trade Zones*, 73rd Cong., 2nd sess., March 6, 1934, 13; James T. Patterson, *The New Deal and the States: Federalism in Transition* (Princeton, NJ: Princeton University Press, 1969).
40. Claudius T. Murchison, "Creation of Free Ports Holds a Serious Problem," *New York Times*, July 22, 1934. See also "4 Trade Groups Act to Speed Free Port," *New York Times*, December 10, 1932.
41. "A Lesson from Seattle," *San Francisco Daily News*, October 2, 1936. This mentality dated to the early 1920s and "the new science of port salesology." See E. W. Zimmerman's review of Roy MacElwee's *Port Development* in *American Economic Review* 16, no. 2 (1926): 308.
42. W. C. Bickford to B. M. Patton, August 3, 1937, folder 2 (Foreign Trade Zones), box 1, Seattle Port Commission Records, University of Washington (hereafter Seattle Port Commission Records).
43. Armistead Leake to Bibb Graves, November 30, 1937, folder 15, box SG12221, Alabama Department of Archives and History (hereafter State Docks Files).
44. "Port Control: Private? Municipal? State? Federal?," *The Commonwealth—Part Two* 10, no. 50 (December 11, 1934): 199–226.
45. Port of New York Authority, *Report on Proposed Foreign Trade Zone at Elizabeth, New Jersey* (October, 15, 1935). On Jamaica Bay, see Henry A. Meyer, "The World's Future Harbor," in *Looking Through Life's Window: Personal Reminiscences* (New York:

Coward-McCann, 1930). See also the clippings files in the Personal Papers of Cyrus A. Potts Relating to Jamaica Bay, Long Island Division, Queens Borough Public Library. On Jersey City, see US Department of Commerce, September 20, 1937, 3, box 9, Celler Papers; "Local Shore Best Suited, Says Expert," *Jersey Journal*, November 30, 1935; "Free Port Planned at $50,000,000 Cost," *New York Times*, December 14, 1935.

46. C. C. Kirkpatrick to William J. Sheehan, July 20, 1936, folder 3413-1587, box 4, SF Harbor Records.
47. Lane Cricher, "Transcript of Proceedings of the Examiners Committee, Foreign-Trade Zones Board," November 12, 1935, 108, folder 4, box 12, Free Port Records; William M. Park to Joseph A. Mack, March 28, 1944, file 045, Free Ports-U.S.-General, 1939–1950, BFDC Records.
48. H. C. Lewis to Daniel C. Roper, August 30, 1935, folder 4, box 2, Free Port Records.
49. "Free Port Project Attacked by Bush," *New York Times*, February 23, 1933; "Port Zone Opposed by State Chamber," *New York Times*, April 3, 1934; "Chamber's Survey Opposes Free Port," *New York Times*, November 6, 1935. La Guardia, in turn, made no secret of his irritation with the warehousemen. See "Free Port Plan of La Guardia," *Washington Post*, November 15, 1933; and "La Guardia Assails Foes of Free Port," *New York Times*, April 19, 1934.
50. "U.S. Asks That City Move, He Declares," *Staten Island Advance*, January 9, 1937; Emanuel Celler, Foreign Trade Zone Committee to the Board of Estimate and Apportionment of the City of New York, May 21, 1937, folder 6, box 9, Free Port Records.
51. "Open for Business," *Staten Island Advance*, February 3, 1937; "Free Port Contract Plan Is Hit," *Staten Island Advance*, July 15, 1937. In exchange for managing and marketing the zone, the operators received 30% of the gross revenue.
52. *American Dock Company v. City of New York*, 21 NYS 2d 943 (1940). The lawsuit prompted the WPA to pull workers from the zone. "WPA Halts Work in Free Port Area," *New York Times*, January 9, 1941; "Waterfront Project," *New York Times*, October 12, 1941. The Docks Department responded to the AWA's criticisms in a lengthy report, William B. Herlands and John McKenzie, *Administration of the Foreign Trade Zone in New York City: Report to Honorable Fiorello F. H. La Guardia* (New York, August 5, 1940).
53. AWA, *Proceedings of the Fifty-Second Annual Meeting* (Chicago: AWA, 1943), 258–60; AWA, *Proceedings of the Fifty-Eighth Annual Meeting* (Washington, DC: AWA, 1949), 340–42; AWA, *The Case for Extension of Foreign-Trade Zone Privileges to Customs Bonded Warehouses* (Chicago: AWA, 1946); AWA to Emanuel Celler, August 20, 1945, box 9, Celler Papers.
54. J. H. Boyd, "Report for the Year of 1947," Foreign Trade Zone No. 2, Board of Commissioners of the Port of New Orleans, February 29, 1948, 1, Board of Commissioners of the Port of New Orleans Archive.
55. "Foreign Trade Zone Looms for San Antonio," *San Antonio Express*, June 1, 1947.
56. On Pittsburgh, see Ralph R. Eizenberg to Franklin D. Roosevelt, telegram, November 11, 1935, Official File 1687, FDRPL. On Miami, see John Sewell, "Transcript of Proceedings of the Examiners Committee, Foreign-Trade Zones Board," November 13, 1935, 242–43, folder 4, box 12, Free Port Records. On Stockton, see W. H. Daum to Emanuel Celler, February 24, 1936, box 9, Celler Papers. By 1950 (and in most cases by the late 1930s), the FTZ Board would also hear from Portland, Maine; Boston; Providence; Bayonne, Elizabeth, and Jersey City; Camden; Philadelphia and

Chester; Baltimore; Norfolk; Charleston; St. Petersburg; Orlando; Tampa; Key West; San Juan; Mobile; New Orleans; Chicago; St. Louis; Detroit; Minneapolis; Galveston; Houston; Laredo; Brownsville; Oxnard; Los Angeles; Oakland, Richmond, and San Francisco; Portland, Oregon; and Seattle. "New York's No-Tariff Trade Zone a Big Hit; Other Cities to Try It," *Wall Street Journal*, November 14, 1944.

57. C. C. Kirkpatrick to Frederick I. Thompson, May 30, 1936, folder 11, box SG12221, Alabama Governor, State Docks Files, SG12218-SG12224, State Docks Files.
58. H. Fugl-Meyer, *Report to the Boston Port Authority on the Practicability of Establishing a Free Port at Boston, Massachusetts* (Boston: Wright and Potter, February 1935).
59. B. M. Patton to W. C. Bickford, July 26, 1937, 2, folder 2 (Foreign Trade Zones), box 1, and W. C. Bickford to B. M. Patton, August 4, 1936, folder 4 (Foreign Trade Zones), box 1, Seattle Port Commission Records.
60. US Department of Commerce, *Regulations Governing the Establishment, Operation, Maintenance, and Administration in the United States of Foreign-Trade Zones*, iv.
61. Emanuel Celler, "Transcript of Proceedings of the Examiners Committee, Foreign-Trade Zones Board," November 12, 1935, 13, folder 4, box 12, Free Port Records.
62. Emanuel Celler to Franklin D. Roosevelt, March 6, 1934, Official File 614, FDRPL.
63. Howard Cullman, "Free Ports or Foreign Trade Zones," radio address, December 30, 1932, 3, folder 4, box 115, Raymond Moley Papers, Hoover Institution Archives; "A Free Port for New York," *New York Times*, December 9, 1932; "Staten Island Free Port," *New York Times*, December 11, 1932.
64. Major Henry J. Amy, "Transcript of Proceedings of the Examiners Committee, Foreign-Trade Zones Board," November 12, 1935, 41, folder 4, box 12, Free Port Records.
65. John McKenzie, "Transcript of Proceedings of the Examiners Committee, Foreign-Trade Zones Board," November 12, 1935, 8, folder 4, box 12, Free Port Records.
66. Daniel Lidz, "Putting White Elephants to Work," letter to the editor, *New York Times*, October 1, 1932.
67. "White Elephants," *New York Times*, September 14, 1932. Popularized in the imperial vernacular of Victorian England, "white elephant" referred to the custom of gifting an albino elephant to an enemy and thereby bankrupting him—because such elephants were sacred, the animal was unable to labor and to earn its keep.
68. "Hog Island May Be Huge Freeport," *Somerset Daily Herald*, July 26, 1934.
69. The WPA covered 76% of a second round of improvements at Zone 1. George Peter Champion, "The Foreign-Trade Zone and Hampton Roads: Its Commercial, Industrial, and Military Possibilities" (MA thesis, College of William and Mary, 1954), 29. In targeting buildings for improvement—rather than for demolition—the Staten Island proposal broke with what Brian Goldstein has termed "the New Deal spatial order." See Goldstein, "Planning's End? Urban Renewal in New Haven, the Yale School of Art and Architecture, and the Fall of the New Deal Spatial Order," *Journal of Urban History* 37, no. 3 (May 2011): 400–422. On La Guardia's mobilization of WPA workers see Mason B. Williams, *City of Ambition: FDR, La Guardia, and the Making of Modern New York* (New York: W. W. Norton, 2013), chapter 5.
70. "Free Port Scheme Pushed by Palma," *New York Times*, May 27, 1934.
71. "Operation Ordered by October 30 Now Impossible," *Staten Island Advance*, October 17, 1936; "Free Port Dredging Bids Asked," *Staten Island Advance*, November 13, 1936.
72. "Sold Down the River?," *Staten Island Advance*, November 30, 1936; "Will Island Lose Free Port Permit?" *Staten Island Advance*, November 30, 1936.

73. "A Dreary Spectacle," *Staten Island Advance*, February 1, 1937.
74. "U.S. Closes Free Port," *Staten Island Advance*, February 10, 1937; "Sprinklers at Free Port Found Active—In Fact, Too Active," *Staten Island Advance*, February 24, 1938.
75. "Bungled," *Staten Island Advance*, May 15, 1937.
76. Albert Parry, "New York Becomes a Free Port," *American Mercury*, November 1934, 368–70.
77. John McKenzie, "Transcript of Proceedings of the Examiners Committee, Foreign-Trade Zones Board," November 12, 1935, 10, folder 4, box 12, Free Port Records.
78. R. W. Patterson, "Transcript of Proceedings of the Examiners Committee, Foreign-Trade Zones Board," November 12, 1935, 156, folder 4, box 12, Free Port Records.
79. Federal Writers' Project, *New York Panorama: A Companion to the WPA Guide to New York City*, new ed. (1938; New York: Pantheon Books, 1984), 333. Stephen V. Ward characterizes the hub map—usually grossly distorted—as a staple of industrial promotion in *Selling Places: The Marketing and Promotion of Towns and Cities, 1850–2000* (New York: Routledge, 1998), 166.
80. In 1937, for instance, fifty-nine trucks and twenty-one lighters docked at Zone 1, versus only four steamships. By 1940, the gulf had widened even further, with 1,812 trucks and 535 lighters versus 31 steamships. City of New York, "Report for the Year of 1940," July 1, 1941, 10, folder 13, box 3, Free Port Records.
81. On lighterage, see Roy S. MacElwee, *Port Development* (New York: McGraw-Hill, 1925), 303–39.
82. "Free Port Chick Pea Cargo Here," *Staten Island Advance*, October 19, 1937.
83. "City Free Port Profit Below Mayor's Hope," *New York Sun*, December 26, 1936.
84. The *Advance* tracked these appropriations diligently, explaining the minutiae of the zone's revenue stream. "$875,000 Authorized to Develop Free Port," *Staten Island Advance*, May 14, 1936.
85. In 1940, the city netted $79,890, while in fiscal year 1939, it lost $47,423. These figures do not include the expenditures on infrastructure. City of New York, "Report for the Year of 1940," July 1, 1941, 16, folder 13, box 3, Free Port Records.
86. Frank Dixon to Thomas Lyons, February 28, 1939, folder 17, box SG12221, State Docks Files. The notorious dealmaker Congressman Frank Boykin secured Mobile's grant, urging Governor Bibb Graves to adopt it. At the Alabama State Dock Commission, Governor Graves appointed a group of men who loathed each other, and this strife influenced the gubernatorial election. Graves's opponent and successor, Governor Frank Dixon, abolished the commission and replaced it with a state department, axing projects like the zone. Frank M. Boykin to Bibb Graves, July 15, 1936, folder 3413-1587, box 4, SF Harbor Records; Earle L. Rauber, *The Alabama State Docks: A Case Study in State Development* (Federal Reserve Bank of Atlanta, January 1945), 12–13.
87. Samuel Richard Bram, "An Examination of the Free Port / Foreign-Trade Zone Concept—With Particular Emphasis on Its Application and Future in the United States" (MBA thesis, Boston University, 1960), 171.
88. "Foreign-Trade Zone Liquidated at Harbor," *Los Angeles Times*, February 2, 1956.
89. Richard S. Thoman, *Free Ports and Foreign-Trade Zones* (Cambridge, MD: Cornell Maritime, 1956), 154. When I interviewed Professor Thoman at his nursing home in 2007, he was shocked to learn of the growth of the zone system since the 1950s (assuming it was dead on arrival, he had moved on to other topics).
90. Louis K. Comstock, "Proposed Contracts for Operation of the Foreign Trade Zone," undated (May 1938), 5, folder 7, box 10, Free Port Records. Comstock chaired the Mayor's Advisory Committee on the Foreign Trade Zone.

91. Ross Myron Trump, "The Port of New Orleans with Special Reference to Its Foreign Trade Zone" (PhD diss., Ohio State University, 1947), 144. Trump's advisor was the prominent economic geographer Eugene Van Cleef, who questioned the wisdom of the zone concept in *Geography for the Businessman* (New York: Harper and Brothers, 1943), 136–39. Van Cleef had previously overseen two master's theses on the zone concept: Hibbert D. Corey, "American Foreign Trade Policy and Its Application to Hampton Roads" (MA thesis, Ohio State University, 1930); and Karl D. Reyer, "Free Ports: The Importance of Geographic Factors in Determining Their Successful Operation, with Special Reference to the Establishment of Free Ports in the United States" (MA thesis, Ohio State University, 1925).
92. William C. Farrer, "The Foreign-Trade Zone," June 4, 1948, 61, folder 3413-1620, box 4, SF Harbor Records.
93. Cornelius G. Kolff, *The Free Port or Foreign Trade Zone of New York* (New York: Cornelius G. Kolff, 1936). Educated in Germany and married to a woman from Hamburg, Kolff was a devout proselytizer for the zone concept (and, according to the *Staten Island Advance*, "possibly the only man on Staten Island who can wear a red tie without being accused of Communistic sympathies"). A real estate developer, he ran a "Free Port Bureau of Information" out of his office and pestered Mayor La Guardia about inadequate promotion of Zone 1. "Hamburg's Free Port Map Shown," *Staten Island Advance*, April 28, 1936; "In the Doldrums," *Staten Island Advance*, September 25, 1936. See also Cornelius G. Kolff Papers, Staten Island Historical Society.
94. US Department of Commerce, *Regulations Governing the Establishment, Operation, Maintenance, and Administration in the United States of Foreign-Trade Zones*, 10–11.
95. Samuel B. Sprinz to John McKenzie, reprinted letter, "Transcript of Proceedings of the Examiners Committee, Foreign-Trade Zones Board," November 12, 1935, 64, folder 4, box 12, Free Port Records.
96. "Halfway House of Trade," *Christian Science Monitor*, March 9, 1938.
97. Paul Goetz, "N.Y. Foreign Trade Zone Seeks Bigger Role in Post-War Commerce," *Wall Street Journal*, October 26, 1945.
98. Emanuel Celler to John W. Snyder, April 18, 1947, box 10, Celler Papers.
99. "Hammond Bans Honey Making by Bees in Residential Area," *Sun*, July 1, 1931; "Owner Fights Ban on Bees as 'Manufacturing' in Home," *New York Times*, July 2, 1931; "The Bees and the Law," *Sun*, July 3, 1931.
100. Ure quoted in "Manufacture" in Robert H. Inglis Palgrave, *Dictionary of Political Economy* (London: Macmillan and Co., 1894), 2:688. See also Lawrence A. Peskin, *Manufacturing Revolution: The Intellectual Origins of Early American Industry* (Baltimore: Johns Hopkins University Press, 2003); Laura Rigal, *The American Manufactory: Art, Labor, and the World of Things in the Early Republic* (Princeton, NJ: Princeton University Press, 1998).
101. Chapter 14 of *Capital* begins, "That form of co-operation which is based on division of labor assumes its classical shape in manufacture. As a characteristic form of the capitalist process of production it prevails throughout the manufacturing period properly so called, which extends, roughly speaking, from the middle of the sixteenth century to the last third of the eighteenth century." Marx, *Capital* (New York: Vintage Books, 1977), 1:455. Fredric Jameson remarks that this "crucial"—albeit ambiguous—chapter unsettles the assumption "that manufacture fully deserves the characterization as capitalist" and confirms "only that genuine capitalism drives it out and destroys all traces of it, just as the Cro-Magnons supplanted the Neander-

thals and obliterated all memory of them." Jameson, *Representing Capital: A Reading of Volume One* (New York: Verso, 2011), 76.

102. Marx, *Capital*, 1:287. For a case study of commodity classification, see Barbara Hahn, *Making Tobacco Bright: Creating an American Commodity, 1617–1937* (Baltimore: Johns Hopkins University Press, 2011).
103. *Tide Water Oil Co. v. United States* 171 US 210 (1898). The court echoed Ure and Marx in pointing out that machinery now superseded hands in the operations of "manufacturing": "The primary meaning of the word 'manufacture' is something made by hand, as distinguished from a natural growth; but as machinery has largely supplanted this primitive method, the word is now ordinarily used to denote an article upon the material of which labor has been expended to make the finished product." In this formulation, "labor" implies machines.
104. Philip Scranton decenters the Chandlerian firm, too, except that he chooses the city as his unit of analysis and neglects the internationalization of production in the late nineteenth century. Scranton, *Endless Novelty: Specialty Production and American Industrialization, 1865–1925* (Princeton, NJ: Princeton University Press, 1997).
105. Tussles over customs law have spilled out into other domains, most famously in the case of Constantin Brancusi, whose bronze sculpture *Bird in Space* was assessed a duty of 40% under the category of "kitchen utensils and hospital supplies" when it was imported into New York City in 1927 by the photographer Edward Steichen, who had presented it as "an original work of art" and hence as duty-free. The trial that ensued after Brancusi appealed to the US Customs Court drew headlines as a referendum on what constituted "art." (In a victory for modernism, Brancusi won.) See T. D. M., "The United States Government and Abstract Art," *Bulletin of the Museum of Modern Art* 3, no. 5 (1936): 2–6.
106. General Traffic Department to J. W. Connolly, October 29, 1937, box 16, accession #712, Cologne-US Customs Data, Benson Ford Research Center, Dearborn, Michigan. Most exporters opted to forgo the rebate, complaining that "the amount of drawback very often does not pay for the labor and cost of collecting it." Lomax, *The Foreign-Trade Zone*, 20. Only those with large-scale, standardized operations, like Ford, pursued it.
107. Margaret Newell, "The Free Port in American Commercial Policy" (MA thesis, Clark University, 1940), 66.
108. Walter P. Hedden, "Transcript of Proceedings, U.S. Department of Commerce," February 24, 1947, 70, box 12, Celler Papers.
109. *Anheuser-Busch Brewing Association v. the United States*, 207 US 556 (1908).
110. US Bureau of Customs, "Memorandum of General Authorities Bearing on the Question of What Constitutes Manufacturing in Connection with Operations Which May Be Carried on within a Foreign-Trade Zone," August 6, 1934, 1, folder 16, box 3, Free Port Records.
111. US Department of Commerce, *Regulations Governing the Establishment, Operation, Maintenance, and Administration in the United States of Foreign-Trade Zones*, 11.
112. Treasury Department to New York Collector of Customs, December 23, 1946; Sterling St. John to FTZ Board, January 14, 1947; Treasury Department to New York Collector of Customs, December 3, 1946; Sterling St. John to FTZ Board, January 14, 1947; Treasury Department to New York Collector of Customs, December 18, 1946; Sterling St. John to FTZ Board, January 14, 1947; and Emanuel Celler to Robert P. Patterson, June 4, 1947, all box 10, Celler Papers.

113. "President Signs Bill Permitting Manufacturing," *Daily Commercial News*, June 21, 1950.
114. Sterling St. John, "Transcript of Proceedings, U.S. Department of Commerce," February 24, 1947, 50, box 12, Celler Papers.
115. Benjamin Altschuler, "Transcript of Proceedings, U.S. Department of Commerce," February 24, 1947, 121, 136, box 12, Celler Papers.
116. Foreign-Trade Zones Board, *Annual Report to Congress for the Fiscal Year Ended June 30, 1947* (Washington, DC: Government Printing Office, 1948).
117. Walter P. Hedden, "Transcript of Proceedings, U.S. Department of Commerce," February 24, 1947, 71, box 12, Celler Papers.
118. Thomas E. Lyons to Emanuel Celler, June 20, 1944, box 9, Celler Papers.
119. Ellsworth Buck, "Transcript of Proceedings, U.S. Department of Commerce," February 24, 1947, 70, box 12, Celler Papers.
120. City of New York, "Report for the Year of 1940," July 1, 1941, 9–10, folder 13, box 3, Free Port Records. Journalists exoticized the Chinese workers as evidence of the otherness of the zone: "Trade Zone Facilities Inspected," *Staten Island Advance*, May 15, 1941; "Like the Pea in the Shell Game," *Foreign Commerce Weekly*, February 21, 1942.
121. "New Free Port Blunder Revealed," *Staten Island Advance*, May 14, 1937.
122. Jesse H. Jones to F. H. La Guardia, September 19, 1944; F. H. La Guardia to Emanuel Celler, October 16, 1944; John McKenzie to Emanuel Celler, October 16, 1944, all box 9, Celler Papers.
123. G. Joseph Minetti to John S. Graham, June 28, 1949, box 10, Celler Papers. Minetti attributed the rising costs to greater involvement of the customs guards in the zones.
124. G. Joseph Minetti to John S. Graham, June 28, 1949, box 10, Celler Papers.
125. "Shackles on Foreign Trade Zone," *San Francisco Chronicle*, December 26, 1951.
126. "Invisible Fences," *Science News Letter*, December 13, 1941.
127. "Electric Eyes Stand Guard," *ADT Transmitter*, February 1937, 7.
128. John N. Dick to Fiorello H. La Guardia, November 8, 1935, 2, folder 2, box 2, Free Port Records; John N. Dick to John McKenzie, December 11, 1935, folder 1, box 1, Free Port Records.
129. Edward S. Carey, "Notes on Some Engineering Problems and Progress Report," memorandum, July 23, 1936, 3, folder 4, box 4, Free Port Records.
130. "Sprinklers at Free Port Found Active—In Fact, Too Active," *Staten Island Advance*, February 24, 1938. *Advance* editors had mocked the device during Zone 1's sluggish start: "And through it all the electric goggle-eye beams benignly across the entrance to the Free Port piers, so that no bold, bad smugglers will sneak out those two bales of braw, bonnie tweeds fra the Scottish isles." "Glass Buttons," *Staten Island Advance*, February 11, 1937.
131. "False Alarm," *New Yorker*, December 23, 1939, 13. For a wire-service treatment of the same vignette, see "It Happens in New York," *Sikeston Standard*, January 19, 1940.
132. "New Free Port to Be Guarded by Electric Eye," *Herald Tribune*, January 27, 1937; "Free Port Guarded by 'Electric Eye,'" *National Labor Tribune*, April 10, 1937.
133. "'Electric Eye' Equipment Placed on Free Port Piers," *Staten Island Advance*, April 10, 1936. Founded in 1874, ADT sold call boxes to monitor "lazy watchmen." "They Make Life Tough for Burglars," *Saturday Evening Post*, May 29, 1954, 22–23, 65–66.

134. Catherine L. Nevins and New York Foreign Trade Zone Operators, *Foreign Trade Zone No. 1* (New York: New York Foreign Trade Zone Operators, 1943), 18.

135. In this instance, the zone facilitated collateralization, freeing up the $100 million in US capital that was frozen in foreign banks due to exchange controls. In 1934, an American merchant with money in a Brazilian bank was unable to convert his milreis to dollars. But if he used his Brazilian currency to buy a load of Brazilian nuts, which he then shipped to Zone 1 to be stored indefinitely, duty free, he could use his nuts as coins. Bankers applauded this prospect. "Such a plan would be virtually impossible without the free port," one insisted to the *New York Times*. "It goes without saying that no bank here would loan a nickel on products stored abroad, but would be perfectly willing to extend credits on the same goods at this port." "Free Port Will Aid Exchange Release," *New York Times*, February 2, 1936. Zone grantees understood this principle: John Dick to Oswaldo Arnha, February 14, 1936, folder 8, box 1, Free Port Records.

136. "Electric Eye Becomes Aid to the Busy Housewife," *Boston Globe*, May 4, 1941.

137. "Now the All-Electric House Evolves," *New York Times*, November 8, 1931.

138. D. S. Harder, as quoted in L. Landon Goodman, *Man and Automation* (New York: Penguin, 1957), 24.

139. On the workerist 1930s, when pride in the "laboring of American culture" drowned out murmurs about automation, see Michael Denning, *The Cultural Front: The Laboring of American Culture* (New York: Verso, 1997). For a brief cautionary comment about the electric eye, see the AFL's William Green, "National Planning: Labor's Point of View," *New York Times*, December 17, 1933.

140. "Mechanical Hands," *Business Week*, May 30, 1936, 13.

141. Labor activists uttered nary a peep about zones during this first phase of the system's evolution. Although Joseph Ryan, head of the International Longshoremen's Association, spoke in favor of Staten Island at the FTZ Board hearing on Zone 1, he and the ILA were absent from planning discussions. "Longshore Chief Backs Free Port," *Staten Island Advance*, n.d., folder 3, box 6, Free Port Records.

CHAPTER FIVE

1. This implosion is forecast in Henri Lefebvre, *The Urban Revolution* (1970; Minneapolis: University of Minnesota Press, 2003).

2. Saskia Sassen-Koob, "Recomposition and Peripheralization at the Core," *Contemporary Marxism* no. 5 (Summer 1982): 88–100; and Peter Kwong, *The New Chinatown* (New York: Hill and Wang, 1988).

3. David Harvey, *The Condition of Postmodernity* (Oxford: Blackwell, 1990), 299.

4. Edward W. Soja, *Postmodern Geographies: The Reassertion of Space in Critical Social Theory* (London: Verso, 1989), 193.

5. Roger Rouse, "Mexican Migration and the Social Space of Postmodernism," *Diaspora: A Journal of Transnational Studies* 1, no. 1 (1991): 8.

6. For a reminiscence on Harvey in 1989, see Andy Merrifield, "The Entrepreneur's New Clothes," *Geografiska Annaler: Series B, Human Geography* 96, no. 4 (2014): 389–91.

7. Harvey, *The Condition of Postmodernity*, 302.

8. Harvey, *The Condition of Postmodernity*, 295.

9. Harvey, *The Condition of Postmodernity*, 240; Fredric Jameson, "The Cultural Logic of Late Capitalism," in *Postmodernism, or, The Cultural Logic of Late Capitalism* (Dur-

ham, NC: Duke University Press, 1991). Jameson's essay first appeared in the *New Left Review* in 1984. He toured the Bonaventure with Lefebvre and Soja.

10. Fredric Jameson, "Spatial Equivalents in the World System," in *Postmodernism, or, The Cultural Logic of Late Capitalism*, 128. On the contrast between Jameson and Soja, see Victor Burgin, *In/different Spaces: Place and Memory in Visual Culture* (Berkeley: University of California Press, 1996), 25–26. More recently and in a related vein, Anna Tsing has emphasized the heterogeneity of the niches and zones of the global assembly line to argue that "diversity forms a part of the *structure* of capitalism rather than an inessential appendage." Tsing, "Supply Chains and the Human Condition," *Rethinking Marxism* 21, no. 2 (2009): 150.
11. MOMA included Gehry in an exhibition on deconstructivist architecture in 1988. On the eighties, see Daniel T. Rodgers, *The Age of Fracture* (Cambridge, MA: Belknap, 2012).
12. See, for instance, Edward Dimendberg, *Facing the Music: Documenting Walt Disney Concert Hall and the Redevelopment of Downtown Los Angeles; A Project by Allan Sekula* (Valencia, CA: East of Borneo Books, 2015).
13. Joseph Helewicz, "Trade Tour Set to Draw Japanese Car Exports, Containerships to City," *Baltimore Sun*, August 31, 1970.
14. Ann Haskell, "Visual Excitement," *Baltimore Sun*, June 21, 1981.
15. Nina Martin, "Artsy Building Boosts Production, Morale," *Baltimore Sun*, November 3, 1982. The open office is expressive of the supremacy of communication in post-Fordism. "Communication—and its productive organization as information flow—has become as important as electricity once was in the age of mechanical production," Christian Marazzi writes in *Capital and Affects: The Politics of the Language Economy* (1994; Los Angeles: Semiotext(e), 2011), 21.
16. Martin Filler, "Perfectly Frank," *Progressive Architecture*, July 1979, 63.
17. Martin, "Artsy Building Boosts Production, Morale."
18. Filler, "Perfectly Frank," 65. As Jameson writes of the use of these same materials in Gehry's house, "The corrugated aluminum, the chain-linked balcony above, are . . . the junk or Third World side of American life today—the production of poverty and misery, people not only out of work but without a place to live, bag people, waste and industrial pollution, squalor, garbage, and obsolescent machinery." Jameson, "Spatial Equivalents in the World System," 128. On export-processing zones in Asia, see note 132.
19. Jameson, "Spatial Equivalents in the World System," 125.
20. Fredric Jameson, "Periodizing the 60s," *Social Text* no. 9/10 (Spring–Summer 1984): 178–209.
21. Linda Liston, "Plant Your Plant at a Home Away from Home, at Home," *Industrial Development*, November/December 1967, 13.
22. George L. Bell, House Committee on Ways and Means, "Foreign-Trade Zones," 80th Cong., 2nd sess., May 10, 1948, 25.
23. Ellsworth Buck, House Committee on Ways and Means, "Foreign-Trade Zones," 80th Cong., 2nd sess., May 10, 1948, 6.
24. Emanuel Celler to Hale Boggs, January 27, 1949, folder 1000-5-6, box 5, Boggs Papers, Tulane University Special Collections, New Orleans, LA (hereafter Boggs Papers). PL81-566 (enacted June 17, 1950) / 81 HR 5332. Initial bills were HR 2158 (Boggs), HR 2163 (Celler).
25. Joseph McCarthy, "Establishment of Foreign-Trade Zones," 81st Cong., 1st sess., *Congressional Record* 95, October 14, 1949, 14507.

26. Arthur Perrin Jr. to Hale Boggs, January 14, 1950, subject files: fur industry, Boggs Papers.
27. Vice President Alben W. Barkley cast a tie-breaking vote to advance the Boggs bill. "Barkley Breaks Tie on Trade Zone Bill," *New York Times*, June 6, 1950. Two months later, longshoremen blocked the boats. "Airport Workers Bar Soviet Cargo," *New York Times*, August 22, 1950; Charles Egan, "Longshoremen Aid Propaganda Fight," *New York Times*, August 27, 1950; "Truman Assails Ban by Dockers on Reds' Goods," *New York Herald Tribune*, September 1, 1950.
28. Joseph A. Sinclair to Hale Boggs, March 7, 1949, folder 1000-5-6, box 5, Boggs Papers; Jay Weil Jr., "The Case for H.R. 4723," *Storage and Distribution*, May 2, 1950.
29. Philip B. Fleming to R. L. Doughton, November 22, 1950, box 346, RG 151, BFDC Records.
30. Foreign-Trade Zones Board, *Laws, Regulations, and Other Information Relating to Foreign-Trade Zones in the United States* (Washington, DC: Government Printing Office, 1966), 27.
31. Foreign-Trade Zones Board, "Minutes of the Meeting of the Committee of Alternates," May 7, 1963, 5, box 35, Central Correspondence, Records of the US Customs Service, RG 36, NARA (hereafter Central Correspondence RG 36).
32. Foreign-Trade Zones Board, "Minutes of the Meeting of the Committee of Alternates," February 2, 1965, 16, box 35, Central Correspondence RG 36. The "sub" in "subzone" likely drew on the nomenclature of the "sub-port of entry," a designation dating to the 1880s in the Treasury Department. See Treasury Department, *Authorization for Establishment of Customs Ports*, vol. 1, RG 56, Entry 349, Records of the Department of Treasury, NARA II.
33. Emanuel Celler to Joseph Marrone, February 9, 1955, folder 2, box 266, Celler Papers.
34. In *Buy American: The Untold Story of Economic Nationalism* (Boston: Beacon, 1999), chapter 5, Dana Frank shows, though, that union leaders, in embracing trade, often broke with rank-and-file members.
35. Emanuel Celler, "Strength through Trade and Aid," March 14, 1958, 1, box 250, Celler Papers.
36. Joseph M. Marrone, "Foreign Investment Services of the Department of Commerce," September 9, 1955, 13–14, box 1, RG 476, Records of the Bureau of Export Administration, Foreign-Trade Zone History Files, 1964–1970, NARA II (hereafter BEA FTZ History Files). "Most Americans," after World War II, according to Douglas A. Irwin, supported the lowering of tariffs via reciprocal trade agreements. Irwin, *Clashing over Commerce: A History of US Trade Policy* (Chicago: University of Chicago Press, 2017), 493.
37. Charles E. Egan, "U.S. Agency to Aid Investing Abroad," *New York Times*, April 27, 1955.
38. For a wild sample that likens the United States to a grocer who doubles as a banker, see "Hurray for Those Jobs We Are 'Exporting'!" *Baltimore Sun*, November 29, 1949.
39. Joseph Hansen, "Eisenhower Chips Away at McKinley's Ramparts," *Militant*, January 17, 1955.
40. "'Protection' Held Not Good for U.S.," *New York Times*, January 14, 1955.
41. On Cold War Keynesianism, see Judith Stein, *Pivotal Decade: How the United States Traded Factories for Finance in the Seventies* (New Haven, CT: Yale University Press, 2010).

42. FTZ Board, Meeting Minutes, November 9, 1955, 8, folder 5, box 1, FTZ Files RG 36.
43. Raymond Kieferle to Lloyd Sanderson, June 14, 1957, 4, box 1, BEA FTZ History Files.
44. Frank Dow to [no name], May 5, 1955, folder 5, box 1, FTZ Files RG 36; Robert Chambers to D. L. Ritger, September 14, 1954, folder 3, box 2, FTZ Files RG 36.
45. Joseph Marrone to Theodore Lyons, March 11, 1957, 2, folder 3, box 1, FTZ Files RG 36.
46. [No name], January 5, 1956, folder 5, box 1, FTZ Files RG 36.
47. Franklin D. Roosevelt to Daniel Roper, November 5, 1934, folder "Puerto Rico," box 251, RG 151, BFDC, NARA II.
48. Abe Fortas to Emanuel Celler, June 1, 1944, box 9, Celler Papers.
49. Leon Falk to B. W. Thoron, June 5, 1944, box 9, Celler Papers. Falk was also instrumental in the establishment of another type of enclave in the Caribbean, an agricultural settlement in the Dominican Republic for Jewish refugees from Nazi Germany. Allen Wells, *Tropical Zion: General Trujillo, FDR, and the Jews of Sosúa* (Durham, NC: Duke University Press, 2009).
50. Overall, eight had opened, but three—in Mobile, San Antonio, and Los Angeles—had closed.
51. FTZ Board, Minutes of the Committee of Alternates, February 2, 1965, 3, box 35, Central Correspondence RG 36.
52. The Shannon Free Zone in Ireland opened in 1959. See George Horne, "Ireland Mounts Economic Drive," *New York Times*, August 28, 1958.
53. "Free Port Factory City?," *Christian Science Monitor*, April 1, 1960; "Mayaguez, P.R., Names New Trade Zone Chief," *New York Times*, February 2, 1961; see also "Puerto Rico Offers a Free Zone as an Attraction for Exporters," *New York Times*, February 25, 1960.
54. Leon Falk to B. W. Thoron, June 5, 1944, box 9, Celler Papers.
55. "Puerto Rico, Si!," *Barron's National Business and Financial Weekly*, May 8, 1961, 19.
56. See "Now Puerto Rico Offers 100% Tax Exemption to New Industry," *New York Herald Tribune*, January 3, 1955, 49; on Ogilvy and PRIDCO, see Dennis Merrill, *Negotiating Paradise: U.S. Tourism and Empire in Twentieth-Century Latin America* (Chapel Hill: University of North Carolina Press, 2009), 203–5.
57. According to Merrill, *Negotiating Paradise*, this advertisement's omission of any explicit visual reference to business was typical of Ogilvy's strategy for fashioning Puerto Rico as a "New Deal Formosa."
58. The historiographic treatment of Zone 7 is an example of why we need a proper typology of the zone concept, and from the ground up. Puerto Rico is sometimes said to have entered the zone world in 1947, in the sense that Operation Bootstrap, by granting island-wide tax incentives for industrial production, is said to have ushered in an "EPZ regime." Patrick Neveling, "Export Processing Zones, Special Economic Zones and the Long March of Capitalist Development Policies during the Cold War," in *Decolonization and the Cold War: Negotiating Independence*, ed. Leslie James and Elisabeth Leake (London: Bloomsbury, 2015), 68. But this claim misses the mark. It ignores the first actually existing zone in Puerto Rico, Zone 7, which was only one of many projects under the umbrella of Operation Bootstrap, and which, to reiterate, opened in 1960. Consequently, it also slights the distinction between Zone 7 and Subzone 7A, or the general-purpose zone and the subzone. And more broadly, it fails to address the boundedness of the spatial form of the export-processing zone, which is almost never without a fence. See also Vanessa Ogle, "Ar-

chipelago Capitalism: Tax Havens, Offshore Money, and the State, 1940s–1970s," *American Historical Review* 122, no. 5 (2017): 1455. Greater exactitude can only enhance the notion of an EPZ regime as it is articulated by Neveling in his valuable scholarship on the zones of decolonization.

59. Here I draw on Richard Walker, "The Geography of Production," in *A Companion to Economic Geography*, ed. Eric Sheppard and Trevor Barnes (Oxford: Basil Blackwell, 2000), 113–32.
60. Ricardo Campos and Frank Bonilla, "Bootstraps and Enterprise Zones: The Underside of Late Capitalism in Puerto Rico and the United States," *Review* 5, no. 4 (1982): 580; Roger Benedict, "Carbide to Raise Plant Outlay to $90 Million if Facility Is Part of 'Foreign Trade Zone,'" *Wall Street Journal*, December 15, 1964; "Connor Authorizes New Trade Zone on Saginaw Bay," *New York Times*, September 18, 1966.
61. Udall quoted in Roger W. Benedict, "Oil Import Impasse," *Wall Street Journal*, July 20, 1965; see also "Chemical Firms Push for Lower-Cost Naphtha," *Chemical & Engineering News*, January 4, 1965, 18–19; and "Fighting for Low-Cost Feeds," *Chemical Week*, June 19, 1965.
62. B. H. Flinn to W. E. Higman, May 19, 1965, and W. M. Caviston to Lester Johnson, October 13, 1965, box 36, Central Correspondence RG 36.
63. "Factions Clash on Occidental's Trade Zone Bid," *Los Angeles Times*, October 11, 1968. For an entertaining study of the Machias affair, see Peter Amory Bradford, *Fragile Structures: A Story of Oil Refineries, National Security, and the Coast of Maine* (New York: Harper and Row, 1975).
64. "Muskie Vows Oil Lobby Fight," *Boston Globe*, January 14, 1969.
65. "'Retired' Oilman Rocks Industry with Northeast Refinery Plan," *Washington Post*, October 28, 1968.
66. Thomas J. McIntyre, "The Secret Government of Oil," *Boston Globe*, November 2, 1969.
67. "When Phillips Petroleum won permission to set up a refinery and free zone in Puerto Rico recently"—following the example of Union Carbide—"it set up a terrible howl. But opposition was muted on the basis that Puerto Rico is only a territory and not part of the continental United States. Now Occi Pete has genuinely thrown the overalls into the domestic oil chowder," wrote Peter Greenough in "The Big Wind in Machiasport," *Boston Globe*, October 2, 1968.
68. Frederick L. Strong, letter to the editor, *New York Times*, January 6, 1969.
69. Gardiner C. Means, "Exploratory Analysis of the Proposal for a Foreign Trade Zone and Oil Port at Machiasport," August 1968, box 75, series 5, Gardiner C. Means Papers, FDRPL.
70. "Oil Imports Drain U.S. Supplies," *Chicago Tribune*, August 23, 1968; William D. Smith, "Imports Program Roils Top Oil Men," *New York Times*, November 21, 1968.
71. "Maine's Oil-Port Plan Stirring a Controversy," *New York Times*, October 6, 1968.
72. Bradford, *Fragile Structures*, 2; "Maine Refinery Has Fan in Area's Top Oil Dealer," *Boston Globe*, October 2, 1968.
73. Peter Greenough, "The Big Wind in Machiasport," *Boston Globe*, October 2, 1968.
74. William Smith, "Imports Program Roils Top Oil Men," *New York Times*, November 21, 1968.
75. "Machiasport Ranks as Region's Top Economic Story," *Boston Globe*, January 5, 1969.
76. Rich Spencer, "Udall Move May Affect Machias," *Boston Globe*, January 22, 1969.
77. "Foreign-Trade Zones Are Gaining Visibility," *New York Times*, December 8, 1968.

78. Peter Greenough, "Sinclair Suit Poses Question: 'What Do We Do Now?'" *Boston Globe*, November 1, 1968.
79. "Armco Sues to Block Plan to Import Steel Duty-Free," *Wall Street Journal*, November 8, 1968.
80. *Armco Steel Corporation v. Stans*, 303 F. Supp. 262 (SDNY 1969); see also *Armco Steel Corporation v. Stans*, 431 F.2d 779 (1970).
81. "Maine's Oil Port Plan Facing Tough Fight," *Boston Globe*, October 27, 1968; Peter Greenough, "Occidental to Press on through Machiasport's Hornet's Nest," *Boston Globe*, December 2, 1968.
82. Leroy F. Aarons, "Change in the Offing for Machias," *Washington Post*, February 5, 1969.
83. George Wilson, "Maine's Oil Dilemma: Money or Nature," *Washington Post*, April 4, 1970; see also Christopher R. W. Dietrich, *Oil Revolution: Anticolonial Elites, Sovereign Rights, and the Economic Culture of Decolonization* (Cambridge: Cambridge University Press, 2017).
84. Peter Greenough, "The Big Wind in Machiasport," *Washington Post*, October 2, 1968. Greenough's barb anticipates Fernando Coronil's take on the mystifications of oil wealth in *The Magical State: Nature, Money, and Modernity in Venezuela* (Chicago: University of Chicago Press, 1997).
85. On economic development on the frontiers of decolonization, see Nils Gilman, *Mandarins of the Future: Modernization Theory in Cold War America* (Baltimore: Johns Hopkins University Press, 2003).
86. Emanuel Celler before the US Tariff Commission, August 5, 1969, 2, box 342, Celler Papers.
87. Keller Easterling, *Enduring Innocence: Global Architecture and Its Political Masquerades* (Cambridge, MA: MIT Press, 2005).
88. David Harvey, "From Managerialism to Entrepreneurialism: The Transformation in Urban Governance in Late Capitalism," *Geografiska Annaler* 71, no. 1 (1989): 10.
89. Roger W. Benedict, "Oil Import Impasse," *Wall Street Journal*, July 20, 1965.
90. On the Balancing Agriculture with Industry program in Mississippi, see James C. Cobb, *The Selling of the South: The Southern Crusade for Industrial Development, 1936–1980* (Baton Rouge: Louisiana State University Press, 1983)—a book written amid the brinksmanship of the seventies and eighties.
91. Alan J. Wyner, "Governor—Salesman," *National Civic Review* 56, no. 2 (February 1967): 81–86.
92. Blaine Liner, "States and Localities in the Global Marketplace," *Intergovernmental Perspective* 16, no. 2 (Spring 1990): 11; "Holton to Direct Tour Seeking German Investment in Virginia," *Washington Post*, April 13, 1971.
93. James Rusk, "Michigan Is Luring Canadian Businessmen," *Globe and Mail*, May 10, 1972.
94. These comprador summits were likely reacting as much to the anticapitalist urban revolutions around the globe as to disinvestment by the US federal government. On the former, see Vijay Prashad, *The Darker Nations: A People's History of the Third World* (New York: New Press, 2007).
95. Dorothy Parker, "Comment about Camden," *Afro-American*, July 30, 1977; "Reverse Plan for South Bronx," *New York Amsterdam News*, June 23, 1979; "New York Legislator Seeks Japanese Aid for the Bronx," *New York Times*, August 23, 1979; Lucia Mouat, "US Cities Reach Out for Overseas Trade," *Christian Science Monitor*, August 9, 1984; Ben Bradlee Jr., "Mayor with a Foreign Policy: Atlanta's Andy Young

Opening Doors Overseas," *Boston Globe*, August 28, 1983. On Atlanta, see also Jessica Ann Levy, "Selling Atlanta: Black Mayoral Politics from Protest to Entrepreneurialism, 1973 to 1990," *Journal of Urban History* 41, no. 3 (2015): 420–43.

96. My thanks to Jay Driskell for this excellent phrase.
97. Ronald C. Kysiak, "A History of CUED," *Commentary* 15, no. 4 (Winter 1992): 4; see also Barbara Block, *Foreign Trade Zones* (Washington, DC: National Council on Urban Economic Development, 1975). Donald Haider, "Place Wars: New Realities of the 1990s," *Economic Development Quarterly* 6, no.2 (1992): 128.
98. Harvey Molotch, "The City as a Growth Machine: Towards a Political Economy of Place," *American Journal of Sociology* 82, no. 2 (1976): 312, 310.
99. Harvey, "From Managerialism to Entrepreneurialism," 16. Harvey identifies the Hanseatic League as an early version of this boosterism. See also Peter K. Eisinger, *The Rise of the Entrepreneurial State: State and Local Economic Development Policy in the United States* (Madison: University of Wisconsin Press, 1988).
100. Dan Balaban, "Site Selection: Industrial Gamesmanship," *Dun's Review & Modern Industry*, March 1966, 111. On post–World War II industrial promotion in the history of a single city, see J. Mark Souther, *Believing in Cleveland: Managing Decline in "The Best Location in the Nation"* (Philadelphia: Temple University Press, 2017), chapter 3.
101. Leonard Sloane, "Regional Agencies Find New Ways to Woo—and Win—Industry," *New York Times*, May 29, 1966.
102. Walter H. Diamond, *One of a Kind: Learning the Secrets of World Leaders*, ed. Dorothy B. Diamond (Syracuse, NY: Syracuse University Press, 2005); Penny Singer, "Scrutinizing the World of Taxation," *New York Times*, October 29, 1989. For an example of the Diamond publishing empire, see Walter H. Diamond and Dorothy B. Diamond, *Tax Havens of the World*, rev. ed. (Albany, NY: Matthew Bender, 1997).
103. Marshall V. Miller, "Foreign-Trade Zone Manufacturing: The Emergence of a Free Trade Instrument," *Virginia Journal of International Law* 9, no. 2 (1969): 444–77.
104. Altogether, by the end of 1979, fifty-eight zones had opened: three closed before 1969, and one closed in 1973.
105. "Foreign-Trade Zones in U.S.—How They Work," *U.S. News & World Report*, November 8, 1976.
106. David Garino, "Duty-Free Trade Zones Gain Popularity As Firms, Cities Realize Their Benefits," *Wall Street Journal*, September 26, 1975.
107. "Foreign-Trade Zones in U.S.—How They Work," *U.S. News & World Report*, November 8, 1976.
108. Gerald R. Ford, "Remarks at a Luncheon in Honor of the Dedication of the San Jose Foreign Trade Zone," May 25, 1976, *Public Papers of the Presidents of the United States, Gerald R. Ford: Containing the Public Messages, Speeches, and Statements of the President, August 9, 1974 to January 20, 1977* (Washington, DC: Government Printing Office, 1975), 2978–80.
109. "Bell and Scissors Trouble for Ford," *Atlanta Constitution*, May 26, 1976.
110. "Benefits Foreseen in Duty-Free Zone Here," *Chicago Tribune*, April 30, 1975.
111. Austin Wehrwein, "Great Lakes Ports Push Bid for Bigger Share of World's Trade," *New York Times*, May 31, 1962; Isadore Barmash, "No. 1 Builder of Shopping Malls," *New York Times*, April 29, 1973.
112. "Arizona Duty-Free Zone Is First on Tribal Lands," *Wall Street Journal*, April 4, 1979.
113. "Kansas City: Foreign Trade Zone on the Prairie," *Business Week*, May 11, 1974.
114. "Zone Sought to Lure Imports to Kansas City," *Los Angeles Times*, November 23, 1972.

115. Judith Frutig, "Kansas City's Fresh Face," *Washington Post*, June 29, 1974.
116. Meg Cox, "Kansas City Businesses Move Underground to Stay Cool, Ease Expansion, Save on Rent," *Wall Street Journal*, June 26, 1981; Joe Roberts, "Trade Zone Facility Concept Unique," *Kansas City Star*, April 8, 1973; "Going Underground Appeals to Firms," *Washington Post*, June 4, 1977.
117. John Crown, "A Start—Shenandoah and Solar Energy," *Atlanta Constitution*, February 5, 1977; "Foreign Trade Zone Predicted for City," *Atlanta Constitution*, March 5, 1975.
118. Tom Walker, "Foreign Trade Zone to Benefit State," *Atlanta Constitution*, February 16, 1975.
119. Anita Sharpe, "Foreign Trade Zones May Connect Companies Here with Higher Profits," *Atlanta Business Chronicle*, January 24, 1983.
120. Newt Gingrich to Michael Lott, May 26, 1981, file 7, box 1, MS 250, Cecil Alexander Papers, Cuba Family Archives for Southern Jewish History, Breman Museum, Atlanta.
121. "Georgia Opens First Foreign Trade Zone," *Atlanta Constitution*, February 19, 1978. On El Salvador's zone in San Bartolo, see Ethel C. Brooks, *Unraveling the Garment Industry: Transnational Organizing and Women's Work* (Minneapolis: University of Minnesota Press), 105–6. In general, see Greg Grandin, *Empire's Workshop: Latin America, the United States, and the Rise of the New Imperialism* (New York: Henry Holt, 2006).
122. "Oil Refinery in Hawaii Gets Permit," *Wall Street Journal*, April 22, 1970.
123. "Foreign Trade Zones—Good Places to Do Business," *Nation's Business* 66, no. 11 (November 1978): F83.
124. Terry Brown, "Chasing the Rabbit," *Wall Street Journal*, April 22, 1976.
125. "In Northeast: A Challenge to the Growing Muscle of the 'Sunbelt,'" *U.S. News & World Report*, October 18, 1976.
126. "Behind Fresh Interest in Duty-Free Zones," *U.S. News & World Report*, November 24, 1980.
127. On capital flight to the Sunbelt, see Larry Sawers and William K. Tabb, eds., *Sunbelt/Snowbelt: Urban Development and Regional Restructuring* (New York: Oxford University Press, 1984); Elizabeth Tandy Shermer, *Sunbelt Capitalism: Phoenix and the Transformation of American Politics* (Philadelphia: University of Pennsylvania Press, 2013).
128. *The Global Assembly Line*, directed by Lorraine Gray (New York: New Day Films, 1986); Folker Fröbel, Jürgen Heinrichs, and Otto Kreye, *The New International Division of Labour: Structural Unemployment in Industrialised Countries and Industrialisation in Developing Countries*, trans. Pete Burgess (Cambridge: Cambridge University Press, 1977); Rachel Grossman, "Women's Place in the Integrated Circuit," *Southeast Asia Chronicle* no. 66 (January–February 1979): 2–17. Grossman's metaphor is tweaked in M. Patricia Marchak's *The Integrated Circus: The New Right and the Restructuring of Global Markets* (Montreal: McGill-Queen's University Press, 1991) and is adopted as a heuristic for the political economy of technoculture in Donna Haraway's "A Cyborg Manifesto: Science, Technology, and Socialist-Feminism in the Late Twentieth Century," in *Simians, Cyborgs, and Women: The Reinvention of Nature* (New York: Routledge, 1991), 149–81.
129. Doreen Massey, *Space, Place, and Gender* (Minneapolis: University of Minnesota Press, 1994), 23; on deskilling, see Harry Braverman, *Labor and Monopoly Capital: The Degradation of Work in the Twentieth Century* (New York: Monthly Review Press, 1974).
130. Marlene Dixon, Susanne Jonas, and Ed McCaughan, "Reindustrialization and the

Transnational Labor Force in the United States Today," *Contemporary Marxism* no. 5 (Summer 1982): 103.

131. Leslie Sklair, "Foreign Investment and Irish Development: A Study of the International Division of Labour in the Midwest Region of Ireland," *Progress in Planning* 29, part 3 (1988): 147–216. On vanishing mediators, see Fredric Jameson, "The Vanishing Mediator: Narrative Structure in Max Weber," *New German Critique* no. 1 (Winter 1973): 52–89.

132. Ho Kwon Ping, "Birth of the Second Generation," *Far Eastern Economic Review,* May 18, 1979. On EPZs in Asia, also see Xiangming Chen, *As Borders Bend: Transnational Spaces on the Pacific Rim* (New York: Rowman and Littlefield, 2005); and Leslie Sklair, "Shenzhen: A Chinese 'Development Zone' in Global Perspective," *Development and Change* 16, no. 4 (1985): 571–602. On sovereignty and the spatial form of the zone, see Aihwa Ong, *Neoliberalism as Exception: Mutations in Citizenship and Sovereignty* (Durham, NC: Duke University Press, 2006); and Christopher Miller, "From Foreign Concessions to Special Economic Zones: Decolonization and Foreign Investment in Twentieth-Century Asia," in *Decolonization and the Cold War: Negotiating Independence,* ed. Leslie James and Elisabeth Leake (London: Bloomsbury), 239–54.

133. "American Nations Setting Up Free Zones to Spur Trade," *World Report,* August 15, 1946, 14–15.

134. The OEEC expedition resulted in a book, *Foreign-Trade Zones in the United States. Technical Assistance Mission #28* (Paris: OEEC, 1954).

135. On Panama, see Thomas E. Lyons, *Report on Proposal to Create a Foreign-Trade Zone (or Free Port) in the Republic of Panama* (Washington, DC: US Department of Commerce, 1946); on Liberia, see Foreign-Trade Zones Board, *Annual Report to Congress for the Fiscal Year Ended June 30, 1948* (Washington, DC: Government Printing Office, 1949), 2. James J. Hennelly, "The Free Port of Monrovia and Its Impact on the Republic of Liberia" (PhD diss., St. John's University, 1973). Liberia's free port was located at docks that the United States constructed in 1943 for the Firestone Rubber Company.

136. Colón Free Zone, *Increase Your Export Trade through Panama's Colon Free Zone* (Colón: Colón Free Zone, 1960); Philippe Nourry, "In Canal Zone, U.S. Has Trained 25,000 Latin Americans," *Boston Globe,* October 13, 1968.

137. Emanuel Celler to Vijaya Lekahmi Pandit, July 2, 1949, and Eliahu Eilat to Emanuel Celler, August 3, 1949, box 10, Celler Papers. On India's EPZs, see Jamie Cross, *Dream Zones: Anticipating Capitalism and Development in India* (London: Pluto, 2014); and Megan Maruschke, "Zones of Reterritorialization: India's Free Trade Zones in Comparative Perspective, 1947 to the 1980s," *Journal of Global History* 12, no. 3 (2017): 410–32.

138. Diamond, *One of a Kind,* 116, 160, 221, 179, 153, 228, and 242.

139. US Department of Commerce, *Free Trade Zones and Related Facilities Abroad* (Washington, DC: Government Printing Office, 1970). On Bangladesh, see, e.g., Richard L. Wilson to A. S. C. Fuller, December 17, 1970, box 1, Records Relating to East Pakistan/Bangladesh, 1968–1975, Bureau of Near Eastern and South Asian Affairs, RG 59, General Records of the Department of State, NARA II.

140. Colonel Robert W. Patterson, "Free Export Zones in the Republic of China" (USAWC Research Element, US Army War College, December 15, 1973).

141. Egypt-US Business Council, "Joint Communique," October 12–13, 1977, box 32, Ralph James Watkins Papers, Hoover Institution Archives, Stanford University.

142. Dan S. McMillin to William F. Buckley, September 18, 1975, box 114, Marvin Lieb-

man Papers, Hoover Institution Archives, Stanford University; Tyler Bridges, "Chile Trade Zone Turns Small Town into Booming City," *Christian Science Monitor*, November 24, 1987.

143. On Bolin, see Leslie Sklair, *Assembling for Development: The Maquila Industry in Mexico and the United States* (Boston: Unwin Hyman, 1989).
144. F. J. Spencer, "Foreign-Trade Zones—Loopholes or Gateways?" *Hydrocarbon Processing* 46, no. 1 (January 1967): 161–66; Gary Taylor, "Houston's Multi-Site Foreign Trade Zone Unique," *Journal of Commerce*, March 12, 1987. On Houston and engineers like Spencer, see also Betsy A. Beasley, *Expert Capital: Houston and the Making of a Service Empire* (Cambridge, MA: Harvard University Press, forthcoming).
145. "Letters of Intent Boost Zone Hopes," *Valley Evening Monitor*, August 7, 1966.
146. Sklair, *Assembling for Development*, 133.
147. "Trade Zone Would Be Big Asset," *Monitor*, June 24, 1970; "McAllen Trade Zone Plan Took Time, Work, Cash," *Corpus Christi Times*, October 29, 1970. McAllen's zone operators planned to publicize the prospect of subzones as a way to generate revenue (via leases). K. Mack Sisk, "Trade Zone on Border Acclaimed as Passport to Profits for Texans," *Dallas Morning News*, January 10, 1971.
148. "Echeverria Goes to Rio Grande," *Washington Post*, August 3, 1971.
149. Arelo Sederberg, "Set Up Satellite Plants over Border, Regional Firms Urged," *Los Angeles Times*, November 17, 1966; Sklair, *Assembling for Development*, 48.
150. Cowie, *Capital Moves*, 108–13; Sklair, *Assembling for Development*, 44.
151. Cowie, *Capital Moves*, 113; see also Sklair, *Assembling for Development*, 10.
152. My privileging of form over content is influenced by Fredric Jameson, whose interventions on this score happen to have coincided with the globalization of the zone concept. As Jameson wrote in 1971, "Not whether the street fighter or urban guerilla can win against the weapons and technology of the modern state, but rather precisely where the street *is* in the superstate, and, indeed, whether the old-fashioned street as such still exists in the first place in that seamless web of marketing and automated production which makes up the new state: such are the theoretical problems of Marxism today, at least in what might be termed the overdeveloped countries." Jameson, *Marxism and Form* (Princeton, NJ: Princeton University Press, 1971), xviii.
153. For discussion of the legislative history of the line between assembling and manufacturing in 807.00, see US International Trade Commission, *Production Sharing: U.S. Imports under Harmonized Tariff Schedule Subheadings 9802.00.60 and 9802.00.80, 1985–1988* (Washington, DC: United States International Trade Commission, December 1989), A24–26.
154. Cowie, *Capital Moves*, 113.
155. David Harvey, "Notes Toward a Theory of Uneven Geographical Development," in *Spaces of Global Capitalism: Towards a Theory of Uneven Geographical Development* (London: Verso, 2006), 85.
156. "Summary of Program on Mexican Border Problem to Be Discussed with AFL-CIO," March 29, 1968, 1–2, declassified NND46228, box 6, Records Relating to Mexico, 1946–1975, Bureau of Inter-American Affairs / Office of the County Director for Mexico, RG 50, Department of State, NARA II (hereafter BIAA Records).
157. Harry R. Turkel, "Memorandum on U.S.-Mexican Bi-National Free Zone Industrial Parks," December 15, 1966, box 6, declassified NND46228, BIAA Records.
158. "Sioux City Workers Victims of Trade Battle," *Chicago Tribune*, April 3, 1978.

159. Speech by James Wengert, filmed in the documentary *We Didn't Want It to Happen This Way*, directed by George Lindblade (Sioux City, IA: Carroll House, 1978).
160. DeVier Pierson to Anthony Solomon, February 14, 1968, declassified NND46228, box 6, BIAA Records.
161. "Possible Public Statement on 'Runaway Plants,'" March 29, 1968, declassified NND46228, box 6, BIAA Records.
162. "Summary of Program on Mexican Border Problem to be discussed with AFL-CIO," March 29, 1968, 1–2, declassified NND46228, box 6, BIAA Records.
163. "Possible Public Statement on 'Runaway Plants.'"
164. A. Sivanandan, "Imperialism in the Silicon Age," *Monthly Review* 32, no. 3 (July–August 1980); Tsuchiya Takeo, "Free Trade Zones in Southeast Asia," *Monthly Review* 29, no. 9 (February 1978): 31.
165. Oscar Rojo of Ans, "Philippines Sets Up Foreign Trade Zone," *South China Morning Post*, July 27, 1971.
166. Jack Egan, "Ford Plant in Philippines: Small Profit, Large Suit," *Washington Post*, August 1, 1978. A shareholder lawsuit claimed that Henry Ford II bribed the Filipino government to clinch the deal.
167. Walden Bello, "Building on Martial Law," *Multinational Monitor* 2, no. 2 (February 1981): 9.
168. "Free Trade Zones: A Capitalist Dream," *Race and Class* 22, no. 2 (October 1980): 191.
169. Padlocked gates at shuttered factories in Canada and the United States, as Steven High points out, mirrored this imagery. High, *Industrial Sunset: The Making of North America's Rust Belt, 1969–1984* (Toronto: University of Toronto Press, 2003), 39.
170. Peter F. Drucker, "The Rise of Production Sharing," *Wall Street Journal*, March 15, 1977. Sklair notes that the term was "floating around" corporate boardrooms in the 1960s but credits Drucker for popularizing it. Sklair, *Assembling for Development*, 8. The term appears to have surfaced first as a synonym for profit sharing between employers and employees, as spelled out in J. J. Jehring, "A Contrast between Two Approaches to Total Systems Incentives," *California Management Review* 10, no. 2 (Winter 1967): 7–14. Arguably, the power imbalance in this workplace scenario was then scaled up into a model for "sharing" between overdeveloped and underdeveloped nations.
171. Peter F. Drucker, "The Economy's Dark Continent," *Fortune*, April 1962.
172. Fröbel, Heinrichs, and Kreye, *The New International Division of Labor*, 297.
173. Annette Fuentes and Barbara Ehrenreich, *Women in the Global Factory* (Boston: South End, 1983), 10.
174. Lloyd Sanderson to Raymond Kieferle, July 26, 1957, box 1, BEA FTZ History Files.
175. Foreign-Trade Zones Board, *Annual Report of the Foreign-Trade Zones Board to the Congress of the United States for the Fiscal Year Ended June 30, 1965* (Washington, DC: Government Printing Office, 1966), 28.
176. A. Kent MacDougall, "U.S. Foreign Trade Zones: Boon or Bane for Production, Jobs?" *Los Angeles Times*, April 18, 1982.
177. See, for example, Lawrence Fellows, "Wooing Industry from Abroad," *New York Times*, March 6, 1977; Robert Jordan, "Trade Zones Seen Bringing 1500 Jobs," *Boston Globe*, April 7, 1977; and "Foreign Trade Zones—Good Places to Do Business," *Nation's Business*, November 1978.
178. Tim Waters, "Wave of Imported Autos Floods Ports," *Los Angeles Times*, June 5, 1986.

179. Martin Merzer, "30 States Seek to Win Japan Auto Factories," *Los Angeles Times*, November 8, 1978.
180. Daniel Machalaba, "More Companies Find Duty-Free Zones Yield Benefits in U.S. Market," *Wall Street Journal*, December 4, 1978.
181. By the late eighties, the race was crowded, and it was cutthroat. An economic development official in Michigan put it starkly: "In the late 1970s, when [Jim] Hettinger made the first of his 12 trips to Japan on behalf of Battle Creek, 'you could turn over any rock and find three companies' looking to locate in the U.S. market, he said. Today, however, Hettinger said, 'turn over any rock in Japan and you'll find three state agents' trying to lure Japanese firms to Kentucky or Tennessee or Indiana." Janet Braunstein, "Tending to the Care and Feeding of Foreign Businesses," *Washington Post*, October 22, 1989.
182. "Customs Rule Is Eased to Spur Output in U.S. by Foreign Companies," *Wall Street Journal*, March 19, 1980.
183. Barry Bluestone and Bennett Harrison, *The Deindustrialization of America: Plant Closings, Community Abandonment, and the Dismantling of Basic Industry* (New York: Basic Books, 1982), 166.
184. Soon Kyoung Cho makes this argument in "The Labor Process and Capital Mobility: The Limits of the New International Division of Labor," *Politics & Society* 14, no. 2 (1985): 185–222; see also Laurie Graham, "How Foreign-Owned Auto Plants Remain Union-Free," *New Labor Forum* 17, no. 3 (Fall 2008): 59–66. On Japanese automakers in the US South, see Sayuri Guthrie-Shimizu, "From Southeast Asia to the American Southeast: Japanese Business Meets the Sun Belt South," in *Globalization and the American South*, ed. James C. Cobb and William Stueck (Athens: University of Georgia Press, 2005), 135–63; Karsten Hülsemann, "Greenfields in the Heart of Dixie: How the American Auto Industry Discovered the South," in *The Second Wave: Southern Industrialization from the 1940s to the 1970s*, ed. Philip Scranton (Athens: University of Georgia Press, 2001), 219–54; and Ann E. Kingsolver, "Tobacco, Textiles, and Toyota: Working for Multinational Corporations in Rural Kentucky," in *Anthropology and the Global Factory: Studies of the New Industrialization of the Late Twentieth Century*, ed. Frances Abrahamer Rothstein and Michael L. Blim (New York: Bergin and Garvey, 1992), 191–205.
185. "Tenn. County OKs Bonds for Datsun Plant," *Atlanta Constitution*, October 1, 1980; "America Starts Bouncing Back," *Nation's Business*, November 1981.
186. Docket No. 23-81, 46 *Federal Register* 62487 (December 24, 1981).
187. Martin Tolchin and Susan Tolchin, "Cultivating Japan," *Washington Post*, March 6, 1988.
188. John Egerton, *Nissan in Tennessee* (Smyrna, TN: Nissan Motor Manufacturing Corporation, 1983), 37.
189. Leslie Bow, *Partly Colored: Asian Americans and Racial Anomaly in the Segregated South* (New York: New York University Press, 2010), 235.
190. John Egerton, *The Americanization of Dixie: The Southernization of America* (New York: Harper's Magazine Press, 1974), 9; see also Charles Stevens, "Nissan Truck Plant Ground Breaking Rite Draws Angry Crowd," *Wall Street Journal*, February 4, 1981.
191. Egerton, *The Americanization of Dixie*, 71.
192. Mike Parker and Jane Slaughter, *Choosing Sides: Unions and the Team Concept* (Boston: South End, 1988), 9, 220.

193. Terry Abrams, "Nissan and the Security Zone," *Security Management*, August 1989, 46, 48.
194. Peter Meredith, "Jobs? Or the Illusion of Jobs," *Sun*, March 7, 1982.
195. Andrew Mair, *Honda's Global Local Corporation* (New York: St. Martin's, 1994), 87–111.
196. Marian Courtney, "Key Role for the State in Trade Zones," *New York Times*, November 29, 1987.
197. Joseph Kraft, "The Downsizing Decision," *New Yorker*, May 5, 1980, 162.
198. Tom Redburn, "U.S. Holds Key to '90s Economics," *Los Angeles Times*, December 30, 1987.
199. George Galster to John Da Ponte, 2, July 3, 1984, files on Zone 78A at the FTZ Board, Washington, DC.
200. On the racialization of Asiatic capital, see Iyko Day, *Alien Capital: Asian Racialization and the Logic of Settler Colonial Capitalism* (Durham, NC: Duke University Press, 2016).
201. Frank, *Buy American*, 160.
202. Frank, *Buy American*, 178; Ronald Takaki, "Who Really Killed Vincent Chin?" *Asian Week*, November 29, 1983.
203. Masao Miyoshi, "Race, Trade, and Nationhood," *San Francisco Review of Books*, November–December 1993, 43. In the film version of Crichton's pulp thriller, a white sex worker who dies at the hands of a Japanese mogul met him not, as in the book, while attending college in Texas, but while "working in that Toyota plant back there in Kentucky"—a.k.a. Subzone 29E.
204. General Accounting Office, "Foreign Trade Zone Growth Primarily Benefits Users Who Import for Domestic Commerce," March 2, 1984 (GAO/GGD-84-52), i, 9, 11; United States International Trade Commission, "The Implications of Foreign-Trade Zones for U.S. Industries and for Competitive Conditions between U.S. and Foreign Firms," February 1984 (USITC Publication 1496).
205. Marcy Kaptur, House Subcommittee of the Committee on Ways and Means, *Operations of the Foreign Trade Zones Program of the United States and Its Implications for the U.S. Economy and International Trade*, 101st Cong., 1st sess., October 24, 1989, 10; Sander Levin, House Subcommittee, *Operations of the Foreign Trade Zones Program*, 33.
206. Benjamin Cole, "Foreign-Trade Zones: Why the Uproar," *U.S. News & World Report*, February 27, 1984.
207. "I agree with the last 45 years of trying to get all world markets open," Kaptur testified. "The free trade theory, I agree with that as an American because I think that's how we think, it's how we operate, and I would hope that 100 years from now the world would be there and that we would have set the right example." Kaptur, House Subcommittee of the Committee on Ways and Means, *Operations of the Foreign Trade Zones Program of the United States and Its Implications for the U.S. Economy and International Trade*, 101st Cong., 1st sess., October 24, 1989, 25. On the persistence of blind faith in free trade (in the Global North), see Eric Sheppard, "Constructing Free Trade: From Manchester Boosterism to Global Management," *Transactions of the Institute of British Geographers* 30, no. 2 (2005): 151–72.
208. William M. Thomas, House Subcommittee of the Committee on Ways and Means, *Operations of the Foreign Trade Zones Program of the United States and Its Implications for the U.S. Economy and International Trade*, 101st Cong., 1st sess., 30.

209. Hyperbole aside, President Carter had hoped to form a federal board to underwrite labor unions in deploying pension funds into redevelopment of the Rust Belt. See Michael A. McCarthy, *Dismantling Solidarity: Capitalist Politics and American Pensions since the New Deal* (Ithaca, NY: Cornell University Press, 2017), 114–21.
210. Michael Brody, "What Kind of Climate?," *Barron's National Business and Financial Weekly*, June 6, 1977, 22.
211. Sander Levin, House Subcommittee of the Committee on Ways and Means, *Operations of the Foreign Trade Zones Program of the United States and Its Implications for the U.S. Economy and International Trade*, 101st Cong., 1st sess., October 24, 1989, 167; Tommy Lee Berry, House Subcommittee, *Operations of the Foreign Trade Zones Program*, 172; Allan I. Mendelowitz, House Subcommittee, *Operations of the Foreign Trade Zones Program*, 70.
212. Steven Wein, House Subcommittee of the Committee on Ways and Means, *Operations of the Foreign Trade Zones Program of the United States and Its Implications for the U.S. Economy and International Trade*, 101st Cong., 1st sess., October 24, 1989, 235.
213. *Business Week* popularized the term *reindustrialization* in a special issue, "The Reindustrialization of America," June 30, 1980. A review called the compendium "fascinating, both for its data and for its unblinking assertion that what's good for internationally competitive capital is good for America." Review of "The Reindustrialization of America," special issue of *Business Week*, *Politics and Society* 10, no. 1 (1980): 122.
214. Michael Hardt and Antonio Negri, *Empire* (Cambridge, MA: Harvard University Press, 2000), 287.
215. Sassen-Koob, "Recomposition and Peripheralization at the Core," 95. The spatial form of the enterprise zone targeted tax breaks at designated urban districts (it contrasted with the foreign-trade zone in that it covered strictly domestic taxes). Promoted by Jack Kemp, Housing and Urban Development director under Reagan, the term first took off in the United Kingdom, where it was floated as a variant of the zone concept: "As a point of intellectual history, the foreign trade zone is the original enterprise zone. In 1977, a British urban planning expert, Peter Hall, took the existing free-trade zone concept, added other forms of tax and regulation abatement, and the enterprise-zone idea was born." "The Original Enterprise Zone," *Sun*, February 1, 1982. Another variant that emerged at the same time was the IBF, or international banking facility. The IBF was a spatial form that allowed US banks to deal in Eurodollars on US soil—in essence, the Bahamas in Manhattan. It was likened to a foreign-trade zone, as in Richard F. Janssen, "Fed Ponders Idea of Declaring New York a 'Free Zone' for International Banking," *New York Times*, April 25, 1979. The enterprise zone and the IBF call out for historicization. For an article that links both of them to the zone concept, see Herbert G. Grubel, "Towards a Theory of Free Economic Zones," *Weltwirtschaftliches Archiv* 118, no. 1 (1982): 39–61; see also Alan C. Hudson, "Off-Shores On-Shore: New Regulatory Spaces and Real Historical Places in the Landscape of Global Money," in *Money and the Space Economy*, ed. Ron Martin (New York: John Wiley and Sons, 1999), 139–54; and Ogle, "Archipelago Capitalism," 1452–53.
216. See, for example, Marlene Dixon, Susanne Jonas, and Ed McCaughan, "Reindustrialization and the Transnational Labor Force in the United States Today," *Contemporary Marxism* no. 5 (Summer 1982): 101–15. André Gorz is credited with popularizing "South Africanization," which he used to describe "a dualization of society," "the

realization of the colonial model within the metropolitan heartland." Gorz, *Critique of Economic Reason*, trans. Gillian Handyside and Chris Turner (London: Verso, 1989), 156.

CONCLUSION

1. Marc Levinson, *The Box: How the Shipping Container Made the World Smaller and the World Economy Bigger*, 2nd ed. (2006; Princeton, NJ: Princeton University Press, 2015); Bill Gates, "Innovation, Disruption, and Progress: What Do Vaccines, Software, and Shipping Containers Have in Common?," August 9, 2013, https://www.gatesnotes.com/Books/The-Box. See also Thomas Birtchnell, Satya Savitzky, and John Urry, eds., *Cargo Mobilities: Moving Materials in a Global Age* (New York: Routledge, 2015); Michael Shane Boyle, "Container Aesthetics: The Infrastructural Politics of Shunt's *The Boy Who Climbed Out of His Face*," *Theater Journal* 68, no. 1 (2016): 57–77; Charmaine Chua, "Slow Boat to China," February 7, 2015, https://thedisorderofthings.com/tag/slow-boat-to-china/; Charmaine Chua, "The Container: Stacking, Packing, and Moving the World," *Funambulist* no. 6 (2016): 40–45; Martin Danyluk, "Capital's Logistical Fix: Accumulation, Globalization, and the Survival of Capitalism," *Environment and Planning D: Society and Space* 36, no. 4 (2018): 630–47; Alexander Klose, *The Container Principle: How a Box Changes the Way We Think* (2009; Cambridge, MA: MIT Press, 2015); and Craig Martin, *Shipping Container* (New York: Bloomsbury, 2016). Lastly, a classic—and an inspiration—is Allan Sekula, *Fish Story* (Düsseldorf: Richter Verlag, 1995).
2. The business of air cargo took off soon after World War II and accelerated during the jet age, but it relied on a much older legal framework. In 1926, Congress passed the Air Commerce Act, paving the way for airports of entry, and in 1928 federal agencies drafted regulations. Bonded routes for the skies shortly followed. Walter Wager, "Airline Frontier Formalities and Customs-Free Airports," *Journal of Air Law and Commerce* 20, no. 4 (1953): 416–37. For a sampling of press coverage, see "Key West Becomes Airport-of-Entry," *Christian Science Monitor*, January 16, 1928; William Ullman, "Inland Cities Are Aspiring to Be 'Airports of Entry,'" *Washington Post*, March 24, 1929; and "Eastern Air Lines Made First Air Bonded Carrier," *Atlanta Constitution*, September 29, 1934. For an excellent map of "sky-roads of commerce," see Thomas E. Lyons, "Foreign-Trade Zones on Great-Circle Routes," *Foreign Commerce Weekly*, January 29, 1944. On air freight in the age of Fed-Ex and UPS, see Barry Lopez, "Flight," in *About This Life: Journeys on the Threshold of Memory* (New York: Vintage, 1998), 73–112; and John McPhee, "Out in the Sort," in *Uncommon Carriers* (New York: Farrar, Straus and Giroux, 2006), 153–84.
3. Levinson's second edition of *The Box* concludes with a new chapter that addresses zones, nodding to the *zona libre* at Colón, Panama, and sketching the free trade zone at Jebel Ali in Dubai—albeit, oddly, without citations, when there were many sources to consult. See, e.g., Mike Davis, "Fear and Money in Dubai," *New Left Review* 41 (September–October 2006): 47–68; Keller Easterling, "Extrastatecraft," in *Re_Urbanism: Transforming Capitals, Perspecta* 39, ed. Kanu Agrawal, Melanie Domino, and Brad Walters (Cambridge, MA: MIT Press, 2007): 2–16. See also Laleh Khalili, *Sinews of War and Trade* (New York: Verso, forthcoming); and Rafeef Ziadah, "Transport Infrastructure and Logistics in the Making of Dubai Inc.," *International Journal of Urban and Regional Research* 42, no. 2 (2018): 182–97.
4. This definition of mystification is from John Berger, *Ways of Seeing* (1972; New York: Penguin, 1977), 15–16.

5. Anson M. Titus, "Observations in Warehouse Practices," *Proceedings of the Thirty-Second Annual Meeting of the American Warehousemen's Association* (Pittsburgh: American Warehousemen's Association, 1923), 191–92.
6. On soldiers, see "When Warriors Hurt Themselves," *New York Times*, September 2, 2010. Calibrating "dwell time" has been an acute challenge for the US military within the parameters of permanent war after 9/11.
7. For a riff on the foreign-trade zone's link to the duty-free boutique, which was born in 1947 at the Shannon Airport in Ireland and in 1962 migrated to the United States, see William Yates, "From a Travel-Log," *Chicago Daily Tribune*, June 23, 1957; and on duty-free shopping at JFK Airport, see box 343, Celler Papers. On airports as sites of dwell time, see Marc Auge, *Non-Places: Introduction to an Anthropology of Supermodernity* (New York: Verso, 1995); Gillian Fuller and Ross Harley, *Aviopolis: A Book about Airports* (London: Black Dog, 2004); and Martha Rosler, *In the Place of the Public: Observations of a Frequent Flyer* (Ostfildern-Ruit, Germ.: Cantz, 1998).
8. This argument is elaborated in Joseph H. Beale, "The Situs of Things," *Yale Law Journal* 28, no. 6 (1919): 525–41. As Jack M. Balkin notes, the legal doctrine that the stream of commerce ends at the factory—that commerce and industry are separate spheres—is a relic of the US Supreme Court's efforts in the early nineteenth century "to maintain distinctions between local and national power." Balkin, "Commerce," *Michigan Law Review* 109, no. 1 (2010): 64. Barry Cushman argues that during the New Deal the stream of commerce threatened to breach the local/national divide, compromising the industry/commerce divide, in *Rethinking the New Deal Court: The Structure of a Constitutional Revolution* (New York: Oxford University Press, 1998), 152.
9. In this vein, I query whether the binary categories of "merchant" and "manufacturer" can register the centrality of logistics in the evolution of supply-chain capitalism. In favor of them is Nelson Lichtenstein, "The Return of Merchant Capitalism," *International Labor and Working-Class History* 81 (Spring 2012): 8–27.
10. Relationships nurtured by tax incentives were not long-term commitments, as city and county executives were learning in situations like that of Subzone 37A. "North Tarrytown Loses Largest Taxpayer as GM Announces Shutdown," *Westchester County Business Journal*, March 2, 1992.
11. Anthony DePalma, "Earth Movers Carving Free-Trade Zone," *New York Times*, April 3, 1983; see also Carter B. Horsley, "Industrial Zones Gain New Stature," *New York Times*, September 20, 1981.
12. "Rockefeller City a 'Free Port,'" *Hartford Courant*, July 29, 1932. Per the Exhibition Act of 1932, Rockefeller Center doubled as "a sort of commercial museum with exhibitions," where foreign commodities were allowed to sit duty-free for up to two years. Congressman Fiorello La Guardia, Entry of Exhibits Under Bond, 72nd Cong., 1st sess., *Congressional Record* 75, July 13, 1932, 15248.
13. After World War II, warehousemen in western states began to pitch transitional storage to long-haul truckers. In 1948, as the story goes, a warehouseman in Reno, Nevada, realized that he could dominate the business if he could dodge inventory taxes. Reading about the foreign-trade zone or "free port" in New Orleans, he decided to lobby for Nevada to be designated a free port—"the whole State." The law that he instigated reorganized "landlocked" Nevada into "as free a port as any on the seacoast," permitting goods from out of state that were destined for other states to be deposited tax-free, and allowing manipulating of them while they were in storage. L. C. Finnell, "Land-Locked Free Port," *Rotarian*, September 1956, 40–41. This law transformed the Nevada desert into an oasis for distribution centers, and

it prompted dozens of other states to approve "free port" laws over the next decade, for a total of thirty-four by 1964. Donald Moffitt, "More States Cancel Inventory Tax on Items for Sale Elsewhere," *Wall Street Journal*, January 15, 1964. Each state relied on the same legal fiction that was first formalized in federal law with the invention of in-bond transport in 1870—the displacement of "situs" by "transit."

14. On trade corridors, see Jean-Paul Rodrigue, *The Geography of Transport Systems*, 4th ed. (New York: Routledge, 2017); and Ishita Dey and Giorgio Grappi, "Beyond Zoning: India's Corridors of 'Development' and New Frontiers of Capital," *South Atlantic Quarterly* 114, no. 1 (2015): 153–70. On AllianceTexas, see www.alliancetexas.com and news coverage such as Bob Davis and Jackie Calmes, "Perot Family's Airport Project Gets a Little Nafta of Its Own from U.S.," *Wall Street Journal*, September 9, 1993.
15. Keller Easterling, *Extrastatecraft: The Power of Infrastructure Space* (New York: Verso, 2014), 63.
16. Susan Nigra Snyder and Alex Wall, "Emerging Landscapes of Movement and Logistics," *Architectural Design* 68, no. 7/8 (1998): 19; Stephen Graham and Simon Marvin, *Splintering Urbanism: Networked Infrastructures, Technological Mobilities, and the Urban Condition* (New York: Routledge, 2001). In the Rust Belt, exurbs sprinkled with industrial parks are of a piece with downtowns dominated by banks and "eds-and-meds." See Tracy Neumann, *Remaking the Rust Belt: The Postindustrial Transformation of North America* (Philadelphia: University of Pennsylvania Press, 2016); and Gabriel Winant, *Crucible of Care: The Fall of Steel, the Rise of Health Care, and the Making of a New Working Class* (Cambridge, MA: Harvard University Press, forthcoming).
17. Juan D. De Lara, *Inland Shift: Race, Space, and Capital in Southern California* (Berkeley: University of California Press, 2018); see also Edna Bonacich and Jake B. Wilson, *Getting the Goods: Ports, Labor, and the Logistics Revolution* (Ithaca, NY: Cornell University Press, 2008); Genevieve Carpio, "From Citrus Belt to Inland Empire: Race, Place, and Mobility in Southern California, 1880–2000" (PhD diss., University of Southern California, 2013); and Thomas C. Patterson, *From Acorns to Warehouses: Historical Political Economy of Southern California's Inland Empire* (New York: Routledge, 2016). See also Boris Vormann, *Global Port Cities in North America: Urbanization Processes and Global Production Networks* (New York: Routledge, 2015).
18. Aerial photographs serve as evidence in Alan Berger, *Drosscape: Wasting Land in Urban America* (New York: Princeton Architectural, 2006).
19. John Da Ponte Jr., "Updated Rules for Foreign-Trade Zones Reflect Big Increase in Zone Activity," *Business America*, November 4, 1991.
20. Keith Bradsher, "Perot Stake under Pact Is Not Clear," *New York Times*, November 11, 1993.
21. Kevin McDermott, "A Customs Dodge Catches On," *D & B Reports* 43, no. 1 (1994): 48. "Logistics cluster" is the business-school term of art for the supply-chain entrepôt, such as in Yossi Sheffi, *Logistics Clusters: Delivering Value and Driving Growth* (Cambridge, MA: MIT Press, 2012).
22. UPS Zone Solutions, "Harness the Advantages of Foreign Trade Zones (FTZ)," https://www.ups.com/us/en/services/international-trade/brokerage/foreign-trade-zone-solutions.page. Zone 29 arrived well ahead of UPS, an early facet of Jefferson County's strategy for a logistics cluster avant la lettre. See John Finley, "State to Help City Become Foreign Trade Zone," *Louisville Courier-Journal*, December 12, 1970; and Leslie Ellis, "Trade Secrets . . . County Warehouse May Soon Hold Exotic Goods," *Louisville Courier-Journal*, December 4, 1979.

23. On Walmart's subzones, apart from the FTZ Board's online database, see Alan L. Gilman, "Retailers Enter Foreign Trade Zones," *Chain Store Age* 69, no. 11 (1993): 118; Richard Halverson, "Logistical Supremacy Secures the Base—But Will It Translate?," and Halverson, "Wal-Mart 'Walks the Walk' of a Global Retailer; Eyes All Corners of the World," *Discount Store News*, December 5, 1994. On Walmart's distribution centers, see Jesse LeCavalier, *The Rule of Logistics: Walmart and the Architecture of Fulfillment* (Minneapolis: University of Minnesota Press, 2016); on Amazon's fulfillment centers, see Claire Lyster, *Learning from Logistics: How Networks Change Our Cities* (Basel: Birkhäuser, 2016); and an acclaimed large-format photograph that depicts the algorithmic anarchy of an Amazon warehouse in Phoenix, Arizona (the photograph is viewable in George Shankar, "Snapshot: *Amazon* (2016) by Andreas Gursky," *Financial Times*, July 1, 2016, https://www.ft.com/content/9c915e52-3ec3-11e6-9f2c-36b487ebd80a).
24. Marco D'Eramo, "Dock Life," *New Left Review* 96 (2015): 85–99; Matthew Hockenberry, "Material Epistemologies of the (Mobile) Telephone," *Anthropological Quarterly* 91, no. 2 (2018): 485–524; Miriam Posner, "See No Evil," *Logic* 4 (2018), https://logicmag.io/04-see-no-evil/; Alberto Toscano and Jeff Kinkle, *Cartographies of the Absolute* (Hants, UK: Zero Books, 2015). For a multimedia meditation on Zone 22 as "the closest you'll get to globalization in your backyard," see the field research by Rozalinda Borcila, Brian Holmes, and Southwest Corridor Northwest Passage, http://southwestcorridornorthwestpassage.org.
25. On Walmart's "import distribution centers," see MWPVL International, "The Walmart Distribution Center Network in the United States," http://www.mwpvl.com/html/walmart.html, accessed October 10, 2018. On Columbus, see John Lasker, "US Foreign Trade Zones: Connecting Labor Exploitation in a Global Race to the Bottom," February 5, 2016, https://towardfreedom.org/archives/labor/us-foreign-trade-zones-connecting-labor-exploitation-in-a-global-race-to-the-bottom/. On Chicago and Joliet, see Kevin Gosztola, "Security Force Arrests Supporters of Striking Walmart Warehouse Workers," October 1, 2012, https://shadowproof.com/2012/10/01/private-security-force-arrests-supporters-of-striking-walmart-warehouse-workers/; Alexander Sammon, "Elmwood, Illinois (Pop. 2,200) Has Become a Vital Hub of America's Consumer Economy. And It's Hell," *New Republic*, January 9, 2019; and Warehouse Workers for Justice, www.ww4j.org. De Lara recounts parallel struggles on the West Coast in *Inland Shift*. On outsourcing, see Louis Hyman, *Temp: How American Work, American Business, and the American Dream Became Temporary* (New York: Penguin, 2018); and Jamie Peck, *Offshore: Exploring the Worlds of Global Outsourcing* (Oxford: Oxford University Press, 2017). The literature on logistics is extensive. Deborah Cowen's *The Deadly Life of Logistics: Mapping Violence in Global Trade* (Minneapolis: University of Minnesota Press, 2014) is foundational, along with Jasper Bernes's "Logistics, Counterlogistics and the Communist Prospect," *End Notes* 3 (2014), https://endnotes.org.uk/issues/3/en/jasper-bernes-logistics-counterlogistics-and-the-communist-prospect, in addition to titles cited earlier. For an overview, see Charmaine Chua, Martin Danyluk, Deborah Cowen, and Laleh Khalili, "Turbulent Circulation: Building a Critical Engagement with Logistics," *Environment and Planning D: Society and Space* 36, no. 4 (2018): 617–29; and the fabulous website-clearinghouse maintained by Matthew Hockenberry, https://supplystudies.com.

INDEX

Page numbers in italics refer to figures.